P9-BZX-722

Encyclopedia of
Allegorical
Literature

ABC-CLIO LITERARY COMPANION

Encyclopedia of
Allegorical
Literature

David Adams Leeming
Kathleen Morgan Drowne

ABC-CLIO

Santa Barbara, California
Denver, Colorado
Oxford, England

Library of Congress Cataloging-in-Publication Data

Leeming, David Adams, 1937–
    Encyclopedia of allegorical literature/David Adams Leeming, Kathleen Morgan Drowne.
        p.   cm.—(ABC-CLIO literary companion)
    Includes bibliographical references and index.
    1. Allegory—Encyclopedias. 2. Literature—History and criticism.
I. Drowne, Kathleen Morgan. II. Title. III. Series.
PN56.A5L44   1996   809'.915—dc20   96-31909   62.59

ISBN 0-87436-781-6 (alk. paper)

02   01   00   99   98   97   96   10   9   8   7   6   5   4   3   2   1

ABC-CLIO, Inc.
130 Cremona Drive, P.O. Box 1911
Santa Barbara, California 93116-1911

This book is printed on acid-free paper ∞.

CONTENTS

INTRODUCTION

The word *allegory* comes from the Greek *allos* meaning "other" and *agoria* meaning "speaking." Allegoria or other-speaking, then, refers originally to a mode of expression in which a secondary ("other") level of meaning takes precedence over the surface level. It might be argued that as a symbolic representation of ideas, any work of art, or any dream, is to some extent allegorical. Characters in *Madame Bovary* are in part personifications of ideas conceived by Gustave Flaubert. My dreams are projections of my psychic life. The paintings of Picasso literally re-present the artist's vision of reality. But having said this, it is important to recognize the universal and pervasive presence of allegory as a more specifically defined approach to both literature and painting and, to a lesser extent, to other areas of human creativity. When we speak of an allegory as opposed to something merely allegorical we refer to a work of art in which the author consciously uses characters, situations, and actions to stand for specific abstractions or for certain generalizations about human life. Personification is perhaps the primary device of the mode. In this sense allegory is closer to metaphor than symbol. But to define allegory as extended metaphor, as some have done, is to lose sight of the fact that in creating a metaphor—for example, "love is a game"—the author's intention is to add a dimension to our immediate understanding of the actual experience of life whereas allegory leads us to a secondary meaning (the *allos*) that the surface of the work only represents.

Merely symbolic or metaphorical characters and situations have connotations or possible meanings, some of which might not even have been intended by the artist. In allegory the secondary meaning must be clear for the intention of the work to be achieved. The lighthouse in Woolf's *To the Lighthouse* or Raskolnikov's agony in Dostoevsky's *Crime and Punishment* or the billboard in Fitzgerald's *Great Gatsby* are clearly symbolic; they lead us to speculate about what they might represent, and they might represent several things at once. In each of these cases the author's primary concern is the particular characters, milieu, and situation he is describing. On the other hand, the human figure named Good Deeds in the medieval morality play *Everyman* is a clear personification for the abstraction called good deeds, and the situation of the figure called Everyman represents the universal human reckoning with the fact of death. These characters and their actions are devoid of the differentiating details that writers and painters use to establish personality, place, and particular context because the playwright is more concerned with abstractions being represented than with the depiction of specific individuals in real-life situations and places. In short, allegory is always didactic; symbolism is not.

There are, of course, gray areas between allegory and symbolic literature. There are those who would say that Hawthorne's *Scarlet Letter* crosses the boundary between symbol and allegory. The gray area is perhaps especially evident in what we call modernism. In the paintings of Edward Munch or the novels of Franz Kafka we sense that we are experiencing the allegorical mode—that idea is clearly taking precedence over realistic depiction—but we are confronted by an essential ambiguity that distances works by Kafka and Munch from a play like *Everyman* or from art such as the carvings of the great medieval cathedrals in which each element has a specific meaning intended by the carver and recognized by the religious initiate. It is fair to say that although allegory is alive in modernism, it is a bit uncomfortable there.

Not surprisingly, allegory in its purest form has been most popular in societies motivated by particular ideologies. The clearest kind of allegory appeals to those who place the importance of particular ideas over the what might be called the beauty of life's vicissitudes. In the western world the allegorical mode achieved its zenith in the Middle Ages when it became a primary means of representing and clarifying Christian concepts for people who lacked education. Allegory has proved to be useful for perpetrators of more modern ideologies as well. The straw-stuffed effigies of Jimmy Carter and Uncle Sam burned by Shiite Iranian revolutionaries were vehicles for allegory, as were the boy and girl on the tractor and the red sunset in the social "realism" of Marxism.

As is the case with any artistic mode, there is good allegory and bad allegory. To reach an audience successfully, allegory must work on two levels. On the primary or surface level, characters and situations must be sufficiently believable, sufficiently human to hold the attention of other humans. On the secondary or didactic level, the ideas must be clear enough to reach the particular society addressed.

This brings us to the question of the audience for allegory. For the peasant family of medieval Chartres, *Everyman* would be received in the context of already known truth. The secondary meaning would be at least as important as the performance. For the Moslem tourist witnessing the same play in present-day Salzburg, success would presumably have to depend much more on the performance. In the latter case much of the purpose for allegory is necessarily lost. The tourist might well watch the play as a quaint example of the art of a former age and a distinctly alien society. At worst the play might be judged to be simplistic, unappealing to the modern sensibility attuned to relativity and uncertainty.

The three closest ancient relatives of allegory—they might even be called types of allegory—are myth, fable, and parable. Allegory also plays a significant role in epic, and later popular vehicles for the mode include the medieval morality play and the romance. But allegory appears in many other forms as well: in philosophical models such as Plato's cave, in the satirical fiction of Jonathan Swift, in biblical hermeneutics, in the modern novel.

The connection between myth and allegory lies in the definition of myth itself as a system of narrative by which a given culture "dreams" its understanding of the mysterious source of life. Myth is necessarily concerned with secondary meaning—with the "other." Characters in myth are personifications who stand for secondary meaning that lies within or behind the surface text of the myth. So it is that Athena is wisdom born mytho-logically out of the head of Zeus, divine power. And so it is that the story of Persephone's abduction and periodic return to her mother is an allegorical tale of the seasonal cycle.

There are always those who would turn what was perhaps not intended as an allegorical work into one. A good example is that of the early Christians who read allegory into the Old Testament Song of Songs, a work derived from ancient Near Eastern erotic marriage poetry. For the early Church this poetry could only be absorbed as an allegory of Christ's relationship with his "bride," the Church. The ancient Greeks, too, practiced allegorical exegesis in their reading of Homer. Scholars referred to the *hyponoia*—the "hidden thought" beneath the texts. It was a way of defusing some of the more antisocial practices of the Homeric heroes. Modern psychoanalytic theorists such as Freud have read dreams and works of literature allegorically so that *Hamlet*, for example, becomes for Freudians an allegory of the Oedipus complex.

Fable (Latin *fabula*, "telling") began in the Western world with the works of Aesop but was taken up later by writers such as La Fontaine and Tolstoy and the creators of the African and African American animal-trickster tales such as those about Br'er Rabbit. Using the popular device of personifying abstractions in animals, it is traditionally used to teach people proper behavior. The typical fable, in which an abstraction such as wisdom is personified by owls or foxes and foolishness by crows, ends with a clear moral that makes the allegory evident to all. The parable (Greek *parabole*, placing next to—"Let me give you an example") is a form traditionally used by gurus or wise people to illustrate abstract concepts. In Western culture the primary parable teller is Jesus. Lao Tsu, the founder of Taoism, told parables in ancient China, and Gautama the Buddha told them in India. Zen masters still tell them in Japan. The typical parable is different from the fable in that the moral it contains is not as explicit. The genre assumes an audience of initiates who can use the parable to turn from sin by being reminded of an essential truth revealed by the narrative.

The generally didactic purpose of allegory can, in short, take many forms. In the articles that follow we will find examples of moral, spiritual, political, psychological, philosophical, and typological (the prophetic meaning behind the lives of actual people) allegories. We will discover allegories in prose as well as in poetry, in gardens and buildings as well as in literature and painting, in Greece as well as in Africa, in the late twentieth century as well as in the Middle Ages. In the process we will come to understand better the mode that more than any other contains the human drive to teach the "truth."

ABC-CLIO LITERARY COMPANION

Encyclopedia of
Allegorical
Literature

ABSALOM AND ACHITOPHEL

An allegorical poem by John Dryden (1631–1700), published anonymously in 1681. John Dryden (1631–1700) was a prolific poet, essayist, and dramatist whose works include *Annus Mirabilis* (1667), *All for Love* (1677), *An Essay of Dramatic Poesy* (1668), *Mac Flecknoe* (1682), *The Medal* (1682), and translations of Virgil (1697), among many others. He was a member of the Anglican church and defended it vehemently while Charles II was alive, but when the Catholic James II succeeded him in 1685, Dryden quickly converted to Catholicism and remained loyal to the Church of Rome for the rest of his life.

Absalom and Achitophel (1681) was written in response to extreme political turbulence in England; the prerogatives of the crown were being challenged and Dryden, who was deeply loyal to King Charles II, felt compelled to promote political reform through his writing. Between 1679 and 1681 a bitter political struggle developed between Charles II (and his Tory followers) and the Earl of Shaftesbury, leader of the Whigs. The issue was royal succession, which became somewhat complicated since Charles had no legitimate children. The Tories believed that Charles's openly Catholic brother, James, Duke of York, was the rightful heir to the throne; the Whigs wanted Charles's illegitimate (but Protestant) son, the Duke of Monmouth, to be the next king. Dryden carefully and tactfully allegorized this conflict through the re-creation of the biblical story of Absalom's revolt against his father, King David (2 Samuel 13–18).

The poem is set in Israel, which becomes an allegorical representation of England. It begins with a satiric reference to David's [Charles II's] virility, which produces numerous illegitimate offspring. David's handsomest, noblest, and most-favored illegitimate child is Absalom [Duke of Monmouth]. David is a wise and virtuous king and has given his people no reason for insurrection; nevertheless, some unhappy Jews [Whigs] decide to rebel against him. Wiser Jews [Tories] advise against rebellion, citing that David has done nothing to provoke such action. But the rebels find a reason in the alleged Jebusite [Catholic] plan to convert Israel to the religion of the Egyptians [French]. The rebellion fails overall, but results in the creation of various political factions whose leaders are deeply dissatisfied with David and eager to end his reign.

In the next part of the poem the ambitious Achitophel [the Earl of Shaftesbury] emerges as the leader of these dissenting political groups. He tries to convince Absalom to overthrow his father's government and seize the throne. He flatters Absalom, telling him that the citizens want him to be their king. Absalom at first resists, recognizing that David is a wise king and that the legal successor to the throne is David's brother [the Duke of York], not himself. But Achitophel persists, telling Absalom that the country needs his strength, that the legal heir is planning his murder, and that David himself secretly wants Absalom to be the next king. Eventually, Absalom succumbs to these deceitful arguments, and Achitophel promptly begins drawing all political dissenters into one revolutionary party supporting Absalom.

As this party comes together, Dryden satirically portrays the misguided and ridiculous motives of these seditious leaders. The character of Zimri, a zealous and fickle rebel, represents Shaftesbury's Whig lieutenant, Buckingham. Shimei becomes the Sheriff of London, who betrayed Charles, and Corah allegorizes Titus Oakes, an infamous renegade Catholic who falsely testified to the existence of a plan to burn London, persecute Protestants, and restore the Catholic church to England.

Absalom, now convinced of his right to become king, travels across Israel to determine how strongly the citizens support his illegal claim to the throne. He presents himself to the people as their friend, deeply opposed to Egyptian domination and the alleged Jebusite plan, but unable to act because of his filial loyalty and the laws of royal succession. The gullible Jews embrace Absalom and proclaim him a new messiah. The conservative Dryden satirically attacks these naïve Jews (Whigs) for their unquestioning support of Absalom and their willingness to sacrifice the laws of legal succession.

In contrast to this stinging portrayal of the Jews, Dryden very sincerely depicts the admirable qualities of some of David's most loyal supporters. Barzillai [the Duke of Ormond] is especially noted for his devotion to David's cause and his true patriotism. Dryden also particularly praises two clergymen, the Sagan of Jerusalem [the Bishop of London] and Zadoc [the Archbishop of Canterbury], for their services to the crown. Other loyal patriots who are commended for staunchly serving their king in Sanhedrin [Parliament] include Hushai [Laurence Hyde], Jotham [the Marquis of Halifax], Adriel [the Earl of Musgrave], and Amiel [Edward Seymour]. They help convince David that his beloved son is being used by the traitorous Achitophel.

The final section of the poem, in which David gives a long and powerful speech, reasserts the royal prerogative and demonstrates David's strength as king. He refuses to excuse disloyalty within his kingdom, scorns the rebellious rationales of Achitophel and his seditious counterparts, disparages their claims that his brother was scheming to become king, and asserts his willingness to protect forcibly the established lawful rights of kings. As David finishes his speech, the Almighty shakes the earth with roaring thunder to demonstrate heavenly approval of David's words and to usher in a new era of legitimate kingly authority.

The allegory of *Absalom and Achitophel* is especially convincing because Dryden manages to promote the ideals of English political reform without relying on direct satire. It is certainly no secret that the poem is intended to disparage the radical Whig position and to encourage the conservative Tory declaration that the legal heir to the English throne must be Charles II's brother and not his illegitimate son. By using the biblical story of David and Absalom, Dryden superficially masks the identities of the English politicians he wants to denounce, thereby increasing the effectiveness and intensity of his attack.

Nahum Tate wrote a second part to *Absalom*. It was edited by Dryden and published in 1682. (Schilling 1961; Thomas 1978; Zwicker 1984)

See also Dryden, John.

ADAMS, RICHARD

British fantasy writer Richard Adams (b. 1920) was born in Newbury, England. Adams spent a great part of his early years exploring the rolling hills and fields of his native Berkshire, and, not surprisingly, his best works are full of that landscape and the animals that live in it. His works include *Shardik* (1977) and the now-classic *Watership Down* (1972). Adams uses the animal world in novels that speak at least indirectly to issues that concern contemporary human beings. Adams's work does not, however, employ the specific one-to-one correspondence that is characteristic of traditional allegory.

See also Watership Down.

THE ADVANCEMENT OF LEARNING

In this work the English philosopher Sir Francis Bacon (1561–1626) suggests in Book II that the purpose of allegory in both "Divine Poesie" and "Heathen Poesie" is to "retire and obscure" the contained message. The point would seem to be that allegory creates an intellectual puzzle that the reader can solve to his or her benefit and that the method can be applied not only to religious questions but to secular ones dealing with "Pollicy or Philosophy."

See also Bacon, Sir Francis.

THE ADVENTURES OF HUCKLEBERRY FINN

The Adventures of Huckleberry Finn (1885) is perhaps the most widely read novel of Mark Twain (Samuel Clemens, 1835–1910), who remains one of America's most beloved authors of stories that appeal to children and adults alike. The novel tells the story of young Huck Finn and his friend, a runaway slave named Jim. Huck, the narrator of the tale, stages his own murder in order to escape imprisonment by his drunken, blackguard father. Fleeing to Jackson Island, he encounters Jim, the slave of his adoptive family, who has decided to run away after overhearing plans to sell him. Huck discovers that his own "murder" has been blamed on Jim, and so the two resolve to leave their old lives behind and travel together down the Mississippi River on a raft.

As they journey down the river, Huck and Jim encounter feuding clans, mobs, criminals, and frauds, surviving each episode with daring and luck. In Arkansas, two rascals, hoping to cash in on a reward, reveal to a local farming family that Jim is a runaway slave. The farmer and his wife happen to be the uncle and aunt of Tom Sawyer, Huck's best friend. Posing as Tom, Huck tries to free his friend and, through a series of misadventures, Huck's true identity is revealed and Jim is told that he was legally freed when his owner died. At the end of the novel, Huck decides to head for the western territories rather than live with Tom's aunt Sally, who wants to "sivilize" him.

In spite of the satiric humor that pervades the novel, Huck and Jim's journey is a daring quest for freedom; it is this journey-quest motif which most obviously suggests an allegorical reading of the novel. But beyond the level of a personal quest, *Huckleberry Finn* has been loosely interpreted by some critics as an allegory of the development of the young American democracy. In this context, Huck represents a new American consciousness that is not afraid to turn away from established "civilization" in order to accept a new morality based on humanism and not on artificial social constructs. A somewhat more radical interpretation suggests that *Huckleberry Finn* is a religious allegory, in which Huck embodies the rejection of conventional Christianity and the acceptance of a less hypocritical, more moral position. (Doyno 1991; Lettis 1962)

See also The Quest as Allegory; Twain, Mark.

AENEID

Like most epics, the great Roman epic, the *Aeneid,* by Virgil (or Vergil, whose full name is Publius Vergilius Maro, 70–19 B.C.E.) has allegorical aspects. Most notably, the descent into the underworld in Book VI is an allegory of necessary renewal and rebirth. Here the hero, Aeneas, must atone for having lost sight of his duty, which was to found Rome, by searching out his destiny in the Underworld and, more importantly, by suffering the difficult process of returning to the world and his divinely appointed task. In modern terms the journey is a "dark night of the soul" or "night journey" in which one's psychological horrors are confronted and defeated so that true selfhood can be achieved.

In a more general sense, the whole poem could be called an allegory of Rome's divine mission to civilize the world. The poem had been commissioned by Augustus to celebrate that mission. The first six books tell the "history" of the Trojan Aeneas's travels after the sack of Troy. This is an allegory of the Roman spirit in search of its body—Rome, the "New Troy." The last six books depict Aeneas's battles with those who would prevent his mission. On the allegorical level, these books depict the struggles between barbarism—however heroic—and the new heaven-based Roman power and civilizing law. Aeneas himself is a model for the ideal Roman, more a priest than the hero that Ezra Pound suggested.

See also Epic as Allegory; The Quest as Allegory; Virgil.

AENIGMA

The sixteenth-century Englishman Henry Peacham, in *The Garden of Eloquence*, defines aenigma as "a kind of allegorie, differing [from other kinds] only in obscuritie, for Aenigma is a sentence or forme of speech, which for the darknesse, the sense may hardly be gathered" (27). An aenigma (enigma) in this sense is much like what we would call a riddle. It stands as a challenge to those who would find hidden meaning—allegory—within it. (Fletcher 1964)

AESOP

In the thirteenth century, a Byzantine monk, Planudes Maximus, wrote a *Life* as a preface to his Latin version of a collection of tales translated from the original Greek and attributed to a certain Aesop. Whether such an individual ever existed is open to question, but because of the biography by Planudes and earlier comments by the Greek historian Herodotus, who mentions a slave called Aesop, "the maker of fables," it is generally accepted that Aesop was indeed a slave, who was born on the island of Samos and who died in Delphi in the sixth century B.C.E.

AESOP'S FABLES

No more than a dozen fables can be definitely traced to the source identified as Aesop. The first collected fables attributed to Aesop were printed by Demetrius of Phalerum in the late fourth century B.C.E. Many of the tales usually attributed to him are probably of ancient Indian and even Egyptian origin. Still, it seems fair to say that Aesop, or the source referred to as Aesop, was the first great master of the allegorical fable—especially the animal fable—in the Western world. Although the animal fable existed in earlier times, in the Aesopian form it achieved, as the Greek philosopher Aristotle suggested, a certain instructional seriousness which the earlier, more humorous forms, had lacked. In fact, according to legend, Aesop was put to death for using his allegorical fables to criticize those in power in his day.

The typical Aesopian tale, then, is a satirical allegory in which animals often represent human characteristics. For example, in the famous tale of the fox and the fleas (attributed in Aristotle's *Rhetoric* [II, xx] to Aesop), it seems there once was a flea-infested fox who refused to allow a hedgehog to remove his tormentors. "Do not remove these fleas," said the fox to his friend, "they have

7

already had their fill of my blood; if you take them away other more hungry fleas will take their place." It seems that Aesop told this fable to suggest obliquely to the people of Samos that they not remove a certain politician from office because he had already embezzled what he wanted whereas any new politician would begin the whole process over again.

In another tale some frogs who asked for a king to rule them were sent a stork who ate them up. Supposedly this fable was told to suggest that removing the Athenian leader Pisistratus in favor of a stronger figure was probably not a good idea.

Not all Aesopian tales are animal fables. A well-known story is the one about the Goods and the Ills. Until the Ills forced the Goods out of the world of humans, the Goods and the Ills had an equal place in that world. But the Ills were present in greater numbers and so were able to drive the Goods out. The Goods made their way to Mount Olympus to ask God to avenge the crime done to them. Zeus granted their request that they be separated once and for all from the Ills and he decreed that from then on when the Ills visited the earth, they would have to go in groups, but that the Goods should visit one by one. So it is that there are more Ills than Goods in the world and that when Ills occur they do so in large numbers, whereas good things come singly and only to those who are able to recognize them.

See also Aesop; Fable as Allegory.

THE AFRICAN-AMERICAN CHURCH, ALLEGORY IN

African Americans have traditionally used allegory in religious practices and rhetoric. This is especially evident in sermons and gospel songs, where the condition of the biblical Hebrews becomes an allegory for the plight of the black slaves and their descendants. When the words "Let my people go" are sung in the black church, the words themselves are recognized as those of Moses and the people as the Hebrews in Egypt, but no one misses the real intention of the song in relation to the captivity of Africans in America. The same is true of the use in the black church and the black vernacular in general of such places as the Jordan River and the "Promised Land." To "cross over" the Jordan is to move on to a better life than the one lived in captivity here. The "Promised Land" is literally Israel but allegorically a land of "milk and honey" in the afterlife:

> I looked over Jordan and what did I see,
> Coming for to carry me home?
> A band of angels comin' after me,
> Coming for to carry me home.

AFRICAN-AMERICAN MUSIC AS ALLEGORY

In *Blues, Ideology and Afro-American Literature*, Houston A. Baker, Jr., reminds us that blues songs, the direct descendants of African-American slave songs, are inevitably about "something else," something other than what they literally say. In short, they are in some sense allegorical. Henry Louis Gates, Jr., in *The Signifying Monkey*, makes a similar assertion. He calls the rhetorical playing with words that characterizes the African-American vernacular in general, and the slave songs in particular, "signifying." Behind signifying is the slaves' practice of using songs, stories, and various other forms of "tricking the words"—really a form of coded speech—to comment to each other on their condition and their masters. As is often the case with allegory, the transference of meaning or signification depends on an audience that is aware of certain symbolic structures. The Christian can understand Bunyan's *Pilgrim's Progress* in ways that the Hindu cannot. The African-American slave could understand the real meaning of the slave songs in ways that the white master could not. And it can be argued that the same applies to the African American's understanding of blues as opposed to the white American's only partial understanding. Allegory depends on a "knowing" audience to whom others are in a sense unknowing outsiders. A blues song to the African American may be at once a lament and an expression of survival. It signifies the painful process of "coming through" in the face of an intolerable social situation. For the white nightclub audience the blues song might well be simply a sad and sexy song about the trials and tribulations of love.

An example of signifying allegory in songs sung by the slaves is the well-known spiritual "Steal Away to Jesus." To the ignorant listener this is a touching example of the deep spirituality of the slaves. According to the ex-slave Wash Wilson, writing in the 1930s, the song had an entirely different and much more pragmatic meaning:

> When de niggers go round singin' "Steal Away to Jesus," dat mean dere gwine be a 'ligious meetin' dat night. Dat de sig'fication of a meetin'. De masters 'fore and after freedom didn't like dem 'ligious meetin's, so us natcherly slips off at night, down in de bottoms or somewheres. Sometimes us sing and pray all night. (Gates 1988)

ALAN OF LILLE

A French humanist and Platonist scholar of the twelfth century, Alan of Lille (or Alain de Lille) wrote *Anticlaudianus*, an allegory in verse on the origins of the soul and *De Planctu Naturae [Complaint of Nature]*, a poem in which the allegorical figure of Nature complains about the human breaking of her laws and the separation between man and Nature that leaves the former in a depraved state. (Bloomfield 1981)

ALBEE, EDWARD

Edward Albee was born in 1928 in Washington, D.C., and was raised by his wealthy adoptive family in Larchmont, New York. His academic career was erratic; after being dismissed from two prep schools, he eventually was graduated from Choate and attended, but did not graduate from, Trinity College in Hartford, Connecticut. His parents owned a chain of vaudeville theaters, and Albee was surrounded by theater and theater people throughout his childhood. Since his first play, *The Zoo Story*, opened in 1959, Edward Albee has been considered one of the more inventive and influential American playwrights. Often compared with the great modern American dramatists Eugene O'Neill, Arthur Miller, and Tennessee Williams, Albee's caustic social criticism and biting wit have created for him a permanent spot in the canon of American drama. His plays are haunted by the recurring themes of loneliness, alienation, and the illusions that people create to protect themselves from the reality of their empty lives.

　　See also Tiny Alice; Who's Afraid of Virginia Woolf?

ALCHEMY AND ALLEGORY

See The Chemical Wedding.

ALGER, HORATIO

Horatio Alger (1832–1899) was an American writer of books for boys. His 100 or more books were widely read in the late nineteenth and early twentieth centuries. Born in Revere, Massachusetts, Alger attended Harvard, worked for a newspaper, and later was ordained a Unitarian minister. In 1866 he gave up his ministry and moved to New York where he began a long association with the Newsboys' Lodging House, a rich source for his many portraits of homeless boys who, through the virtues of hard work and individualism were able eventually to "make good." (Alger also wrote biographies of actual self-made men, most notably, of Abraham Lincoln and James A. Garfield.)

　　A great deal of apocryphal material surrounds Alger's life. A now-discredited 1928 biography by Herbert Mayes presents a picture of a repressed child of a Unitarian minister who fled to Paris in rebellion and later became chaplain of a boys' lodging house and began writing the books that made him one of the most popular writers of his time. The facts are unclear. What is sure is that he did write the *Ragged Dick* series (1867 ff.), the *Luck and Pluck* series (1869 ff.), and the *Tattered Tom* series (1871 ff.). All of these books were based on the American Dream—the "rags to riches" dream. While not, strictly speaking, allegories, they are clearly representative of that dream. The basic plot of all of the books is the same: poor boy works hard and is rewarded by material success. The "Horatio Alger hero," who has become what might be called an American archetype, is symbolic of the idea prevalent in Alger's time—a time of vast and rapid commercial growth in America—that immense success was possible for any hardworking, honest, and moral American boy, however poor.

　　The most famous of the Alger novels was *Ragged Dick; or Street Life in New York with the Boot-Blacks.* Dick Hunter is the persona taken by the Alger hero in this story of a New York City shoe shine boy who works hard, takes advantage of opportunities, remains pious and moral in spite of many deprivations, and eventually rises to a position of respect and wealth in society.

In current literary circles Horatio Alger is not held in high esteem. Some criticize his stock characterization and plot making. Some find fault with his blind acceptance of the American capitalist ethic. Some have pointed to what they see as simplistic Freudian allegory—Alger's heroes represent the author in his struggle against his father, who takes form as the villain who always attempts to thwart and take advantage of the hero.

ALICE'S ADVENTURES IN WONDERLAND

Originally published as *Alice's Adventures under Ground* (1865), *Alice's Adventures in Wonderland* is certainly the most famous children's story written by the Reverend Charles Lutwidge Dodgson, better known as Lewis Carroll (1832–1898), and is perhaps one of the most widely read children's tales of all time. The dream-fantasy of seven-year-old Alice, who falls down a rabbit hole and encounters all kinds of fantastic adventures and remarkable characters, charmed and fascinated adults as well as children, making it an immediate best-seller. Memorable characters such as the White Rabbit, the Mad Hatter, the March Hare, and the King and Queen of Hearts satirize Victorian education, literature, politics, and life in general.

The tale begins with a young girl called Alice following a white rabbit in his descent down a rabbit hole. In fact, Alice falls down the hole and when she comes to the bottom she tries to follow the rabbit, who rushes on ahead of her complaining that he will be late. Finding herself before a set of locked doors, Alice discovers a little key and uses it to open one of the doors. Beyond the tiny door is a beautiful miniature garden. Alice is bemoaning the fact that she is too large to enter it when a bottle appears. She drinks its contents and becomes too small to reach the key she has left on a table. When she eats a piece of cake nearby she grows too large even to stand up. All of this is the beginning of a series of adventures including falling into a pool made of her own tears, confronting a rude caterpillar who, from his perch on a mushroom, challenges her to recite "You are old, Father William," which she does. She also meets a duchess holding a baby, and the baby turns into a pig. And there is a Cheshire Cat who grins at her. She attends a tea party given by the Mad Hatter, who, with his guests, the March Hare and the Doormouse, talk sheer nonsense. She is introduced by the Duchess to a character called the Mock Turtle. Finally, the Queen of Hearts, in a bizarre trial, orders that the girl's head be cut off. As the entire court rushes toward Alice she accuses them of being nothing but a pack of cards and she awakens from her dream, one that would be continued in a sequel called *Through the Looking Glass*.

Critics have suggested that *Alice in Wonderland* symbolically represents everything from a Freudian dreamscape to a psychedelic drug "trip." Allegorically, the novel has been associated with the Oxford or "High Church"

The Queen of Hearts orders that Alice's head be cut off in *Alice's Adventures in Wonderland*.

movement of the mid–nineteenth century, partly because of Carroll's position as a don at Christ Church. In this interpretation, Alice allegorically depicts an innocent everyman who encounters characters and situations symbolizing religious and political excesses in various ways. For example, the White Rabbit is an English clergyman, the Caterpillar stands for Oxford philosophy, the King and Queen of Hearts are Royal Supremacy, the Mock Turtle is the Victorian Church of England, and so on. Other critics maintain that *Alice's Adventures* may be read as a radical parody of the morally allegorical stories that were standard reading fare for Victorian children. Instead of learning from her mistakes and evolving into a more mature, morally upstanding girl (as was most often the case in children's literature of the time), Alice does not progress morally. She is not punished for the curiosity that initially leads her down the rabbit hole, and she does not seem to acquire any sort of moral code as a result of her adventures. (Leach 1971; Leslie 1971)

See also Carroll, Lewis; *Through the Looking Glass.*

ALL HALLOWS EVE

While not strictly speaking an allegory, Charles Williams's last novel, *All Hallows Eve* (1948), has much in common with allegorical literature in that a primary purpose of the book is to illustrate Williams's particular mystical brand of Christianity. Thus, although the main character, Lester Furnival, cannot be said to stand for everyman in the way that Everyman in the medieval morality play of that name does, her passage through the mysterious events of the novel is certainly meant to represent what Williams sees as the possible triumph of Christian love over evil.

The plot of the novel is suffused with the presence of the dead Lester. She finds herself fully conscious but for the most part invisible in the London world in which she had lived before her death in a plane crash. As it turns out, her mission in the world of the living is a purgatorial one that will lead to her salvation and that of her still-living husband, Richard. The evil that Lester's love must overcome is represented by a corrupt faith healer called Simon the Clerk and his devoted follower, Lady Wallingford. Among the redeemable living are Richard and his Christian friend Jonathan, who is in love with Lady Wallingford's daughter, Betty. When Jonathan paints a commissioned portrait of Simon that reveals the subject's evil nature, Lady Wallingford, in a rage, takes her daughter away. Allegorically speaking, then, Betty becomes the human soul over which the powers of evil and good do battle.

Embodying Williams's theory that one who loves deeply enough can relieve a loved one of spiritual and emotional burdens, Lester in a mysterious way is able to visit Betty and to save her from Simon's evil machinations. In this, Lester is Christlike. As Lester saves Betty, she also saves her husband, appearing to him in various ways during the novel and causing him to understand the profundity of her love for him. Only when Richard and Lester understand each other fully can Lester be released into the light of eternal life.

It must be noted that *All Hallows Eve,* like most of Williams's work, is not so much allegorical as symbolic. In it one finds the ambiguity of realistic fiction, the development of complex characterization that is not a characteristic of traditional allegory. And most of all, the setting is contemporary and realistic. We are in London, with real people, facing real problems. Although the reader is led to look for secondary meaning in the presence of a dead protagonist, it can certainly be argued that the effectiveness of the novel does not depend on our believing or even understanding Williams's doctrines.

See also Williams, Charles.

ALLEGORESIS

Allegoresis, as opposed to allegory, is a term used most often by deconstructionists to differentiate the role of the reader from the writer in the process by which meaning is transferred in allegory. Allegoresis in its most basic sense is literary criticism which is, in fact, the subjectively imposed meaning of the reader. Thus, in his *Allegories of Reading,* Paul de Man stresses the impossibility of coming to a full understanding of an allegorical text because of the "structural interference of two distinct value systems"—the writer's and the reader's. In fact, says de Man, "allegorical narratives tell the story of the failure to read" (205). (de Man 1979; Hunter 1989; Quilligan 1979)

See also de Man, Paul.

ALLEGORIA

The Greek term for allegory.

ALLEGORY

Allegory, from the Greek *allegoria* (Latin *alia oratio),* means "other-speaking." The Greeks tended to associate allegory with the philosophical idea of hyponoia, the hidden meaning of myths, and our sense of allegory comes from that association. In allegory, literal meaning gives way to secondary meaning; it is the secondary meaning which takes precedence. The journey of Spenser's Red Crosse Knight is on the literal or primary level of meaning a journey from one place to another, but it is clear to the reader that the secondary meaning—the spiritual, political, and philosophical journey represented by the knight's travels—is the more important meaning. In allegory we are somehow made aware that we should be concentrating on that secondary level of meaning even when the primary or literal level works perfectly well as fiction. Swift's *Gulliver's Travels* works well on the literal level and contains sufficient characterization and suspense to interest us directly, but we never lose sight of the fact that we should be looking for the political and philosophical meaning contained in Swift's plots, settings, and characters.

THE ALLEGORY OF LOVE

The subtitle of this important critical work by C. S. Lewis is "A Study in Medieval Tradition." Lewis, better known for his *Chronicles of Narnia* and his space trilogy, was a scholar of medieval literature at Oxford University. In *The Allegory of Love,* he outlines the development of allegory. He begins by analyzing the medieval concept of courtly love and moves by way of a consideration of the use of allegory in love poems to a discussion of *The Romance of the Rose,*

Chrétien de Troyes, and Spenser's *Faerie Queene*. He makes the point that Chrétien's work evolves from the adventure tale *Erec*, to the high point of courtly love poetry in *Launcelot*, in which religious feeling is represented allegorically. The allegorical *Romance of the Rose* Lewis sees as a major influence on the thinking of the major English writers of the fourteenth to seventeenth centuries, establishing an allegorical mind-set that made possible the literary expression of the great moral themes contained in medieval love poetry. In *The Faerie Queene* of Spenser, for instance, Lewis concerns himself not so much with what he sees as the inferior political allegory as with the deep moral allegory he finds there, allegory that speaks to an essential need of the human imagination, a need also expressed in mythology. Not surprisingly, Lewis applies many of his theories fictionally in his *Narnia Chronicles* for children and his space trilogy for adults.

    See also Chrétien de Troyes; *The Chronicles of Narnia; Erec and Énide; The Faerie Queene;* Lewis, C. S.; *The Romance of the Rose; The Space Trilogy.*

ANDREAS CAPELLANUS

Known also as Andre le Chapelain, the Frenchman Andreas lived in the late twelfth and early thirteenth centuries. While serving as chaplain to the king, Andreas also found time to write an important book on courtly love, *The Art of Love.*

    See also *The Art of Love.*

ANIMAL FARM

Animal Farm is the best known work of George Orwell, who was born Eric Arthur Blair in 1903 in Bengal, India. *Animal Farm* was first published in 1945, in spite of many rejections from publishers who thought the book incendiary, considering England's alliance with Russia since 1941. However, *Animal Farm* became a huge success, making Orwell both internationally famous and financially secure. George Orwell lived to complete one other literary masterpiece, *Nineteen Eighty-Four*, before he died of tuberculosis in London in 1950.

    Animal Farm is the story of a rural farm whose overworked and underfed animals revolt against their owner, Mr. Jones. After overthrowing Jones and expelling him from the farm, the animals, who can think rationally and communicate with each other, establish a government of their own. The pigs of the farm, empowered by their ability to read and write, lead the new government and place themselves in powerful and prestigious roles. The other animals, who banded together in good faith at the beginning of the revolution, are eventually betrayed by the power-crazed pigs, especially their leader, Napoleon. They are forced to return to their former servitude, again overworked and underfed, this time enslaved not by a human being, but by one of their former allies. The novel ends with the recognition that the condition of the animals has not improved and in fact may have worsened; only the leadership of the farm has changed.

Animal Farm is a beast fable, a form traditionally used to satirize human vices and folly by representing them in the characters of animals. But Orwell's beast fable can be interpreted as a political allegory with definite historical references. The animals on the farm, who journey from political naïveté at the beginning of the tale to political sophistication at the end, are closely based on the historical characters or character types prevalent during the first 30 years of the Soviet Union. Manor Farm, later to be renamed Animal Farm, becomes Russia itself, and Mr. Jones becomes Tsar Nicholas II. Old Major, the elderly white boar who both predicts and inspires the revolution, is a combination of Marx and Lenin. Napoleon, the power-hungry boar and eventual leader of the farm, is Joseph Stalin; the select group of pigs that surrounds him is the Politburo. Snowball, the boar who rivaled Napoleon's popularity and was consequently expelled from the farm, is Leon Trotsky. The propagandists of the Soviet regime are represented by Squealer, the pig whose role is to justify the actions of Napoleon and his associates to the other animals of the farm. The general pig population, capable of reading, writing, and planning, are the Bolshevik intellectuals who led the revolution in Russia and dominated the Soviet bureaucracy. The ferocious dogs, trained by Napoleon himself, represent the Soviet secret police who helped to maintain Stalin's power. These animals situate themselves for much of the story in Jones's farmhouse: the Kremlin.

Other animals in the novel fill the roles of people and groups who were less powerful in the Communist regime of the Soviet Union. Boxer, the carthorse, represents the decent, loyal, hardworking proletarian who will willingly kill and die for his land and beliefs. Clover, the mare, portrays the protective, gentle, motherly, hardworking woman of the laboring class. Mollie, the vain and self-indulgent mare who eventually flees the farm, characterizes the White Russians who opposed the revolution and escaped the country. Benjamin, the donkey, one of the smarter animals on the farm, depicts the average man who becomes cynical through his recognition of invidious government corruption. Moses, the tame raven, forever preaching about Sugarcandy Mountain (Heaven) to the animals, represents the Russian Orthodox church and to some extent the Roman Catholic church. Finally, the extensive sheep population on the farm signifies the ignorant public who are easily led and willing to repeat thoughtlessly any fragment of propaganda.

Even the neighbors of Animal Farm assume allegorical roles consonant with the historical referents of the story. Farmer Pilkington represents Churchill's England, and Farmer Frederick, known for his cruelty to the animals on his farm, symbolizes Hitler's Germany. Individual events of the story also parallel events following the 1917 Russian Revolution: the Windmill and its destruction represent the failed plan for rapid Soviet industrialization, the hens' revolt signifies the resistance of the peasants to collective farming, the animals' false criminal confessions suggest the Purge Trials of the 1930s, and the counterfeit money that Farmer Frederick exchanges for the animals' corn depicts Hitler's betrayal of the Nazi-Soviet Pact of 1939.

Similarly, the internal conditions of the farm allegorize most effectively the internal conditions of Soviet Russia after the Revolution. The pigs' acquisition of luxuries, privileges, and power on the farm parallels the rise of the Communist party in the Soviet Union. The pigs first break and then alter each of the Seven Commandments upon which Animal Farm was founded, but with each betrayal they assume more rewards: apples, milk, the farmhouse, beds, alcohol, clothes, and, essentially, the power to murder indiscriminately and with impunity. Similarly, the Communists under Stalin reaped many benefits for their exploitation and abuse of the proletariat workers, taking for themselves and enjoying what they had outlawed for the rest of the population.

Orwell's *Animal Farm* is certainly an allegory about the effects of the establishment of the Soviet Union, written to expose the cruelties and injustices of a regime supposedly dedicated to equality for all. Yet the novel may also be interpreted as a political allegory targeting not just the Russian Revolution, but all political revolutions. Orwell reveals, through his animal characters, a world that is unable to live up to its own ideals. Allegorically speaking, this vision may be applied to the inability of any human community to live in harmony, equality, and peace according to an idealized set of moral edicts. (Greenblatt 1974; Lee 1969; Meyers 1991; Smyer 1988)

See also Orwell, George.

ANTICLAUDIANUS

See Alan of Lille.

APULEIUS, LUCIUS

The Latin writer Apuleius, best known as the author of *Metamorphoses*, better known as *The Golden Ass,* one of the earliest Roman novels, was born in North Africa—probably Carthage—in about 125 C.E. What we know of the life of Apuleius is slight. It seems he was born of well-to-do parents and educated in Carthage and Athens. In Athens he studied poetry, philosophy, music, and geometry and later moved to Rome, where he achieved a reputation as a great stylist among the literary set. He also became a follower of the Egyptian goddess Isis and began a long study of magical rites associated with her cult. In 156 Apuleius began a long journey around the empire only to become involved in a strange situation in which he agreed to marry a wealthy woman older than himself, was accused of seducing her by black magic and murdering her, and was tried. Eventually he found his way back to Carthage, where he gained a reputation as a great orator and an advocate of emperor worship. He died in Carthage in about 175 C.E.

See also *Cupid and Psyche; The Golden Ass.*

AQUINAS, THOMAS

The Christian theologian and philosopher Thomas Aquinas (1225–1274) was born of a noble family near Aquino. He became a Dominican friar in 1244 and studied in Cologne and Paris before being called to teach in the papal Curia. Aquinas was particularly interested in the Greek philosopher Aristotle and was able to apply Aristotelian thought to Christian theology. His most famous work is the *Summa Theologia,* in which he discusses many aspects of the relationship between faith and reason. He reminds us that "God is the author of Holy Scripture," that it is in God's power to signify meaning in scripture both by words and by things described by words. In the "science" of holy doctrine signification is literal and historical, but also spiritual. In the spiritual aspect, elements of the Old Testament are representative of the New and they refer also to the life of the soul in Christ and to the larger world of God's "eternal glory." These levels of the spiritual nature of the science of holy doctrine are all contained in the term *allegory,* says Aquinas.

Aquinas, now Saint Thomas Aquinas, is generally considered the greatest of Catholic theologians. His followers are called Thomists.

See also Bede, The Venerable; The Bible and Allegory; Dante Alighieri.

ARCHITECTURE AND ALLEGORY

See Church Architecture and Allegory; Painting and Sculpture, Allegorical.

ARGENIS

An allegorical Latin prose romance by the seventeenth-century writer John Barclay, *Argenis* was once universally praised; it was translated into English by Ben Jonson. Since the nineteenth century, however, it has received little notice. The plot of *Argenis* concerns the complicated adventures of a young man who becomes involved in a war between the king of Sicily and a rebel faction. The young man, Archombrutus, supports the king, along with another young man, Policharus. Both fall in love with the king's daughter, Argenis, who loves Policharus. The dispute between the two erstwhile friends is resolved when it is revealed that Archombrutus is in reality the king's son by an earlier secret marriage and thus the half-brother of Argenis. Archombrutus becomes heir to the throne, but Policharus wins his Argenis.

The story of *Argenis* is a political allegory. Its subject was believed to be the political struggles in France before the Concordat of Henry IV. Sicily represented France, Argenis was the French throne, and the rivals to her hand represented two factions supporting Henry IV.

It was not for the allegory that *Argenis* was ever read, however. The praises heaped on the work in the two centuries after its publication were based almost exclusively on the brilliance of the author's Latin style.

See also Barclay, John.

☖ ARMAH, AYI KWEI ☖

Born in 1939 in the seaport of Sekondi-Takoradi, Ghana, Ayi Kwei Armah was educated in Ghana, at Harvard University, and in New York. He worked as a writer, translator, journalist, and lecturer in Ghana, Algeria, France, and the United States before settling for some time in Tanzania. His first novel, *The Beautyful Ones Are Not Yet Born* (1969), takes its title from a slogan the author saw on a Ghanaian bus. Armah frequently addresses, in his fiction and in his many essays, his disillusionment with postcolonial Africa. His other novels include *Fragments* (1970), *Why Are We So Blest?* (1972), *Two Thousand Seasons* (1972), and *The Healers* (1975). Armah has lived in Dakar, Senegal, since 1982.

    See also The Beautyful Ones Are Not Yet Born.

☖ *THE ART OF LOVE* ☖

Following in the tradition of Ovid's *Ars Amoris*, Andreas Capellanus or Andre le Chapelain (late twelfth century) wrote this Latin dialogue on courtly love. While not an allegory, the work is, as Paul Piehler suggests (94), at times a parody of religious allegory in which Andreas uses the allegorical method to speak clearly about the joys of erotic and courtly love. The nobleman, who in *The Art of Love* attempts to seduce a "lady," depicts an allegorical landscape dominated by such figures as Rex Amoris (the "King of Love") and Love's militia, and the *via quaedam pulcherrima* (the "most beautiful path"). (Piehler 1971)

    See also Andreas Capellanus.

☖ ARTHURIAN ALLEGORY ☖

During the Middle Ages, King Arthur, the legendary king of the Celtic Britons, and his court, especially Sir Lancelot, came to be associated allegorically with the noble possibilities of life in this world as opposed to the next. The chivalry and dedication of the knights of the Round Table represented a kind of medieval humanism that was bound to give way to the darker side represented by Sir Mordred and Morgan Le Fey, who would be responsible for Arthur's death. The spiritual gap in the Round Table, expressed in the tendency of the knights to become gradually complacent in their noble status and by the illicit and therefore unchivalric relationship between Lancelot and Arthur's queen, Guinevere, eventually had to be filled by the interjection of the nontemporal. The quest for the Holy Grail—the cup used by Jesus at the Last Supper—was caused by the appearance of the Grail itself among the knights during the Feast of Pentecost, the celebration of the coming of the Holy Spirit to the disciples of the dead Christ. And it is the gentle Christlike Galahad, the illegitimate son of Lancelot, rather than Lancelot himself, who in most versions of the story finally finds the Grail and brings the spiritual essence back to the lost temporal world represented by Arthur and his original company. (Honig 1966; Mac-Queen 1970)

See also Chrétien de Troyes; *Erec and Énide; The Idylls of the King; Le Morte d'Arthur*.

ATTIS MYTH

There are many versions of the story of Attis, the sacrificial god of ancient Phrygia in Anatolia. Attis and his mother, Cybele, became important cult figures in Rome. The philosopher Sallustius provides us with the classic allegorical reading of the myth in question.

According to the story told by Sallustius, Cybele, the Great Mother, fell in love with the beautiful boy Attis as he lay by the Gallus river. She crowned him with her cap of stars and took him to herself. But Attis dallied with a nymph and deserted the Mother. As a punishment Cybele made the boy go mad; he cut off his genitals, gave them to the nymph, and returned to the Goddess.

For Sallustius, the Great Mother is the life force, the source of generation. Attis is a metaphor for the creation of things that are death-defined, things that live and die. He is a necessary adjunct to the Mother. He was discovered lying by the river Gallus, because Gallus represents the galaxy—the Milky Way—which represents the fluid of passion. Attis loves a nymph because nymphs are the guardians of generation, generation being based in fluid (it is said that Attis as a child had been suckled on "he-goat's milk"). In the end, Attis sacrifices his genitals because generation must be stopped at some point. His return to the Mother recognizes the source of all creation in the gods.

Sallustius goes on to suggest a more human level of allegory for the myth, one that explains a Roman, Easter-like ritual of Attis:

> At first we, having fallen away from the gods
> and living with a Nymph, are despondent. We
> abstain from corn and all rich foods, because
> they are not good for the soul. Then we cut
> down the tree of Attis and we fast totally; this
> represents the cutting off of further generation.
> Then we drink the milk and are born again. We rejoice
> and symbolically return to the gods. (In Murray 1951)

(MacQueen 1970; Murray 1951)

See also Sallustius.

AUGUSTINE

Aurelius Augustinas (354–430 C.E.) was one of the early "church fathers," a theologian and philosopher best known for *The Confessions, The City of God,* and *On Nature and Grace.* While Augustine is not known as an allegorist, a title such as *The City of God* suggests allegory—the city standing for the heavenly kingdom—and Augustine spoke often of the joy of seeking meaning beneath the obscure surfaces of scripture. In *The City of God*, he writes, "The *Song of Songs* is a certain spiritual pleasure of holy minds, in the marriage of that King and Queen-city, that is, Christ and the Church. But the pleasure is wrapped up in allegorical veils, that the bridegroom may be more ardently desired, and more joyfully unveiled, and may appear" (XVII, 20). (Fletcher 1964)

See also The Song of Songs.

AUSTEN, JANE

The English novelist Jane Austen (1775–1817) was the sixth of seven children born to the Reverend George Austen in Steventon, Hampshire. Austen's personal life appears relatively uneventful; she never married but did develop extremely close ties with her family, particularly with her sister Cassandra. Austen's literary career began at the age of 15 with a burlesque of Samuel Richardson called *Love and Friendship*. Soon after, she embarked on fiction writing with a keen eye for that which she found ridiculous in contemporary society. Austen's novels are characterized by their portrayals of middle-class provincial families, acute psychological analysis of the characters, and often humorously satiric examinations of courtship and social conventions. Her published novels include *Sense and Sensibility* (1811), *Pride and Prejudice* (1813), *Mansfield Park* (1814), and *Emma* (1816), as well as *Northanger Abbey* and *Persuasion*, both published posthumously in 1818. Austen's novels were not especially successful during her lifetime, but she is now recognized as an important contributor to the maturing of the English novel. Austen died at the age of 41 and is buried in the cathedral in Winchester.

See also Mansfield Park.

AUTO SACRAMENTALE

The *auto sacramentale* (sacramental mystery play) was a form of allegorical Eucharist play popular in Spain in the sixteenth, seventeenth, and eighteenth centuries. It was derived from the religious drama of the Middle Ages. The purpose of the *auto* was theological and philosophical. Allegory was present not only in the plots and characters but in stage action and dialogue. Like the mystery plays of that period, the *autos* were performed for the feast of Corpus Christi (Body of Christ). Lope de Vega (1562–1635) and Rojas Zorrilla (1607–1648) had written *autos sacramentales* earlier, but it was Pedro Calderón de la Barca (1600–1681) who made the most of the form. Calderón is generally considered to be the greatest dramatist of Spain's Baroque Golden Age. A soldier and playwright, he became a priest in 1651 and after that wrote for the most part only *autos sacramentales*. One of the most famous of his plays is *El Gran Teatro del Mundo [The Great Theater of the World]* (ca. 1637), which in itself suggests an allegorical intention. (Frye 1957; Parker 1943)

See also Calderón de la Barca, Pedro; *The Great Theater of the World.*

BACON, SIR FRANCIS

The London-born philosopher, lawyer, statesman, translator, and essayist (1561–1626) thought of himself as a "second Aristotle" and set out through his writings to reconsider the science and philosophy of his day. Much of his time was spent in politics. Before being imprisoned for bribery, he achieved the high position of Lord Chancellor in 1617. Bacon was so successful a writer that in the great controversy that has raged over the authorship of Shakespeare's plays he has been mentioned more often than most other candidates as the true bard.

See also *The Advancement of Learning*.

BALE, JOHN

John Bale (1495–1563) was an English playwright who, after converting to Protestantism, enthusiastically supported the English Reformation. Five of his plays, all anti-Catholic morality plays, have survived: *Three Laws, God's Promises, John the Baptist, The Temptation of Our Lord*, and his most important work, *King John*.

See also *King John;* Morality Plays.

BARAKA, AMIRI

Born in Newark, New Jersey, in 1934, the then–Leroi Jones achieved fame as a poet and later as a radical crusader for African-American rights. Not long after off-Broadway success with his one-act play *Dutchman* in 1964, Jones changed his name to Amiri Baraka to emphasize his struggle against the white power structure that had given him his old "slave name." Baraka's writings are not allegory, but their dependence on highly symbolic and representative characters gives them an almost surrealistic effect that sometimes seems to call for allegorical interpretation. In *Dutchman*, for example, a young black man in a grey flannel suit, who is seduced into violence by a provocative white woman, seems to represent the African American who can only succeed in the white world by wearing its psychological, emotional, and even physical "uniforms" while hiding a deep hatred and righteous anger within.

See also The System of Dante's Hell.

BARCLAY, JOHN

John Barclay (1582–1621) was a Scottish writer, born in France, who composed poetic romances and satires in Latin. He died in Italy. Barclay was influenced by the work of Petronius, the Latin writer of the picaresque novel *Satyricon*. In fact, Barclay wrote his own version of *Satyricon* but was best known for the allegorical prose romance *Argenis*.

See also Argenis.

BAUM, L. FRANK

Lyman Frank Baum (1856–1919), the son of a wealthy New York businessman, worked at a variety of jobs before finding lasting success as a writer of children's literature. The stories he told to his own children formed the foundation for his first published children's tales, *Mother Goose in Prose* (1897). One of the characters introduced in this book was Dorothy Gale, the farm girl from Kansas who became the heroine of *The Wonderful Wizard of Oz* (1900). After its remarkable and immediate success, Baum wrote 14 more tales about the adventures of Oz. Indeed, the adventures of this fantasy world did not end with Baum's death in 1919; 26 more books about Oz appeared between 1919 and 1951, written by various authors. *The Wonderful Wizard of Oz*, by far the most memorable of all Baum's tales, has been immortalized by the 1939 musical film called *The Wizard of Oz*, starring Judy Garland.

See also The Wonderful Wizard of Oz.

THE BEAUTYFUL ONES ARE NOT YET BORN

This 1969 novel of the Ghanaian author Ayi Kwei Armah is a searing attack on Nkrumah's postcolonial betrayal of the Ghanaian people. Set in Accra, the story depicts an anonymous Man with a meaningless job whose strong sense of personal integrity forces him to resist accepting bribes and other forms of social corruption. The man struggles to support his family honestly, while all around him is evidence that everyone else has succumbed to the corrupt social and political system. He is despised by his family and overlooked by the world; he suffers in private anguish, wondering about his own penchant for stoic endurance in the face of wicked humanity.

While not a pure allegory, *The Beautyful Ones Are Not Yet Born* is in some ways an allegorical rendering of the bleak conditions in postcolonial Ghana. Few characters are named and locations are not specific. The unnamed hero becomes the Everyman character, trying to remain true to his own personal morality and make sense of a corrupt world (denoted by the images of filth, pollution, and excrement that dominate descriptions of the city). Material success has become the only measure of a person's worth, which has led to total disregard of any ethical or community considerations. Critic Shatto Arthur Gakwandi suggests that *The Beautyful Ones Are Not Yet Born* "is only valid when it is distanced as an allegory or when it is presented as an aspect of the man's mind. . . . The more universal concerns of the novel are the effects of human lust for power and money when these are given free rein in a society. Then the sense of community and mutual respect is shattered and every man relies on the self-seeking unscrupulous aspects of his nature to secure his position in that society" (Gakwandi, 107). Thus, Armah seems to be saying with his allegory, it is not human nature itself that ought to be condemned, but the social situations that elicit the cruelty and greed inherent in all people. (Fraser 1980; Gakwandi 1992)

See also Armah, Ayi Kwei.

BECKETT, SAMUEL

Samuel Beckett (1906–1989) was born near Dublin, graduated from Trinity College in 1927, and moved to Paris. He spent the rest of his life in France, writing plays and fiction and teaching in the French *lycées.* Beckett's first major success as a playwright came with the 1952 release of *Waiting for Godot,* a despairing comedy about waiting for something that never appears. Later plays, including *Endgame* (1958), also wrestle with the themes of negation, disappointment, and nonexistence. Along with his writing, Beckett contributed his talents to stage and radio drama, film, and mime; he received the Nobel Prize for Literature in 1969.

See also Endgame; Waiting for Godot.

BECKFORD, WILLIAM

Beckford (1760–1844) is a major figure among gothic novelists. His *Vathek: An Arabian Tale* (1786), which, though he was English, he wrote in French, is a classic in the genre—one that emphasizes the mysterious and the bizarre and is an allegory. Beckford liked all things gothic; he created a gothic estate at Fonthill Abbey in England.

See also Vathek.

BEDE, THE VENERABLE

An Anglo-Saxon scholar, historian, and theologian, The Venerable Bede (673–735) discussed allegory in various ways, bringing together classical and

Christian approaches. His *De Schematibus et Tropis Sacrae Scripturae [Concerning the Figures and Tropes of Holy Scriptures]* (ca. 700) contains a chapter called "De Allegoria" in which the writer follows in the tradition of classical writers such as Quintilian who tie allegory to irony. In a chapter called "De Asteismo" ("Concerning Wit"), he discusses the classical idea of allegory as a kind of witty double meaning and applies the idea to biblical allegorical interpretation. Allegory, says Bede, has a factual and a verbal side, verbal allegory using imagery to convey prophetic meaning, factual allegory using Old Testament facts to represent later Christian ones. The image in Isaiah XI of the "rod out of the stem of Jesse" is purely verbal, referring allegorically to Christ being born via the line of David through Mary. Factual allegory is contained, for example, in the Genesis 37 story in which Joseph was sold to the Ishmaelites for "thirty pieces of silver," representing for Christians the later selling of Christ. Bede also takes up the four levels of meaning outlined by John Cassian: the literal or historical, the purely allegorical, the moral or tropological, and the anagogical.

> Take, for instance, the phrase, "the Temple of the Lord." In terms of history, it is the house which Solomon built: in terms of allegory, it is the body of the Lord, about which John speaks in his second chapter, "Destroy this temple, and in three days I will raise it up." Or it is his Church, to whom is said, "The temple of God is holy, which temple ye are." By tropology it is each of the faithful, to whom it is said in I Corinthian III, "Know ye not that your bodies are the temple of the Holy Spirit, which is in you?" By anagogy, it is the mansions of joy above, to which aspired the man who said, "Blessed are they who dwell in thy house, O Lord; they will praise thee for ever and ever." [John MacQueen translation, 51–52.] (MacQueen 1970)

See also The Bible and Allegory; Cassian, John; Fourfold Allegory; Quintilian; Satire and Allegory.

 # BELLOW, SAUL

Born in Quebec in 1915 to immigrant Russian parents, Saul Bellow and his family moved to Chicago in 1924. Bellow was educated at the University of Chicago, Northwestern University, and the University of Wisconsin. Since then he has pursued an academic career and has written numerous novels, short stories, plays, academic publications, and a travel book about modern Israel. His well-deserved place in the canon of American literature was sealed when he was awarded the Nobel Prize for Literature in 1976.

See also Henderson the Rain King.

"BELOW THE MILL-DAM"

Rudyard Kipling (1865–1936), an English Victorian poet and storyteller, is perhaps best remembered for his two *Jungle Books* (1894, 1895) and *Kim* (1901). Yet Kipling's 1902 story "Below the Mill Dam" is a particularly good example of an allegorical tale that offers important insights into the political and industrial state of England at the turn of the century. It may be read as the story of a revolution culminating in the triumph of new populism in England, directed by right-wing radicals such as Kipling himself. Much of the story involves conversations between a Black Rat and a Grey Cat, who live in an ancient water mill. The Waters and the Wheel (of the mill) also function as characters in the story, and together they discuss (among other things) the possible advantages and disadvantages of the Miller using the mill to generate electricity.

Politically, the Black Rat may represent Lord Salisbury and, more generally, members of Britain's upper class, who were gradually losing their social prominence. This group deeply resented any infringement on what they believed to be their traditional role in society. The Grey Cat, it has been argued, allegorizes Alfred Balfour, Lord Salisbury's nephew and a member of the Parliament. The Cat is connected to Balfour through its color (Balfour's hair turned gray during his four years at the Irish Office), its demeanor (both are somewhat antisocial), and its ability to survive (the Cat withstands being doused in the Waters; Balfour weathered many vigorous political conflicts). The Waters figure into this allegorical interpretation as a representation of the masses, a voting bloc large enough to be worthy of some concern to the powerful political parties. The old mill itself, and its eventual ability to generate electricity, allegorizes the conservative Kipling's vision of an England in which the modernization of political thought and action was long overdue. (Parry 1988)

See also Kipling, Rudyard.

BENITO CERENO

See Melville, Herman.

BENJAMIN, WALTER

Walter Benjamin (1892–1940) is generally thought to be one of the greatest of German cultural critics. A Jew who exiled himself from his native Germany during the early Hitler years, Benjamin was a Marxist who championed fellow–Marxist exile Bertolt Brecht and argued for the necessity, in the context of depersonalized modern life, of moving beyond what he called "auratic appreciation" of works of art to a more socioeconomic understanding of what the surfaces of works signify. By "auratic appreciation," Benjamin meant the traditional reverential—what he would call "bourgeois"—approach to art.

In a deconstructionist sense, Benjamin's approach might be called allegorical. The purpose of his analysis is to break down traditional perceptions of the world by exposing the socioeconomic thought-structure behind the linguistic and "allegorical" masks of modernist writers. What the critic eventually derives, says Benjamin, is a new sociohistoric aura—leading to an exposé of the horrors of modern life—to replace the old "auratic appreciation." Some of

Benjamin's most important works include the essays "The Work of Art in the Age of Mechanical Reproduction" and "The Author as Producer."
  See also Allegoresis; Brecht, Bertolt.

BEOWULF

Although many of the details surrounding the composition of *Beowulf* remain a mystery, the poem has come to be regarded as a great masterpiece of Anglo-Saxon literature. The author of this heroic epic is unknown, and scholars differ greatly as to when it was actually composed. Speculations range from the early eighth to the tenth century, but the years between 700 and 850 are often regarded as the most probable approximate date of composition; the extant manuscript of *Beowulf* was written in approximately the year 1000. In 1731, this manuscript was badly damaged in a fire in the London library where it and many other medieval English manuscripts were housed. A number of words, lines, and even an entire passage of the poem were destroyed in the fire; nevertheless, considering the condition of other extant medieval manuscripts, the text of *Beowulf* is remarkably complete.

The story is set in the sixth century, before the migration of Germanic tribes to Britain, and offers rare insight into the Anglo-Saxon culture of the time. Through the adventures of the warrior-hero Beowulf, the poet highlights the importance of such qualities as loyalty, honor, fidelity, and courage in battle. Although an inherently pagan story, Beowulf is largely informed by the Christian tradition which had already spread to England by the time the poet composed his epic. Specific references to the Old Testament occur throughout the work, and some critics explain that this decidedly Christian influence functions as an allegory of Christian salvation.

The story of Beowulf is the story of brave and noble battles fought against evil and threatening forces. Hrothgar, King of the Danes, is terrorized by a monster named Grendel, who steals into his kingdom during the night and devours or carries off his warriors. This carnage continues for 12 years, until finally a man of great bravery and strength, Beowulf of the Geats, hears of Hrothgar's plight. Beowulf travels to Denmark to battle Grendel and free the Danes of this threat to their safety. Hrothgar and his men welcome Beowulf with a great feast, but after the festivities end and the warriors fall asleep, Grendel appears. Beowulf attacks the monster, twisting off his right arm. Grendel, mortally wounded, flees from the hall.

The next evening, Grendel's mother appears at Hrothgar's hall to avenge her son. She seizes a warrior and escapes into the night; Beowulf does not awaken in time to stop her. The next morning, Hrothgar leads his men to the mere, or marsh, where Grendel and his mother live. Beowulf swims to the bottom of the mere, assaulted on every side by serpent-monsters of the water. Finally, he arrives at the lair of Grendel's mother. He attacks her with a sword that has been given to him by one of Hrothgar's men, but it fails to harm her. Desperate, Beowulf wrestles the monster to the ground. Spying a sword hanging on the wall of the cave, he seizes it and slays Grendel's mother. Then he turns and severs the head of the wounded Grendel, who is lying close by. Taking the giants' sword and Grendel's head as prizes, Beowulf begins to swim back to the surface of the mere. As he swims, the sword disintegrates until all that is left is the hilt. This he presents to Hrothgar at the feast that celebrates his brave and glorious victories.

Beowulf leaves Denmark and returns to his homeland, the land of the Geats. He is welcomed there by King Hygelac and rewarded for his acts of bravery with riches and a high position in the kingdom. After many years pass, Beowulf himself becomes the king of the Geats, and is a noble and generous ruler. During his reign, one of the Geat warriors discovers a dragon's treasure-trove and steals a golden goblet to present to Beowulf. The dragon, in his outrage at being robbed, devastates the entire land. Beowulf, in spite of his advancing age, vows to rid his kingdom of the dragon. He approaches the dragon's lair with a number of warriors, but after it becomes apparent that Beowulf's sword has no effect on the dragon, all but one warrior flee the scene. The loyal Wiglaf remains, and with his help Beowulf deals the dragon a mortal knife-blow. However, Beowulf himself has been deeply wounded in the fight. Weak and dying, his final act is to bestow upon Wiglaf a king's gold collar. The other warriors return to the scene, burn the body of their dead king, and bury the dragon's treasure along with Beowulf's ashes. All the Geats mourn their beloved lord and hero, who has died protecting his kingdom and his people.

Beowulf has been interpreted as Christian allegory for several reasons. First, the opening situation of the story parallels the coming of the Christian Savior. Hrothgar and his people are crippled by a destructive and ferocious monster who is described as the offspring of Cain and an inmate of hell. Then Beowulf arrives from afar, a savior who has the power to destroy their nemesis. The obvious Christian conclusion is that if Grendel is so closely associated with Cain and hell, then his vanquisher, Beowulf, may rightly be associated with Christ the Savior. Thus the first episode in the epic allegorizes the coming of Christ to a people who desperately need to be "saved."

Second, the episode involving Beowulf's slaying of Grendel's mother may be interpreted as an allegorical rendering of the Christian notion of baptism. Beowulf immerses himself in the mere water, infested with serpents, and emerges having rid the mere of both Grendel and his dam, identified as the poisonous powers of hell. This episode also lends itself to allegorical interpretation insofar as the description of the cave where Grendel and his mother lived corresponds closely with the way that hell itself was described before and during the Middle Ages. In early Christian gospel, an event called the Harrowing of Hell was described as a descent that Christ made into hell to confront Satan. Allegorically, Beowulf's descent into the fiery underwater cave and subsequent victorious ascent parallel Christ's descent into hell and his triumphant resurrection.

Third, Beowulf's final battle against the fire-dragon may be recognized as allegorically depicting the high price of salvation: the life of the Savior. Beowulf is led to the dragon by the guilty thief of the goblet, just as Christ was led to his death by the guilty Judas. Beowulf brings 12 warriors to help him fight the dragon, paralleling Christ's 12 disciples. Beowulf was deserted by all but one warrior, Wiglaf, just as Christ was left with only one truly faithful disciple, Saint John. Beowulf dies at the ninth hour of the day, just as Christ did. Ultimately, Beowulf vanquishes the fire-breathing dragon (an ancient representation of the creatures of hell) and saves his kingdom and his people, but his victory comes at the expense of his own life. The Savior gives his life so that others might be saved.

Many critics have been reluctant to equate firmly the character of Beowulf with the representation of Christ, but the episodes in Beowulf do function as allegories of Christian doctrine. This, however, does not diminish the pagan aspects of this story. Rather, *Beowulf* must be seen as a poem that combines elements of the pagan Germanic tribal traditions with the newly assimilated Christian doctrine that was spreading through Europe at the time of the poem's composition. (Bloomfield 1981; Goldsmith 1970; McNamee 1963)

BERNARDUS SILVESTRIS

Bernardus Silvestris was the twelfth-century French author of a philosophical allegory called the *Cosmographia [On Cosmogony]*. He also wrote the *Mathematicus [On Destiny]*. Bernardus, who died in about 1160, was a teacher at St. Martin in Tours. In the *Cosmographia* the author attempts to make sense of the idea that a given reality is defined by its opposite, that man and the universe are intricately interrelated, and that the universe, which he allegorizes in a sense, is almost like a conscious organism full of unformed material that desires form—a kind of Mother Nature. (Bloomfield 1981)

BESTIARIES

Bestiaries became popular in the Middle Ages as a means of conveying moral lessons by way of animal figures. These were books of stories and poems richly illustrated with the animal figures. The animals stood allegorically for certain human characteristics—the wily fox, the wise owl, and so forth. These bestiaries are probably the source for many later children's stories. The earliest examples of Christian bestiaries occur in Greek in the fourth century. These were translated into Latin as *Physiologus* by Theobaldus in the eleventh century. There is also a famous bestiary by an Anglo-Norman poet, Phillippe de Thaun, in the thirteenth century. (Benet 1965)

BETWEEN THE ACTS

Published in 1941, Virginia Woolf's last novel is a symbolic tale with elements of allegory. The action of the plot takes place in one day, the day of the village pageant written and directed by the somewhat androgynous Miss La Trobe, the "womanly-manly" who clearly represents Virginia Woolf herself in that she strives, as Woolf had done, for instance, in *Orlando,* to use the sweep of English history to achieve a certain harmony in a fragmented modernist world on the brink of further disintegration. The pageant, performed "between the acts" of the dysfunctional modern people who make up the household from whose perspective we enter the story, begins with the age of Chaucer and moves in the first act to the Elizabethan period. Between the acts of the pageant, our corrupt and squabbling household, representing "modern civilization," continues to act out its own ancient pageant of jealousy, anger, and attempted communication. Other scenes in the pageant—the Age of Reason, the Victorian Age—refer to both the earlier order and later disintegration of society and indirectly to the same disintegration of the household that is our focus. At the end of the play, the characters come running forward holding mirrors in which the members of the audience are reflected, indicating the allegorical purpose of the play. In the evening the people of the house in question continue their domestic drama, but the pageant, by revealing their larger history, has provided a perspective—even a purgation—that somehow brings them together and makes their lives more possible.

See also Woolf, Virginia.

BHAGAVAD GITA

The philosophical book central to the Indian epic *The Mahabharata,* the *Gita* is an allegory in the sense that the hero Arjuna represents all heroes and, in turn, all of us as we make our way to self-knowledge. When he asks his charioteer, who is in reality the god Krishna, why he should fight in the battle between the two ruling families of India, Krishna reveals himself as Time itself and exhorts Arjuna to express himself as a warrior so as to "win a prosperous kingdom," that is, to realize himself. "Time am I, wreaker of the world's destruction," he says. An interesting allegorical element in the *Bhagavad Gita* is the cosmic tree. The tree stands for the universe and for humankind's condition. We humans are in the tree but cannot perceive its dimensions, for it is the manifestation of Brahman, ultimate reality itself.

See also The Mahabharata.

THE BIBLE AND ALLEGORY

Religious texts are sometimes interpreted allegorically as opposed to fundamentally or literally. This is especially so when the literal content or tone of the given text is incompatible with the beliefs of a cult for whom the text is sacred.

The Hebrew Bible or Old Testament has always been considered sacred by Christians, along with the later New Testament. But for the earlier Christian interpreters of the Old Testament, a book such as the erotic Song of Songs or

Song of Solomon—based on ancient Egyptian marriage poetry—could only be acceptable as allegory, the story of Christ's relationship with his church. This kind of allegory is known as typological allegory; it is particularly characteristic of Christian readings of the Old Testament. Old Testament events or figures are seen as "types" of corresponding aspects of the New Testament. St. Paul in his Epistles was a leading early Christian typological allegorist. This is how Paul, in 1 Corinthians 10, reads the story of the Hebrew exodus from Egypt (Old Testament Book of Exodus, chapters 14 and 16), in which the Children of Israel escape from their pursuers when Yahweh causes the Red Sea to open for them and later sends them manna to eat and water to drink from the Rock. First, the story from Exodus:

> And the LORD said unto Moses, Wherefore criest thou unto me? speak unto the children of Israel, that they go forward: But lift thou up thy rod, and stretch out thine hand over the sea, and divide it: and the children of Israel shall go on dry ground through the midst of the sea. And I, behold, I will harden the hearts of the Egyptians, and they shall follow them: and I will get me honour upon Pharaoh, and upon all his host, upon his chariots, and upon his horsemen. And the Egyptians shall know that I am the LORD, when I have gotten me honour upon Pharaoh, upon his chariots, and upon his horsemen. And the angel of God, which went before the camp of Israel, removed and went behind them; and the pillar of the cloud went from before their face, and stood behind them: And it came between the camp of the Egyptians and the camp of Israel; and it was a cloud and darkness to them, but it gave light by night to these: so that the one came not near the other all the night. And Moses stretched out his hand over the sea; and the LORD caused the sea to go back by a strong east wind all that night, and made the sea dry land, and the waters were divided. And the children of Israel went into the midst of the sea upon the dry ground: and the waters were a wall unto them on their right hand, and on their left. And the Egyptians pursued, and went in after them to the midst of the sea, even all Pharaoh's horses, his chariots, and his horsemen. And it came to pass, that in the morning watch the LORD looked unto the host of the Egyptians through the pillar of fire and of the cloud, and troubled the host of the Egyptians, And took off their chariot wheels, that they drave them heavily: so that the Egyptians said, Let us flee from the face of Israel; for the LORD fighteth for them against the Egyptians. And the LORD said unto Moses, Stretch out thine hand over the sea, that the waters may come again upon the Egyptians, upon their chariots, and upon their horsemen. And Moses stretched forth his hand over the sea, and the sea returned to his strength when the morning appeared; and the Egyptians fled against it; and the LORD overthrew the Egyptians in the midst of the sea. And the waters returned, and covered the chariots, and the horsemen, and all the host of Pharaoh that came into the sea after them; there remained not so much as one of them. But the children of Israel walked upon dry land in the midst of the sea; and the waters were a wall unto them on their right hand, and on their left. (Exodus 14:15–29)

> And the LORD spake unto Moses, saying, I have heard the murmurings of the children of Israel: speak unto them, saying, At even ye shall eat flesh, and in the morning ye shall be filled with bread; and ye shall know that I am the

LORD your God. And it came to pass, that at even the quails came up, and covered the camp: and in the morning the dew lay round about the host. And when the dew that lay was gone up, behold, upon the face of the wilderness there lay a small round thing, as small as the hoar frost on the ground. And when the children of Israel saw it, they said one to another, It is manna: for they wist not what it was. And Moses said unto them, This is the bread which the LORD hath given you to eat. (Exodus 16:11–15)

And all the congregation of the children of Israel journeyed from the wilderness of Sin, after their journeys, according to the commandment of the LORD, and pitched in Rephidim: and there was no water for the people to drink. Wherefore the people did chide with Moses, and said, Give us water that we may drink. And Moses said unto them, Why chide ye with me? wherefore do ye tempt the LORD? And the people thirsted there for water; and the people murmured against Moses, and said, Wherefore is this that thou hast brought us up out of Egypt, to kill us and our children and our cattle with thirst? And Moses cried unto the LORD, saying, What shall I do unto this people? they be almost ready to stone me. And the LORD said unto Moses, Go on before the people, and take with thee of the elders of Israel; and thy rod, wherewith thou smotest the river, take in thine hand, and go. (Exodus 17:1–5)

Paul interprets the story:

Moreover, brethren, I would not that ye should be ignorant, how that our fathers were under the cloud, and all passed through the sea; and were all baptized unto Moses in the cloud and in the sea; and did all eat the same spiritual meat; and did all drink the same spiritual drink: for they drank of that spiritual Rock that followed them; and that Rock was Christ. But with many of them God was not well pleased: for they were overthrown in the wilderness. (1 Corinthians 10:1–5)

Although Paul accepts the historicity of the events of Exodus, he sees them as an allegorical representation of Christian reality. So the wilderness becomes the place of spiritual struggle, Egypt the old sinfulness, the Red Sea and the cloud pillar the promise of baptism, the manna the bread of the Christian communion, the water from the Rock the communion wine.

In Galatians 4, Paul interprets the story from Genesis of how the patriarch Abraham had two sons, Isaac (Israel) by his apparently barren wife Sarah and Ishmael, who was exiled with his slave mother, Hagar (Agar). This is the Old Testament story:

And the LORD visited Sarah as he had said, and the LORD did unto Sarah as he had spoken. For Sarah conceived, and bare Abraham a son in his old age, at the set time of which God had spoken to him. And Abraham called the name of his son that was born unto him, whom Sarah bare to him, Isaac. And Abraham circumcised his son Isaac being eight days old, as God had commanded him. And Abraham was an hundred years old, when his son Isaac was born unto him. And Sarah said, God hath made me to laugh, so that all that hear will laugh with me. And she said, Who would have said unto Abraham, that Sarah should have given children suck? for I have born him a son in his old age. And the child grew, and was weaned: and Abraham made a great feast the same day that Isaac was weaned. And Sarah saw the son of Hagar the Egyptian, which she had born unto Abraham, mocking. Wherefore she said unto Abraham, Cast out this bondwoman and her son: for the son of this bond-woman shall not be heir with my son, even with Isaac. And the thing was very grievous in Abraham's sight because of his son. And God said unto Abraham, Let it not be grievous in thy sight because of the lad, and because of thy bond-woman; in all that Sarah hath said unto thee, hearken unto her voice; for in Isaac shall thy seed be called. And also of the son of the bondwoman will I make a nation, because he is thy seed. (Genesis 21:1–13)

This is Paul's interpretation:

Which things are an allegory: for these are the two covenants; the one from the Mount Sinai, which gendereth to bondage, which is Agar. For this Agar is Mount Sinai in Arabia, and answereth to Jerusalem which now is, and is in bondage with her children. But Jerusalem which is above is free, which is the mother of us all. For it is written,

> Rejoice, thou barren that bearest not;
> break forth and cry, thou that travailest not:
> for the desolate hath many more children than she which hath a husband.

Now we, brethren, as Isaac was, are the children of promise. (Galatians 4:24–29)

For Paul, then, Ishmael and Hagar represented the old law of the Jews, while Sarah and Isaac represent the new Christian vision; Sarah as the Church gives miraculous birth to the new law represented by Isaac, who in typological terms is Christ.

Other New Testament writers made use of the typological method. Matthew in chapter 12 of his gospel remembers the Old Testament story of Jonah's three days and nights in the belly of the whale (Jonah 1) and points to the allegory: "For as Jonas [Jonah] was three days and three nights in the whale's belly; so shall the Son of man [Jesus] be three days and three nights in the heart of the earth."

Closely related to—even an offshoot of—typological allegory is what has been called prophetic allegory. In this tradition the early Christians saw the Israel of the Old Testament as an allegory for the Kingdom of God to come. As John MacQueen and others have pointed out, such prophetic allegory was also common in the Old Testament.

The prophet Isaiah (5:1–7) writes a prophetic allegory that speaks to differences between Israel and Judah during the eighth century B.C.E.:

Now will I sing to my wellbeloved a song of my beloved touching his vineyard. My wellbeloved hath a vineyard in a very fruitful hill: And he fenced it, and gathered out the stones thereof, and planted it with the choicest vine, and built a tower in the midst of it, and also made a winepress therein: and he looked that it should bring forth grapes, and it brought forth wild grapes. And now, O inhabitants of Jerusalem, and men of Judah, judge, I pray you, betwixt

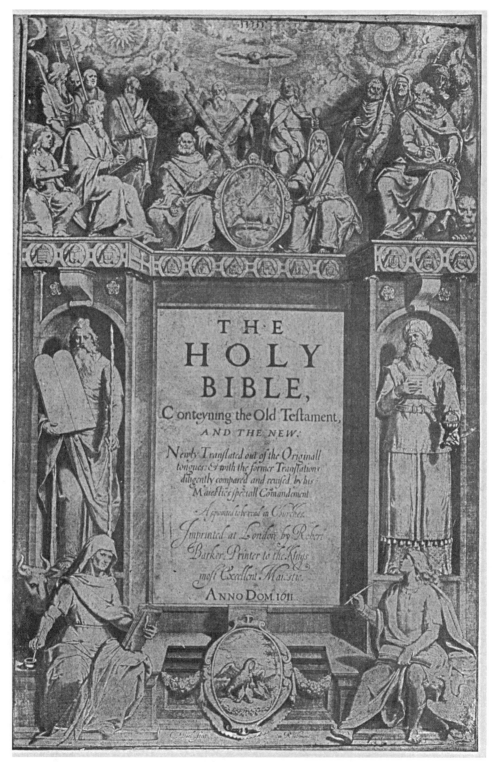

THE
HOLY
BIBLE,
Conteyning the Old Testament,
AND THE NEW:

Newly Translated out of the Originall
tongues: & with the former Translations
diligently compared and reuised, by his
Maiesties speciall Comandement

Appointed to be read in Churches.

Imprinted at London by Robert
Barker, Printer to the Kings
most Excellent Maiestie.

ANNO DOM 1611.

Title page of the *Bishops' Bible,* an English Bible published in 1611

me and my vineyard. What could have been done more to my vineyard, that I have not done in it? wherefore, when I looked that it should bring forth grapes, brought it forth wild grapes? And now go to; I will tell you what I will do to my vineyard: I will take away the hedge thereof, and it shall be eaten up; and break down the wall thereof, and it shall be trodden down: And I will lay it waste: it shall not be pruned, nor digged; but there shall come up briers and thorns: I will also command the clouds that they rain no rain upon it. For the vineyard of the LORD of hosts is the house of Israel, and the men of Judah his pleasant plant: and he looked for judgment, but behold oppression; for righteousness, but behold a cry.

As John MacQueen suggests (27), the vineyard here is Palestine, the land occupied by Judah and Israel. The vine is Judah, the tower Jerusalem. The wild grapes represent the oppression inflicted upon the people by the kings of Judah.

In the Old Testament book of Daniel, we find the prophet Daniel interpreting a dream of King Nebuchadnezzar allegorically. This was the dream of the statue with the golden head, the silver chest and arms, the brass midsection, the iron legs, and the iron and clay feet. The statue was destroyed by a stone.

Then Arioch brought in Daniel before the king in haste and said thus unto him, I have found a man of the captives of Judah, that will make known unto the king the interpretation. The king answered and said to Daniel, whose name was Belteshazzar, Art thou able to make known unto me the dream which I have seen, and the interpretation thereof? Daniel answered in the presence of the king, and said, The secret which the king hath demanded cannot the wise men, the astrologers, the magicians, the soothsayers, shew unto the king; But there is a God in heaven that revealeth secrets, and maketh known to the king Nebuchadnezzar what shall be in the latter days. Thy dream, and the visions of thy head upon thy bed, are these; As for thee, O king, thy thoughts came into thy mind upon thy bed, what should come to pass hereafter: and he that revealeth secrets maketh known to thee what shall come to pass. But as for me, this secret is not revealed to me for any wisdom that I have more than any living, but for their sakes that shall make known the interpretation to the king, and that thou mightest know the thoughts of thy heart. Thou, O king, sawest, and behold a great image. This great image, whose brightness was excellent, stood before thee; and the form thereof was terrible. This image's head was of fine gold, his breast and his arms of silver, his belly and his thighs of brass, His legs of iron, his feet part of iron and part of clay. Thou sawest till that a stone was cut out without hands, which smote the image upon his feet that were of iron and clay, and brake them to pieces. Then was the iron, the clay, the brass, the silver, and the gold, broken to pieces together, and became like the chaff of the summer threshingfloors; and the wind carried them away, that no place was found for them: and the stone that smote the image became a great mountain, and filled the whole earth. This is the dream; and we will tell the interpretation thereof before the king. Thou, O king, art a king of kings: for the God of heaven hath given thee a kingdom, power, and strength, and glory. And wheresoever the children of men dwell, the beasts of the field and the fowls of the heaven hath he given into thine hand, and hath made thee ruler over them all. Thou art this head of gold. And after thee shall arise another kingdom inferior to thee, and another third kingdom of brass, which shall bear rule over all the earth. And the fourth kingdom shall be strong as iron: forasmuch as iron breaketh in pieces and subdueth all things: and as iron that breaketh all these, shall it break in pieces and bruise. And whereas thou sawest the feet and toes, part of potters' clay, and part of iron, the kingdom shall be divided; but there shall be in it of the strength of the iron, forasmuch as thou sawest the iron mixed with miry clay. And as the toes of the feet were part of iron, and part of clay, so the kingdom shall be partly strong, and partly broken. And whereas thou sawest iron mixed with miry clay, they shall mingle themselves with the seed of men: but they shall not cleave one to another, even as iron is not mixed with clay. And in the days of these kings shall the God of heaven set up a kingdom, which shall never be destroyed: and the kingdom shall not be left to other people, but it shall break in pieces and consume all these kingdoms, and it shall stand for ever. Forasmuch as thou sawest that the stone was cut out of the mountain without hands, and that it brake in pieces the iron, the brass, the clay, the silver, and the gold; the great God hath made known to the king what shall come to pass hereafter: and the dream is certain, and the interpretation thereof sure. Then the king Nebuchadnezzar fell upon his face, and worshipped Daniel, and commanded that they should offer an oblation and sweet odours unto him. (Daniel 2:25–46)

For Daniel, this was prophetic allegory of the coming of the Kingdom of God, represented by the stone, which destroys the four preceding kingdoms. For Christians, the stone became the coming of Christ.

A particularly popular form of Christian biblical allegory is found in the parables of Jesus. These exemplary stories—the Prodigal Son, the Good Samaritan, and many others—are clearly didactic and are used by Jesus to illustrate ideas.

The writer John Cassian (560–435), in his *Collationes* (XIV, 8), formulated four levels of biblical meaning: the literal, the purely allegorical, the moral, and the anagogical. The purely allegorical level of an Old Testament text refers to Christ and his work; the moral level refers to the life of the Christian soul; the anagogical refers to higher cosmic realities. (MacQueen 1970)

See also Bede, The Venerable; Cassian, John; Figural Allegory; Fourfold Allegory; Parable as Allegory; Paul as an Allegorist; The Song of Songs.

BIDPAI

Sometimes spelled Bidpay or Pilpay, Bidpai is said to be the author of the *Fables of Bidpai,* a collection of allegorical fables—often but by no means always beast fables—originally from the third-to-fifth-century Sanskrit collection called the *Panchatantra.* A popular Arabic version, *Kalilah and Dimnah* (ca. 750 C.E.) was a translation of an earlier Pahlavi or Persian version (ca. 55 C.E.). The name Bidpai means "scholar," and Bidpai's *Fables* were supposed to have been commissioned by an Indian king to aid in his sons' education. Bidpai's *Fables* are generally thought to have influenced those of La Fontaine.

One Bidpai fable tells how a good man was awakened by the noise of a thief robbing his house during the night and decided to wait before accosting him so that the thief could be caught red-handed with his loot. But unfortunately, the man fell asleep again and the thief got away with everything. In the morning the good man bemoaned both the loss of his goods and the fact of his own sloth, which had caused him to let the thief go unchallenged.

The moral allegory here is clear enough. The good man is everyman, his failure to do anything is our inherent tendency to be slothful, the loss of the goods is representative of anything—spiritual or material—that we might lose by not being "awake." (Benet 1965; Leach 1984)

See also Aesop; Fable as Allegory; La Fontaine, Jean de.

BILLY BUDD, SAILOR

See Melville, Herman.

THE BIRTHDAY PARTY

This first full-length play by British playwright Harold Pinter (b. 1930) is a good example of absurdist drama with a tendency toward allegory; another example is *Waiting for Godot*. The setting for the play is a run-down boarding-house by the sea. The establishment is run by Meg, an unkempt but motherly woman whose husband Petey is kindly and quiet. They have a boarder named Stanley, who had once given a piano recital only to be locked out of his next scheduled event. Into this world come an unpleasant Irishman and a falsely friendly Jew who, it appears, are out to get Stanley for reasons that we never find out. They arrange a birthday party for him, but Stanley insists it is not his birthday. The strangers then interrogate him in a particularly cruel and absurd manner. In this aspect the play is reminiscent of the situation of Joseph K. in Kafka's *The Trial*. The birthday party takes place and during a game of blindman's buff, Stanley's glasses are stolen, leading to his losing mental control of himself. The two mysterious strangers drive him upstairs and, in the end, they take him away in a black car. He is dressed in a mourning suit, holding his broken glasses and bereft of speech. After Stanley's departure, the motherly Meg, happy with the party that has taken place, comes downstairs, oblivious to what has really gone on.

If this play is an allegory—and Pinter claimed it was not—Stanley is the artist forced into conformity by the philistines represented by the stangers. Or, Stanley could be any of us searching for security in a chaotic world and discovering, like Kafka's Joseph K., that we are always at the mercy of irrational forces and that those who might support us are silent and/or incompetent. (Esslin 1961)

See also Kafka, Franz; Pinter, Harold; *Waiting for Godot*.

BLACKMORE, SIR RICHARD

The author of the somewhat allegorical epic *Prince Arthur* (1695), Blackmore wrote a preface to this epic in which he treated allegory from a purely secular as opposed to the traditionally religious point of view. Blackmore (ca. 1650–1729) was an English physician and a prolific writer. He was honored by being made physician to William III and then knighted.

BLAKE, WILLIAM

William Blake (1757–1827) was the great poet, painter, and engraver who led the way to the high period of English romanticism. Blake was a mystic and an antinomian who created his own mythology for expressing his religious views. The visionary work of Blake is always symbolic and often approaches allegory. The title of the prophetic book *The Marriage of Heaven and Hell* is an example of the use of personification for allegorical purposes. In Blake's *Songs of Innocence* and *Songs of Experience* allegory is often evident.

THE GARDEN OF LOVE

I went to the Garden of Love,
And saw what I never had seen:
A Chapel was built in the midst,
Where I used to play on the green.

And the gates of this Chapel were shut,
And "Thou shalt not" writ over the door;
So I turn'd to the Garden of Love,
That so many sweet flowers bore,

And I saw it was filled with graves,
And tomb-stones where flowers should be:
And Priests in black gowns, were walking their rounds,
And binding with briars, my joys & desires.

Here Blake uses the garden to represent the pure visionary life "where I used to play on the green"—a life of innocence and openness. The chapel, with its closed gates and its signs of "Thou shalt not," represents the repressiveness and mundaneness of organized religion and the status quo. That world is further personified in the "priests in black gowns" who bind "with briars" the innocent "joys and desires."

Blake called allegory an "inferior kind of poetry" but once said, "Allegory addressed to the Intellectual Powers, while it is altogether hidden from the Corporeal Understanding, is my Definition of the Most Sublime Poetry." So it is, perhaps, that critics have been led to allegorical interpretations of Blake. One of the most popular objects of such interpretations has been *The Book of Thel*, which has been seen by many as an allegory of the struggle between things physical and things spiritual, a story of the Soul's unwillingness to give up Eternity for the World. (Fletcher 1964; MacNeice 1965; MacQueen 1970)

See also *The Book of Thel.*

BLUES AS ALLEGORY

See African-American Music as Allegory.

BOCCACCIO, GIOVANNI

Best known for his collection of tales called *The Decameron,* Boccaccio (1313–1375) was an Italian man of letters born in Certaldo. He spent much of his life in Florence, where, through many works of prose and poetry in the vernacular Italian, he contributed, with his countrymen Dante and Petrarch, to the evolution of the Italian Renaissance.

In a work called *De Genealogia Deorum Gentilium [Concerning the Genealogy of the Pagan Gods],* Boccaccio in effect justified Christian use of pagan mythology in schools by providing it with "politically correct" allegorical meaning. Boccaccio argued that all myth was fable—that myths, like fables, were masks for serious meaning.

So, for example, stories like that of Odysseus tied to the mast of his ship so he can listen with impunity to the songs of the sirens, or of Aeneas tossed by the storm are literally untrue, but they conceal "universal" truths about the individual's struggle with life's dark side. Boccaccio also points out that Christ made use of this fable method in his parables.

The Decameron, Boccaccio's major work, is written in the realistic mode and is not an example of allegory. (MacQueen 1970)

See also Fable as Allegory; Medieval Art and Allegory; Myth as Allegory.

BOETHIUS, ANICIUS MANLIUS SEVERINUS

Boethius (ca. 480–524) was a Roman philosopher who acted as a statesman for the Roman emperor Theodoric until he fell out of favor and was executed. As a scholar he influenced medieval thinking on a variety of subjects, including Aristotle, music, and mathematics. His most important work, *De Consolatione Philosophae [The Consolation of Philosophy],* written during his imprisonment before execution, brings together Christian values and humanistic ones from the classical tradition.

See also *The Consolation of Philosophy.*

THE BOOK OF MARGERY KEMPE

Most information about the life of Margery Kempe (ca. 1372–1438) comes from her autobiography. We know that she was born and raised in Norfolk, England,

and after the difficult delivery of her first child and the stinging response of a priest to her confession, she suffered some form of mental breakdown. She began to recover from this breakdown when she saw the first of many religious visions. In spite of continuous domestic conflict, she bore her husband 13 more children. When she was about 40 years old, Kempe arranged a vow of celibacy with her husband and left on a pilgrimage to the Holy Land. There, she saw many visions of Christ and the Virgin Mary, which continued throughout her life.

The Book of Margery Kempe is a spiritual autobiography that details Kempe's efforts to live a holy life as she was instructed to do in her visions of Jesus Christ and the Virgin Mary. Kempe, an illiterate medieval housewife for most of her life, dictated her story to two scribes; the latter one revised the entire text but seems to have remained true to Kempe's original expression. *The Book of Margery Kempe* may be interpreted as an allegory of Christian love in that Jesus Christ is portrayed as Kempe's lover/bridegroom in a way similar to the biblical Song of Songs as interpreted by early Christians. Kempe, as the allegorical bride of Christ, renounces her worldly relationships, "marries" Christianity, and becomes a representation of human salvation.

Another allegorical element of *The Book of Margery Kempe* involves the description of her pilgrimage to Jerusalem. As a religious pilgrim, Kempe's journey may represent the spiritual quest that all Christians must undertake to reach the Holy Land of religious salvation.

See also The Quest as Allegory; The Song of Songs.

THE BOOK OF THEL

Based in part on Milton's *Comus*, Blake's *Book of Thel* is an allegorical poem, the first of his prophetic books. It tells the story of a girl about to become a woman. Thel still lives in the Vale of Har, which in Blake's mythology signifies self-love, but she is considering the value of her virginity, represented by the lily. She meditates on the impregnation and fertilization of the lily, represented by the Cloud. Thel becomes aware of her senses and escapes in fear back to the land of self-love. Hers is an awakening not yet ready for fruition. (Damon 1971)

See also Blake, William; *Comus*.

BORGES, JORGE LUIS

The fictional works of the Argentine writer Jorge Luis Borges (1899–1986) brought him international recognition. Borges himself was international in background and outlook. His grandmother was English; he spoke English, French, and German; and he was well read in all of these languages. Borges lived at various times in Switzerland and Spain as well. While in Spain he became part of a group called ultrists, which was influenced by modernist movements such as expressionism and surrealism. This association was certainly in part reflected in Borges's use of fantasy and Kafkaesque distortion in his fiction. His works are often called allegories because of their evident symbolism and their surrealistic plots and characters. A title such as *Borges and Myself*—by Borges—itself suggests an allegorical puzzle about the nature of identity and the inner self.

La muerte y la brujula [Death and the Compass] (1942) is one of Borges's masterpieces and has definite allegorical aspects. The plot involves a detective named Lonnrot, who, in the course of attempting to solve crimes committed by one Scharlach, traps himself in a labyrinth built by his own too-complex reasoning powers. Allegorically, the labyrinth is life itself, and the detective's reason is the illusion by which we all attempt to make sense of the meaninglessness of existence. As many critics have pointed out, however, Borges's work is itself an allegory of the possibility of achieving meaning through art.

A dissenting voice on the question of Borges and allegory is that of Maureen Quilligan, who finds in the "dense web of extremely self-conscious correspondences" in Borges's fiction a "finished self-sufficiency" which is different from what she sees as the "open-endedness" of true allegory (220). Still, it can reasonably be said that Borges's texts are allegories for the failure of modern people to find meaning and significance in a fragmented world; his narrators themselves often seem to have little idea of the facts surrounding their narratives. His texts seem to suggest the impossibility of comprehending meaning in a universal context that is itself meaningless. (Quilligan 1979)

See also Allegoresis.

BRECHT, BERTOLT

The German playwright Bertolt Brecht (1898–1956) studied in his youth to become a doctor, served as a medical orderly in World War I, and eventually gave up medicine for theater in the 1920s in Munich. He moved to Berlin and came under the influence of Max Reinhardt at the prestigious Deutsches Theater. Brecht worked with the composer Kurt Weil and with the great director Erwin Piscator during the late 1920s. When Hitler came to power, Brecht left Germany and lived first in Denmark, then Sweden, Finland, and finally the United States. Forced by a reaction against his Communist leanings to leave America after the war, he moved to Switzerland and then to Communist East Germany, where he became artistic director and resident playwright at the Berliner Ensemble Theater in East Berlin. Brecht died suddenly in 1956.

Brecht's name is nearly always associated with a new form of drama called "Epic Theatre." In epic theatre we find the concept of "alienation," in which the audience must remove itself from any kind of sentimental identification with the characters or actions depicted on the stage in order to view the given play for its Marxist meaning. Plays such as *The Caucasian Chalk Circle* and *Mother Courage* become, in the context of "alienation," parables to illustrate political and social ideas. Or, they may even be said to become allegories in which characters are embodiments or personifications of certain abstractions.

See also Benjamin, Walter; *The Caucasian Chalk Circle.*

BROWNING, ROBERT

Robert Browning (1812–1889) was born in Camberwell, England, the son of an educated bank clerk. He attended the University of London briefly, but his education resulted mostly from reading his father's extensive library. He published his first poem, "Pauline," when he was 21; its personal, confessional nature was not very well received and Browning resolved to avoid such intimacy with his readers in the future. In 1836, he began writing plays, but none were successful on stage. Nevertheless, scriptwriting taught Browning the potential power of dramatic monologues; unfortunately, his first published collection of such monologues, *Dramatic Lyrics* (1842), was no more successful than his plays had been.

In 1845 Browning met Elizabeth Barrett, a semi-invalid six years his senior. They fell in love and eloped to Italy, where they lived for 15 years. During this time, Robert Browning published *Men and Women* (1855), an impressive collection of poems. This happy time in Browning's life ended with Elizabeth's death in 1861, but he continued to write for appreciative audiences for the next two decades. A collection of monologues called *Dramatis Personae* (1864) and his vast poetic masterpiece *The Ring and the Book* (1868) were well received by critics, but his final few volumes of poetry were considered to be less remarkable than those he wrote during his marriage and in the years immediately following Elizabeth's death. Since Robert Browning's death in 1889, scholars have come to consider his work as foreshadowing the trends of twentieth-century poetry. In some poems, such as "Childe Roland to the Dark Tower Came," there are allegorical aspects.

See also "Childe Roland to the Dark Tower Came."

BUNYAN, JOHN

John Bunyan (1628–1688) was an early English Puritan whose humble parentage in no way suggested his ultimate fame as the author of one of the most popular allegories ever written in English. The son of a Bedfordshire tinker, Bunyan had little formal schooling and his youth was spent learning his father's trade. In 1653 he was converted to a Nonconformist Baptist sect and began preaching; in 1660 the Anglican church began persecuting such dissenters. Bunyan chose imprisonment over conformity and was incarcerated in the Bedford jail from 1660 until 1672. During his imprisonment he preached to the other inmates and wrote his spiritual autobiography, *Grace Abounding to the Chief of Sinners* (1666). In it he includes only sparse details of the events of his

An engraving of John Bunyan from *The Pilgrim's Progress*, a work he composed while imprisoned in 1675.

life, including his family background, his marriage, and his military service. Instead, he chooses to trace his complex spiritual growth from sinful tinker to devout Baptist preacher.

After his release from prison, Bunyan resumed his role as Nonconformist preacher and was again imprisoned in 1675. During this second incarceration he composed his greatest work, *The Pilgrim's Progress from This World to That Which Is To Come* (1678), which has become perhaps the most widely read allegory written in English. The second part of *The Pilgrim's Progress*, which relates the journey of Christian's family, was published in 1684. Other allegorical tales by Bunyan include *The Life and Death of Mr. Badman* (1680) and *The Holy War* (1682).

See also *The Holy War; The Life and Death of Mr. Badman; The Pilgrim's Progress.*

BUTLER, SAMUEL

Samuel Butler (1835–1902) was born to a clergyman's family in Nottinghamshire. He attended St. John's College, Cambridge, but refused to take holy orders, as his father wished. He emigrated to New Zealand, became a successful sheep farmer, and embarked on what would become a prolific writing career. He returned to England in 1865, enrolled in Heatherley's Art School, and became a relatively successful painter and, eventually, an art critic. His diverse interests and talents also surfaced through music, science, philosophy, literary study, and satire. Butler never achieved greatness through any of his eclectic activities during his lifetime and could not have known that his posthumously published, semiautobiographical novel *The Way of All Flesh* (1903) would become his most influential work.

See also *Erewhon.*

CALDERÓN DE LA BARCA, PEDRO

Calderón (1600–1681) is one of the greatest of Spanish dramatists and writers. He was born in Madrid of an aristocratic family, was educated by Jesuits, and eventually became a priest. It was after his ordination that he wrote a type of religious and allegorical play called the *auto sacramentale* (sacramental mystery play). His most popular work in this genre was his *Great Theater of the Western World*. Calderón was prolific. At the center of his concerns was the tradition of honor or *pundonor* (according to which, for example, a man could kill his wife for infidelity) and his belief that without Christian directions humans invariably lose sight of reality. (Benet 1965)

See also *Auto Sacramentale; The Great Theater of the World.*

CAMUS, ALBERT

One of the best-known French writers of the twentieth century, Albert Camus (1913–1960) was born and raised in North Africa. After the start of World War II, Camus moved to Paris to work as a journalist and a writer. In 1942 he published the highly successful *L'Etranger* (translated as *The Outsider* in England and *The Stranger* in the United States, 1946) and *Le mythe de Sisyphe* (translated as *The Myth of Sisyphus*, 1955). His fame from these books continued as a result of the editorials he published in *Combat*, a popular French newspaper. His novel *La Peste* (1947), translated as *The Plague*, is often treated allegorically. Many considered Camus's voice to be the voice of France's national conscience. Both the man and his work became increasingly controversial during his lifetime. Camus, who won the Nobel Prize in 1957, was an undeniably important contributor to literature of the human conscience and remains a popular and influential writer both in France and abroad. (Benet 1965)

See also *The Plague.*

CANDIDE

Candide is the best-known work by the French philosopher and satirist Voltaire. Published in 1759, with the subtitle *Optimism*, the philosophical and somewhat allegorical novel is an attack on the optimist philosophy of Gottfried Wilhelm Leibniz (1646–1716), whose ideas are represented by the absurdly optimistic Dr. Pangloss. Pangloss is tutor and companion to the hero, Candide, and even as unspeakable events destroy the societies and friends around him, he mouths the Leibnizian theory that "all is for the best in this best of all possible worlds." Candide himself is an everyman figure, blessed or cursed with the kind of naïveté, curiosity, and innocence that allow him to become the victim of each of the injustices and catastrophes that Voltaire throws in his way. His travels through the world are not realistic; they are carefully staged by the author in support of his overall satire on humanity. Candide is expelled from the castle of his adoption for making love with the baron's daughter, Cunegonde; he is forced to fight in a meaningless war; he learns that his girlfriend has been massacred; he undergoes the horrors of the Lisbon earthquake, suffers under the Inquisition, watches his old tutor hanged, discovers Eldorado and riches, has his riches stolen from him, and finally finds his way to Turkey where, with the miraculously still-alive Pangloss (he was not properly hanged, it seems) and a now very ugly Cunegonde (she was not properly massacred) whom he marries, he settles down in relative seclusion to "cultivate our garden"—the only thing left to do in such a world.

See also Voltaire.

THE CANTERBURY TALES

The Canterbury Tales, begun probably in 1386, is the best-known work by Geoffrey Chaucer (ca. 1343–1400); it details the journey of a group of medieval religious pilgrims to Canterbury. Along the way, the pilgrims—a group that includes Chaucer himself—tell stories to pass the time and, sometimes, to teach moral lessons; these stories make up the great majority of the text of the *Tales*. Many of these stories have been interpreted allegorically; indeed, the entire journey (which is never actually completed in the *Tales*) may be understood as an allegory of every person's pilgrimage (however incomplete) toward spirituality.

An example of a tale that incorporates allegorical elements is the Clerk's tale of Walter and his wife, the patient Griselda. Walter, an unreasonably demanding husband, tests his wife's loyalty and patience by treating her poorly, even to the point of stealing her children and faking their deaths. After Griselda's years of steadfast loyalty and fidelity, Walter rewards her by presenting her with her grown children, unharmed. Allegorically, this tale has been read as the Christian story of virtue and reward. Griselda is the Christian soul who endures her earthly hardships painfully but without complaint. In this view, Walter is a god-figure who tests Griselda's faith and then rewards her for her unwavering virtue.

Another tale with an allegorical flavor is the Pardoner's tale of three drunkards who, upon hearing of their friend's death, vow revenge upon Death himself. A mysterious man advises the trio that they will find Death if they walk

∴ Prima pars ∴

Here begynneth the Segye of Thebes ful
lamentably tolde by John lidgate monke of
Bury annexynge it to ye tallys of Cauntbury

S Irs quod I. sith of youre Curtesye
I entrede am · in to youre Companye
And admytted · a tale for to telle
By hym that hath power to compele
I mene oure hoste governere and gyde
Of youre erskone · rydenge here by syde
Thogh my wit bareyne be and dulle
I wolle reherce · a stoory wonderfulle
Touchenge the syege and destruccyon
Of worthy Thebes · the myghty royale Ton
Bilt and bygonne of olde antiquite
Vpon the tyme of worthy Iosue
By diligence of kynge Amphion
Cheeff cause first of this foundacyon

Chaucer's pilgrims tell tales as they journey to Canterbury. Originally, each of the 30 pilgrims was to tell 4 stories apiece. The feat proved too large, however, and Chaucer composed only 24 of the 120 tales he set out to complete.

along a path and look under a tree. They follow these directions, but instead of Death, they find a great basket of treasure. In order to keep the treasure from being evenly divided, the three greedy friends all kill each other, and the mysterious man's prophecy is realized. Allegorically, this story has been interpreted as a moral exemplum equating the figure of Death with Avarice, one of the Seven Deadly Sins.

Other tales that have been read as allegorical include Chaucer the pilgrim's Tale of Melibee, in which Melibee's wife, Prudence, counsels him against taking revenge on those who attacked his daughter, Sophie ("Wisdom"). Allegorically, the tale explains that when "wisdom" is attacked, one ought to use "prudence" to assess the situation. The Parson's tale, the Manciple's tale, the Canon's Yeoman's tale, the Nun's Priest's tale, and the Merchant's tale, among others, have also been interpreted by scholars to contain elements of allegory. (Koonce 1966; Neuse 1991)

See also Chaucer, Geoffrey; *The Hous of Fame; The Parlement of Foules.*

CAPEK, KAREL

A Czech writer who used a great deal of fantasy in his novels and plays, Capek (1890–1938) was a nationalist and an idealist who fought with the literary sword against those who threatened his homeland. Much of his work has been seen as political allegory, including his most famous play, *R.U.R.*

See also R.U.R.

CARLYLE, THOMAS

A Scottish essayist, historian, and social critic, Thomas Carlyle (1795–1881) was, until the end of the nineteenth century, one of the most well-known and well-respected thinkers and writers in Britain. Born in Ecclefechan, Scotland, to a Calvinist peasant family, Carlyle was educated at the University of Edinburgh. He decided against joining the ministry, and for several years he worked in law, mathematics, teaching, and journalism, trying to find for himself a permanent vocation. In 1821 he suffered a sort of spiritual crisis; he describes this experience in the somewhat allegorical *Sartor Resartus* (1833) but attributes it to the main character, Professor Diogenes Teufelsdröckh.

Carlyle was made famous by *The French Revolution* (1837), an examination of the annihilation of the French aristocracy and a warning to England to avoid a similar fate. He is also remembered for *Heroes and Hero-Worship* (1841), *Past and Present* (1843), *Cromwell* (1845), and *Frederick the Great* (1858–1865). By 1848, Carlyle was deeply discouraged by the corruption of English society, and after his wife died in 1866 he retreated into seclusion for the rest of his life. He continued to write, however, and his *Reminiscences* were published posthumously in 1881. Carlyle remains a profoundly important figure in British literature and history; as one of the earliest Victorian social critics, Carlyle influenced and contributed to the shape of Victorian thought.

See also *The French Revolution; Sartor Resartus.*

CARROLL, LEWIS

The Reverend Charles Lutwidge Dodgson (1832–1898), who wrote under the pen name of Lewis Carroll, was a humorist and writer of literature for children. Carroll studied mathematics at Christ Church, Oxford, but because of his pronounced stammer and intense shyness he struggled with the teaching and lecturing that were a part of his university post. For the same reason, he rarely preached after his ordination in 1861. His 1865 masterpiece, *Alice's Adventures in Wonderland* (originally titled *Alice's Adventures under Ground*), was an instant success. Carroll's other well-known literary achievements include *Through the Looking Glass* and *What Alice Found There* (1871), and *The Hunting of the Snark* (1876), a long nonsense poem.

See also *Alice's Adventures in Wonderland; Through the Looking Glass.*

CASSIAN, JOHN

The Latin writer Cassian (360–435), in his *Collationes*, is said to have been the first formulator of fourfold allegory—the literal, the allegorical proper, the tropological (moral), and the anagogical.

See also Bede, The Venerable; The Bible and Allegory; Fourfold Allegory; Sallustius.

THE CASTLE OF PERSEVERANCE

A morality play written early in the fifteenth century, *The Castle of Perseverance* has as its hero a character called Mankind. From the Castle, which is at once his world and his soul, the hero succeeds with the help of the personified virtues in expelling six of the seven personified deadly sins. But when he is old, he falls victim to Avarice and himself abandons the Castle. Beware of the evils of avarice—especially in old age—the playwright tells us through his allegory.

The allegory is evident throughout the plot. At the beginning of the play the character World is richly enthroned and is being flattered by his cronies, Lust and Folly; his treasurer, Covetousness; and his messenger, Backbiter. Next we are introduced to the Devil and his attendants, Pride, Envy, and Wrath. Flesh is revealed with his followers, Gluttony, Sloth, and Lechery. All of the characters in the play are costumed allegorically. Lechery is a sexy woman, Gluttony and Flesh are corpulent, and so forth. Now little Mankind appears, followed by Good Angel and Bad Angel, the embodiments of the war in his (and the spectator's) soul. Bad Angel succeeds in leading Mankind to where

World sits with his evil attendants who dress Mankind appropriately, as a dandy, after he forsakes God in favor of their wares; the bad characters all seduce Mankind with the qualities they represent. But Good Angel and her helping virtues, Shrift and Penance, arrive to save him. They convince him to abandon the throne of World and to return through confession and forgiveness to God by going first to the Castle of Perseverance, where he is trained in proper ways by ladies who are the seven major virtues: Meekness, Patience, Charity, Abstinence, Chastity, Industry, and Generosity. Now squabbling breaks out among the evil forces before they agree to attack the Castle to win back Mankind. The attack fails until Covetousness is sent to convince Mankind—now an old man—to leave the Castle. And, indeed, Mankind gives in to the lure of wealth. Death comes to take him, however, and his future falls to the hands of Bad Angel, who is taking him off to Hell when she is interrupted by the "daughters of God": Mercy, Truth, Righteousness, and Peace. Righteousness and Truth argue that he should be punished while Peace and Mercy argue for forgiveness. God is called on to judge, and He takes Mankind's soul to himself.

The "theater" used for this play was itself allegorical (see diagram below). In the center of a circle formed by a ditch or moat in the town square was a platform on stilts representing the castle. At the edge of the circle in each of the four directions stood platforms that served as stages for characters representing the Devil, the World, the Flesh, and God. There was an added platform in the northeast for Covetousness (Avarice). Sitting within the circle, the audience experienced directly the conflict or *agon* between the forces of evil and sin and the power and love of God for the soul of Mankind. The play and its theater were allegories for the great cosmic battle and the battle within each individual as understood by the medieval mind. (Hardison 1965; MacQueen 1970)

See also *Everyman;* Morality Plays; Personification.

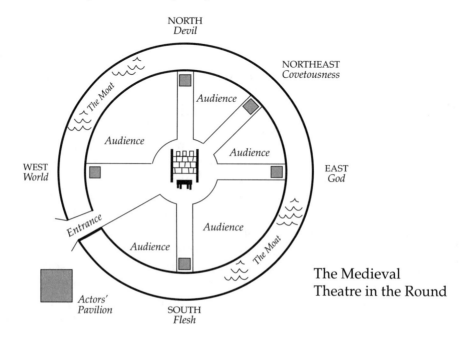

The Medieval
Theatre in the Round

THE CAUCASIAN CHALK CIRCLE

In *The Caucasian Chalk Circle* by Bertolt Brecht, there are allegorical elements associated with Brecht's "epic theatre" idea that drama should be used to bring political and social consciousness to the audience. The central figure in the play is a peasant woman, Grusha, who rescues the child of a self-centered and corrupt governor from war and takes him away to the provinces. Grusha is an allegorical representation of the Marxists' belief in the potential essential nobility of the peasant class and, in a sense, she is "Mother Russia," who struggles at the end of the play with the old order, represented by the governor's wife, for possession of the child. When the two women are told to pull on the child from two directions to see who can "win" him from the chalk circle in which he stands, the governor's wife is perfectly willing to pull, even if it means the death of the child. Grusha would rather give up the child than kill it and refuses to pull. A rogue named Azdak, who has become a judge after a revolution, is proletarian justice. The struggle between Grusha and the governor's wife for custody of the child is class struggle for the new generation, and he decides, according to the new justice of Marxism, that the child, in spite of original ownership, should belong to Grusha.

See also Brecht, Bertolt.

CHAUCER, GEOFFREY

Geoffrey Chaucer (ca. 1343–1400) was the son of an affluent London wine merchant; he was educated at the Inner Temple and was placed, while in his teens, as a page to Elizabeth, Countess of Ulster, and Prince Lionel. In this aristocratic household he undoubtedly learned the manners and skills of the ruling class. He became involved in King Edward III's military campaigns of the Hundred Years War and was captured and ransomed by the French in 1359. In 1366 he married Phillipa, the daughter of a knight, and entered King Edward's household in 1367. Chaucer traveled on several diplomatic missions to Spain, France, and Italy during the following few years, and then worked as a customs official in London from 1374 to 1385. He served as a member of Parliament for the county of Kent for one session (1385–1386) and served the nobility in varying capacities for much of the rest of his life. He died in 1400 in Westminster; he is buried in Westminster Abbey, where his tomb is the heart of Poets' Corner.

Chaucer is generally considered the greatest English poet of the Middle Ages. Some of his writing is allegorical. Written in English instead of Anglo-Norman (a version of French) or Latin, as most court poetry was at that time, Chaucer's literary contributions hastened the acceptance of English as the language of literature. Even during his lifetime Chaucer was recognized as an important and influential writer, and his influence endured throughout the fifteenth century and beyond.

See also The Canterbury Tales; The Hous of Fame, The Parlement of Foules.

THE CHEMICAL WEDDING

The *Chymische Hochzeit Christiani Rosencreutz* (1616), as it is called in the original German, is an allegorical work published by the followers of Christian Rosencreutz ("Rose-Cross"), the founder of a semimystical religious group called the Rosicrucians. Rosencreutz's thoughts were influenced by alchemy, Jewish mysticism, Gnosticism, and other esoteric traditions. Rosicrucians were supposed to travel in order to learn, to provide knowledge, and to help the sick. *The Chemical Wedding* is an allegorical representation of an alchemical Rosicrucian initiatory process in which the actual wedding of Frederick V and Princess Elizabeth (daughter of James I of England) serves as the literary vehicle.

In the story, Rosencreutz is called from his preparation for Easter celebrations to go to a magical castle. There he takes part in a wedding and is initiated during Holy Week into the mysteries of a new way of seeing. The marriage of the bride and groom is an allegory of the Rosicrucian marriage of the soul, which involves the alchemical turning of base metal into gold or, in spiritual terms, the turning of the merely material self into something godly. (Eliade 1987)

See also Gnosticism and Allegory.

CHESTERTON, G. K.

Gilbert Keith Chesterton (1874–1936) was a prolific English poet, journalist, essayist, novelist, and critic. Born in London, he was educated at St. Paul's school and at the Slade. He published several collections of poetry and essays, and his contributions to literary criticism, including work on Dickens, Shaw, Blake, and Chaucer, were highly influential. Of his extensive writings, Chesterton is remembered most for his popular series of detective stories which began with *The Innocence of Father Brown* (1911) and for the somewhat allegorical *The Man Who Was Thursday: A Nightmare* (1908). The detective series focuses largely on a Catholic priest who is able to solve complex mysteries because of his keen insight into the workings of evil. Chesterton himself converted to Roman Catholicism in 1922. (Benet 1965)

See also The Man Who Was Thursday: A Nightmare.

CHESTNUTT, CHARLES

Charles Chestnutt (1858–1932) was an African-American short-story writer and novelist who was born to a family of free blacks in Cleveland, Ohio. After the Civil War, when Chestnutt was eight years old, his family returned to their previous home in Fayetteville, North Carolina. There, he worked in his parents' store and attended a Freedmen's Bureau school. While still a teenager he began his teaching career and in 1880 became the principal of the Fayetteville State Normal School for Negroes. In 1883 he returned to Ohio, settled his own family in Cleveland, and shortly thereafter passed the state bar exam. He founded his own court reporting firm and soon became one of Cleveland's more prominent, successful, and respected citizens. Chestnutt's first literary success was his 1899 short story "The Goophered Grapevine," which was the first story by an African American to be published in *The Atlantic Monthly*. In the same year, Chestnutt published two collections of short fiction: *The Conjure Woman* and *The Wife of His Youth and Other Stories of the Color Line*. His first novel, *The House behind the Cedars,* was published in 1900; his second, *The Marrow of Tradition*, with some allegorical elements, was released the following year; and his final novel, *The Colonel's Dream,* appeared in 1905. Most of Chestnutt's stories portray various aspects of Southern black folk culture, and many wrestle with the social and psychological consequences of blacks "passing" for white, an issue in which he, a fair-complexioned person, was deeply interested.

See also *The Marrow of Tradition*.

"CHILDE ROLAND TO THE DARK TOWER CAME"

"Childe Roland to the Dark Tower Came" (1852) is one of the more enigmatic dramatic romances by Robert Browning (1812–1889). The poem is a sort of dream vision in the tradition of Bunyan's *Pilgrim's Progress.* But Browning's dream-poem soon takes on nightmarish qualities; the landscape through which Childe Roland passes is both frightening and dangerous. Childe Roland is a pilgrim who undertakes a journey to the mysterious Dark Tower; the result of this journey-quest is ambiguous, but many critics agree that the poem's central themes are the problems of saving one's own soul and living a meaningful life. Among various other conflicting readings, Childe Roland's journey has been interpreted as an allegory of dying, an allegory of rebirth, an allegory of spiritual growth, and an allegory of man's limitations. (Jack 1973; Shaw 1968)

See also Browning, Robert.

CHOPINEL, JEAN

Jean Chopinel, or Chopinel, known as Jean de Meun[g] (c. 1250–c. 1305) was the French poet and scholar who completed the last 18,000 lines of the great French poem, *Le Roman de la Rose* [*The Romance of the Rose*], a poem begun by Guillaume de Lorris.

See also Guillaume de Lorris; *The Romance of the Rose*.

CHRÉTIEN DE TROYES

Chrétien lived during the twelfth century and was perhaps the greatest of the many compilers of the Arthurian legend. A Frenchman and court poet, Chrétien wrote several of the best known of the tales of King Arthur's court. His *Perceval* was the first version of the Grail story. Another important work is *Lancelot, ou le chevalier de la charrette* (Launcelot, or the Knight of the Cart). His most allegorical work is *Erec and Énide.* (Benet 1965)

See also *Erec and Énide.*

 # THE CHRONICLES OF NARNIA

The Chronicles of Narnia is a collection of seven books for children by C. S. Lewis (1898–1963). Most of the events take place in a fantasy land called Narnia, which was created by the great lion king Aslan. In *The Lion, the Witch, and the Wardrobe,* four English children, who enter Narnia by way of a magical wardrobe, find themselves involved in the liberation of Narnia from a wicked witch. Eventually they become the rulers of Narnia for Aslan before they find themselves back in "real time," in England, or perhaps it is unreal time, since no English time has passed during their adventures in Narnia.

The inhabitants of Narnia are both humanlike (but not actually "Sons of Adam" and "Daughters of Eve" like the four Pevensie children) and animal—usually talking animals. When Aslan created his paradise land of Narnia, it was almost immediately infected by the evil witch, who found her way there with the help of a human boy. So it was that in the various adventures of the books, other human children must help redeem the land.

That there is allegory in this story is clear enough. The connection between Aslan and Christ is evident in spite of disclaimers by Lewis—himself a Christian apologist. In the series Aslan is, by his own consent, ritually murdered in order to pay for the sins of a human—one of the four Pevensies. And he rises from death in a particularly stirring scene that captures the essence of the Easter message as well as any in literature. The Judeo-Christian allegory is evident in many details of the books. The wardrobe through which the children enter Narnia, for instance, is made of the apple tree grown from the apple that had been given to the first human sinner in Narnia—the one who had provided entry to the wicked witch. It is difficult not to associate the first sinner with Adam, the witch with Satan, the apple with the forbidden tree, and the wardrobe that comes from the original apple with the pathway to righteousness and redemption that is given by the "New Adam," Christ. Still, it must be said in support of Lewis's disclaimers that the *Narnia* books read perfectly well without any allegorical interpretation. They are by no means suitable only for Christian readers.

See also Lewis, C. S.

CHRYSIPPUS

Chrysippus of Soli in Cilicia (280–207 B.C.E.) was the leader of the Stoic philosophers in Athens in ca. 230 B.C.E. He was an early allegorist in that he suggested connections between the gods and certain natural phenomena and moral ideas. He was fond of allegorical statements such as "Reason *(logos)* is man's governing ship." Chrysippus also articulated a doctrine of world citizenship—the universe, he believed, was a *polis* (city) of gods and humans, who communicated by way of reason. It was the existence of reason as demonstrated by the order of the universe *(logos)* that served as Chrysippus's primary argument for the existence of God. (Eliade 1987)

CHURCH ARCHITECTURE AND ALLEGORY

The French art historian Emile Male rightly paints a picture of the medieval church building as, to quote John MacQueen, a "historical allegory, written in stone, glass, and wood" (40). Built in the form of the cross, the building represents the body of Christ, the east end or sanctuary being the head, where the communicant becomes one with Christ in the ritual of Holy Communion. The windows and carvings tell allegorical tales of the life of the Church and the Christian's journey through life. (MacQueen 1970)

See also Medieval Art and Allegory; Painting and Sculpture, Allegorical; Ritual as Allegory.

CICERO, MARCUS TULLIUS

Cicero (106–43 B.C.E.) was the greatest of the Roman orators. Born of an equestrian family, Cicero became a successful lawyer at a relatively early age and then went into politics, where his oratory skills served him well. For his part in suppressing a conspiracy, he was honored as "father of the country." Eventually he became involved in the power struggles that followed the assassination of Julius Caesar and was murdered by followers of Marc Antony, whom he had condemned in several famous speeches (the *Philippics).*

Cicero was a noted philosopher, most famous for his *De Natura Deorum [Concerning the Nature of the Gods].* The *De Natura* speaks to the question of allegorical interpretation. The author presents us with a conversation between representatives of three schools of ancient Greek philosophy: the Epicureans, the Academics, and the Stoics, who were known for their allegorical approach to myth and literature. The Stoics' position is represented by one Balbus, who presents the gods as, in a sense, personifications of elements of nature and human experience. Ceres (Demeter) is grain, Liber is wine, Saturn's Greek name is Kronos, or Time. When Kronos eats his sons he eats up the years, expressing his Latin name, which means "filled up."

Cicero was deeply influenced by the Stoics. He believed in the dignity of each human being, whether slave or freeman, whether Roman or non-Roman. This belief arose from his view of an ordered universe based on reason—a *logos*-based cosmos. In short, Cicero believed in natural law. In *The Republic* he wrote, "True law is correct reason that agrees with nature." For Cicero there was universal and timeless right and wrong based in the laws of nature or *logos*. A major part of Cicero's discussion of what might be called the natural republic is to be found in his *Dream of Scipio,* a philosophical fable in the general tradition of Plato's myths. Some have gone so far as to call this work allegory, probably because of the fantastic or mythic setting, in which Scipio Africanus is visited by his grandfather in a dream and is given a vision, from somewhere in space, of the earth, the stars, and the other planets in proper perspective. This vision becomes, in a sense, an allegory for Cicero's view, expressed by Scipio in the dream, of the vanity of humanity in the face of the immensity and finely tuned order of the universe. But it must be pointed out that there is little on the surface of this work of what we would call traditional allegory. Abstractions are not personified. It is simply that Cicero uses a fantasy vision to speak to the human condition. (Eliade 1987)

See also Chrysippus; Cleanthes; *Hyponoia*; Painting and Sculpture, Allegorical; Plato.

CLEANTHES

Cleanthes of Assos (331–232 B.C.E.) preceded Chrysippus as head of the Stoics in Athens and looked at the world through allegorizing eyes. His most famous work is the *Hymn to Zeus,* a study of the stoics' understanding of Fate and its importance in the relationship between humanity and the gods. To quote Gilbert Murray, he saw the universe as a "mystic pageant, in which the immortal stars were the dancers and the Sun the priestly torch-bearer" (165). (Murray 1935)

See also Chrysippus.

CLEMENS, SAMUEL

See Twain, Mark.

COCTEAU, JEAN

Jean Cocteau (1889–1964) was a French novelist, screenwriter, poet, and essayist who was at the very center of the modernist movement in the arts. Born to a wealthy Parisian family, Cocteau did poorly at school and dabbled somewhat successfully in poetry until he was moved by a performance of Stravinsky's ballet *The Rites of Spring* to take up the challenge of modernism in the arts. Almost immediately Cocteau began creating poems, plays, novels, and essays that caught the attention of the great artists of his day—Proust, Picasso, Apollinaire, to mention only a few. It is perhaps for his films that Cocteau will be most remembered. His most famous work for the screen is *Orphee* (Orpheus), based on the myth of Orpheus and Eurydice. Cocteau continued working on the Orpheus theme in various media until his death. His interest in the theme can be called allegorical in that the Orpheus story, involving the descent of the singer Orpheus into the underworld in search of his lost bride, is representative of Cocteau's central concern. This concern is that of the poet, who has a mysterious power to see and in a sense to move beyond the borders of the here-and-now and to create, but who is misunderstood by those around him. The tragedy of Orpheus and of the poet—including the avant-garde Cocteau—is that they are doomed to explain the world beyond to the nonlistening Philistines for whom they create.

See also Orpheus Myth.

COETZEE, J. M.

John Michael Coetzee, a descendant of seventeenth-century Afrikaner settlers, was born in 1940 in Cape Town, South Africa. He came to the United States in 1965 to begin his doctoral work in English language and literature at the University of Texas at Austin and later accepted a teaching position at the State University of New York at Buffalo (1968–1971). There, he completed most of his first novel, *Dusklands* (1974). A writer of considerable international acclaim and the author of several novels and over 40 scholarly articles, he is currently a professor of general literature at his undergraduate alma mater, the University of Cape Town.

See also Foe; In the Heart of the Country; Waiting for the Barbarians.

COLERIDGE, SAMUEL TAYLOR

Samuel Taylor Coleridge (1772–1834) was born in rural Devonshire, but was educated in London and then attended Jesus College in Cambridge. In spite of an unhappy marriage and a debilitating addiction to opium, Coleridge maintained close relationships with such writers as William Wordsworth and Charles Lamb and produced several of the masterpieces of Romantic poetry, including "The Ancient Mariner," "Christabel," "Kubla Khan," and "Dejection: An Ode." A great English Romantic poet and literary critic, Coleridge attempted to differentiate between allegory and symbol. He saw the symbolic in literature as "organic" rather than "mechanic," as "always . . . a part . . . of the whole of which it is representative." Thus, " 'Here comes a sail' (that is, a ship) is a symbolic expression." But if, in referring to a hero, we say "Behold our lion!" we are using allegory. Allegory is "the employment of one set of agents and images with actions and accompaniments correspondent, so as to convey, while in disguise, either moral qualities or conceptions of the mind" (30). For Coleridge it was important to point out that in allegory the correspondences appeal to our mental faculties even as the differences are clear to our senses and imaginations. It is evident that a hero, as far as our senses and our imaginations are concerned, cannot be a lion, but the mechanical and mental connection made by the writer between the hero and the lion sends a clear mental message as to the writer's opinion of the hero.

Some critics have interpreted certain of Coleridge's poems as historical or political allegories. For example, in "Recantation: Illustrated in the Story of the Mad Ox" (published in *Sibylline Leaves*, 1817), Coleridge allegorizes the story of the French Revolution, justifying to his audience his own condemnation of the revolution although he originally supported it. In the poem, the ox (the French Revolution) is owned by "Old Lewis" (the French King Louis XVI). At the beginning of the story, the newly freed ox is happy and playful, capering about the meadow. But the parish, mistaking the ox's activity and energy for madness, chase and pester the bull until he is truly driven mad. In this way, Coleridge demonstrates his vision of a revolution gone wrong through misunderstandings and overzealousness. (Coleridge 1936; Fletcher 1964; Honig 1972; Kitson 1991)

COMUS

The great English poet John Milton (1608–1674) composed the masque *Comus* in 1634. Masques were essentially court entertainments which in England first took place during the reign of Henry VIII and became particularly popular under James I early in the seventeenth century. It was then that they developed, under the particular direction of the architect and designer Inigo Jones and the playwright Ben Jonson, into the elaborate form that Milton inherited. The seventeenth-century English masques were plays that pointed in their love-oriented plots, elaborate pastoral sets, lyrical songs, ornate costumes, and dances back to the fertility rites from which the form probably evolved.

Milton called his *Comus* a mask (masque), and in terms of its plot, setting, and elaborate language it certainly fits the definition. Masques sometimes have allegorical aspects; this is true of Milton's play, which represents the eternal struggle in youth between chastity and sexuality. The plot of *Comus* is simple and the allegory relatively obvious. The play takes place in the woods, which stand, as they often do in literature, for the state of being spiritually lost or in limbo. In these woods a young virgin is left by her two virtuous brothers, who go off to hunt up food. But the lady is found by Comus (from the Greek *komos*, meaning "revel"), who represents the pleasures of sex and tempts her to become his bride. Comus is the son of Bacchus and Circe and behaves, therefore, as might be expected. With the help of her brothers and the river nymph Sabrina, who represent strong virtue, the lady is finally saved. A few of her words, through which moral abstractions are personified, will convey the clear allegorical intentions of the poem:

> These thoughts may startle well, but not astound
> The virtuous mind, that ever walks attended
> By a strong siding champion Conscience.—
> O welcome pure-ey'd Faith, white-handed Hope,

Thou hov'ring Angel girt with golden wings,
And thou unblemish't form of Chastity . . . (Benet 1965)

See also Blake, William; Milton, John.

THE CONFIDENCE MAN

The Confidence Man, published by Herman Melville (1819–1891) in 1857, has intrigued scholars for generations by its quietly bitter assault on the political and moral crises of the mid–nineteenth century. The story takes place onboard a steamboat, the *Fidele,* as she travels from St. Louis to New Orleans. The passengers, one by one, are approached by a confidence man who assumes a variety of clever disguises. The confidence man succeeds in duping a number of passengers, cheating them out of both money and sympathy through his elaborate ruses. Other passengers refuse to be persuaded by his stories; their deep cynicism protects them from the confidence man's manipulations. Thus the *Fidele* and her passengers become a microcosm, representing the broad spectrum of political attitudes and religious beliefs of mid–nineteenth-century America.

The Confidence Man has been interpreted as both historio-political allegory and religious allegory. Historically, the novel seems to be based loosely on the political movements in America from the mid-1840s until the mid-1850s. Critic Helen P. Trimpi suggests that the seven or perhaps eight personae of the confidence man onboard the *Fidele* may reflect historical figures who manipulated public and philanthropic opinion on the issue of slavery during this tumultuous decade. The deaf-mute, considered by many to be the first appearance of the confidence man, may allegorize the person of Benjamin Lundy, the nearly deaf Quaker founder of the antislavery periodical *The Genius of Universal Emancipation.* The second persona of the confidence man, Black Guinea, may be understood to allegorize the issue of slavery as an important (and manipulative) issue; Black Guinea's legless condition underscores the immobility of African Americans at the time and suggests also their lack of political influence. John Ringman, the Man with the Weed, is the third disguise of the confidence man and may be intended to allegorize the character of William Cullen Bryant. His fourth appearance, as the Man in Gray Coat and White Tie, the charity agent for the "Seminole Widow and Orphan Asylum," could be Theodore Parker, a preacher, pamphleteer, and supporter of the "Free Kansas" movement, which preceded the founding of the Republican party. His fifth disguise, as John Truman, may perhaps represent Thurlow Weed, politician, newspaper editor, and cofounder of the Republican party. The sixth persona of the confidence man, the Herb-Doctor, may suggest Charles Sumner, Massachusetts senator, antislavery orator, and another cofounder of the Republican party. The seventh persona, that of the Philosophical Intelligence Office agent (the "PIO Man"), may be interpreted as an allegorization of Horace Greeley, the powerful and influential newspaper editor and member of the fledgling Republican party.

The final manifestation of the confidence man as Frank Goodman, the Cosmopolitan, may suggest the character of Henry Ward Beecher, the Liberal Congregationalist preacher and political speaker for the Republican party. In the novel, all of the manifestations of the confidence man argue for the innate goodness in mankind, progress, and Providence. Yet, based on the allegories of historical and political figures, all the confidence man's personae are really trying to solicit support for themselves and donations to their causes.

Many of the other characters onboard the *Fidele* whose personal philosophies allow them to resist being duped by the confidence man seem to allegorize important figures of the mid–nineteenth century. For example, Mark Winsome may represent Ralph Waldo Emerson, Egbert may be Henry David Thoreau, the Crazy Beggar could suggest Edgar Allan Poe, and the Gentleman in Gold Sleeve-Buttons is probably the wealthy manufacturer, politician, and philanthropist of Boston, Abbott Lawrence.

The Confidence Man may also be interpreted on a more general level as a religious allegory, revealing the disparity between man's profession of Christianity and his practice of it. The form-changing confidence man in this context takes on the characteristics of Satan by masquerading as faith, hope, or charity while actually embodying the opposite of these ideals. Contrasting the deaf-mute's slogans of charity, taken from 1 Corinthians 13, with the barber's direct proclamation of "No Trust," Melville allegorizes both Christian love and the evil that preys on human weakness and gullibility. In spite of the atmosphere of "No Trust" onboard the *Fidele* ("faith"), the confidence man elicits a great deal of "trust" by victimizing those who are persuaded by his often "charitable" causes. The diabolic aspect of the confidence man is revealed to the reader as character after character either falls for the clever con games or, through deeply cynical and un-Christian misanthropy, rejects the confidence man entirely. The novel ends with the confidence man victimizing an old man reading his Bible; the final action is that of the confidence man extinguishing the only light. Thus, Melville's allegory may suggest the sad impossibility of a world based on Christian ideals and principles, and the reality of a world in which the evil conquer the vulnerable. (Trimpi 1987)

See also Melville, Herman.

CONRAD, JOSEPH

Teodor Josef Konrad Korzeniowski (1857–1924) was born in Poland to an aristocratic family. Young Teodor had an adventurous nature; he took up smuggling for a while and then became a seaman on British ships, where he took the name Joseph Conrad. Already well read in Polish and French, young Conrad took to the English language well and soon was speaking and reading it with enthusiasm. He became so proficient in his adopted language, in fact, that he wrote all of his major works in it. These include such classics as *Typhoon*, *Lord Jim*, *Nostromo*, *Victory*, and *Heart of Darkness*.

Critics have always recognized the symbolic in the work of Conrad, and many have suggested that his penchant for symbolism leads him naturally into allegory. Certainly Conrad's settings, described as they are sometimes in almost surrealist terms, seem to demand special attention as carriers of meaning. When we read *Heart of Darkness* we realize that the jungle where Mr. Kurtz lives is an embodiment of something in the human soul. In *Victory* the island retreat of Heyst and Lena that is invaded by the evil Mr. Jones signals the Garden of Eden to the mind bent on allegory. Without doubt it would be fair to suggest the presence of the *paysage moralisé,* or "moralized landscape," in Conrad's work. Yet Conrad himself cautions us against allegorical interpretations. In a letter to Barrett H. Clark about *Victory,* he points out that "a work of art is very seldom limited to one exclusive meaning"; it is the symbolic, he says—not the allegorical—that provides complexity and depth in art. And in another letter he speaks of "the majestic overpowering tediousness of an existence full of allegoric visions." No serious reader of Conrad can deny the presence of a strongly symbolic and archetypal level of meaning, but to call this level allegory is to ignore the essentially realistic surface of his work and the notable lack of didactic intention. (Yelton 1967)

See also *Heart of Darkness; Paysage Moralisé; Victory.*

THE CONSOLATION OF PHILOSOPHY

De Consolatione Philosophae, or *The Consolation of Philosophy,* by Boethius, is an allegory in which Philosophy is personified as a beautiful woman. Boethius tells how, as he sat bemoaning his fate in prison, the woman appeared to him:

> Her face inspired deep respect. In her glance
> there was a light that saw deeper than any mortal
> eye could see. She had all of the features of
> youth and vitality, though one sensed that
> her age was beyond the measurements of time. It
> was difficult to know her height because she was
> sometimes of our size and sometimes she seemed
> so tall that her head disappeared from sight
> among the clouds.

Boethius goes on to describe the artful and delicate gown worn by Philosophy—a gown damaged "by hands that had ripped away whatever they could." The description of the woman clearly represents the various characteristics of philosophy—its vigor, its mysteriousness, its ability to touch matters of this world and to reach into the heights beyond, its timelessness. The rent garment reveals the attacks on philosophy by rough and ignorant humans. (MacQueen 1970)

See also Boethius, Anicius Manlius Severinus.

COOPER, JAMES FENIMORE

James Fenimore Cooper (1786–1851) is best known for his *Leatherstocking Tales,* a collection of five novels: *The Pioneers* (1823), *The Last of the Mohicans* (1826), *The Prairie* (1827), *The Pathfinder* (1840), and *The Deerslayer* (1841). *The Leatherstocking Tales* relate the adventures of Natty Bumppo, an American wilderness man, whose stories take on mythic proportions as he aligns himself with the forces of nature and virtue in order to combat evil in its many forms. With his faithful Indian companion, Chingachgook, Natty Bumppo allegorically represents the American ideals of pure morality, true Christianity, and natural integrity. Consequently, the *Leatherstocking Tales* have been interpreted as an indictment of civilization, since the violence and ruthlessness of the white settlers stand in direct opposition to the forces that Natty Bumppo represents.

While the *Leatherstocking Tales* embody certain allegorical aspects, Cooper did undertake a series of stories that were consciously allegorical. *The Bravo* (1831) is a politically allegorical tale, in which the dark corridors of Venice represent widespread and invidious political corruption. *The Heidenmauer* (1832), a historical allegory, features two hills that suggest the twin powers of church and state in ancient Germany. *The Monikans* (1835), an extremely unpopular and virtually unreadable political allegory, depicts the hypocritical governments of England and the United States, called "Leaphigh" and "Leaplow," respectively. *The Sea Lions* (1849) tells the story of two ships on parallel journeys to the Antarctic, allegorizing two contrasting ways of life. And the island setting in the novel *The Crater* (1847) allegorizes the social development of America. (Peck 1977; Rans 1991; Shulenberger 1955)

COOVER, ROBERT

Robert Lowell Coover (b. 1932) is an American novelist born in Iowa and educated at the universities of Southern Illinois, Indiana, and Chicago. He served in the U.S. Navy from 1953 to 1957 and has taught philosophy at several universities. Considered a postmodernist writer, he won the William Faulkner Award for best first novel for *The Origin of the Brunists* (1966). Other novels by Coover include *The Universal Baseball Association, Inc., J. Henry Waugh, Prop.* (1968), *The Public Burning* (1977), *Spanking the Maid* (1981), *Gerald's Party* (1986), and *Pinnochio in Venice* (1991).

See also The Universal Baseball Association, Inc., J. Henry Waugh, Prop.

CORNUTUS, ANNAEUS

Sometimes called Phornutus, Cornutus (ca. 20–ca. 67 C.E.) wrote the *Commentary on the Gods,* an allegorical reading of the Greek religion. He is one of the several classical allegorizers of whom Rabelais is so disdainful in the prologue to *Gargantua,* where he asks whether we can truly believe that when Homer wrote his epics that he had in mind the allegorical meanings with which these classical writers have burdened him. (MacQueen 1970)

See also Rabelais, François.

COSMOGRAPHIA

See Bernardus Silvestris.

CRATES

Crates of Thebes (365–285 B.C.E.) was a beggar-philosopher and the teacher of Zeno, the founder of Stoicism. Crates interpreted Homer allegorically and was an important influence on the *Homeric Allegories* by the first-century B.C.E. thinker Heraclitus.

See also Homeric Allegories.

THE CRYING OF LOT 49

Published in 1966 by American author Thomas Pynchon, *The Crying of Lot 49* tells the story of Mrs. Oedipa Maas, a California housewife who is, to her great surprise, named executrix of the extensive estate of Mr. Pierce Inverarity, her former lover. In trying to unravel the mysteries surrounding Inverarity's legacy, Oedipa learns of a secret postal service, Trystero, which operates in defiance of the federal monopoly on mail delivery and through which many Americans communicate. Allegorically, Oedipa's quest for the meaning of the Inverarity estate becomes "a quest for the 'meaning' of America itself, including the 'other' America of the disinherited and the drifters" (Buning, 145). Other allegorical readings include Oedipa's quest as a journey toward self-knowledge and understanding and as a quest to somehow "heal" the diseased and corrupted city of San Narciso through Oedipa's modern-day search for the "Holy Grail." (Buning 1992; Madsen 1991)

See also Pynchon, Thomas.

CUPID AND PSYCHE

The well-known tale of Cupid (Eros) and Psyche takes its fullest form in Books IV–VI of *The Golden Ass,* the Roman satirical romance by Apuleius.

Psyche was the beautiful youngest of three daughters born to a king and queen. She was so beautiful, in fact, and so often compared to Venus (Aphrodite), that the goddess became jealous and ordered her son Cupid to make the girl fall in love with an ugly and worthless man. As it turned out, Cupid himself fell in love with Psyche.

Cupid brings Psyche back to life with the kiss of amour. The sculpture, by Antonio Canova (1757–1822), is housed by the Louvre, Paris.

When Psyche remained unmarried, her father consulted the oracle, who ordered that the girl be laid out corpselike on a mountaintop where a terrifying serpent would marry her. On the mountain, Psyche fell into a deep sleep and was magically removed to a beautiful palace where she was visited each night by an unnamed bridegroom who left each morning before she could see him.

Psyche's sisters set out in search of her, but the mysterious husband warned his bride not to respond to them in any way should they find her. Finally, he allowed his wife simply to meet her sisters in return for a promise that she not heed their appeals to learn his identity. The women did visit and they were overcome with jealousy when they saw the lavish surroundings in which their younger sister lived. Psyche's husband warned her that her sisters' plan was to force her to see his face and that should they succeed he would have to leave her. He also revealed that she was pregnant.

The sisters visited twice more and told Psyche that her husband was a terrible serpent that would devour her when her child was born. Psyche was horrified and agreed to a plan whereby she would shine a light on her husband and kill him with a knife.

But when one night she raised the lamp over her sleeping lover she saw not a serpent but Cupid. Ashamed of having broken her promise, she thought of killing herself but instead she leaned down to kiss the beautiful god. As she did so she spilled some hot oil from her lamp on his shoulder and he awoke. Furious and sad at once, he flew away, vowing revenge on the sisters—they soon paid with their lives—and scolding Psyche for having exposed him to Venus's ire by revealing him as her husband.

It was the god Pan who convinced Psyche not to take her own life but to try to win back the love of Cupid. Psyche searched the earth for her love, but he lay moaning in his angry mother's quarters. Venus demanded that Jupiter have the girl brought to her for punishment. The punishment consisted of several impossible tasks, which the girl accomplished only with the magical help of sympathetic beings in nature. The final task was a descent into Hades. Take a box to Persephone, she was told, and have her place in it a bit of her beauty. Despairing, Psyche tried to leap off a tower, but the tower told her how to get to, survive in, and return from the Underworld. Most important, she was not to look into the box. Not surprisingly, this was one instruction she could not follow. She opened the box only to be enveloped, not by beauty but by the sleep of death.

But Cupid, now cured of his burn, flew down to save his love. He replaced the sleep of death in the box and appealed to Jupiter to allow his marriage. Venus finally agreed to the marriage as well, and Mercury was sent to bring Psyche to heaven, where she was given the gift of immortality. A child was soon born to the happy couple; she was named Voluptas (Pleasure).

The allegory behind this complicated story was clear to Apuleius's readers. Cupid is from the Latin *cupido*, meaning "love" or "desire." Psyche is the Greek for "soul." Venus means "sexual love" or "charm." And Voluptas, as has been noted, means "pleasure." Treated as gods, these personifications of abstract ideas are players in a morality drama that reads something like this: The pure soul struggles with sexual passion and jealousy for union with love. Only through real suffering and the facing of ultimate loss itself and only with the help of natural forces can soul and love be united. The natural child of such a union is true Pleasure.

See also Apuleius, Lucius; *The Golden Ass*; Personification.

CYNEWULF

Cynewulf was an Old English poet of the late eighth and early ninth centuries. Some critics have noted that this medieval poet, recognizable by the inscription of his name in runic characters after several poems, incorporates a form of psychomachian allegory into texts such as "Christ II," "Juliana," and "The Phoenix." "Christ II," also called "The Ascension," is the second part of a three-part poem preserved in the *Exeter Book*, and is based on a homily of Pope Gregory the Great. Also preserved in the *Exeter Book*, "Juliana" is a short poem which, closely following its Latin source, retells the story of the martyrdom of a Christian virgin who was persecuted in 303 c.e.. The poem describes Juliana's torture and imprisonment after she refuses marriage and a pagan lifestyle. She is visited in prison by a devil disguised as an angel, but she recognizes him and forces him to tell her about the evildoing of Satan. Juliana's executioners are converted and martyred after their first attempts to martyr her fail. "The Phoenix," another poem in the *Exeter Book*, attributes Christian significance to the myth of the phoenix by developing an allegorical relationship between the bird and Christ.

Scholars consider Cynewulf's poetry to be allegorical primarily because it describes spiritual conflicts between Christianity and paganism in terms of warfare; saints are depicted as allegorical soldiers of Christ battling against demonic opponents who represent particular vices or the Devil himself. (Irvine 1981)

See also Prudentius, Aurelius Clemens.

DANTE ALIGHIERI

Dante (1265–1321), Italy's greatest poet and one of the great masters of all time, is best known for his monumental literary epic *Divina Commedia [The Divine Comedy]*—a primary example of allegory. Dante lived and worked during the period when the Middle Ages became the Renaissance. Born in Florence, Dante was given a thorough classical and Christian education and early on became involved in the political and religious wars between various factions in Italy at the time. In about 1300 he began work on his *Comedy*, which was not completed until just before his death. In 1274 he had met a woman named Beatrice. He met her again when he was 18; she became the idealized muse for all of his work and the primary inspiration for *The Divine Comedy*.

Dante's work indicates the transition to a Renaissance mode in that he is the first poet to apply religious theories of allegory to the study of literature in the vernacular. In his *Convivio* (ca. 1306) he asserts that it is proper for vernacular literature to be both literal and allegorical. The literal level is a *bella menzogna*—a "beautiful lie"—under which is hidden a truth. As Dante notes, this is a poet's rather than a theologian's way of understanding allegory, as the beauty of the literal level is as important to him as the truth of the allegorical. And, he notes, allegory itself is complex and many-layered, not simplistic.

As an example of the literal level, Dante gives us Ovid's description of Orpheus taming the beasts with his music. At the simplest—one might say factual—allegorical level this means that those who are wise can tame those who are wild and cruel. Another allegorical level, Dante tells us, is the moral level, which has to do with lessons that can be applied to our behavior. When Christ takes only three of his apostles to the mountain for his transfiguration, we understand that for our most important acts we should have only a few companions.

The fourth level of understanding for Dante is the anagogic, a high spiritual level that transcends the literal but in no way contradicts it. When the Hebrews left the captivity of Egypt, Judea literally became free, but just as true is the fact that is represented by the story of that event—namely, that when the soul departs from sin it becomes holy and free.

In a famous letter in Latin to Con Grande della Scala on *The Divine Comedy*, Dante broadens the traditional medieval view of allegory by discussing the degrees of allegory and the possibility that allegory can be ambiguous, that although its purpose is didactic it must function in such a way as to recognize the stylistic and rhetorical requirements of literary art. Dante seems to have wanted to be thought of first as a poet and only secondarily as a philosopher-theologian. For Dante, allegory takes on respectability as a literary form whereas in earlier allegories literature had taken a distinctly secondary role to the didactic purpose. (Fletcher 1964; MacQueen 1970; Quilligan 1979)

See also *The Divine Comedy;* Fourfold Allegory.

 # THE DAY OF THE LOCUST

The last novel by Nathanael West (1903–1940), *The Day of the Locust* (1939) has been interpreted as a loose allegory of the distinctly American pursuit of stardom and glamour. *The Day of the Locust* recounts the experiences of Tod Hackett, a young man drawn to what he believes to be the alluring possibilities of life in Hollywood. What he finds there is a disturbingly brutal and nightmarish world, in which individual identities are virtually erased, people are routinely violated both physically and emotionally, and human compassion is virtually nonexistent. The final scene, a violent mob riot in which several characters are killed or maimed and Tod is driven insane, recalls the chaos wrought by the biblical locusts, which punished humans for their sins. Allegorically, Tod becomes everyman, lost in a seductive but terrifying world of sexuality, violence, and victimization. (Hyman 1986)

See also West, Nathanael.

DE LILLE, ALAIN

See Alan of Lille.

DE LORRIS, GUILLAUME

See Guillaume de Lorris.

DE MAN, PAUL

In his influential *Allegories of Reading* (1979), Paul de Man takes a deconstructionist, postmodernist approach, seeing allegory as a genre that questions its own validity. Allegory "simultaneously asserts and denies the authority of its own rhetorical mode."

Like so many students of allegory, de Man makes a distinction between symbol and allegory. A symbol is based on the sense of identity between the sign and that to which it refers. There is an almost metaphysical connection between the two entities. In allegory, argues de Man, there is no such link. Rather, the allegorical text always points back to a different text, and given the problems of interpretation in particular political and social contexts, signs both refer to something and illustrate what the deconstructionist sees as the basic failure of language to be a reliable vehicle for meaning. (Johnson 1994; Quilligan 1979)

See also Allegoresis.

DE MEUN[G], JEAN

See Chopinel, Jean.

DE PLANCTA NATURAE

See Alan of Lille.

DEAD SOULS

The satiric novel *Dead Souls* (1842) is the most well known work by the Russian writer Nikolai Gogol (1809–1852). The story centers around the likable Chichikov, a poor Russian who designs the clever scheme of buying the names of dead "souls" (serfs) from estate owners in order to mortgage them and acquire fraudulent funds. Critic James B. Woodward argues that *Dead Souls* may be read as a moral allegory of "the perversion of the 'Russian soul' and a prediction of its eventual rebirth—an allegory that hinges on the portrayal of spiritual perversion as a divergence from the symbolic ideal of 'pure femininity'" (Woodward 252). Chichikov's journey through the Russian countryside thus becomes an allegorical pilgrimage during which he must confront his own moral corruption. (Woodward 1978)

See also Gogol, Nikolai.

DEFOE, DANIEL

Daniel Defoe (ca. 1660–1731) was born to a middle-class Presbyterian English family and spent his early adulthood working as a small-scale merchant. He was rather successful for a time, but eventually found himself deeply in debt. He then turned to writing and to politics, publishing and distributing political pamphlets and verses that championed the Whigs. After being jailed briefly for one of his more incendiary pamphlets, he became a political spy under the guidance of Robert Harley, an influential politician and benefactor of Defoe's. When he was nearly 60, Defoe began a new chapter in his career by writing a series of adventure tales. *Robinson Crusoe* appeared in 1719 and, while not received very well by the bourgeoisie at the time, became a favorite with the working classes and remains to this day his most widely read tale. Like many moralistic works of the period, *Robinson Crusoe* leaves ample room for an allegorical reading.

    See also Robinson Crusoe.

DEGUILEVILLE, GUILLAUME DE

Deguileville (c. 1294–1360) was the author of an allegory called *Pilgrimage of the Life of Man,* as translated from the French by John Lydgate (ca. 1370–1450). In its emphasis on the quest aspect of the human life, it is an ancestor of Bunyan's *Pilgrim's Progress.* (MacQueen 1970)

    See also Piers Plowman; The Pilgrim's Progress.

DEKKER, THOMAS

Thomas Dekker (ca. 1572–1632), English playwright and pamphleteer, was probably a Londoner by birth and upbringing. Little is known of his life, other than that he was plagued by financial troubles and is thought to have authored or contributed to about 50 plays, 20 of which have survived. *Old Fortunatus* (1599) is the earliest surviving play; the second, *The Shoemaker's Holiday* (1599), is considered by many to be his finest work. Dekker's pamphlets indulge in more explicit moralizing than do most of his plays; examples include *The Wonderful Year* (1603), *The Seven Deadly Sins of London* (1606), and *Lantern and Candlelight* (1608). But the plays, particularly *Old Fortunatus,* can be said to be allegorical in part.

    See also Old Fortunatus.

DINESEN, ISAK

Isak Dinesen, the pseudonym for Karen Blixen (1885–1962), was a Danish short-story writer and novelist who often wrote in English. Born into an affluent family, she studied art at the Royal Academy of Fine Arts in Copenhagen, then traveled to Paris and Rome to continue her education. She married her cousin in 1913, and moved to Kenya to farm coffee, but the marriage foundered, and in 1931 she returned to Denmark, divorced and bankrupt. She published her first book, a collection of macabre neogothic short stories called *Seven Gothic Tales* (which includes the allegorical story "The Monkey"), in 1934. Her highly successful novel *Out of Africa* followed in 1937; other acclaimed works include *Winter's Tales* (1942), *Angelic Avengers* (1944), and *Anecdotes of Destiny* (1958).

    See also "The Monkey."

Isak Dinesen

DISRAELI, ISAAC

In a chapter entitled "Allegory" in his *Amenities of Literature,* Disraeli, or D'Israeli (1766–1848), the father of the British Prime Minister Benjamin Disraeli, calls allegory "art in which one thing is related, and another understood," but he suggests that this definition is not sufficient to cover the "multiform shapes which allegory assumes. . . ." (Fletcher 1964)

THE DISTINCTIONES ABEL

See Peter the Chanter.

THE DIVINE COMEDY

The *Divina Commedia* (ca. 1300–1321), by the Italian Dante Alighieri, is one of the world's greatest allegorical poems. In a letter to Can Grande della Scala, the poet announced that his work was "polysemous," that it had several levels of meaning. The reader, he said, should consider the poem first from the point of view of the literal meaning—the condition of souls after death. It is that subject on which the work as a whole stands. The *Commedia* could, however, be taken allegorically, in which case the subject would become, said Dante, "man according as by his merits or demerits in the exercise of his free will he is deserving of reward or punishment by justice."

The *Commedia* is also a political allegory. That is, the fate of certain historical and contemporary figures in the epic reflect Dante's attitudes toward people and situations in his own society. It should be pointed out, too, that in some ways the *Commedia* is Dante's own spiritual autobiography—the record of a midlife reassessment—and that this autobiography can be seen as a level of allegory. In the same way, the epic can be seen as the spiritual autobiography of any who would follow in Dante's path.

Dante thought of his poem as an epic in the sense that the protagonist—Dante himself—goes on a journey to the farthest reaches of reality—Hell, Purgatory, and Paradise—in search of destiny and wholeness. Dante's allegory is sophisticated in that on the literal level it is meant to be a true story: Dante, the "hero" of the epic, is real; the time, 1300, is real; and for the Christian of Dante's time, Hell, Purgatory, and Paradise are real. All of this makes the work different from an allegory such as *Everyman,* in which there is no pretense of literal reality. Furthermore, whereas in *Everyman* we have personified abstractions as characters—Good Deeds, Everyman, and others—in the *Commedia* the characters are real personages, historical and contemporaneous, with symbolic aspects only suggesting allegorical interpretation at various levels.

At the beginning of the epic, in Canto 1, the poet Dante finds himself in the middle of life "in a dark wood" on the eve of Good Friday. To escape he attempts to climb a beautiful mountain but is prevented from doing so by fierce beasts. At this point the Roman poet Virgil—Dante's historical inspiration—appears and offers to guide Dante to his beloved Beatrice. Throughout the poem the real Dante is present as a distinct personality, but as the dark wood and his time of life suggest, he is also, like Everyman in the northern allegory, a representative of the "lost" Christian sinner in search of the grace of God and, archetypally, of any human being who begins the pilgrimage from brokenness to wholeness, the one who wishes to ascend the mountain to God or to individuation. Virgil, too, is a historical figure, but he is also an archetypal allegory for human wisdom, who speaks to all humans. Beatrice is a real woman known to Dante, but in the Christian allegory she is divine grace and archetypally she might be called the hero's lost inner self, which must be found if wholeness is to be achieved. It might well be said that it is only on the archetypal allegorical level that the poem can be meaningful to the reader who is not medieval or Christian.

After the introductory canto, the poem is divided into three parts—the *Inferno* (Hell), the *Purgatorio* (Purgatory), and the *Paradiso* (Paradise)—each made up of 33 cantos. Dante must journey through Hell and Purgatory before he can attain Paradise. For the Christian, Hell is the place of suffering after death for the evil committed in life. Allegorically speaking, it is the condition of the lost soul. As Dante, led by Virgil, descends more deeply into the Inferno, he meets friends, enemies, and historical figures who represent particular types of sin in the Christian context; in the personal context, they represent various aspects of our brokenness as we confront the realities of our inner selves. The Virtuous Pagans in Limbo serve as an allegory of classical humanism. While virtuous, they lack the faith of Christ or, archetypally speaking, faith in the mystery of life.

Hell is made up of a series of circles. In circles two through five, Dante meets those who have sinned through choice. The first sin is that of lust, and the primary representatives are Francesca da Rimini and her lover. In real life Francesca had been married to a deformed man, only to fall in love with his handsome younger brother Paolo. The lovers were discovered and stabbed to death. In Hell they drift aimlessly together. Allegorically they represent the sin of adultery and, more profoundly, the aimlessness of self-indulgence. Next the poet confronts the gluttons, the hoarders, and the wrathful before entering the sixth and seventh circles, where he meets, among others, the heretics, the violent, the blasphemers, and the sodomites—including several popes. In the eighth and ninth circles he meets the fraudulent and the malicious. All of these sins must be seen in light of the politics and religion of Dante's day, but also in light of the tendencies which confront anyone attempting the passage to self-realization.

Purgatory in Catholic theology is the place where the redeemed prepare for eventual Paradise. In Dante's geography it is a mountain to be climbed. In religious allegory it is the place of repentance. Archetypally it is an allegory for the losing of the old self in order to find the new. As in the case of Hell, there is suffering in Purgatory, but suffering with a productive purpose. Each section of Purgatory is protected by an allegorical angel: the Angel of the Church, the

Angel of Peace, the Angel of Temperance, the Angel of Chastity, and so forth. A specifically Christian allegory is evident when we note that Dante and Virgil depart from Hell and enter Purgatory on Easter morning, representing, as was the case with their descent into Hell during Good Friday and Holy Saturday, the path of Christ.

Paradise is the reward for having climbed the mountain of Purgatory, and there Virgil, as human wisdom, gives way to Beatrice or Divine Grace, who now becomes Dante's guide through the joys of revelation and the eventual union with God. In terms of the anagogic or spiritual and archetypal level of meaning, the achievement of Paradise is the achievement of self-realization or wholeness. (Fletcher 1964; Honig 1966; MacQueen 1970)

See also Dante Alighieri; Epic as Allegory; Virgil.

DODGSON, CHARLES LUTWIDGE

See Carroll, Lewis.

DR. FAUSTUS

The Tragical History of the Life and Death of Dr. Faustus, a play by the English dramatist and poet Christopher Marlowe (1564–1593), was probably first performed in 1588. The character of Faust has long fascinated writers, and given the tradition of the medieval morality play with which Marlowe would have been familiar, it is not surprising that we find elements of allegory in a plot so steeped in questions of sin and damnation. But Marlowe was no Christian apologist, and to the extent that *Dr. Faustus* is allegory it reflects the inclinations of Marlowe himself. Marlowe's play is based on the traditional story of the brilliant man whose excessive knowledge and the pride that derives from it lead him to sell his soul to the devil. To the medieval mind the allegorical uses of this story would be obvious. Faust would represent human pride and dangerous knowledge and his sin would lead to the loss of his soul. In the Renaissance view of the highly individualistic and perhaps atheistic Marlowe, however, Faust is someone to be admired and pitied as he attempts to stand against the repressive, anti-intellectual requirements of God. Thus, Faust comes to stand in this play for humankind's understandable thirst for knowledge, even though he must pay the old medieval price for that knowledge.

See also The Castle of Perseverance; Everyman; Marlowe, Christopher; Morality Plays.

DR. JECKYLL AND MR. HYDE

The famous dual character in the novel *The Strange Case of Dr. Jeckyll and Mr. Hyde* (1886), by Robert Louis Stevenson (1850–1894), has acquired significant

The Tragicall History
of the Life and Death
of *Doctor Faustus*.

Written by *Ch. Marklin*.

LONDON,
Printed for *Iohn Wright*, and are to be sold at his shop
without Newgate, at the s: .. .. the
Bib¹ 1616.

The original frontispiece from the 1616 edition of *Dr. Faustus*

connotative meanings even for many who have never read the story. The plot, Stevenson maintained, came to him in a dream; readers maintain that the horrors of *Dr. Jeckyll and Mr. Hyde* have haunted their dreams ever since. Stevenson's novel helped to popularize the concept of a divided self with separate personalities, and, in the century since its publication, the names of Jeckyll and Hyde have generally come to represent any sort of good/evil duality.

The novel traces the story of the socially upstanding physician Dr. Henry Jeckyll, who develops a potion by which the good and the evil in men can be separated into two independent bodies. Drinking one dose of the potion transforms the good and handsome Dr. Jeckyll into the evil and hideous Edward Hyde. Drinking an additional dose of the drug returns him to the body and identity of Dr. Jeckyll. After Mr. Hyde murders the father of the woman Dr. Jeckyll loves, Dr. Jeckyll shuts himself up in his laboratory. Ultimately, Jeckyll and Hyde become inseparable, and Hyde's suicide results in their dual destruction. Many critics have interpreted *Dr. Jeckyll and Mr. Hyde* as an allegorical depiction of the duality of man's moral nature. Dr. Jeckyll represents the good in man, Mr. Hyde represents the evil, and the allegorical strategy of the doppelgänger, or reflected, "doubled" character, produces the tension between conflicting sides of one mind. (Tymms 1983)

See also Stevenson, Robert Louis.

DREAM AND ALLEGORY

In ancient times dreams tended to be treated as literal messages, dream visions from the supernatural, rather than as allegory, but there have always been people who would "read" dreams for deeper meanings. There has always been an assumption that, given the strange juxtapositions and the unrealistic atmospheres of dreams, there might be something more in them than meets the eye. In modern psychiatry, especially, dreams are seen as symbolic messages—not necessarily from the supernatural but from the unconscious to the conscious world. Under the influence of the prevailing psychological view we go so far as to believe that we ignore our dreams at our own psychological peril. Dreams are seen, in short, as allegories of the psyche.

Several major allegorical works make use of a dream to take the reader into the allegorical world. The events of *Alice's Adventures in Wonderland* take place during a dream, the plot of *Piers Plowman* is contained in a dream of its author, and Chaucer's *Hous of Fame* and Cicero's *Dream of Scipio* use the same dream device. (Eliade 1987)

In many religious traditions dreams are themselves allegorical. In the Bible there are several instances of dreams by which God sends messages to humans, messages that have to be interpreted allegorically. One of the best known occurs in Genesis 41 (1–38):

> And it came to pass at the end of two full years, that Pharaoh dreamed: and, behold, he stood by the river. And, behold, there came up out of the river

seven well favoured kine and fatfleshed; and they fed in a meadow. And, behold, seven other kine came up after them out of the river, ill favoured and leanfleshed; and stood by the other kine upon the brink of the river. And the ill favoured and leanfleshed kine did eat up the seven well favoured and fat kine. So Pharaoh awoke. And he slept and dreamed the second time: and, behold, seven ears of corn came up upon one stalk, rank and good. And, behold, seven thin ears and blasted with the east wind sprung up after them. And the seven thin ears devoured the seven rank and full ears. And Pharaoh awoke, and, behold, it was a dream. And it came to pass in the morning that his spirit was troubled; and he sent and called for all the magicians of Egypt, and all the wise men thereof: and Pharaoh told them his dream; but there was none that could interpret them unto Pharaoh. Then spake the chief butler unto Pharaoh, saying, I do remember my faults this day: Pharaoh was wroth with his servants, and put me in ward in the captain of the guard's house, both me and the chief baker: And we dreamed a dream in one night, I and he; we dreamed each man according to the interpretation of his dream. And there was there with us a young man, an Hebrew, servant to the captain of the guard; and we told him, and he interpreted to us our dreams; to each man according to his dream he did interpret. And it came to pass, as he interpreted to us, so it was; me he restored unto mine office, and him he hanged. Then Pharaoh sent and called Joseph, and they brought him hastily out of the dungeon: and he shaved himself, and changed his raiment, and came in unto Pharaoh. And Pharaoh said unto Joseph, I have dreamed a dream, and there is none that can interpret it: and I have heard say of thee, that thou canst understand a dream to interpret it. And Joseph answered Pharaoh, saying, It is not in me: God shall give Pharaoh an answer of peace. And Pharaoh said unto Joseph, In my dream, behold, I stood upon the bank of the river: And, behold, there came up out of the river seven kine, fatfleshed and well favoured; and they fed in a meadow: And, behold, seven other kine came up after them, poor and very ill favoured and leanfleshed, such as I never saw in all the land of Egypt for badness: And the lean and the ill favoured kine did eat up the first seven fat kine: And when they had eaten them up, it could not be known that they had eaten them; but they were still ill favoured, as at the beginning. So I awoke. And I saw in my dream, and, behold, seven ears came up in one stalk, full and good: And, behold, seven ears, withered, thin, and blasted with the east wind, sprung up after them: And the thin ears devoured the seven good ears: and I told this unto the magicians; but there was none that could declare it to me. And Joseph said unto Pharaoh, The dream of Pharaoh is one: God hath shewed Pharaoh what he is about to do. The seven good kine are seven years; and the seven good ears are seven years: the dream is one. And the seven thin and ill favoured kine that came up after them are seven years; and the seven empty ears blasted with the east wind shall be seven years of famine. This is the thing which I have spoken unto Pharaoh: What God is about to do he sheweth unto Pharaoh. Behold, there come seven years of great plenty throughout all the land of Egypt: And there shall arise after them seven years of famine; and all the plenty shall be forgotten in the land of Egypt; and the famine shall consume the land; And the plenty shall not be known in the land by reason of that famine following; for it shall be very grievous. And for that the dream was doubled unto Pharaoh twice; it is because the thing is established by God, and God will shortly bring it to pass. Now therefore let Pharaoh look out a man discreet and wise, and set him over the land of Egypt. Let Pharaoh do this, and let him appoint officers over the land, and take up the fifth part of the land of Egypt in the seven plenteous years. And let them gather all the food of those good years that come, and lay up corn under the hand of Pharaoh, and let them keep food in the cities. And that food shall be for store to the land against the seven years of famine, which shall be in the land of Egypt; that the land perish not through the famine. And the thing was good in the eyes of Pharaoh, and in the eyes of all his servants. And Pharaoh said unto his servants, Can we find such a one as this is, a man in whom the Spirit of God is? (Genesis 41:1–38)

Among Native Americans and other shamanic peoples, dreams play an important role in revealing the wishes of the spirit world. The tradition of the vision quest involves the allegorical use of dreams. In this tradition a boy on the brink of manhood fasts in a place isolated from his fellow tribesmen. He waits for dreams which, if they are good dreams, will bring him into contact with the Great Mystery and bring something good to his people. Some tribes have dream doctors who interpret the allegory of the questor.

See also Alice's Adventures in Wonderland; The Bible and Allegory; Cicero, Marcus Tullius; Freud, Sigmund; *The Hous of Fame*; Native American Allegory; *Piers Plowman*.

THE DREAM OF SCIPIO

See Cicero, Marcus Tullius.

DRYDEN, JOHN

John Dryden (1631–1700) is considered to be the foremost English literary figure in the latter half of the seventeenth century. Educated at Westminster School and Trinity College, Cambridge, Dryden enjoyed great success as both a poet and a playwright; he excelled at comedy, heroic tragedy, translations, literary criticism, essays, and satires. He published his first notable poem, "Heroic Stanzas," to commemorate the death of Oliver Cromwell. In 1667 he published "Annus Mirabilis," a poetic description of the English navy's defeat of the Dutch and a celebration of the fortitude of the English during the great fire of London in 1666. Dryden was subsequently named poet laureate in 1668, but in 1688 he was removed from this position after the Protestant William and Mary took over the English throne. Financially strapped, Dryden returned to writing plays and translations to support his family. Just two months before his death he finished *Fables Ancient and Modern* (1700), composed of translations of Ovid, Chaucer, and Boccaccio. Many of Dryden's important literary contributions were written while he was poet laureate, including *Absalom and Achitophel* (1681), *Mac Flecknoe* (1682), and *The Medal* (1682). Dryden sometimes made use of allegory, as, for instance, in *The Hind and the Panther* (1687), in which the newly converted Dryden's Catholic beliefs are evident. In the work, a pure-white hind

John Dryden

(representing the Catholic church) and a spotted panther (the Anglican church) discuss theology; the hind's argument is clearly superior.

See also *Absalom and Achitophel.*

THE DYNASTS

The Dynasts, written in the first decade of the twentieth century by English novelist and poet Thomas Hardy (1840–1928), is a historical epic drama that makes use of both prose and poetry to illustrate, by way of a chronicle of the Napoleonic wars, the author's well-established view that mankind is completely at the mercy of Fate. Hardy comments on the events in the plot by way of an allegorical choral entity made up of beings whose names clearly point to their significance. The chorus, somewhere above the earth, observes the events over which humans believe they have control and, like a Greek tragic chorus, it comments on those events and reminds us of the control of destiny, personified as Immanent Will. The choral allegorical characters are The Spirit of Years, Shade of Earth, Spirit Sinister, Spirit Ironic, and Spirit of Pities. The spirits laugh at Napoleon's pomposity and at the various strategies of war and politics. At the end of the war, the Spirit of Years points to the fact that throughout the hundred days of turmoil humans have lived puppetlike in a dream, being manipulated by Immanent Will. Napoleon, for all the effect he seemed to have on the world, was of little consequence in the context of time. The Spirit of Pities wonders why, then, the events of the war have taken place. The Spirit Ironic, speaking for the author, suggests that the events have occurred for no reason at all. (Benet 1965)

See also Hardy, Thomas.

THE ECLOGUES

See Virgil.

ELIOT, T. S.

Thomas Stearns Eliot (1888–1965) was born in St. Louis, Missouri, and educated at Harvard University. He settled in London in 1915 and became a British subject and a member of the Anglican Church in 1927. In addition to his many notable poems, such as "The Waste Land" and "The Love Song of J. Alfred Prufrock," Eliot wrote numerous essays and plays, including *Murder in the Cathedral* (1935) and *The Family Reunion* (1939). He was awarded the Nobel Prize for literature in 1948, and since then has come to be recognized as a leader in modern Symbolist poetry.

It is tempting to read the poetry of T. S. Eliot allegorically because of the dreamlike juxtaposition of the real and the apparently symbolic in works such as "The Waste Land" and *Four Quartets*. Certainly the waste land itself can be seen as a metaphor for the interior landscape of both the poet and the morally bankrupt civilization in which he lives. But to seek specific didactic meanings for the characters and incidents in the poem is to challenge its essential ambiguity and to lose sight of its vitality. It seems more accurate to call "The Waste Land" a symbolic poem rather than an allegorical one. In the case of Eliot's plays, especially, perhaps *The Family Reunion*, there is ample justification for allegorical reading.

See also The Family Reunion.

ELLISON, RALPH

Ralph Ellison (1914–1994), though anything but prolific, is generally considered to be one of the greatest American writers of the first half of the twentieth century. An African American who studied at Tuskegee Institute and taught in various colleges, he is best known for his first and only completed novel, *Invisible Man*, a work that makes use of allegory among other techniques to expose the inner condition of the African American in American society.

See also Invisible Man.

EMBLEMS

The art critic Erwin Panofsky defines emblems as "images which refuse to be accepted as representations of mere things but demand to be interpreted as vehicles of concepts . . ." (148). In this sense, the emblem has long been a weapon in the arsenal of allegorists. In the Middle Ages emblems such as the Lamb, the Dove, and the Fish were widely used, their significance lying in their theological meaning rather than in the representation of particular natural species. Poets

Engraving for "Emblem VII" in an 1861 collection of Francis Quarles's emblematic poetry.

have sometimes attempted to be emblematic even in the arrangement of their words. Thus George Herbert in the seventeenth century had his printer arrange two stanzas of "Easter Wings" in the shape of a dove's wings. This approach is a logical development of the commonplace Renaissance use of a motto with a highly stylized or explanatory picture, sometimes accompanied by an emblematic poem.

A well-known English emblematic poet was Francis Quarles (1592–1644), from whose *Emblemes* the example shown on the facing page is taken. The image of the child hiding his face stands over three allegorical objects—themselves emblems in the broad sense—the butterfly (Psyche/Spirit), labelled *Vita [Life]*; the cross, labelled *Via [The Way]*; and the cross as lamp, labelled *Lux [The Light]*. The significance of the emblem is made clear in lines from the Book of Job, and the emblematic poem by Quarles, the first four stanzas of which appear below, makes the allegory clearer still:

EMBLEM VII

Wherefore hidest thou thy face, and holdest me for thine
*enemy? —*Job 13, 24

Why dost thou shade thy lovely face? O why
Does that eclipsing hand so long deny
The sunshine of thy soul-enlivening eye?

Without that light, what light remains in me?
Thou art my life, my way, my light; in thee
I live, I move, and by thy beams I see.

Thou art my life; if thou but turn away,
My life's a thousand deaths: thou art my way;
Without thee, LORD, I travel not, but stray.

My light thou art; without thy glorious sight,
My eyes are darkened with perpetual night.
My GOD, thou art my way, my life, my light.

More modern examples of the use of emblem are the rosebush outside of the prison and the letter A worn by Hester Prynne in Hawthorne's *The Scarlet Letter*. Edwin Honig suggests that the sign outside the inn in *Moby-Dick* where Ishmael stays before boarding Captain Ahab's ship is an emblem—the sign's words "Spouter Inn" and the owner's name, Peter Coffin, prefigure the "two symbols of the quest: the whale itself and the coffin-turned-lifebuoy through which Ishmael is finally saved." (Fletcher 1964; Honig 1966; Panofsky 1955)

See also Herbert, George; *Moby-Dick*; Quarles, Francis; *The Scarlet Letter*.

ENDGAME

In 1958, the Irish playwright Samuel Beckett (1906–1989) released *Endgame*, another play, like *Waiting for Godot* (1952), about waiting. In this case, Hamm,

Clov, Nagg, and Nell are waiting both for their own deaths and the extinction of life on earth. Nagg and Nell are presumably Hamm's parents, and it is hinted that Clov may be Hamm's adopted son. Set in a tiny cell-like room, all the characters but Clov are immobile; Nagg and Nell are legless and confined to dustbins, and Hamm is restricted to his wheelchair. A darker play than *Waiting for Godot, Endgame* is full of images of physical degeneration: Nell actually dies in her dustbin and Nagg falls into complete silence. As in *Godot,* the end of the play leaves the three remaining characters in a perpetual state of waiting.

Endgame has been read as an allegory of the profound physical and psychological devastation resulting from atomic warfare. Interestingly, Hamm and Clov see the end of all life on earth as a positive development, and thus *Endgame* may also be read as a sort of inverse creation myth. It should be made clear that Beckett would almost certainly have rejected any of these readings. (Kennedy 1989; Mercier 1977)

See also Beckett, Samuel; *Waiting for Godot.*

ENDIMION

A play by the Englishman John Lyly (1554–1606), *Endimion* (1591) is a complicated love story that incorporates relatively little action. Endimion, a courtier, falls in love with Cynthia, Goddess of the Moon. Tellus, Goddess of the Earth, loves Endimion; Corsites, a soldier, loves Tellus; and Euménides, Endimion's friend, loves Semele. In response to being spurned by Endimion, Tellus vengefully arranges for a sorceress to place Endimion under a spell of everlasting sleep. Euménides, Endimion's friend, learns from a magic fountain that a kiss from Cynthia will combat the spell and awaken Endimion. Through a series of complex events and subplots, Cynthia kisses Endimion and seals their love, while the other characters eventually pair off into happy couples.

In numerous conflicting allegorical readings, *Endimion* has been the subject of historical, psychological, and religious interpretations. Historically, critics have claimed that Cynthia is Queen Elizabeth I; Tellus is Mary, Queen of Scots; Endimion is the Earl of Leicester or the Earl of Oxford; and Corsites is Sir Edward Stafford or Sir Henry Lee. Psychologically, Cynthia has been equated with virtuous love and Tellus with earthly passion. In a religious context, the fifth act of *Endimion* has been read as an extension of the Christian allegory of the Four Daughters of God (Mercy, Truth, Justice, and Peace) derived from Psalm 85:10. (Houppert 1975; Hunter 1962; Saccio 1969)

See also Lyly, John.

ENDYMION

In 1817 the English Romantic poet John Keats (1795–1821) wrote a 4,000-line allegorical romance called *Endymion,* based on the Greek myth of the youth

Endymion who was loved by Diana, the moon goddess. The poem tells of Endymion's quest for union with the goddess, whom he knows from visions. In the course of his search he falls prey to sensual pleasures with a young mortal woman. In so doing Endymion fears he has betrayed his noble ideal, but the woman finally reveals her true identity as the goddess Diana herself.

The poem is an allegory of the poetic quest—specifically, Keats's quest—for the highest of ideals embodied in art. The moon goddess is that ideal, and the poet (Endymion) finds that she can be clothed in mortal dress (the young woman), that the materials for the expression of the ideal are of this rather than a visionary world.

See also Keats, John.

ENUMA ELISH

The *Enuma Elish* is the epic of the ancient Babylonian people of the Fertile Crescent, the valley of the Tigris and Euphrates Rivers in what is now Iraq. The poem takes its name from its first words, "Enuma elish" ("When on high") and was composed in the Semitic Akkadian language in the third millennium B.C.E. and preserved on clay tablets. The *Enuma Elish* is in some ways allegorical, representing the change during the period in question from a matriarchal or at least matrilineal system to the patriarchal system of the Semitic nomadic invaders from the north.

An important part of the Babylonian epic is the story of the war between Tiamat, the great "All Mother" primordial waters from which life had sprung, and her descendant, Marduk, the new creator god of the Babylonians. In her anger at the young gods for having killed her consort, Tiamat created monsters to fight against them and herself became a giant monster. Marduk then became a warrior and succeeded in cutting the goddess in half to make heaven and earth. Out of the various parts of her body he built an ordered creation which stood in contrast to the old chaotic world of the Mother.

Joseph Campbell and others have suggested that the Tiamat-Marduk myth is not only an allegory of the defeat of the old matriarchy but of a battle between "two aspects of the human psyche at a critical moment of human history" (80–82). The myth reflects the new male-oriented interest in reason and war, represented by the male hero, as opposed to the old commitment to the mysteries and the agricultural activities represented by the goddess. In short, in the defeat of Tiamat we have an allegorical record of the devaluation of the female by newly dominant male power. (Campbell 1970; Leeming 1994)

EPIC AS ALLEGORY

To the extent that epics are quest narratives they are allegorical. That is, the epic hero, whether Odysseus, Gilgamesh, Jason, Aeneas, or the Indian Rama who embarks on a journey in search of something—home, eternal life, the

Golden Fleece, the new Troy (Rome), or his lost love—is an allegorical representation of the human quest for wholeness or fulfillment. The hero's journey is an extended metaphor for life's journey.

In another sense, too, epics are allegorical. Epics reflect the values and aspirations of particular cultures. A given epic might be said to project the "soul" of a culture. In this sense, the *Odyssey* and the *Iliad* are allegories of the Mycenean world's search for its identity. Virgil's *Aeneid* reflects a new Roman duty-oriented value system for which the older Homeric system based on individual pride (*arete*) is outmoded.

See also Aeneid; Gilgamesh; The Odyssey; The Quest as Allegory; *Ramayana*.

EPIC THEATRE

See Brecht, Bertolt.

EREC AND ÉNIDE

A chivalric romance by Frenchman Chrétien de Troyes (1150–1190), *Erec et Énide [Erec and Énide]* is the earliest known Arthurian romance. The Arthurian court described by Chrétien is one that represents the medieval ideals of chivalry and courtly love. What allegory there is in the romance speaks to that representation and to the conflict between marital duties and knightly ones.

The story tells how one of Arthur's knights, Erec, marries the beautiful Énide and loves her so much that he neglects his knightly duties in favor of domestic ones. Énide is upset with her husband because his reputation is at stake. When he overhears his wife complaining about his inactivity, he becomes furious and forces her to go on a series of knightly adventures with him. Erec succeeds in proving his valor but he is unfairly harsh with his wife, and eventually she is kidnapped by a wicked baron. When it seems that Erec is about to die of wounds suffered, he revives and rescues his wife.

Marguerite Murphy has noted particularly the allegory in the last part of the tale, in which the hero, Erec, attempts the passage called the "Joy of the Court." After prevailing in a fight with a mysterious knight and liberating him from enchantment, Erec blows the horn of joy, signifying his success, and returns, in honor, to King Arthur's court. Murphy suggests that in his struggle with and freeing of the strange knight, Erec has found expression for the chivalric code and his knightly duties; he has found true joy. In breaking the knight's spell he reunites a court. His act brings about the essence of courtly love—the "joy of the court." That joy is itself represented in the final scene, when Erec and his long-suffering wife Énide, now fully reconciled, in the presence of King Arthur are crowned rulers of Erec's father's land. (Bloomfield 1981)

See also Chrétien de Troyes.

EREWHON

Erewhon is an allegorical work by Samuel Butler (1835–1902), a prolific English writer who was largely misunderstood and unappreciated during his lifetime. His posthumously published novel *The Way of All Flesh* (1903) and *Note Books* (1912) are perhaps his best-remembered literary contributions. *Erewhon* (1872) was by far the most successful of Butler's books during his life, perhaps due partly to its anonymity and partly to its cleverly satirical portrait of life in nineteenth-century England. Butler spent much of his life in New Zealand, and the setting for *Erewhon* (1872) takes many of its details from his experiences there. But *Erewhon*, an anagram for "nowhere," is a biting allegory of the religious, political, ethical, and educational institutions that he sees ravaging his native Britain. *Erewhon* is not Butler's utopian "ideal state"; rather, it is a place in which Butler can effectively comment upon those attitudes and accomplishments that the English value but that he sees as corrupt and ridiculous.

Erewhon begins as an adventurous and highly realistic travel narrative; the main character, Thomas Higgs, traverses oceans, mountains, and rivers to arrive in the mysterious country of Erewhon. He awakens one morning in this unfamiliar land, surrounded by a herd of goats and two shepherdesses. Seeing him, the girls run away and return with some men to investigate the intruder. They take Higgs to a nearby town, where they search his clothing and confiscate his watch. After an intense and thorough physical examination, he is jailed.

While imprisoned, Higgs begins to learn the language and customs of this strange country called Erewhon. He learns that physical beauty, strength, and health are valued by the Erewhonian culture above all else. Disease is considered criminal, and those who fall ill are tried and jailed. Conversely, those who commit crimes such as murder or robbery are hospitalized and treated with unlimited sympathy and understanding by "straighteners" who represent modern psychologists. The victims of such crimes, however, are severely punished for allowing themselves to be so victimized. Allegorically, Butler attacks what he perceives to be the extremely liberal British notion of aiding those who victimize others, while neglecting to help the truly innocent victims of disease, crime, or other social misfortunes.

Higgs is released from prison into the custody of Nosnibor, an embezzler who is recovering from his "illness." Higgs learns a great deal about the history of Erewhon, as well as about the social and educational values of the country. He also learns the reason that his watch was taken when he first encountered the Erewhonians. Two hundred years before, a scientist purported that machines had minds and emotions and had the potential to become the ultimate rulers of the earth. As a result, all forms of machinery had been eliminated from Erewhon; the only surviving bits are relegated to a machinery museum. Advancing mechanical technology embodies a threat to the Erewhonians that Butler uses to allegorize modern man's enslavement to scientific "progress."

Higgs finds the economy of Erewhon to be particularly unusual. The Erewhonians have two separate currencies; one is used for trade and the other has only spiritual value. Yet the spiritual currency is more respected, and the

Erewhonians use this monetary system at Musical Banks, where coins are exchanged for music. Money, like good physical health, is treasured in Erewhon; the society honors and rewards those who possess it, even if they did little or nothing to actually earn it. Butler satirizes the British attitude toward wealth as he presents Erewhonians who are respected only for their financial status. Conventional religion is also satirized through the Musical Banks; the number of Erewhonian financial investors was rapidly decreasing because the banks only paid dividends every 30,000 years, and most investors demanded more frequent and tangible returns. Through this depiction, Butler comments on those British who have sacrificed traditional religious faith for worldly rewards.

To learn more about Erewhon, Higgs visits the Colleges of Unreason, the intellectual centers of the country. There, young Erewhonian boys study all that is impractical or useless, including such disciplines as Hypothetical Languages and Hypothetical Sciences. Clearly, these Colleges represent British intellectual communities; Butler allegorizes the uselessness and impracticality of these institutions and the English perversion of what is considered to be academically valuable.

Higgs eventually falls in love with Arowhena, Nosnibor's daughter. Yet he is forbidden to marry her because Nosnibor has an unmarried daughter, Zulora, who is older than Arowhena. Higgs and Nosnibor argue, and Higgs leaves to find a new place to live. Higgs and Arowhena continue to meet in secret at the Musical Banks. At about this time, the king of Erewhon begins to think that perhaps Higgs is a dangerous infiltrator attempting to reintroduce machinery to the culture. Higgs feels he must escape from this strange land, and convinces the queen that he must take a balloon ride in order to speak with the god of the air. Smuggling Arowhena aboard the balloon, the two travel far over the mountains, away from Erewhon, where they eventually land in the ocean and are rescued by a passing ship. The two travel to England, where they are married. Higgs, convinced that the Erewhonians are the lost ten tribes of Israel, plans to return to Erewhon someday to spread Christianity.

Erewhon examines complicated issues of freedom and responsibility by allegorizing aspects of nineteenth-century British religion, education, ethics, and politics. On the surface, the culture of Erewhon is far different from that of England, but careful readers find that many Erewhonian attitudes are embarrassingly similar to those of the English. People are valued for their money and devalued for their illnesses; rewards in the afterlife are sacrificed for rewards in the temporal world; young people study the obsolete rather than the practical; technology is both revered and feared. Through his allegorization of British culture, Butler accuses England of committing the same cruelties, injustices, and stupidities that are so obviously rampant in Erewhon. Yet Butler's message is tempered by his whimsical, often humorous story of the unwitting Higgs, whose encounter with the distorted society of Erewhon helps to clarify Butler's vision of his own distorted culture. (Harris 1916; Stillman 1932)

See also Butler, Samuel.

The first page of *Everyman,* published ca. 1500

 # *EVERYMAN*

Everyman (ca. 1500) is the best-known and perhaps the most important surviving example of the medieval morality play. *Everyman* is purely allegorical; each character's significance is accurately defined by his name. The play teaches the moral lesson that Christians must not fall victim to sin and greed, but must instead lead a righteous life in order to be rewarded in heaven.

The play begins with a Messenger announcing that Everyman will be called before God to account for his life. Then God speaks, explaining how He has been forsaken and forgotten by mankind, and how a reckoning of all men is necessary to prevent further moral decay. He sends Death to summon Everyman, the representative of all humankind, before him.

When approached by Death, Everyman protests that he is not ready for death and asks for some more time on earth so that he may improve his book full of the accounts of his life. Death refuses Everyman's request, but tells him that he may seek companions to accompany him on his journey.

Everyman turns to his friend Fellowship, who refuses to escort Everyman to his death. Likewise, Kindred declines Everyman's request for companionship on his journey. Even Goods, whom Everyman had loved so well, explains that he cannot accompany Everyman to his reckoning with God, since worldly riches are only temporary possessions and do not follow one to the grave.

Distraught, Everyman turns to Good Deeds for help. Good Deeds is weak from Everyman's long neglect, bound to the ground by Everyman's sins, and unable to rise. Good Deed's sister, Knowledge, stays with Everyman until Good Deeds can regain his strength. Knowledge takes Everyman to Confession, who offers Everyman penance for his sins. Joyfully, Everyman scourges his flesh, and Good Deeds rises from the ground, healthy and strong. Knowledge gives Everyman a garment of sorrow that will deliver him from pain, and the three companions prepare to go before God.

As they begin their pilgrimage, Good Deeds explains to Everyman that other companions may accompany them: Strength, Beauty, Discretion, and Five Wits. Everyman pays a visit to a priest to receive the seven sacraments, and when he returns the seven travelers begin their journey to Death.

As Everyman nears his destination, all of his companions abandon him with the exception of Good Deeds. Together, the two descend into the grave. An Angel announces that Everyman's soul is pronounced virtuous, and a Doctor concludes the play by proclaiming that all Christians must live wisely and remember that only Good Deeds can accompany one to the final judgment. (Cawley 1956)

See also Morality Plays.

EXTENDED METAPHOR

Metaphor is a device by which an implied comparison is made between two unlike things which are, nevertheless, in some way alike. Thus, in the phrase a "gem of an idea," we know that gems and ideas are entirely different categories in the literal sense but figuratively we are able to see that a great idea can have real value that can be conveyed by a mental association with a gem, which also has value. Allegory may be seen as extended metaphor in that a metaphor is extended into a developed narrative with characters, plot, settings, and so forth. A character's journey, for example, might be seen as a metaphor for life (the road of life) and the adventures the character experiences are the experiences of life, perhaps representing such things as temptation, pleasure, pain, or goodness. Characters the hero meets might even be named Temptation, Pleasure, Pain, or Goodness. Settings in which the questor finds himself can be a part of the extended metaphor as well—a valley might represent a descent into the depths of the soul, a garden might be a place of temptation or of joy, a mountain might be representative of divine revelation. In extended metaphor, then, implicit comparisons are made between abstractions and characters, settings and ideas. That is, characters and incidents in allegory have at least one level of meaning other than the literal. Insofar as *Gulliver's Travels* is allegory, for instance, the fantasy lands described by Swift and the people in them are compared to Swift's world and the people in it. It is this allegorical level, the level of the extended metaphor, that will be meaningful to the mature reader—even if the immature reader sees only the fantasy world depicted.

See also Metaphor as Allegory.

A FABLE

William Faulkner labored for years on his intentionally allegorical novel, *A Fable* (1954), which he believed would be his greatest masterpiece. Although it received the National Book Award and the Pulitzer Prize in 1955, it has not earned him the lasting fame of some of his other novels. Set in World War I France, *A Fable* points to the life of Christ, specifically to the events surrounding and the significance of his death.

The plot of *A Fable* begins on Wednesday as the people of a French town, as if driven by some power, converge on Allied Headquarters. Only gradually does Faulkner reveal the events that have led up to this movement of the people. It seems that a corporal and his 12 followers, by refusing an order to attack the enemy, had caused other regiments on both sides of the lines to refuse to fight and a cessation of hostilities had taken place. The leader of the mutinous group has been brought to the town to be executed. This is the bare outline of a plot suffused with complex subplots, all suggesting the story of Christ's passion.

Critics have recognized *A Fable* as a modern morality play; in this religious allegory, both the men and the war represent the ways in which humanity becomes tragically involved in evil. The men, many of whom are not named and are addressed only by their military position (e.g., the Sentry, the Quartermaster General, the Corporal), compositely represent everyman. The conflicts that arise among themselves allegorize the internal struggle between good and evil that exists within every person. The war itself takes on the significance of what Christian theology calls Original Sin. More specific to the Christian gospel, some critics suggest that the old general in the novel first represents God, then the devil, or Evil; a Runner represents Saint Paul; the Corporal—who was born in a stable, has 12 close companions, leads an anti–status quo movement, and is executed on a Friday between two thieves—becomes the modern incarnation of Christ.

Scholars disagree on the extent to which *A Fable* may be considered purely allegorical, although Faulkner's intentional casting of the character of Christ in the form of the Corporal is universally accepted. *A Fable* is a complicated novel open to varying allegorical readings; however, its theme of humankind's struggle to extricate itself from evil and find salvation lends itself to didactic moral and mythic interpretations. (Roma 1972; Urgo 1989)

See also Morality Plays.

FABLE AS ALLEGORY

The word "fable" comes from the Latin *fabula*, meaning "telling." When used as a literary term, "fable" refers to little tales—often involving talking animals—used to teach some moral or appropriate conduct. Often the tale ends with a proverblike summary of the lesson intended. No one knows when fables were first used. They are found in the ancient writings of the East and the West. Among the Greeks, Hesiod (eighth century B.C.E.) and especially Aesop (sixth century B.C.E.) told them. The ancient Buddhists of India used fables to illustrate the ideas of the Buddha in the *Panchatantra*, a work with origins perhaps nearly as old as the Greek fables. In twelfth-century France, Marie de France collected more than 100 fables. The twelfth century also saw a development of the beast fable, a type of extended satirical tale involving such familiar medieval animals as Renart the Fox and Chanticleer the Rooster, whose escapades were used to teach lessons. Perhaps the most famous of Western fable writers is the Frenchman Jean de La Fontaine, whose *Fables* were published in the seventeenth century as satires on the French court and human society as a whole. Fables have been written by modern writers as well. The American James Thurber (1894–1961) wrote a series called *Fables for Our Time*, a satire on contemporary society through Thurber's eyes.

Fables are allegorical in that particular animals are used to represent abstractions: the owl can be wisdom, for instance, and the fox wiliness. The situations in which the animals find themselves are clearly representative of human situations.

See also Aesop; La Fontaine, Jean de.

FABLES OF BIDPAI

See Bidpai.

THE FAERIE QUEENE

Composed by the English poet Edmund Spenser (1552–1599), *The Faerie Queene* is a national epic that looks back to other great literary epics such as Virgil's *Aeneid* and Tasso's *Jerusalem Delivered* (1575). It is also a Christian epic and, specifically, a Protestant epic that defends and celebrates the position of the English monarchy and the English state against the Roman Catholic Church. The first three books of the epic were published in 1590, a six-book version appeared in 1596, and a posthumous fragment in 1609. In a 1590 letter to Sir

Walter Raleigh that would serve as an introduction to his work, Spenser begins by calling *The Faerie Queene* a "continued Allegory, or darke conceit" and then proceeds to outline his approach and purpose. As a moral allegory the work was intended "to fashion a gentleman or noble person in vertuous and gentle discipline." Certain places and figures, then, would stand for certain virtues and vices. As political and historical allegory the work would contain representations of particular personalities, institutions, and events in Spenser's world. For instance, a character might represent not only the sin of Pride but the institution the poet saw as the political and historical embodiment of that sin, the Roman Catholic Church. About Gloriana, the Faerie Queene herself, Spenser writes, "I meane glory in my generall intention, but in my particular I conceive the most excellent and glorious person of our soveraine the Queene [Elizabeth I], and her kingdome in Faery Land."

Each book of *The Faerie Queene* concentrates on a single virtue, usually embodied in a particular questing knight, whose virtue is challenged by various embodiments of sin. It should be noted that each knight represents in particular one of the many virtues contained in the perfect knight, Prince Arthur, who appears frequently if briefly in the epic and who is the model of the ideal moral being and the ideal nation. The virtues treated in the six books of the epic are Holiness, Temperance (Moderation), Chastity, Friendship, Justice, and Courtesy. Each book also speaks to aspects of the political and historical questions that preoccupied Spenser and his countrymen.

The most widely read book of *The Faerie Queene* is Book I, in which the Red Crosse Knight (a figure of St. George, the patron saint of England) journeys with Una (the true church) to the place where he will finally defeat and kill the dragon (Roman Catholicism) that has imprisoned Una's parents. The path of the quest is representative both of the Christian's moral development and of the development of the English church in the face of what Spenser sees as Catholic duplicity.

When Una appears before Gloriana, the Faerie Queene, to ask for help in the release of her mother and father from the wicked dragon, the Red Crosse Knight volunteers to help her. Thus England, or everyman, and the true church form an alliance against the anti-Christ to free humanity, represented by the first parents, imprisoned by sin. But Una and the Knight are separated by the machinations of the magician Archimago, perhaps the papacy. Deprived of Una (Truth), the Knight falls into the clutches of Duessa, whose outer beauty conceals an essential corruption (Spenser's view of Catholicism). Only with Prince Arthur's help—the help of true Christian faith and morality—is the knight reunited with Una so that he can eventually fight and defeat the dragon in Eden. In the end, Red Crosse and Una—England and the true church, the individual and faith—are married amid much rejoicing.

Book II follows the adventures of Sir Guyon, who represents Temperance. He is accompanied by a Palmer, who is Sobriety but is tricked by the evil Archimago into believing that the Red Crosse Knight has attacked a virgin. A fight between the two is avoided only when the two knights recognize the Christian emblems on each other's shields. Various allegorical characters

The Red Crosse Knight, as depicted in this late sixteenth-century edition of *The Faerie Queene.*

confront Sir Guyon on his adventures: the enchantress Acrasia, who is his opposite, Intemperance; three half-sisters called Medina (or Golden Mean), Perissa (or Excess), and Elissa (or Deficiency); the angry Furor and his mother, Occasion. Guyon defeats all of these forces—reflecting what the poet would have us defeat within ourselves—and finally must fight his natural nemesis—the natural nemesis of Temperance, Pyrocles or Fiery Anger. Loose Living, Wantonness, and Mammon also challenge the virtue of Guyon—all are threats to Temperance. But with Prince Arthur's help, Guyon succeeds in overpowering his enemies and eventually reaches the Bower of Bliss, destroys it, and completes the original purpose of his quest: to restore two lovers to human shape from the beastly condition in which they have been trapped by Acrasia. Thus Intemperance is finally definitively defeated by Temperance.

Book III is the tale of the Lady Britomart, who is Chastity and who, with the help of Sir Guyon and Prince Arthur, defeats such characters as Lust and Jealousy and later rescues Amoret (or Love) from an evil enchanter.

Book IV is the Legend of Gambel and Triamond; its allegorical theme is friendship. Book V is the Legend of Artegal or Justice.

The level of moral allegory, as opposed to political and historical allegory, in Spenser's work is perhaps most fully experienced in Book VI, the book of Courtesy, in which the hero Calidore struggles against and defeats the Blatant Beast:

> A wicked monster, that his tongue doth whet
> Gainst all, both good and bad, both most and least,
> And poures his poysnous gall forth to infest
> The noblest wights with notable defame. (VI, 12)

By means of courtesy—the outward expression of inner grace—Calidore can muzzle and control this beast, who is Scandal. But, sadly, he cannot kill him. In fact, at the end of Book VI the poet bemoans the continued existence of scandal in his world:

> So now he raungeth through the world againe,
> And rageth sore in each degree and state;
> . . .
> Ne spareth he the gentle Poets rime,
> But rends without regard of person or of time. (VI, xii)

(Hamilton 1961; Hankins 1971; Heale 1987; Padelford 1911; Parker 1960)

FAIRY TALES AND ALLEGORY

Fairy tales resemble myths and dreams in that they are particularly unveiled narratives, revealing clearly their archetypal bases. So, for example, we often find a young hero or heroine who, oppressed by a wicked stepparent, wanders in a dark wood and eventually, after difficult adventures, finds, marries, and lives "happily ever after" with a miraculously discovered prince or princess. Over the centuries people have seen in these tales, which are present in every corner of the world, allegories of religious and political beliefs and, more recently, allegories of the development of the psyche. Thus, a Christian or Buddhist or Hindu apologist might see the child lost in the dark wood as a representation of the lost soul, and a Jungian analyst might read the same situation as an image of the psyche in a state of unbalance or brokenness. The quest for the prince or princess might be for medieval readers the process by which the stability of society is achieved while for the modern, psychologically directed reader it might speak to the question of the search for wholeness or "individuation." (Jung 1953–1961; Propp 1958)

See also Grimm Brothers.

THE FAMILY REUNION

A verse drama by the Anglo-American poet T. S. Eliot (1888–1965), *The Family Reunion* (1939) is a modern version of Aeschylus's *Oresteia*, the tragic drama about the House of Atreus. The central character in Eliot's play, like the central ones in the Greek trilogy, is a ritual victim who achieves knowledge and redemption. In a sense, then, the Eliot play is an allegory in that it represents the older trilogy. More important, it is a modern morality play in which allegory plays an important role in the development of a lesson.

Lord Harry Monchensey, like Agamemnon in the first part of the *Oresteia*, has just returned home. There is a curse on his house as there had been on Agamemnon's, and the source of the curse was murder. Harry long ago had murdered his wife and is being haunted, like Orestes in the *Oresteia*—who has murdered his mother— by the Furies or Eumenides. Harry's wise aunt, Agatha, who understands his plight, reveals to him that his father had wanted to kill his mother when she was pregnant with him. Thus Harry is under a family curse. It is Agatha who speaks for Eliot in this play and who orchestrates much of the action.

The moral of this modern morality play is, of course, based in the allegory. The curse of Harry's family (the human family) is not peculiar to Harry or in any direct sense his fault. The curse goes back to his father's sin or, in terms of the Christian point of view Eliot is attempting to convey, Original Sin. Once Harry is enlightened by Agatha (read spiritual enlightenment) and relieved of the onus of personal guilt, he is able to live with the presence of the Eumenides and even welcome them. Once he accepts them, Harry can work against the family curse (Original Sin). *The Family Reunion*, then, is a morality play of spiritual growth and salvation, reflecting Eliot's own conversion to Christianity late in the 1920s. (Benet, Sarkar, and Dale 1988; Headings 1982)

See also Eliot, T. S.; Morality Plays.

FAULKNER, WILLIAM

William Cuthbert Faulkner (1897–1962), born and raised in Mississippi, grew up in a family with a long history of Confederate service and strict adherence to family honor and white supremacy. This background provided Faulkner with much of the material for his greatest novels, including *The Sound and the Fury* (1929), *As I Lay Dying* (1930), and *Light in August* (1932). Faulkner frequently suffered financial crises throughout his life and turned several times to scriptwriting in Hollywood to make money. His enduring fame, however, rests upon his novels, primarily those set in the fictional southern county of Yoknapatawpha. Faulkner was awarded the Nobel Prize for Literature in 1950. At least one of his novels, *A Fable*, is clearly allegorical.

See also A Fable.

FIELDING, HENRY

While not really an allegorist, the English novelist and dramatist Henry Fielding (1707–1754) did make use of allegorical devices in his work—perhaps especially in character names like Squire Allworthy, Fanny Goodwill, Sophis (wisdom), Lady Booby et al., and in the stock plot that involves a young man's "finding himself" by way of various adventures. Fielding's most famous play is the farcical *Tom Thumb* (1730). His greatest novels are *Joseph Andrews* (1742) and *Tom Jones* (1749). Fielding was a highly versatile man. In addition to his writing he worked as a lawyer and a chief magistrate. His literary work reflects both the intellectual eighteenth-century interest in satire and the middle-class interest in what might be called sentimental realism. His novels and plays satirize the hypocrisy of society but uphold the moral values of the middle class. Thus, inner virtue is always rewarded and hypocrites fall from grace. All of this takes place in a setting realistically depicted, complete with violence, sex, and a great deal of low life and local color.

See also Tom Jones.

FIGURAL ALLEGORY

Figural allegory occurs when a particular figure, as opposed to a narrative, stands for something else. It is often personification as in the goddesses Natura and Fortuna or the character Everyman. It could and has been argued that St. Paul's figure of Charity in 1 Corinthians 13 is an example of figural allegory: "Charity suffereth long, and is kind. . . ." In the same way Aristotle makes an allegorical figure of Virtue. A clear example of biblical allegory that is figural occurs in the depiction of Wisdom in Proverbs 8:

> Doth not Wisdom cry? and understanding put forth
>   her voice?
> She standeth in the top of high places, by the
>   way in the places of the paths.
> She crieth at the gates, at the entry of the
>   city, at the coming in at the doors.

Objects as well as abstractions can be allegorical. The Tower of Babel is an allegory for human pride. More often than not, figural allegorical is contained within narrative allegory. The Tower of Babel is understandable in the context of the story about it. The harp of Orpheus is perhaps an example of figural allegory, but it is contained within the larger myth, which is itself a narrative allegory.

See also Fortuna; Personification.

FILM AND ALLEGORY

The cinema has been an effective medium for allegory almost from the beginning. The political films of the early Soviet director Sergei Eisenstein (e.g.,

Battleship Potemkin and *Mother)*, with their abstract imagery and their focusing on clearly symbolic details, almost demand an allegorical reading. Angus Fletcher rightly points to the "iconographic plotting" of these films (186). Fletcher also notes the "emblematic mode" that characterizes the films of the Italians Vittorio DeSica *(Miracle in Milan)* and Federico Fellini *(La Strada, La Dolce Vita)*, the Spaniard Luis Buñuel *(Viridiana)*, the Frenchman Alain Resnais *(Last Year at Marienbad)*, and the great Swedish director Ingmar Bergman *(The Seventh Seal)*. Another filmmaker who makes use of the allegorical iconographic method—throughout his career but particularly in his late films—is the Japanese director Akira Kurosawa *(Dreams, Rashomon)*. It has also been suggested that Oliver Stone has used a "Christian allegorical structure" in *Platoon* (Beck, 213). All of these geniuses of the cinema make use of methods that are roughly analogous to those of the surrealist painters. By forcing us to concentrate on odd details or emblematic scenes that stand out against realistic backgrounds, they lead us to allegorical meanings, however obscure.

It might be argued that animated cartoon films are allegorical, in the same way that the animal fables of Aesop and La Fontaine are. Thus, for instance, the wily mouse, Jerry, represents the crafty intelligence that always overcomes the combination of smugness and voraciousness of the pursuing cat, Tom. (Beck 1992; Fletcher 1964)

FLETCHER, ANGUS

Angus Fletcher's *Allegory: The Theory of a Symbolic Mode* (1964) is a major contribution to and influence on other allegory scholarship that has followed it. In some ways Fletcher's definition of allegory is traditional: "In the simplest terms," he writes, "allegory says one thing and means another. It destroys the normal expectation we have about language, that our words 'mean what they say'" (2). Fletcher considers allegory as a genre in the context of religious ritual, symbolism, and psychoanalysis. He is influenced primarily by myth-oriented critics such as Mircea Eliade and Northrop Frye. Rather than narrowing the definition of his subject, he speaks of it as a wide-ranging art form that addresses our spiritual and social condition.

FOE

J. M. Coetzee's 1986 novel *Foe* retells Daniel Defoe's story of *Robinson Crusoe* from the perspective of a female castaway who was not included in Defoe's original tale. Susan Barton, a white Englishwoman, finds herself put off a ship after a mutiny; she swims to an isolated island occupied by only two other inhabitants: Cruso and Friday. Friday's tongue has been removed, rendering him unable to speak; neither Susan Barton nor the reader ever discover the circumstances surrounding his mutilation. By and by, the three are rescued from the island by a passing ship; Cruso dies onboard, leaving Susan and Friday to make their way to England. After their arrival, Susan writes her memoirs of their ordeal and takes them to a writer, Mr. Foe, to have them published. She struggles with Foe to retain control of her story; ultimately he reshapes her tale into the now-familiar account of Robinson Crusoe's adventures.

Critic David Atwell suggests that *Foe* may be interpreted as an allegory of "the ambiguous condition of postcoloniality that South Africa inhabits" (108). In this reading, the island itself, where the characters are effectively trapped, suggests the confining, restrictive atmosphere of postcolonial South Africa. Cruso becomes representative of white South Africans, the enslaved Friday becomes black South Africans, and Susan Barton, robbed of her authority by Foe, becomes an allegory of the colonial South African settler versus the more powerful, metropolitan white South African. (Atwell 1993)

See also Coetzee, J. M.; *In the Heart of the Country; Robinson Crusoe; Waiting for the Barbarians.*

FORTUNA

The Greeks and even more so the Romans made a practice of personifying abstractions such as war, health, victory, and love. Among the most popular of these allegorical figures was the Roman goddess Fortuna (Fortune). In ancient Rome and medieval Europe, it was customary to attribute all chance happenings to Fortuna. Fortuna is sometimes associated with fate. (Fletcher 1964)

See also The Life of Coriolanus.

FOURFOLD ALLEGORY

The so-called fourfold theory of allegorical interpretation grows out of Platonic ideas of an interrelated hierarchical arrangement in the universe in which we move up a cosmic ladder from a lowly material basis to a pinnacle of spirituality. Another important classical source is Aristotle's idea of the four causes—material, formal, efficient, and final. The early Christian church used a threefold method of interpreting sacred texts, moving from literal to moral and finally to spiritual meanings. The fourfold method emerged in the Middle Ages when scholars suggested that the true Christian should interpret texts first literally, then at the level of what can be called allegory proper—the level of theological meaning—then at the tropological or moral level, and finally at the anagogic or mystical-spiritual level. Dante gave great weight to the fourfold theory in his famous letter to Con Grande and in the allegory of *The Divine Comedy*. (Fletcher 1964; MacQueen 1970)

See also Aquinas, Thomas; Bede, The Venerable; Cassian, John; Dante Alighieri; *The Divine Comedy.*

THE FRENCH REVOLUTION

Scholars have interpreted certain passages and characters in Thomas Carlyle's epic history, *The French Revolution* (1837), as allegorical. The work itself opens with the death of Louis XV in 1774, traces the unfortunate reign of Louis XVI and the Terror, and ends in 1795 with Bonaparte's quelling of the Insurrection of Vendémiaire. Carlyle is by no means an objective chronicler of these turbulent years in France; he manipulates history in an attempt to find symbolic meaning in these events, as well as to advise the British aristocracy to avoid similar bloodshed in England.

Critic Mark Cumming suggests that Carlyle deliberately employed allegorical techniques to moralize the events in France:

> In the allegorical passages of *The French Revolution*, characters are removed for a short time from the fluctuating process of history to static moral pictures. Their internal complexities are temporarily suspended so that an isolated dominant characteristic of their strength (purity, valor, resolution) or, more often, their weakness (vanity, cowardice, indecision) can be depicted; their historical roles . . . are clearly registered in static emblems . . . [which] treat primarily the aimlessness and irrationality of French political life. (139)

In this way, the events of the French Revolution are perceived as more than history; they also become moral allegories of folly, self-delusion, apostasy, and destruction. (Cumming 1988)

See also Carlyle, Thomas; *Sartor Resartus*.

FREUD, SIGMUND

Sigmund Freud (1856–1939), the influential Austrian psychiatrist and founder of psychoanalysis, is directly responsible for much of our contemporary use of allegory in our everyday lives. It is he who taught us to be aware that the literal meaning of our words, our dreams, and our actions might conceal quite different meanings. He taught us, in fact, that nearly everything means something beyond itself. Freud also saw in art a means by which the artist disguised and yet expressed his neuroses. If this is true, all art might be said to be in a sense allegorical. (Freud 1956)

See also Dream and Allegory; Psychoanalysis and Allegory.

FRYE, NORTHROP

The leading "myth critic," best known for his now-classic *Anatomy of Criticism* (1957), Frye reminds us that "all commentary is allegorical interpretation, an attaching of ideas to the structure of poetic imagery" (89). An allegory exists, says Frye, when an author "continuously" tells us—implicitly or explicitly—that although he/she is saying one thing he/she also means something else

(90). Frye distinguishes between sophisticated allegory—a "contrapuntal technique" which enhances the narrative and the meaning—and "naïve allegory," which dominates and makes the narrative secondary to the desired message. The latter sort is "elementary" and is directed to "schoolroom moralities, devotional exempla, local pageants and the like" (90). Such allegory in Frye's opinion is of little interest to the student of literature, whose interest is first awakened by "continuous" allegories such as Bunyan's *Pilgrim's Progress* and Spenser's *Faerie Queene*, both of which "work" on the level of their imagery as well as on the level of allegorical content. The literary commentator's interest continues to develop with the development of literature in general; in fact, it becomes evident to Frye that any literature with a "high degree of thematic content" suggests the presence of allegory. (Frye 1957)

GARCÍA MÁRQUEZ, GABRIEL

See Magic Realism and Allegory.

GARDENS, ALLEGORICAL

The tradition of the allegorical garden is ancient. For instance, the pagan gods had their sacred groves, and in Old Testament times there were groves sacred to the goddess Asherah. A patriarchal ambiguity in relation to such groves is perhaps reflected in the Book of Genesis. There, the Garden of Eden is a space that stands for the perfection of God's creation or nature ordered by divinity. But perfection challenges the natural tendency toward disorder, and the perfect garden is nearly always invaded by disorder or sin. So Satan brings about imperfection in the Garden of Eden by tempting Eve to eat the forbidden fruit, and literary gardens often become the space of witches and enchantresses. Homer's Circe and Calypso live in sacred gardens that serve as appropriate backdrops for the seduction of Odysseus. The Park of Mirth in *The Romance of the Rose [Le Roman de la Rose]* is a dangerous place as, in later literature, is the garden in Hawthorne's "Rappaccini's Daughter," a modern version of the Garden of Eden in which the hero is attracted to the fatally infected inhabitant. Like the walled castle gardens of the Middle Ages, gardens have, over the years, become associated with courting at best and with inappropriate eroticism at worst. Paul Piehler points to the allegory of the enclosed garden in *The Romance of the Rose* as a "symbol of social exclusiveness," the entrance to which is guarded by Oiseuse ("Leisure"), "suggesting the unavailability of courtly love to those who lack adequate leisure and the corresponding vulnerability of the idle to the assaults of sexual temptation" (101).

Traditionally, the garden stands also for the attempts of humans to wall out chaos in favor of order in our lives. As such, the garden can be seen as a microcosm of the walled city, which serves a similar purpose. In the Age of Enlightenment, or the Age of Reason, gardens were created to represent the dominance of human reason over unruly nature. Thus, gardens like the one at the Palace of Versailles are marked by carefully cropped trees and shrubs creating artificial vistas of perfect fountains and classical structures. The garden itself celebrates order and reason. In the Romantic era, gardens were just as carefully created to suggest the dominance of nature; paths were made to appear randomly directed, fountains became rustic grottoes, and the flowerbeds themselves were made to seem wild and natural rather than artificial. (Piehler 1971)

See also The Allegory of Love.

GARGANTUA AND PANTAGRUEL

This great five-part satirical work was written by the French scholar and humanist François Rabelais (1494–1553) between 1532 and the end of his life. The work describes the adventures of Gargantua and Pantagruel, two giants, father and son, and Pantagruel's companion Panurge, who is a personification of wit. The work is not an allegory but there are allegorical moments, especially in Book IV when Pantagruel and Panurge voyage to the Oracle of the Holy Bottle (a parody on the Holy Grail) in order to find out whether Panurge should marry. On the way the heroes meet some people allegorically named the Papimaniacs and the Pope-Figs, who clearly represent the church against which Rabelais was in rebellion and by which he was roundly condemned. (Benet 1965)

See also Rabelais, François.

GILGAMESH

The Babylonian epic of *Gilgamesh,* composed in about 2000 B.C.E., is based on an older Sumerian saga and is perhaps rightly called the oldest of epics. It is allegorical in that its hero, Gilgamesh, goes on a quest for immortality that can serve as a metaphor for the longing of all human beings to escape the power of death. In the end, Gilgamesh, like us, discovers the limitations of the human species and must learn to accept his own mortality.

Gilgamesh, King of Erech, was tyrannizing his people, so the gods sent an animal-like man, Enkidu—a kind of unspoiled, natural side of Gilgamesh—to temper his evil ways. Enkidu and Gilgamesh wrestled and in the end became great friends. Together they set off to do good things. First they cut down a cedar tree in the sacred woods guarded by the monstrous Humbaba—perhaps death—who merely by breathing on humans could turn them to stone. With the help of the gods, who blinded the monster, the heroes killed him, but according to some versions of the tale, Enkidu was infected by his poisonous power. At this point the goddess of love and fertility, Ishtar, attempts to seduce Gilgamesh, but he refuses her, pointing to the fate of others seduced by and then sacrificed for her. In anger, the goddess has the king of heaven send the Great Bull of Storms against the two men, who promptly kill it. Enkidu now dreams of his coming death, decreed by the gods as punishment for his role in

Detail on a limestone panel depicts Assyrian king Ashurbanipal (669–627 B.C.E.). Excavations of the king's library uncovered a large portion of *The Epic of Gilgamesh.*

the killing of the bull. When Enkidu does die, Gilgamesh, in his grief at the loss of his friend, goes on a long quest in search of eternal life. What he learns during his quest—primarily from the immortal Sumerian-Babylonian Noah figure, Utnapishtim—is that immortality is reserved for a special few. Gilgamesh is made to see that, like most humans, he is not one of these. He returns home, sadder but wiser, to tell his story in Erech.

See also Epic as Allegory; The Quest as Allegory.

GILMAN, CHARLOTTE PERKINS

Charlotte Perkins Gilman was born in Hartford, Connecticut, in 1860. Her father abandoned their family when Charlotte was an infant, and her childhood was spent with her mother and brother, moving often and barely avoiding poverty. When she was older, Gilman studied art and became a teacher and a designer of greeting cards. She married Charles Stetson in 1884, in spite of her ambivalence about combining her career with the demands of a domestic life. After her daughter was born a year later, Gilman fell into a deep depression. She was treated by Dr. S. Weir Mitchell, a well-known nerve specialist, who prescribed a "rest-cure" consisting of total bed rest, isolation, and no intellectual work whatsoever. Upon returning home, Gilman found that she could not adhere to her doctor's orders to devote herself exclusively to her home and her child. She separated from her husband and they eventually divorced. In 1890, she married George Houghton Gilman, a first cousin. Gilman found this marriage much more satisfying, and the couple remained together until George Gilman's death in 1934. Gilman, suffering from an inoperable cancer, took her own life in 1935. Perhaps Gilman's best-known work is the classic and somewhat allegorical short story "The Yellow Wallpaper" (1892), based in part on her own dreadful experience with Dr. Mitchell's "rest-cure." But Gilman's intellectual contributions extend beyond literature into sociology and women's issues, and she is now recognized as an important leader in the women's movement from 1890 to 1920.

See also "The Yellow Wall-Paper."

GINSBERG, ALLEN

The American poet Allen Ginsberg (1926–) is most often associated with the "Beat" movement of the 1950s. Influenced by the free form and free living he found in the works of Walt Whitman, Ginsberg achieved a landmark work in the long, perhaps somewhat allegorical poem "Howl" (1956), a satirical and often violent outcry against society and a lament for the Beat generation. (Benet 1965)

See also "Howl."

GNOSTICISM AND ALLEGORY

Gnosticism is a much vilified theological point of view that derived from early Christianity, the philosophies of the Greeks Pythagoras and Plato, and various esoteric traditions of Greece and the East. Gnosticism stressed knowledge rather than belief and was concerned with the allegorical nature of symbols. That is to say, symbols were seen to be allegories of *gnosis* or knowledge. Christ was a personification of a particular characteristic of the "Mind of God." Other personifications of the same reality were Mind, Logos, Truth, the Church, and most important, the figure of Sophia (Wisdom), who is sometimes seen as an allegory for the Mind of God. In the *Wisdom of Solomon*, written in Alexandria in the second century C.E., we learn that Sophia is the divine light within all things, loved by all wise men and the spouse of God himself—the source of *gnosis* (Benet 1965; Eliade 1987; Leeming 1994; Leeming and Page 1994)

GOAT SONG

The Austrian Franz Werfel's *Goat Song: A Drama in Five Acts [Bocksgesang: In fünf Akten]* (1921) has been the subject of numerous, sometimes conflicting, allegorical interpretations. The story is set at the turn of the nineteenth century in a Slavik country; Stevan Milic is about to marry his son, Mirko, to a young woman named Stanja. Mirko has an older brother, born a deformed, goatlike creature, whom the family has hidden in the stable for more than 20 years. One day the physician, after visiting the goat-monster, forgets to lock the door of the stall. The monster escapes and joins a renegade band of social outcasts and gypsies, led by a student named Juvan, who are petitioning the rich for land. Stevan, as spokesperson for the villagers, denies their request; in anger the mob torches the countryside and pillages the town until it is subdued by the military. Juvan, Stanja's secret love, is sentenced to be hanged; Mirko dies trying to protect Stanja; and Stanja reveals that she will soon bear the child of the goat-monster. Amid this chaos, Stevan and his wife, relieved of the guilty burden of their secret son, fall in love with each other once again.

Critics have tended to interpret this play both mythically and socio-politically. Mythically, the goat-monster may be seen as an allegorical representation of the destructive, irrational evil that is inherent in every person. Regardless of how we try to hide it or subdue it, it is an unholy, dangerous force that is always ready to escape from us and devastate our lives and the lives of others.

Sociopolitically, *Goat Song* may be read as a story of the rebellion of the disenfranchised poor against the contemptuous rich. In this interpretation, the goat-monster, aligning himself with the rebellious mob, becomes an allegorical image of revolution, symbolizing all the disenfranchised, weak forces who battle against the politically and financially powerful. Critics have also noted that the story of *Goat Song* prefigures and even prophesies the rampant bloodshed, destruction, and adoration of evil of the Nazi years under Hitler's Third Reich. (Michaels 1994; Wagener 1993)

See also Werfel, Franz.

GOETHE, JOHANN WOLFGANG VON

Perhaps the greatest of German writers, Goethe (1749–1832) contributed to the ever-emerging definition of allegory by commenting as follows: "There is a great difference, whether the poet seeks the particular for the general or sees the general in the particular. From the first procedure arises allegory, where the particular serves only as an example of the general; the second procedure,

Johann Wolfgang von Goethe

however, is really the nature of poetry: it expresses something particular, without thinking of the general or pointing to it." Thus Goethe, like Coleridge, tends to belittle allegory, considering it inferior to symbol in what he sees as "real" poetry: "True symbolism is where the particular represents the more general, not as a dream or a shadow, but as a living momentary revelation of the Inscrutable" (Wellek 1955, I, 211).

Goethe was not above making use of allegory, however. The second part (1832) of his great work the *Tragedy of Faust* has strong allegorical elements. In Part I (1808) Goethe had followed the traditional tale of the brilliant scholar who sells his soul to the devil in return for the granting of his overwhelming desire for knowledge. But in Part II the poet moves away from plot and depicts an older and wiser Faust who returns to his native land as the embodiment of the human desire for achievement. He creates a society which, though not perfect, is a place for activity and creativity. For Goethe Faust here becomes an allegory of the man who learns the value of life itself. But the moment of that realization is the moment when the devil claims his own. We learn too late the value of being. But God intervenes here, taking Faust's soul to himself. In spite of his sins, Faust—the everyman in search of experience—had always possessed a core of goodness. The protests of the forces of evil are rejected and angels take Faust off to the ultimate place of creative activity, God's heaven. (Fletcher 1964; Wellek 1955)

See also Coleridge, Samuel Taylor; *Dr. Faustus.*

GOGOL, NIKOLAI

Russian novelist and short-story writer Nikolai Gogol (1809–1852) was born the son of a petty Ukrainian aristocrat. At the age of 19, Gogol moved to St. Petersburg to pursue a career as a writer. He published his first narrative poem, "Hans Kuchelgarten," in 1829; it met with disastrous reviews and Gogol, deeply embarrassed, bought the unsold copies, burned them, and for a short while became a recluse. He then embarked on a number of short-lived occupations, including acting, painting, and teaching in a girls' boarding school. His first collection of stories, *Evenings on a Farm near Dikanka* (2 vols., 1831–1832), portraying the folklore of the Ukraine, met with great success. He then took a job teaching medieval history at St. Petersburg University and published another collection of Ukrainian stories, *Mirgorod*, in 1835.

Gogol is best remembered for his drama *The Inspector General* (1836) and his partly allegorical novel *Dead Souls* (1842). Each contains elements of the bizarre comic style that characterizes much of Gogol's fiction and has caused him to be celebrated as one of the most gifted nineteenth-century Russian writers.

See also Dead Souls.

THE GOLDEN ASS

The writer of this work was Lucius Apuleius, a Roman rhetorician, philosopher, and some would say magician, who lived in Carthage in the second century C.E. The real title of the book, a satirical and allegorical romance, which is an ancestor of the novel, is *The Metamorphoses*. But it is better known as *The Golden Ass* to differentiate it from the great *Metamorphoses* of the Roman poet Ovid.

The Golden Ass describes a fanciful voyage through Greece. It tells how the licentious and ever-curious Lucius, while visiting the land of wonderful witches in Thessaly, convinces a young woman to steal a magic potion that will turn him into an owl. But somehow he takes the wrong potion and turns into an ass. In this degrading form he continues his travels. Throughout the work there are stories of lust and witchcraft and other subjects. The most famous tale is the one of Cupid and Psyche. In the end, having witnessed the brutality and unbridled licentiousness of humankind, Lucius, with the help of the goddess Isis, eats a rose and is returned to his original state.

William Aldington, who translated Apuleius in the sixteenth century, explains the allegory as follows: The transformation of Lucius into an ass represents the true inner state of mortals. When we allow sensuality—represented by the witches—to overpower our reason and virtue, we naturally become beasts. It is reason and virtue—represented by the rose—that we must imbibe before we can achieve our true humanity. "This book of Lucius," wrote Aldington, "is a figure of a man's life, and toucheth the nature and manners of mortal men, egging them forward from their asinal form to their human and perfect state. . . ." (MacQueen 1970)

See also Apuleius, Lucius; *Cupid and Psyche.*

GOLDEN BOY

This 1937 play by the American playwright Clifford Odets (1906–1963) was subtitled in an early draft "A Modern Allegory"; even without such a broad hint, critics have been able to recognize Odets's story as an American morality play. The main character of the play is Joe Bonaparte, a 20-year-old boy who has a cock-eye, an Italian immigrant father, an enormous talent for playing the violin, and an insatiable need to become a great American success. Not satisfied with the prospect of life as a musician, he is lured into the world of prize-fighting by promises of money, fame, and power. His abandonment of his music becomes irrevocable when he breaks his hands in a prizefight. Eventually, after murdering an opponent in the boxing ring and losing all sense of personal integrity, he destroys himself in a suicidal car accident.

Critics have interpreted *Golden Boy* as a social allegory of the destructive underside of the American Dream. In this vision, artists (such as Joe the violinist) cannot hope to achieve conventional "success" when competing against the violence and greed of twentieth-century America. Furthermore, Joe can be understood as battling, through his boxing, for a sense of individual self-worth which is difficult to find in a social hierarchy based on money and fame. Considered one of the earliest American existentialist plays, *Golden Boy* warns its audience of the dangers on the road to material success. (Brenman-Gibson 1981)

    See also Odets, Clifford.

GOLDING, WILLIAM

Sir William Gerald Golding (1911–1993) was born in Cornwall and educated at Marlborough at Brasenose College, Oxford. His professional life included working as a writer, actor, and producer in the theater; teaching school; and serving in the Royal Navy during World War II. His first publication was the collection *Poems* (1935), but it wasn't until the allegorical *Lord of the Flies* (1936) that Golding's success as a writer was assured. Golding continued to write for the remainder of his life; his works include 13 novels, two essay collections, and a play. He won the Nobel Prize for Literature in 1983 and was knighted in 1988.

    See also Lord of the Flies.

GORMENGHAST TRILOGY

See Peake, Mervyn.

GRAHAME, KENNETH

Kenneth Grahame (1859–1932) was a British essayist and writer of children's literature. Born in Edinburgh, Grahame moved to Berkshire to live with his grandmother after his mother died. He attended school in Oxford, but instead of enrolling in Oxford University, as he wished, he was forced to begin work for the Bank of England. His first publications were two books of essays called *The Golden Age* (1895) and *Dream Days* (1898). After his marriage in 1899, Grahame began writing children's stories for his son Alastair. They formed the basis for his classic novel-length story *The Wind in the Willows* (1908), a work that has allegorical aspects. This was the last important literary work that Grahame would produce; he lived a rather reclusive life after Alastair committed suicide at the age of 19.

    See also The Wind in the Willows.

GRAVITY'S RAINBOW

See Pynchon, Thomas.

THE GREAT GOD BROWN

This 1926 play by Eugene O'Neill (1888–1953), while not nearly as popular with audiences or critics as *The Hairy Ape* and other plays, uses allegory effectively to paint its picture of human suffering. The story follows the lives of four people, but is significantly complicated by the fact that the characters wear masks during most of the scenes. The real faces of the characters represent their true inner selves, while the masks they wear signify the personas they share with the public world. In the story, one man (Dion) dies and his rival in love (Billy) assumes Dion's mask, along with his family and children. Eventually Billy "kills" his own mask, effectively destroying his former identity. He lives on as Dion, but his anguish soon leads to the destruction of his physical self as well. Cybel (the mistress to both men and the symbol of Mother Earth) understands the meaning of the masks and grieves for Billy's anonymous death. At the end, Dion/Billy's wife, Margaret, who never really understands that Billy adopted Dion's identity by wearing his mask, keeps Dion's mask inside her clothes, "under her heart." Allegorically, this play has been interpreted as the story of every person's spiritual conflict between the private self and the public self. While all the characters in *The Great God Brown* don their masks for different reasons, the end result is that each of them suffers from the chasm created between the unmasked, "real" self and the masked, "public" self. (Egri 1984; Miller 1965; Ranald 1984)

See also *The Hairy Ape;* O'Neill, Eugene.

THE GREAT THEATER OF THE WORLD

El Gran Teatro del Mundo (ca. 1637) was the most popular of the *autos sacramentales*—one-act religious dramas—by the great seventeenth-century Spanish playwright Calderón de la Barca (1600–1681). In this play the theater is an allegory for the world. The playwright is, of course, God. As was the case in the medieval morality plays of northern Europe, the characters in this play are the various personified vices and virtues, who express themselves through words and actions appropriate to the qualities indicated by their names. What the play attempts to show is that God orchestrates the events on the stage which is life, and that these events are but temporary. Only God is eternal. (Benet 1965)

See also *Auto Sacramentale;* Calderón de la Barca, Pedro; Morality Plays.

GRIMM BROTHERS

Jacob (1785–1863) and Wilhelm (1786–1859) Grimm were scholars of German philology. They are better known to most of the world as the collectors of *Kinder und Hausmärchen* [*Children's and Household Tales*] or *Grimm's Fairy Tales* (1812 ff.). The Grimm brothers got most of their stories for the book from interviews with peasants. Many of the collected tales are allegorical in nature. Depending on the listener and the historical context, the allegory can be political, philosophical, religious, or, in modern times, psychological. The tales tend to be based on certain formulas. For example: the child is lost in the woods, is accosted by a witch, delivers himself and a princess from the witch, marries the princess, and lives happily ever after. Or, there once were three sons, one was good, two were bad, and so on. One of the best examples is a tale called "The Water of Life." What follows is a psychological-religious allegorical reading of it.

"Once upon a time," there lived a king who was desperately ill. The beginning of this and of most fairy tales involves a ritual placing of a situation in time. It is one-half of a framework that will be completed in the "happily ever after" ending. In the first image of "The Water of Life," the king, as kings nearly always are, is a symbol of the kingdom of humanity on earth at odds with our universal nemesis, mortality. The sick old king who is unwhole and must be made whole again thus evokes the theme of salvation which, with the quest theme, is the religious essence of the fairy tale as a genre.

The king has three sons who weep in the palace garden over their father's condition. As potential saviors the children must remind us of the knights of King Arthur's Round Table, whose adventures can perhaps restore harmony to the Arthurian vision. The symbolic nature of numbers in fairy tales, as in myth and ritual, gives significance to the fact that there are three children. The number four represents quaternity—balance, wholeness, harmony—and four brothers would indicate a common effort to restore harmony to the kingdom. The existence of three sons, however, tends to suggest the discordant situation of two against one.

In the garden an old man appears to the sons to tell them that their father might be cured by the water of life but that the water will be difficult to find. The old man is familiar to us in the almost ritualistic formula that is the traditional fairy tale. He is the "other" interjected into our world; he can be the wise old spirit or the fairy godmother. His function is to point to the solution of the apparently insoluble problem. His way invariably requires the difficult quest.

The oldest son goes to his father to request permission to attempt the search for the water of life. But as he asks and finally receives his loving father's reluctant permission, he is thinking that if he finds the water, his father will reward him by making him his heir. His thoughts mark him allegorically as an embodiment of the sins of greed and selfishness.

The oldest son sets off on his quest and almost immediately meets a dwarf who inquires as to his destination. When the prince answers in a rude manner, the dwarf uses magic to imprison him on his horse between two mountains. The dwarf, like the old man in the garden, is an allegorical embodiment of the "other," complete with deep and dangerous power. The "other" must never be treated lightly. The imprisonment between the mountains suggests the narrow vision of the first prince and is an allegorical morality lesson for all of us. Needless to say, when the first son does not return home, the second son takes up the quest and follows his brother's pattern of behavior, ritualistically, down to

Witches, such as the one pictured in this 1914 edition of *Grimm's Fairy Tales,* often played a large role in the Grimm brothers' stories.

the exact words and movements. So now the two "bad" brothers are imprisoned and we are ready for the quest of the third son. When he asks his father's permission to seek the water of life, he does so with no thought of what he might gain from success. When he meets the dwarf he answers openly and politely. The youngest son is innocence personified. The dwarf appreciates his reply and tells him of the enchanted castle where the water of life flows from a magical fountain. He gives the boy certain magical objects and ritual directions, which the boy accepts on faith. With faith, the storyteller seems to say, comes the power of the "other."

The prince finds the castle, uses the dwarf's magic to overpower its evil guardians, and finds a beautiful princess who immediately offers herself in marriage if the prince will promise to return in a year. He promises to do so and the princess shows him the fountain and the water of life. She reminds him that after taking some of the water he must leave the enchanted castle before midnight.

In terms of psychological allegory, we find many elements here of the traditional mythic hero's descent into the underworld, which is representative of anyone's descent into the locked castle of the unconscious. Our descent, like the hero's, is necessary if the goal of wholeness is to be achieved. The hero descends into the underworld to retrieve someone or something that has been lost. Jesus "retrieves" Adam and Eve, Orpheus tries to retrieve Eurydice. The prince retrieves the enchanted princess, his "other half" without which he cannot be whole, without which he cannot live "happily ever after." There is possibly a complex religious allegory here as well. In terms of the Virgin cult of medieval Christianity the princess takes on particular meaning. The Virgin is the earthly form of the Mother of God, but as the Church—the castle freed from enchantment—she is also his bride. The prince, who is everyman, can only be free and whole when at one with the Church.

The waiting period of one year is, of course, a period of testing and growing. The growth begins immediately when the prince almost fails to leave the castle by midnight and has part of his heel sliced off as he rushes through the closing gate. The ritual wound, like that of the Fisher King in the Arthurian story of the Holy Grail, would seem to stand for the idea of mortality, which is the result of original sin—the sin of Adam and Eve, who ate of the forbidden tree in the Garden of Eden. The prince continues to learn when he is deceived by the wicked brothers after he frees them from their imprisonment. They steal the water of life and turn the king against him and he must wander alone in the dark forest for the year of waiting. Again, the allegory here seems to suggest the necessity of the inner search, the psychological trial.

The two evil princes, who have been told by their brother of the castle and the princess, attempt to enter the castle and are thwarted. Only the worthy can attain the kingdom of God or, psychologicaly speaking, only those who have made the inner journey can attain wholeness. The young prince emerges from the darkness and does just that. He wins the princess, frees the castle, is reconciled with his father, and lives "happily ever after."

See also Fairy Tales and Allegory.

GUILLAUME DE LORRIS

Guillaume was the thirteenth-century French poet who composed the first 4,058 lines of the allegorical *Romance of the Rose [Le Roman de la Rose]*. The poem was completed by Jean de Meung.

See also Chopinel, Jean; *The Romance of the Rose*.

GULLIVER'S TRAVELS

Jonathan Swift (1667–1745) was the Anglican Dean of St. Patrick's Cathedral in Dublin and a well-known political journalist and satirist when his *Gulliver's Travels* was published anonymously in 1726. It was an immediate success, and Swift's authorship soon became widely known. The biting social, moral, and political allegory in *Gulliver's Travels* takes careful aim at humankind in general, and English members of the Whig political party in particular. Through a series of fantastical shipwrecks, Swift's main character, a fairly unremarkable Englishman, encounters cultures and peoples far different from those he knew in England, yet in some ways strikingly similar.

Book I of *Gulliver's Travels* opens with Lemuel Gulliver taking a position as a ship's doctor; shortly thereafter his ship is wrecked in a storm and Gulliver, the only survivor, washes up on an island. He awakens on the beach to discover that he is firmly tied to the ground, captured by a community of tiny humans only six inches tall. These are the people of Lilliput, who, when they realize that the giant Gulliver does not intend to harm them, find him to be a remarkable curiosity. They attend to his needs, teach him the Lilliputian language, and eventually welcome him into the royal court. When Lilliput is endangered by a nearby empire, Blefescu, Gulliver offers to assist the forces of Lilliput. After Blefescu is defeated, the Lilliputian emperor wants to enslave his prisoners. Gulliver argues for their liberty, and eventually prevails. During a later visit to Blefescu, Gulliver finds a damaged boat that had washed ashore. With the help of the Blefescu people, he repairs the boat, sails away, and is eventually rescued by an English ship.

In Book II, after visiting briefly with his family, Gulliver sails away again on a ship bound for India. During a supply stop on the island of Brobdingnag, Gulliver is left behind by his shipmates when a giant human chases the sailors away. Gulliver is captured by a giant farmer, becomes a family "pet," and is particularly befriended by the giant's young daughter. The farmer puts the tiny Gulliver on display in the city of the giants, but Gulliver's health suffers tremendously as a result. The farmer then decides to sell the weak and sickly Gulliver to the queen, who thinks him rather interesting. Eventually Gulliver regains his strength, only to find himself in the midst of dangerous adventures with rats, a dwarf, wasps, apples, and hailstones, all of which seem enormous to him. Gulliver and the king of Brobdingnag discuss their respective countries, but when the king asks questions about the institutions of England, Gulliver cannot help but feel ashamed of his country. After two years, Gulliver is rescued from Brobdingnag when a giant bird picks up his living quarters and drops it into the sea, where he is again rescued by a ship returning to England.

Gulliver soon returns to the sea in Book III, but this time his ship is attacked by pirates and Gulliver is cast away on an island. One day a large floating island descends from the sky and takes Gulliver aboard. This is the flying island of Laputa, inhabited by intellectuals who understand only the abstract and the impractical. When Laputa arrives over the land of Balnibari, Gulliver is permitted to visit. There he sees hundreds of exceedingly impractical projects being developed to improve agriculture and architecture. Next Gulliver travels to Glubbdubdrib, an island of sorcerers. The governor of Glubbdubdrib magically calls forth many historical figures, and Gulliver learns from them that history texts are inaccurate. His next journey takes him to Luggnagg, where he visits a group of immortal beings called Struldbrugs. He then travels to Japan and from there back to England. He has been gone over three years.

Book IV tells how Gulliver sails again shortly after his return to his family, this time as a ship's captain. The crew mutinies, and Gulliver is cast adrift. Landing on an unknown island, Gulliver is frightened and shocked by wild creatures that are half-human, half-ape. He soon realizes that on this island rational horses called Houyhnhnms rule the savage humanlike creatures called Yahoos. The Houyhnhnms are horrified at Gulliver's descriptions of the institutions and lifestyles of England and eventually decide that Gulliver must either be treated as a Yahoo or required to return to his native land. Gulliver is grief-stricken at the prospect of leaving the rational Houyhnhnms, but builds himself a canoe and leaves the island as instructed. He is picked up by a Portuguese vessel, but the disgust he feels toward the barbarous Yahoos carries over into revulsion toward all humans. He sails back to England but is repulsed by the sight of his family. The story ends with the embittered Gulliver's complete denial of human companionship, preferring instead to seek friendship among the horses in his stable.

Allegorically, *Gulliver's Travels* demonstrates the failings of contemporary politicians such as Prime Minister Walpole, King George I, and others. But Swift is not content with merely allegorizing specific personages; his satire attacks not just the embodiment of political corruption in the Walpole administration, but political corruption in general. Furthermore, Gulliver's encounters with the inhabitants of Lilliput, Brobdingnag, and the other fictional lands allegorize what Swift perceived to be an important shortcoming of his age, the "Age of Enlightenment": the inability of many to recognize the irrational side of mankind.

Many critics interpret *Gulliver's Travels*, especially Books I and III, to be allegorical depictions of the scientific, intellectual, and political worlds of eighteenth-century England. Flimnap, a character in Book I, is often connected with Walpole; the colored ribbons in Lilliput signify the major British orders, and the ludicrous and nonsensical conflict between Lilliput and neighboring Blefescu may parallel the historically bitter rivalry between England and France. The King of Laputa in Book III suggests the character of King George I, and

Captain Lemuel Gulliver, of
Redriff Ætat. suæ 58.

Engraved frontispiece to *Gulliver's Travels,* published in 1726

perhaps royal cruelty in general. The infinitely impractical scientists and mathematicians of Laputa and Balnibari parody those members of the Academy who Swift believed were turning away from traditional Christian and humanist thinking. Critics argue that many other incidents and interactions may be directly linked to historical events and personages in eighteenth-century England, thus suggesting that Swift's tale deliberately and accurately depicts his experience as a British subject.

Book IV, a beast fable, incorporates a somewhat less politicized allegorical structure. Instead, Swift creates a social and moral allegory focused around the Houyhnhnms—humanity's rational nature—and the Yahoos, mankind's irrational nature. In the end, Gulliver embraces wholeheartedly the "utopian" culture of the Houyhnhnms and pays sincere obeisance to their leader, the embodiment of Reason. As a result, Gulliver denies the irrational aspects of mankind and rejects all emotionality and intimate personal connections. This leads to his unenviable final situation: alone, he rejects human love and affection from his family, longing only for the pseudo-utopia of the coldly rational Houyhnhnms.

An important aspect of the allegory of *Gulliver's Travels* is that in spite of the many direct connections that can be drawn between fictional characters and encounters and historical people and events, Swift's fiction operates on another level as well. Flimnap may be intended to allegorize Robert Walpole, but he also serves to represent political corruption in general. The characters of the King of Laputa and the Emperor of Lilliput may be connected to England's King George I, but to other kings as well. The ridiculous basis for the war between Lilliput and Blefescu may allegorize the Reformation, but may also represent any futile religious war. Swift's fiction serves to offer his readers both ideals and antitypes, demonstrating simultaneously what man should emulate and what man should denounce. (Asimov 1980; Carnochan 1968; Erskine-Hill 1993; Frye 1961; Kallich 1970; Lock 1980; Varay 1990; Wedel 1968; Williams 1968)

See also Swift, Jonathan; *A Tale of a Tub*.

HAFIZ

Hafiz (or Hafez) is the pen name of Shams-ud-din Muhammad (1300–1388), the Persian Sufi (dervish) poet and ardent student of the Muslim holy book, the Koran. He is best known for his collection of ghazals (odes), the *Divan of Hafiz*. While not strictly allegorical, these poems do have secondary religious or mystical meanings. On the surface they are concerned with love, nature, and other worldly subjects, but they suggest mystical ideas. In the lines that follow, Hafiz uses a depiction of human love—human union—as an allegory for the mystic's quest for union with the eternal:

> Haste, o Saqui! Come fill the cup and pass it round.
> In a love that seemed so easy, alas, what pain I've found!
> Each whiff of musk from those dark curling tresses,
> Each twisted ringlet, for my heart a bleeding wound.
> The wayfarer will know the way, and the customs of each stage.
> Should your guide command it, spill wine upon the prayer ground. (Magill 1987)

THE HAIRY APE

One of the more popular plays by Eugene O'Neill (1888–1953), *The Hairy Ape* (1922) tells the story of Yank, a proud stokeman on a luxury liner, who by chance encounters the daughter of a steel magnate. Her horrified condemnation of him as a "filthy beast" shatters his entire worldview, and through a series of painful events and confrontations, Yank learns that he doesn't "belong" anywhere in society. In the play's final scene, Yank reaches out to what he believes to be a symbol of his own oppression: a caged gorilla in the zoo. Yank releases the gorilla from his cage, but the animal promptly grabs him and crushes him to death. While not an allegorical tale in the strictest sense, *The Hairy Ape* has been interpreted as an allegory of the alienated position of modern man in industrialized society. In this sense, Yank represents not only the disenfranchised worker, but every person who struggles to preserve a sense of personal dignity and "belonging" in a world that cares little for individuality. (Egri 1984; Miller 1965; Ranald 1984)

See also *The Great God Brown;* O'Neill, Eugene.

HARDY, THOMAS

The English novelist and poet Thomas Hardy (1840–1928) was born in Dorsetshire, a section of England on which he based the mythical county of Wessex, the setting for most of his novels. Hardy was an architect who became dissatisfied with his profession and turned to writing novels, including the well-known *Far from the Madding Crowd* (1876), *The Return of the Native* (1879), *The Mayor of Casterbridge* (1887), *Tess of the D'Urbervilles* (1897), and *Jude the Obscure* (1897). After 1897 Hardy turned primarily to poetry, including his allegorical epic drama, *The Dynasts.* Much influenced by the ideas of scientific determinism of the late nineteenth century, Hardy's philosophy, as expressed in his novels, is highly fatalistic. Fate and chance nearly always defeat his characters, who desperately attempt to better their lives against the odds of forces—natural and social—beyond their control. In a sense, all of his novels could be said to be allegories in that they act out the drama of determinism which Hardy sees as the essence of life. (Benet 1965)

See also *The Dynasts.*

HAROUN AND THE SEA OF STORIES

Haroun and the Sea of Stories (1990) is a recent work by the Anglo-Indian novelist Salman Rushdie (b. 1947). Rushdie was born in Bombay but moved to England in his early teens. Much of his work has been concerned with the cultural conflicts and explorations resulting from his background. His novels include *Grimus* (1975), *Midnight's Children* (1981), *Shame* (1983), and more recently *The Satanic Verses* (1989). This last work led to a condemnation by the Ayatollah Khomeini, the leader of the Islamic revolution in Iran, who accused Rushdie of blasphemy against Islam and charged faithful Moslems around the world to hunt down and kill the author.

Haroun, on the public level, is a reaction to Khomeini's condemnation. On the private level Rushdie is responding to his own divorce and his forced seclusion as a result of the threat to his life.

Although Rushdie denies allegorical intention in any of his work, it is evident that *Haroun* is in some sense allegorical. Haroun is a youth whose father, Rashid, is a storyteller who has forgotten to "live in the real world," whose wife has left him, and who has lost his ability to tell tales. "What's the use of stories that aren't even true?" he asks. So it is that Haroun goes on a quest through an ocean of stories, which he must release from the power of one Khattam-Shud. Khattam-Shud in Hindustani is the term used to announce the end of stories and Khattam-Shud is called the "Prince of Silence," the "Foe of

Speech." That he is the Ayatollah Khomeini, the suppressor of Rushdie's voice, is clear enough. He is the Cultmaster of Bezaban ("without a voice"). That is, he is the leader of Iran. His people are the Chupwalas (the "quiet people"), who live in darkness. In opposition to Khattam-Shud are the people of Gup ("gossip" in Hindustani), who live in the light and value free speech above all things. The Chupwalas hate light and turn on darkness with their "darkbulbs" while their leader tells "antitales." The people of Gup City (London/the West) are, with all their freedoms, somewhat disorganized, but when their princess is captured by the dark forces they mobilize and, using the power of their freedom, become a significant force for good. Still, for all the power of Truth, magic is needed to overcome Khattam-Shud. With the help of his guides, Iff the Water Genie and Butt the Hoopeo (there *are* ifs and buts to things), Haroun makes the sun shine on the darkness of the land of the Chupwalas, and there is a meltdown of their static and frozen structures. Allegorically we see that the light of Reason will prevail over the darkness of irrationality. Haroun is able through his work to reunite his family and to release his father's voice. (Cundy 1993; Durix 1993)

HAWTHORNE, NATHANIEL

Nathaniel Hawthorne (1804–1864) was born in Salem, Massachusetts, to a prominent family descended from early American colonists. As an adult, Hawthorne was troubled by his relationship to one particular ancestor, Judge John Hathorne, who presided at the Salem witch trials of 1692. In 1808 Hawthorne's father died; in 1815 Hawthorne and his mother moved to Maine, where he would attend Bowdoin College.

After graduating from college in 1825, Hawthorne returned to Salem, where he began writing short stories and sketches in earnest. In 1828 he paid to have his first novel, *Fanshawe*, published; it received minimal critical attention. Ashamed, he continued writing fiction, focusing mainly on the interrelated themes of guilt and Puritanism. These stories were collected and published in *Twice-Told Tales* (1837; expanded 1842). Hawthorne found work as an editor, writer, and Custom House surveyor. In 1841 he quit his work at the Custom House in order to get married and to invest in the Brook Farm commune, an experiment run by the leading followers of transcendentalism. In 1842 the Hawthornes left Brook Farm and moved to Concord to live in the Old Manse, the former home of Ralph Waldo Emerson. In 1846 he published a collection of short fiction called *Mosses from an Old Manse*, and in 1850 his first important and highly acclaimed novel, *The Scarlet Letter*, appeared. In the next few years he published *The House of the Seven Gables* (1851), *The Snow Image and Other Tales* (1851), *The Blithedale Romance* (1852), *A Wonder Book* (1852), and *Tanglewood Tales* (1853).

In 1853 Hawthorne was appointed American consul at Liverpool by the newly elected President Franklin Pierce, one of Hawthorne's college friends. He lived in England for four years and in Italy for two years before returning home and publishing his final novel, *The Marble Faun* (1860), and a collection of essays called *Our Old Home* (1863). Hawthorne left four novels unfinished at his death in May 1864.

Hawthorne, simultaneously haunted and fascinated by his family's Puritan heritage, earned for himself a prominent position in the canon of nineteenth-century American literature with his powerful psychological tales of guilt, pride, and sin. While *The Scarlet Letter* (1850) is commonly considered to be an American literary masterpiece, Hawthorne's shorter fiction has certainly not gone unnoticed by readers and critics. Scholars, in their enthusiastic efforts to corroborate Hawthorne's professed "inveterate love of allegory" with allegorical readings of his stories, have in some cases attempted to force the tales to fit into any number of prescribed allegorical molds. Yet Hawthorne should not necessarily be considered a traditional allegorist; while his stories contain numerous historical, religious, psychological, and mythic elements of allegory, they are rarely allegories in the strictest sense.

Nevertheless, Hawthorne's favorite writers were Bunyan and Spenser, and he was keenly aware of the usefulness of allegorical strategies in his writing. He incorporates some of these strategies in his short story "My Kinsman, Major Molineaux" (1832), in which a simple farm boy named Robin searches for his influential kinsman, only to find him tarred and feathered and paraded through the town streets in disgrace for being a Tory. Among many other allegorical readings, this story has been interpreted as a journey-quest from innocence to experience, a historio-political rendering of Puritan ideology, and a psychological voyage into the underworld.

"Young Goodman Brown" (1835) has also been the subject of a variety of allegorical interpretations. In this tale, Goodman Brown leaves his wife, Faith, to venture into the forest on a mysterious errand. There, he experiences a revelation that permanently shatters his religious belief. Faith becomes an allegorical figure of religious faith; after Brown "loses faith" in the forest, he can no longer relate to his wife. "Young Goodman Brown" has also been treated as an allegory of the fall of Adam due to the temptation of Eve, in which Brown is the impressionable Adam and Eve is recast as Faith.

"Rappaccini's Daughter" (1844) assumes a particularly allegorical aspect, but although Beatrice recalls Dante's Beatrice in the *Divine Comedy* and Rappaccini's lush garden suggests the Garden of Eden in Genesis, the tale resists being categorized as a sustained retelling of the story of the Original Sin. Yet elements within "Rappaccini's Daughter" often lead readers to a Christian interpretation of the garden, the shrub, and the poison that contaminates it all.

"Lady Eleanore's Mantle," "The Celestial Railroad," "The Gray Champion," and "The Maypole of Merry Mount" are among the many other Hawthorne tales that have been examined through allegorical lenses. All of them, and others, do yield up allegorical interpretations of varying plausibility and strength. Critic Beverly Haviland offers some general insight into the role of allegory in Hawthorne's short fiction, suggesting that "Hawthorne uses allegory to attack the American version of romantic symbolism, transcendentalism, because he saw how vicious idealism could be in practice. His villains—Aylmer, who wants to efface his wife's birthmark ['The Birthmark']; the minister who wants to efface his face with a black veil ['The Minister's Black Veil']; Ethan Brand, who wants to make his mark by discovering the Unpardonable Sin ['Ethan Brand']— have long been recognized as characters whose idealizing heads have repressed their sympathizing hearts" (Haviland, 279). In this way, Hawthorne seems to use allegorical approaches in his fiction to extend his examination into the consequences of sin and pride. (Becker 1971; Haviland 1987; Waggoner 1979)

See also The Marble Faun; The Scarlet Letter.

HEART OF DARKNESS

This 1902 long short story by Joseph Conrad (1857–1924) is a tale told by a seaman named Marlow about an experience during his time as a river steamer captain on the Congo River. Marlow had been fascinated by stories he had heard about a trader called Kurtz who had disappeared into the wilderness upriver. When Marlow finally got to Kurtz he discovered a man who, from the colonial point of view, had "gone native." With great difficulty Marlow had extricated the dying trader from the African people who idolized him—especially from one of the tribeswomen who seemed particularly reluctant to let him go. Marlow is obsessed by Kurtz, by his attachment to the wilderness, and this is the real and the allegorical subject of Conrad's work. Kurtz's last words are ambiguous in terms of his feelings: "The horror! the horror!" In Marlow and the reader's mind Kurtz has experienced "the heart of darkness," the deepest reaches of the human experience. The journey up the river for Marlow had been symbolic of the actual journey taken by Kurtz and had become for him a psychological milestone. (Benet 1965)

See also Conrad, Joseph.

HEMINGWAY, ERNEST

See Paysage Moralisé.

HENDERSON THE RAIN KING

It has been suggested that *Henderson the Rain King,* a novel by the American writer Saul Bellow (b. 1915), is an allegory of a Lacanian quest for the knowledge of one's desire (King 1989). In the novel, the hero, a disillusioned American millionaire named Eugene Henderson, journeys through Africa looking for peace of mind. He makes his way first to the country of the Arnewi, a peaceful people ruled by a queen. After being taken in by the Arnewi, Henderson runs away rather than face the consequences of having inadvertently destroyed their well. Next he is adopted by the warlike Wariri tribe, ruled by King Dahfu, a guru figure who will teach Henderson to accept his animal nature. While in Dahfu's land, Henderson is named rain king because of his having successfully lifted the statue of the rain goddess. But now Henderson, like Dahfu, is at the mercy of the goddess ritual; he can be killed when he is no longer productive as far as the cult is concerned. While with the peaceful Arnewi, Henderson had been told by their queen that his problem was his will to live instead of dying. King Dahfu, before he dies, teaches Henderson the importance of facing death with courage. Not wishing to be made the new sacrificial king of the Wariri, however, Henderson flees to America. Whatever allegory there is here seems to be ambiguous. What we can say is that Henderson at the end of the novel seems, at least, to have accepted his mortality. As a modern disillusioned "hero," he represents all of us in the many ways we choose to find meaning in our lives. (King 1989)

See also Bellow, Saul.

HERACLITUS

See Homeric Allegories.

HERBERT, GEORGE

One of the greatest of the seventeenth-century British metaphysical poets, George Herbert (1593–1633) made frequent use of allegory in his overall exploration of the relationship between the Christian soul and God. An example of an allegorical poem by Herbert is "Love (III)," which begins "Love bade me welcome: yet my soul drew back/Guiltie of dust and sinne," dust being, presumably, existence itself ("Remember O Man that thou art dust and unto dust thou shalt return"). Love here is clearly a personification who also stands specifically for God as Love and who longs to unite with the "bride" who is the human soul. The whole poem is quoted here:

LOVE (III)

Love bade me welcome: yet my soul drew back,
Guiltie of dust and sinne.
But quick-ey'd Love, observing me grow slack
From my first entrance in,
Drew nearer to me, sweetly questioning,
If I lack'd any thing.

A guest, I answer'd, worthy to be here:
Love said, You shall be he.
I the unkinde, ungratefull? Ah my deare,
I cannot look on thee.
Love took my hand, and smiling did reply,
Who made the eyes but I?

Truth Lord, but I have marr'd them: let my shame
Go where it doth deserve.
And know you not, sayes Love, who bore the blame?
My deare, then I will serve.
You must sit down, sayes Love, and taste my meat:
So I did sit and eat.

In "Humilitie," another good example of Herbert's allegory, the traditional virtues vie with each other in their pride, thus representing corrupt court behavior. It is the personified Humilitie who tempers the not-so-virtuous virtues.

HUMILITIE

I Saw the Vertues sitting hand in hand
In sev'rall ranks upon an azure throne,
Where all the beasts and fowl by their command
Presented tokens of submission.
Humilitie, who sat the lowest there,
To execute their call,
When by the beasts the presents tendred were
Gave them about to all.

The angrie Lion did present his paw,
Which by consent was giv'n to Mansuetude.
The fearfull Hare her eares, which by their law
Humilitie did reach to Fortitude.
The jealous Turkie brought his corall-chain;
That went to Temperance.
On Justice was bestow'd the Foxes brain,
Kill'd in the way by chance.

At length the Crow bringing the Peacocks plume,
(For he would not) as they beheld the grace
Of that brave gift, each one began to fume,
And challenge it, as proper to his place,
Till they fell out: which when the beasts espied,
They leapt upon the throne;
And if the Fox had liv'd to rule their side,
They had depos'd each one.

Humilitie, who held the plume, at this
did weep so fast, that the tears trickling down
Spoil'd all the train: then saying, *Here it is*
For which ye wrangle, made them turn their frown
Against the beasts: so joyntly bandying,
They drive them soon away;
And then amerc'd them, double gifts to bring
At the next Session-day.

Through his poem Herbert reminds the court and courtiers of the evils of intrigue and ambition and of the need for humility. (Gottlieb 1989; Williams 1984)
        See also Emblems.

HESIOD

The eighth-century B.C.E. Greek poet Hesiod (Hesiodos), whose *Theogony* and *Works and Days* are primary sources for Greek mythology, is said to have been a farmer in Boetia. Hesiod, with Homer, is responsible for compiling a great part of what we think of as Greek mythology. His works are highly allegorical both in terms of the personification of abstractions and the meaning behind events.

See also Myth as Allegory; *Theogony; Works and Days.*

THE HOBBIT

See The Lord of the Rings; Tolkien, J. R. R.

THE HOLY WAR

The last major work of John Bunyan (1628–1688), *The Holy War* (1682) is a complex allegory that combines clearly religious elements with more subtle political and historical commentaries. The story deals with the city of Mansoul (man's soul) and its builder and rightful king, Shaddai. The city is threatened and finally conquered by the evil Diabolus, who promptly punishes or corrupts the townspeople and many of Mansoul's leaders, including Lord Understanding, Mr. Conscience, Lord Willbewill, Mr. Affection, and Mr. Mind. Diabolus appoints his own men to lead the city, installing Mr. Lustings as Mayor and Mr. Forget-Good as Recorder.

When the news of Mansoul's capture reaches Shaddai, he and his son, Emmanuel, resolve to rescue the city from its evil invaders. Emmanuel arrives at Mansoul with his captains, Credence and Good Hope, Charity, and Innocence and Patience, as well as their squires, Promise and Expectation, Pitiful, and Harmless and Suffer Long. Emmanuel's army is powerful, and Diabolus, to save himself, attempts to compromise. Emmanuel will not agree to any negotiations; after a terrible battle, Diabolus is forced to surrender. The now-repentant citizens of Mansoul fear punishment by Emmanuel's righteous forces and beg for mercy and forgiveness. Emmanuel absolves them of their sins, reinstates his chosen town officials, and sentences Diabolus's servants to crucifixion.

Mansoul is issued a charter of rights, and for a time the town seems secure. But the Diabolians gradually infiltrate the town once more, and the carnal lusts regain control of Mansoul. Emmanuel's forces arrive once more to fight the enemy, and when Emmanuel himself appears, victory is again secured and the enemy chiefs are punished. The story ends with Diabolus still at large, Carnal Security hiding in the town, and Unbelief nowhere to be found. Thus, the citizens of Mansoul learn that they must never let down their guard if they want to protect themselves from the enemy.

Critics argue over the nature and primacy of the allegorical messages in *The Holy War*. In terms of religious allegory, the tale recalls both the transformation of the individual soul and the salvation of all humankind. Further, the events in *The Holy War* correspond to the events of the English Revolution: the first reign of Diabolus is the tyrannical reign of Charles I and his bishops, Emmanuel's first victory is the "rule of the saints" (1649–1653), the second fall of Mansoul is the fall of Cromwell, the return of Diabolus is the English Reformation, the revamping of the town is Charles II's purging of the Nonconformists. In yet another allegorical interpretation, scholars suggest that *The Holy War* might also be read as a chronicle of the political happenings in Bedford, Bunyan's hometown, from 1650 to 1682. (Hill 1989; Sadler 1979; Wakefield 1992)

See also Bunyan, John; *The Life and Death of Mr. Badman; The Pilgrim's Progress.*

HOMER

Traditionally, Homer was a blind Ionian poet who composed the two great epics, *The Iliad* and *The Odyssey*. In fact, we are not even sure there was a single poet called Homer. Homer may be a name applied to two or even several poets. Seven Greek cities claimed him as a native. Whether or not he existed, the genius behind the composition of the two epics remains one of the greatest in world literature.

See also The Odyssey.

HOMERIC ALLEGORIES

A first-century work of a man later wrongly associated with the fourth-century B.C.E. Heraclides Ponticus, a pupil of Plato who had written a work called *Homeric Questions,* or with the early fifth-century philosopher Heraclitus of Ephesus. The *Homeric Allegories* by the pseudo-Heraclitus was an allegorical interpretation of the Homeric epics in which the author followed in the by-then ancient tradition of searching for hidden meanings or *hyponoia* in the works of the great master poet. (MacQueen 1970; Rollinson 1981)

See also Hyponoia.

HONIG, EDWIN

Honig's *Dark Conceit: The Making of Allegory* (1966) is a pioneer book among modern attempts to define the subject. In his book the author defends allegory against what he sees as a biased feeling against it among literary scholars. He suggests that allegory occurs when a narrative uses figurative language and conveys a particular belief. Allegory is no more "old-fashioned" or narrow, he says, than are allegorical works such as Hawthorne's "Rappaccini's Daughter," Kafka's *The Castle*, Swift's *Gulliver's Travels*, or Melville's *Moby-Dick*.

HORACE

See Quintilian.

THE HOTEL NEW HAMPSHIRE

John Irving (b. 1942) is a well-known contemporary American novelist, many of whose novels—including *Setting Free the Bears* (1968), *The World According to Garp* (1978), and *The Hotel New Hampshire* (1981)—have been made into popular films. While *The Hotel New Hampshire* is not an allegory in the strictest sense, it does contain some highly allegorical elements. The most notable of these elements is Sorrow, the Berry family's pet Labrador retriever. Sorrow is put to sleep on Halloween, the same night that the eldest Berry daughter is gang-raped. The eldest son Frank's interest in taxidermy keeps Sorrow's body in the family, and it is the actual body of this dead dog that reappears at several critical moments in the story. Allegorically, Sorrow functions first on the literal level of the family pet, then as a symbol of the evil and violence within the lives of the Berry children, then, ultimately, as a universal symbol of evil, denoted by a lowercase "s" in "sorrow." *The Hotel New Hampshire* depicts the unavoidable appearance of sorrow in the life of every individual and the many guises that sorrow takes; nevertheless, Irving's novel does offer some hope that the struggle to establish one's identity is worthwhile and can be successful. (Miller 1982; Reilly 1991)

See also Irving, John.

"THE HOUND OF HEAVEN"

See Thompson, Francis.

THE HOUS OF FAME

The Hous of Fame, an important narrative poem by Geoffrey Chaucer (ca. 1343–1400), has been interpreted as an example of medieval allegory. Written between 1374 and 1380, the poem is a dream-vision in three parts which ends, incomplete, after 2,158 lines.

The first part of the poem retells the story of the epic quest of Aeneas to found the city of Rome. In the second part, a talking eagle sent by Jove sweeps out of the sky to pick up the dreamer and carry him away. The eagle promises to take the narrator to a place where he can learn about love. He is dropped alongside a tower of ice, upon which the engraved names of the famous are melting away and becoming illegible. He then enters the house of Fame, suspended between earth, sea, and heaven, where a goddess with many ears, eyes, and tongues grants the gift of fame. There, the dreamer learns of the arbitrary nature of fame as he watches the goddess randomly award petitioners fame and notoriety. In the final section of the poem the dreamer encounters, in a valley below the castle, the house of Rumour. This house is 60 miles long, made of twigs, and revolves continually. The eagle lifts the dreamer into the house, where he sees a great throng of people telling news and stories which fly out of the crevices in the walls at random and arrive at the house of Fame to be judged. As an unidentified, imposing figure approaches the scene, the poem breaks off.

The Hous of Fame has been read as a moral allegory of the vanity of worldly fame; the figure of Fame is linked to the figure of Fortune, and the dreamer comes to learn that the distribution of fame, like fortune, is random, unequal, and not necessarily based on merit or justice. It is important for the modern reader to realize that fame in the Middle Ages was a Christian concept which proved quite problematic to those poets, clergy, or rulers who desired both earthly fame and spiritual salvation. B. G. Koonce explains that "outwardly the poem conforms to the principles of allegory in combining heterogeneous elements, both pagan and Christian . . . [b]ut informing these details, and relating them on the level of allegory, is a background of moralized mythography which has transformed such pagan images into symbols pertaining to Christian doctrine" (7). (Koonce 1966; Neuse 1991)

See also *Aeneid*; *The Canterbury Tales*; Chaucer, Geoffrey; *The Parlement of Foules*.

"HOWL"

When *Howl and Other Poems* was published in 1956, the 30-year-old poet Allen Ginsberg was catapulted to a place of honor among the "Beat" poets of his generation. Ginsberg's best-known poem, "Howl," is an angry, confessional piece that details the horrors of modern existence through a nightmarish vision of an America full of suffering and hypocrisy. A catalogue of sexual, political, and narcotic rebellion, "Howl" has been interpreted as a loose political allegory indicting America and Americans for the crimes of excessive materialism, conformity, and mechanization leading inevitably toward war. (Hyde 1984)

See also Ginsberg, Allen.

HURSTON, ZORA NEALE

Zora Neale Hurston (1891–1960) was born in the all-black town of Eatonville, Florida. She attended Howard University and Barnard College, where she studied anthropology with Franz Boas and Gladys Reichard. Living in New York in the 1920s, Hurston became a firsthand observer as well as an important participant in the artistic explosion now called the Harlem Renaissance. After graduating from Barnard in 1928, Hurston spent the next several years collecting folklore from her own hometown and other black communities in Florida,

Zora Neale Hurston

Louisiana, and Mississippi. By the mid-1930s she was publishing not only folklore collections but also novels and travel books. Her reputation as a writer peaked when her autobiography, *Dust Tracks on a Road,* was published in 1942. Yet this point marked the beginning of the end of Hurston's widespread acclaim. She soon dropped out of the public eye, partly due to increasing financial troubles. In 1960 Hurston died in Fort Pierce, Florida, and was buried in an unmarked grave in a segregated cemetery. Since her death, however, Hurston's work has enjoyed a remarkable and deeply deserved resurgence in popularity. Her work illustrates the beauty of the folkloric traditions, the complexities of human relationships, and the power of black southern communities.

    See also *Moses, Man of the Mountain.*

HYPONOIA

Hyponoia is the Greek word for the hidden meaning (literally, "underthought") of a myth or fable. The *rhapsodes,* or professional reciter-singers of epic poetry, made a practice of interpreting Homer by uncovering the *hyponoia* in his work. Later the Stoics took up this tradition, and eventually *hyponoia* was associated with *allegoria* or allegory. The practice of finding *hyponoia* in Homer seems to have been based on a need to make the Homeric stories appropriate for educational purposes. (Fletcher 1964; Rollinson 1981)

    See also Allegory; *Homeric Allegories.*

IBSEN, HENRIK

The influential Norwegian playwright Henrik Ibsen (1828–1906) was born of a middle-class family that suffered extreme financial reverses during his childhood. This family situation would be reflected in several of his plays, especially *The Wild Duck.* After studying medicine for a while, Ibsen acted on his desire to become involved in theater, and by 1851 he had been named manager and playwright at the National Theater in Bergen, Norway. Later he spent many years living in other European countries before returning to Norway in 1891. His best-known plays are *An Enemy of the People, Ghosts, A Doll's House, Hedda Gabler, The Master Builder,* and *The Wild Duck,* all of which deal in one way or another with important social issues: marriage, venereal disease, political hypocrisy, the role of women in society, psychological problems, and the plight of those who lose in the game of capitalism. Ibsen insisted always that he was not a didactic playwright, that his intention was to depict the reality of human life—the complexity of relationships, the conflict between social and individual needs—not to convey any social message. Yet students of Ibsen have more often than not concerned themselves with what they have seen as the playwright's ideas as a social commentator rather than with his art or even his talent as a reader of human nature. Some critics have gone so far as to read Ibsen allegorically. We are told by such readers, for instance, that when Nora leaves her husband in *A Doll's House,* she represents the "new woman," that her husband's house is an embodiment of Victorian patriarchy. In *Peer Gynt*—perhaps the most overtly symbolic of his plays—the hero can be seen as a representation of the split between the animal and the higher ideal in human nature, and the play itself as an allegory of that struggle, a kind of modern morality play. Among the realistic plays, *The Wild Duck* has been most susceptible to allegorical readings.

    See also *The Wild Duck.*

ICONOLOGIA

See Ripa, Cesare.

THE IDYLLS OF THE KING

The Idylls of the King (published separately between 1859 and 1885) by Alfred, Lord Tennyson (1809–1892), is a collection of 12 individual stories that relate, in narrative verse, the story of King Arthur and his Knights of the Round Table. Set in fifth-century England, this chivalric romance is a complex poem of good and evil, love and betrayal, honor and courage. Critics have recognized that while *Idylls* defies simple allegorical interpretations, Tennyson does incorporate various allegorical elements into this highly symbolic and influential work.

The Idylls of the King has been read as an allegory in which King Arthur represents the soul of Everyman struggling for good, and the Round Table is an allegorical rendering of the Order that the soul attempts to impose on its world. The eventual collapse of Arthur's Round Table suggests the return to a chaotic, disordered state in the life of both the individual and the society at large. Guinevere has been interpreted as representing the Body, Modred as the cosmic forces of Evil, Merlin as the Intellect, and the Knights as faculties of the Soul. On a more religious level, critics have claimed that the Lady of the Lake is the Church, and Excalibur is the Word of God, thus proposing that *The Idylls of the King* may be read as a primarily Christian allegory incorporating many aspects of biblical scripture. (Priestley 1973; Robinson 1917)

See also Arthurian Allegory; Tennyson, Alfred, Lord.

IN THE HEART OF THE COUNTRY

J. M. Coetzee's 1977 novel *In the Heart of the Country* (published in the United States as *From the Heart of the Country)* has been interpreted by many critics as an allegory of life under apartheid in South Africa. The story consists of 266 numbered entries, written in the form of a diary. The narrator is an unmarried and seemingly unstable woman of indeterminate age named Magda, who lives with her father on an isolated sheep farm. While it is impossible to be certain whether the events Magda describes happen in reality or merely in her own imagination, it seems that Magda becomes jealous of the relationship she believes her father has with one of their servants, Klein-Anna. Magda first imagines that she murders her father and, later, it appears that she actually does kill him. She then tries to dominate Klein-Anna and her husband, Henrik, and when she finds she cannot, she tries to establish a more equal relationship with them. After this also fails, Magda believes that Henrik rapes her and then leaves the farm with his wife. Ultimately, Magda is left alone on the farm to converse with her dead father and communicate with the "sky-gods" who she believes send her messages.

Some critics interpret Magda's story as an allegory of South Africa's fragmented consciousness. This reading suggests that the remote stone farm stands for all of South Africa, Magda's father represents the Afrikaner government, and Magda herself becomes the embodiment of the oppressed black Africans or, in an alternate reading, the ineffectual South African liberal. Finally, *In the*

Heart of the Country becomes an allegory of apartheid, in which the unhealthy psychological states of the characters reflect the unhealthy reality of an apartheid society. (Penner 1989)

See also Coetzee, J. M.; *Foe*; *Waiting for the Barbarians*.

INVISIBLE MAN

This 1952 novel by Ralph Ellison (1914–1994) has become a classic of American literature. The story is narrated by an unnamed African-American man, who lives in a cellar room lighted by 1,369 bulbs. The tone of the narrative in some ways recalls Dostoevsky's *Notes from the Underground* in its emphasis on the narrator's existential loss of social significance. The narrator recalls incidents from his youth in the South, in which he is initiated into the madness of the white world's view of the "Negro" and through which he learns to hide his feelings and his inner identity. Dismissed from his Negro college in the South, the invisible man comes to New York and becomes a leader of the "Brotherhood" until he realizes how he is being used merely as a token black; once again he is made invisible as a man. Regardless of what he engages himself in—employment, black nationalism, women's rights—he finds himself trapped in a mad dream of invisibility.

Surrealistic in its style and events, *Invisible Man* can be seen as a subtle allegory of the dilemma of African Americans in a country that has tended to render them "invisible" as human beings and visible only as race-defined categories of life. Titles by another African-American writer, James Baldwin, refer to the same invisibility; for example: *No Name in the Street*, *Nobody Knows My Name*, and "Stranger in the Village."

See also Ellison, Ralph.

IRVING, JOHN

John Irving (b. 1942), an American novelist and short-story writer, was born in Exeter, New Hampshire, and attended the universities of Pittsburgh, Vienna, New Hampshire, and Iowa. His first three novels, *Setting Free the Bears* (1969), *The Water-Method Man* (1972), and *The 158-Pound Marriage* (1974), gained Irving little critical attention, but his fourth book, *The World According to Garp* (1978), was highly successful. He followed *Garp* with *The Hotel New Hampshire* (1981), *The Cider House Rules* (1985), *A Prayer for Owen Meany* (1989), *A Son of the Circus* (1994), and a collection of short stories and essays called *Trying To Save Piggy Sneed* (1996).

See also *The Hotel New Hampshire*.

JAMES, HENRY

Henry James (1843–1916) was a major American short-story writer and novelist. Born in New York of a distinguished family that included Henry's brother, William, the philosopher, James moved to France and then to England, where he lived until his death. James was a prolific writer. Among his most famous works are *Daisy Miller, Portrait of a Lady, The Bostonians*, and *The Ambassadors*. Although certainly not in the obvious sense a writer of allegory, Henry James does from time to time treat subjects allegorically. Karen Smythe suggests, for example, that the short story "The Jolly Corner," a ghost tale of sorts in which the Jamesian hero, Brydon, confronts his dark double in an abandoned house, is an "allegory of autobiography." Smythe bases this suggestion on the fact that the story on one level "explores the process of figuration, of writing" (375–376). Central to the story, she says, is Brydon's "failure to read" the situation in which he finds himself. Smythe points to "The Altar of the Dead," "The Aspern Papers," and "The Beast in the Jungle" as other Jamesian works that can be seen as allegories of the writing process. In each of these stories the central character fails to "read" his situation clearly. Indeed, these stories might well be considered allegories of allegoresis, the process by which we attempt to read allegories and, according to Paul de Man and others, invariably fail.

Specifically, Smythe sees in "The Jolly Corner" an allegory of the futility of the writer's attempt to write about himself; it "exemplifies the theoretical problems facing a writer whose goal is textual self-construction." That is to say, the main character—the "writer figure"—is unable to face the self-knowledge which an honest acceptance of his other self might provide.

It might be suggested that something of this allegorical approach can be found in what is perhaps James's greatest novel, *The Ambassadors*, which at its deepest level is about the creation of a story by a sensitive—one might even say "writer-figure"—central character. The most dramatic scene in the novel is one in which that character, Lambert Strether, is forced to face a reality in denial of which he has spent the whole novel creating an elaborate but false plot. In this sense Strether resembles Brydon in "The Jolly Corner" and Marcher, the hero of "The Beast in the Jungle"; he discovers too late the self-blinding role of his own personality in the story he has concocted.

In the scene in question, Strether sits comfortably at a riverside table enjoying the view of the idyllic French countryside. He has come here from Paris in a self-congratulatory mood to celebrate his having understood and supported what he sees as the platonic relationship between his young friend Chad Newsome and Madame de Vionnet, a married French woman from whose "clutches" Strether has been sent to France to rescue the young man. Suddenly on the river Strether notices a boat and in it a man and a woman, obviously lovers, who turn out to be his supposedly "virtuous" friends. But what Strether really sees here in this allegorical emblem of adultery is the failure of his reading, the failure of his creative act, and the significant role of his own unseeing and dangerously innocent personality in that failure.

See also Allegoresis; de Man, Paul.

JEAN DE MEUN[G]

See Chopinel, Jean.

JERUSALEM

For the prophets of the Old Testament and Jews in general, the city of Jerusalem is the physical center of being and the spiritual center of the universe. For Christians, Jerusalem has often been treated more allegorically as the bride of Christ or the Church itself. In Revelation 21, Jerusalem comes down to earth "like a bride adorned for her husband." In this light, Christ's entering the literal Jerusalem in the days before his crucifixion takes on an allegorical meaning with several levels. Later, Jerusalem will become an allegory for the Christian Church itself, also the bride of Christ and "our general mother." Thus, the "New Jerusalem"—the symbolic successor to the literal Jerusalem of the Hebrews—becomes an allegory for Christians of what Northrop Frye calls the "home of the soul" and Jesus calls the "Kingdom of God." Many postbiblical writers have made use of this symbolic and allegorical Jerusalem for their own purposes. William Blake, in his visionary poem "Jerusalem," and in the hymn of the same name, saw in the city a symbol of an eternal world of the imagination beyond life as we know it. T. S. Eliot, in "The Waste Land," uses Jerusalem and other great cities ironically, to stand for the demise of civilization. (Frye 1983)

JESUS

See Parable as Allegory.

JOHNSON, BARBARA

The scholar Barbara Johnson (b. 1947), in her study *The Wake of Deconstruction,* includes an essay entitled "Women and Allegory." Starting from Sir Joshua Reynolds's allegorical portrait of Theory as a woman and considering the allegorical use of the female gender in Cesare Ripa's allegorical moral emblems of the 1600s, Johnson pursues the question of the connection between women and allegory, women, like allegory, being "texts" read, categorized, and usually misread primarily by white men. (Johnson 1994)

See also Ripa, Cesare.

JOYCE, JAMES

It is perhaps tempting to read allegory into *Ulysses,* the great modernist novel by the Irish writer James Joyce (1882–1941). As Maureen Quilligan has suggested, the text of the novel is "marked by the kind of verbal self-reflexiveness characteristic of allegory," and by the tendency to "play self-consciously with the process of reading" the novel as it is "read" (284). Yet, as Quilligan also points out, the characters in *Ulysses* tend to take precedence over the "textual emphasis," thus diminishing any allegorical effect.

In short, it seems fair to say that the "quests" of Leopold and Molly Bloom and Stephen Dedalus—the central figures of *Ulysses*—work on the level of the particular rather than the general. We do not see didactic "meaning" in their stories in the sense that we see such meaning in the quests of the Red Crosse Knight of Spenser's *Faerie Queene* or the pilgrim of Bunyan's great allegory, *The Pilgrim's Progress.* (Quilligan 1979)

See also Allegoresis.

KAFKA, FRANZ

Franz Kafka (1883–1924) was a Czech of German-Jewish descent. He wrote in his spare time from his administrative job in a workers' accident insurance institute. Kafka's family life was somewhat difficult. He admired and even idolized his father, who tended to be critical of his son. The father-son conflict became an important theme in Kafka's work. Religion was a major concern. His disillusionment with the concept of a patriarchal and sometimes arbitrary divine power led him to an interest in Jewish mysticism rather than orthodox religion. There was also a disastrous love affair that failed to some extent because of Kafka's indecisiveness, and most important, there was the author's bad health. Tuberculosis took his life at an early age not long after he had finally settled many of his personal problems, become happily associated with a woman he loved, and begun to spend more time at his writing. Few of his works were published during his lifetime, and Kafka even asked his friend Max Brod to burn the unpublished ones after his death. Brod did not obey, and works such as *The Metamorphosis, The Trial, The Castle,* and "The Country Doctor" have made a reputation which places Kafka among the greatest of modernist writers.

Kafka's method is highly symbolic, abstract, expressionistic, and always veiled in irony. His works have a dreamlike quality that suggests the influence of the new interest in the psyche that came with the work of Freud and psychoanalysts of the period. In some ways his novels and short stories can be said to be allegories of the writer's own psychological state, reflecting the despair and loneliness resulting from his sickness, the difficulties in his love life, and the antagonism of his father. On another level, they are prophetic allegories of the modern condition that took concrete form in the totalitarianism that would gradually emerge in Europe after World War I. They convey a sense of isolation and meaninglessness even as the human consciousness within them looks for some understanding of what seems to be an irrational super-bureaucratic and controlling force. On still another related level, Kafka's works are allegories of the human quest for religious understanding. Kafka himself said he wrote in an attempt to "communicate the impossible."

Edwin Honig, Louis MacNeice, and others have pointed to the parable aspect of Kafka's writing, noting, however, that the Kafka hero, although related

Franz Kafka

to the Bunyanesque or Dantesque allegorical questor, is denied any kind of "supernatural grace." Thus in Kafka we move in the direction of existentialism and absurdism.

In *The Trial*, Joseph K., the central character, is on trial, it seems, simply for being Joseph K. The plot of the novel is a nightmare journey through a labyrinthine bureaucracy, the source of which is never revealed, so that K. can never achieve a sense of valid context and, therefore, self-knowledge. The allegory points to Kafka's personal nightmare and to the dilemma of the new existentialist human.

The Castle has much the same effect. This time the "hero," K, has been called to a castle to serve as a land surveyor, but when he gets to the village where the castle is, he can never find the way to it and eventually doubts its reality, even as it determines his life and undermines his identity. In "The Country Doctor" the doctor is similarly controlled by an irrational authority, reflecting again in nightmare mode a modern condition suffused with anxiety, frustration, despair, and the denial of identity.

Perhaps the most allegorical of Kafka's tales is *The Metamorphosis,* in which the central character, Gregor Samsa, a petty bureaucrat whose life has been a colorless trek through daily routine, awakens one morning to find himself a giant bug possessed, nevertheless, of a heightened consciousness. The story follows the gradual deterioration of Gregor's physical situation and a parallel understanding of the reality of his own inner condition and the overall "human condition" for which it is an allegory. (Clifford 1974; Honig 1966; Hunter 1989; MacNeice 1965)

KALILAH AND DIMNAH

See Bidpai.

KEATS, JOHN

The great English Romantic poet John Keats (1795–1821) was born in London of a modest family. Although he studied to be a doctor, Keats knew early on that he was meant to be a poet. In 1818 his first collection of poems was published. The year after that he began work on his allegorical poem, *Endymion.* During the same year he met Fanny Brawne and soon they were engaged. During his courtship Keats wrote his great odes—"Ode on a Grecian Urn," "Ode on Melancholy," "Ode to a Nightingale"—and poems such as "The Eve of St. Agnes" and "La Belle Dame Sans Merci," works which have made his reputation as one of the greatest of poets. Keats's marriage to Fanny Brawne was never to take place and a brilliant career was cut short when the poet died in Rome of tuberculosis at the age of 26.

See also Endymion.

John Keats

KEMPE, MARGERY

See The Book of Margery Kempe.

KESEY, KEN

Ken Kesey was born in Colorado in 1935 and attended the University of Oregon. In the early 1960s he volunteered to participate in drug experiments carried out by the government, including research on the effects of LSD. Nationally known for his flamboyant cross-country capers with Neal Cassady and "the Merry Pranksters" and his fondness for LSD and other hallucinogenic drugs, Kesey became both a cult hero of the 1960s and a well-respected writer. His first novel, the somewhat allegorical *One Flew over the Cuckoo's Nest* (1962), draws on Kesey's experiences as an aide in a psychiatric ward of a veterans' hospital. The popular novel was admired by both the critics and the public and was eventually turned into a successful film and a stage play. Kesey's more recent works, including *Sometimes a Great Notion* (1964), *Kesey's Garage Sale* (1973), *Demon Box* (1986), and *Sailor Song* (1993), have not managed to rival the widespread popularity of *Cuckoo's Nest*.

See also One Flew over the Cuckoo's Nest.

KING, STEPHEN

Stephen King (b. 1947) has become arguably one of the most popular American fiction writers of this century. While many conventional critics play down King's literary contributions, others have discovered in King's works meaningful social commentary and important allegorical elements. Two of King's works, written under the pseudonym Richard Bachman, may be interpreted as particularly effective allegorical pieces. Both "The Long Walk" and "The Running Man" incorporate biting political and social criticism into the author's frightening vision of America's future.

"The Long Walk," a story of a marathon in which participants walk until they can no longer keep pace and are then executed, offers a vision of a society so dehumanized by government forces and violent lifestyles that people can no longer meaningfully connect with those around them. The walkers in the marathon represent a microcosm of society at large; they come from diverse economic, social, racial, and religious backgrounds, and each symbolizes a particular archetype (the parasite, the loner, etc.). With the exception of the protagonist, Ray Garrity, they all live their lives believing that to help another is to harm oneself. The spectators are bloodthirsty and cruel, the walkers are victimized by the system that traps them, and the overall triviality of the deadly marathon allegorizes the ruthless competitiveness of our own political and corporate worlds.

"The Running Man" also depicts the cruelty of a desensitized and dehumanized society. In this story, a man desperate for money to save his dying child volunteers to compete on one of many game shows that entertain the American public by mutilating or killing the participants. The hero must hide for 30 days from both the police and a team of professional bounty hunters whose job it is to find and kill him as quickly as possible. The television audience supports and abets the hunters and demonstrates virtually no compassion for the hunted. "The Running Man" allegorizes the complacency of the wealthy, the cruelty of the average citizen, and the occasional humanity of the downtrodden and victimized in this shocking representation of a thoroughly sinister America.

Other stories by Stephen King may also be recognized as allegorizing certain aspects of society. For example, "Thinner" may allegorize a corrupt and unjust political system through its portrayal of a highly connected lawyer who attempts to escape the consequences of killing a gypsy woman. And in novels such as *The Stand,* the ancient struggle between Good and Evil is re-created in the barren landscape of a world decimated by an apocalyptic plague. (D'Amassa 1985)

KING JOHN

King John, or *Kynge Johan* (written prior to 1536) has become the best-known work by English playwright John Bale (1495–1563) and was the first morality play used to support Protestant purposes. *King John* combines aspects of the well-established form of the morality play (such as abstract allegorical characters) with elements of the historical play soon to be made popular by Christopher Marlowe and William Shakespeare.

The complicated story, encompassing a large cast of characters, is a scathing attack on the Church of Rome. Taking some liberties with historical events, Bale portrays King John not as knave (as previous dramatists had done) but as a virtuous protector of the English realm from the viciousness of the Church of Rome. Combining moral didacticism with the dramatization of historical events, Bale equates Sedition with Stephen Langton, Private Wealth with Cardinal Pandulphus, and Usurped Power with the Pope. King John becomes the allegorical representative of the ideal monarch, answerable only to God; the widow England appeals to him for protection against the Catholic clergy, who have driven her husband, God, into exile. At the end of the play, after the death of King John, a character called Imperial Majesty (Henry VIII) arrives to crush the evil Church of Rome and, with the help of Nobility and Clergy, save the widow England. (McCusker 1971)

See also Morality Plays.

KIPLING, RUDYARD

Rudyard Kipling (1865–1936) was born in Bombay, India, to British parents and was sent to private school in England, with his sister, when he was six

Little Toomai is lifted to meet the gaze of the elephant catcher Petersen Sahib in the first edition of Rudyard Kipling's *The Jungle Book,* published in 1894.

years old. He returned to his family in India when he was 17, and worked there for seven years as a newspaper reporter and writer. He returned to England in 1889 and established himself as a writer in London. In 1892 he married Caroline Balestier, an American woman, and lived in Vermont, near her family, until 1896. During this time he wrote *The Jungle Book* (1894) and *The Second Jungle Book* (1895). The Kiplings then returned to England, and his most famous novel, *Kim*, was published in 1901. He continued to write collections of short stories for adults for the rest of his life, including *Traffics and Discoveries* (1904) and *A Diversity of Creatures* (1917). In 1907, Kipling became the first English writer to receive the Nobel Prize for Literature.

See also "Below the Mill-Dam."

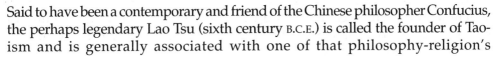

LA FONTAINE, JEAN DE

La Fontaine (1621–1695) was a French writer of ballads, plays, and especially of *Fables choisies, mis en vers [Selected Fables in Verse]*, and the more licentious *Contes et nouvelles en vers [Short Tales in Verse]*. He was generally thought to be a vagabond and parasite who neglected his wife. His wit, however, and his poetry were greatly appreciated, and he was elected to the French Academy in 1683. La Fontaine's fables are allegorical pieces—often beast stories—which are derived directly from the classical fables of Aesop and the Indian ones of Bidpai (Pilpay). What he brought to the tradition was a great facility with verse.

See also Aesop; Bidpai; Fable as Allegory.

LANGLAND, WILLIAM

Very little is known about the life of William Langland (ca. 1330–1387), other than what details can be deduced from his long religious allegory, *The Vision of Piers Plowman*. It seems that Langland came from western England, probably the Malvern Hills area, and that he was familiar with life in London. Scholars speculate that because of his extensive knowledge of the Scriptures he might have intended to become a clergyman; however, through marriage and/or lack of preferment, he was reduced to poverty and never officially entered the church.

See also Piers Plowman.

LAO TSU

Said to have been a contemporary and friend of the Chinese philosopher Confucius, the perhaps legendary Lao Tsu (sixth century B.C.E.) is called the founder of Taoism and is generally associated with one of that philosophy-religion's primary texts, the *Tao te Ching*. The other great text is the *Chuang-tsu*, by the philosopher Chuang Chou (fourth century B.C.E.). Both of these works, like most Chinese philosophical writing, make extensive use of parable and allegory. Often these parables and allegories are brief and to the point; there is little of the Western tendency to give way to the enjoyment of the story itself for its own sake, as, for instance, in Aesop or La Fontaine. For instance, Taoism preaches the *Tao* (the "Way"), which in the *Tao te Ching* (IV) is compared allegorically to an "empty vessel" that, nevertheless, can always "be drawn from" without ever needing to be refilled: "It is bottomless; the very progenitor of all things in the world." (Eliade 1977)

LARKIN, PHILIP

Critics have always discovered allegory in the work of British poet Philip Larkin (1922–1985). John Reibetanz has argued that the basis of Larkin's allegorical approach is the conscious separation of form from content in his poetry. Such separation necessarily focuses our attention on meaning rather than on what might be called primary reality. A good example of the allegorical approach is found in the poem "Toads," which begins:

> Why should I let the toad work
> Squat on my life?
> Can't I use my wit as a pitchfork
> And drive the brute off?

Obviously this is not a poem about a toad; it is about what the toad represents and is, thus, allegorical. (Reibetanz 1982)

LAWRENCE, D. H.

In a work called *Apocalypse*, the English novelist D. H. Lawrence (1885–1930) differentiates between symbol and allegory: "Symbols mean something; yet they mean something different to every man. Fix the meaning of a symbol and you have fallen into the commonplace of allegory" (60). In this comment Lawrence takes the typically anti-allegory view of many modernists and implicitly condemns the frequent attempts among critics to read allegories into his work. For Lawrence, Virginia Woolf, James Joyce, and many of the other great modernists, a symbol—for example, the lighthouse in Woolf's *To the Lighthouse*—adds complexity and the beauty of ambiguity to a text. Allegory—the attaching of specific meanings for a didactic purpose, allowing meaning to take precedence over integrity of form—is for many modernists an inferior kind of literature. (Lawrence 1932)

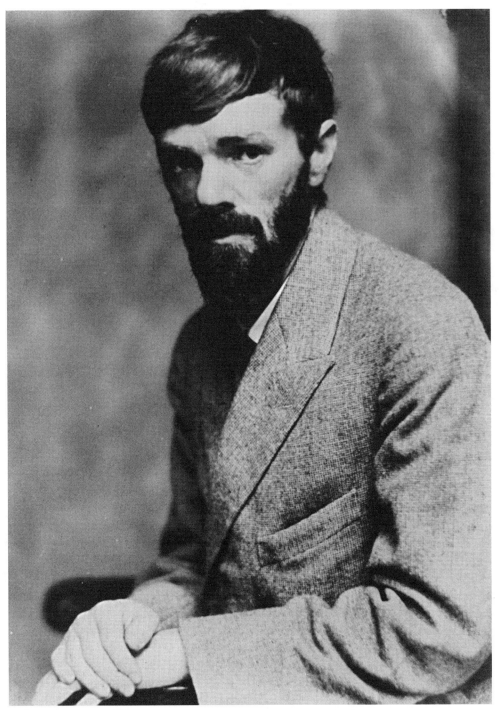

D. H. Lawrence

LEWIS, C. S.

Clive Staples Lewis (1898–1963), literary scholar, Christian apologist, and writer of fantasy fiction for children and adults, is often described as a Christian allegorist. Lewis was born in Belfast, privately educated as a child, attended University College, Oxford; served in and was wounded in World War I; and became a professor of English studies at Magdalen College, Oxford. With his friend J. R. R. Tolkien he was part of a private literary society called The Inklings.

It is in *The Allegory of Love* that Lewis establishes himself as an important theorist of allegory. In this work he develops the idea that as the human became gradually more philosophical during the classical and medieval periods, turning increasingly to inner dialogue, allegory emerged as a tendency for expression. It was primarily on medieval allegory that Lewis focused his attention in *The Allegory of Love*. He stressed his belief that medieval allegory was a "form of expression" through which the writer could use fiction to embody the "internal battles" between good and evil that concerned the Christian, as opposed to the external battles that concerned, for example, Homer.

Lewis's theories are themselves fictionalized in works such as the adult space trilogy that begins with the novel *Out of the Silent Planet*, and the children's series, the *Chronicles of Narnia*. In these works we find somewhat naïve heroes, blind to the truly "real" world that is contained in the science fiction or fantasy worlds they visit. In a sense, the stories become records of allegoresis, of the heroes' gradual "reading" of the allegory in which they find themselves. In every case, the essence of the world visited is the struggle between the forces of good and the forces of evil.

There are those who argue that to read fantasy as allegory is to confuse allegory with symbolism, and Lewis might well have agreed with them. He denied any allegorical intention in his work but did not deny the symbolic element. In *The Allegory of Love*, Lewis distinguished allegory, with its one-to-one object-belief arrangement, from symbolism, which begins with the great mysteries and attempts to find archetypal expression for them. Thus, Good Deeds in *Everyman* is allegorical, but the grave scene in *Hamlet* is symbolic.

The question for the student of allegory reading Lewis, then, is whether Aslan, the "Lion King" in the Narnia chronicles, for example, is allegorical or symbolic. Does he represent Jesus, or is he a symbolic representation of an archetype—of something we might call wholeness? Are the space trilogy and the Narnia series collectively a mask for Christian dogma, or are they symbolic of the less-definable archetypal quest for self-knowledge that transcends Christianity?

The answer to these questions would seem to be sometimes one thing and sometimes the other. When, in the first book of the Narnia chronicles, a family of English children enters the fantasyland of Narnia by way of a wardrobe, we are not necessarily led to a Christian understanding of their action. We do, however, experience an archetypal sense of movement from one kind of reality to a somehow truer one. Yet, when the children witness the terrible sacrifice of Aslan and his resurrection, it is difficult not to think allegorically in the Christian mode. Lewis was committed to his Christian beliefs and was, at the same time, a writer with great evocative abilities who attempted to be loyal to what his friend J. R. R. Tolkien called the "inner consistency of reality" in a fantasy text. Perhaps it would be fair to say that for Lewis the quest for self-knowledge could ultimately only be by way of Christianity and, therefore, not surprisingly, the writer and apologist—the symbolist and the allegorist—sometimes clash in his works. (MacNeice 1965; Matheson 1988; Piehler 1971; Quilligan 1979)

See also The Allegory of Love; The Chronicles of Narnia; The Space Trilogy.

THE LIFE AND DEATH OF MR. BADMAN

An allegorical dialogue by John Bunyan (1628–1688), *The Life and Death of Mr. Badman* illustrates what happens to unrepentant sinners who live a life of evil and depravity. The work takes the form of a dialogue between two Puritans: Mr. Wiseman and Mr. Attentive; the former explains to the latter the events of the recently deceased Mr. Badman's despicable life. It seems that even as a child, Mr. Badman was thoroughly bad. This badness progressed, as sin begets sin, and at the time of his death, his sins included lying, stealing, cheating, swearing, whoring, drinking, adultery, hypocrisy, and many others. Each new mention of a particular sin in Mr. Badman's life elicits a kind of sermon from one of the men, using examples from literature and scripture to depict the tragedies that inevitably befall such sinners. Mr. Badman neither repented during his lifetime nor met with devastating tragedies while he was alive; indeed, for some time he was rather prosperous. But for Bunyan, Mr. Wiseman, and many readers of the seventeenth century, Mr. Badman's infinitely peaceful death, "like a lamb, or, as men call it, a chrisom child, quietly and without fear," meant certain damnation. Ultimately, Bunyan's moral allegory was intended not as an unusual or extreme example of one man's evil lifestyle, but as a warning to the many living relatives of Mr. Badman's, in every town and household, to mend their erring ways and repent their sins. (Wakefield 1992)

See also Bunyan, John; The Holy War; The Pilgrim's Progress.

THE LIFE OF CORIOLANUS

The Life of Coriolanus is one of the famous *Lives* of the Greek biographer Plutarch or Plutarchos (ca. 46–ca. 120 C.E.). Plutarch spent most of his life as a priest of Apollo but visited the great cities of his time—Athens, Rome, and Alexandria. Plutarch's brief biographies of such figures as Julius Caesar, Antony and Cleopatra, and Coriolanus, which were translated into English by Thomas North in 1579, served as source material for later writers, most notably William Shakespeare. Plutarch was not an allegorical writer, but *The Life of Coriolanus* does contain allegorical material. Coriolanus himself is held up as a representation of the Roman ideal of *virtus*. In a series of wars he bravely fights for his countrymen but runs into trouble when he denies what seem to us now the legitimate demands of the masses. Forced into exile by the people, Coriolanus joins the old enemies of Rome and is finally murdered by the jealous among his new allies.

Allegory plays a role in the story when Fortune is invoked by Coriolanus's mother in her successful attempt to dissuade him from attacking his country. In return for the mother's work, the Romans decree that a temple of Fortune be erected and the women of Coriolanus's family build a statue to her. Many stories were told of Fortune's speaking to the people. Through the work of Coriolanus's mother, good Fortune comes to Rome. (Benet 1965)

See also Fortuna.

THE LIGHT PRINCESS

This fantasy for children by George MacDonald (1824–1905) has a definite allegorical side to it. Much of the allegory centers on the meanings of the word "light." The story tells of a young princess who is weightless and, therefore, in danger of floating off on the slightest wind. Her condition is the result of a curse put on her by her wicked aunt, the princess Makemnoit (an allegorical name over which children may puzzle). The little princess's lightness seems to extend to her mental and emotional life as well; she is, in short, "flighty," to put her condition in the best light.

As in most fairy tales—and this story is told very much in the fairy tale mode—it is up to a potential mate to free the bewitched hero or heroine. In this case, a prince arrives—handsome and anything but a lightweight. After various trials and tribulations he is able to free the princess by means of his love for her. That is, his love stimulates love within her and she loses both her physical and emotional weightlessness.

The allegory here would seem to suggest that through love we are able to overcome the meaninglessness and lack of substance in our lives.

See also Lilith; MacDonald, George.

"THE LIGHTNING-ROD MAN"

See Melville, Herman.

LILITH

This most important of the fantasies of George MacDonald (1824–1905) was greatly admired by C. S. Lewis and J. R. R. Tolkien and influenced their work as well as that of later fantasy writers. The central figures in *Lilith* are the student narrator, who is drawn magically into a dreamworld worthy of Kafka or

Freud, and the dominant character in that world, the strange Lilith, the first wife of Adam. The young man is an everyman and Lilith is the trial through which we must pass to achieve self-knowledge. But *Lilith* is a symbolic novel rather than an allegorical one. To attribute allegorical meaning to characters and incidents is to deprive this novel of its mystery and symbolic power. This is a novel about the power of love to redeem, about the need to enter into the inner world of danger and great beauty.

See also *The Light Princess*; MacDonald, George.

LORD OF THE FLIES

William Golding (1911–1993) was a British novelist whose first novel, *Lord of the Flies* (1954), has frequently been interpreted as containing elements of religious, political, social, and psychological allegory.

Set sometime in the future, *Lord of the Flies* tells the story of a group of young British boys (aged six to twelve) who, after being evacuated from an atomically war-torn England, are marooned on a lush deserted island. There, this group of youngsters faces the challenge of creating for themselves an orderly and just society without the guidance or interference of the adult world. At first, the boys are enthralled with the idyllic possibilities of their island life. But soon their group becomes divided, and many of the boys regress from the "civilized" behavior of society to the barbarous, irrational actions of a pack of animals. By the time they are "rescued" by the British navy, most of the boys have become bloodthirsty creatures, worshipping a symbolic "Beast" and murdering their own kind in savage ecstasy. The boat-shaped island suggests that the boys' experiences may typify the journey that all people must take from innocence (or ignorance) to some understanding of human nature.

Lord of the Flies may be recognized as religiously allegorical in that the boys' story may represent the Christian story of Original Sin. The boys find themselves alone in a natural paradise—an Edenic island—which is uncorrupted by human contact. The imagined "snake-thing" which some of the children fear is present on the island suggests the beginning of their ultimate corruption. Soon Ralph, the protagonist of the tale, is identified to the reader as a sort of good-intentioned "everyman," the red-haired and physically unattractive Jack allegorizes the Devil, and the introspective, gentle Simon becomes a prophetic Christ-figure who is mercilessly sacrificed at the hands of Jack and his followers. This story of human depravity and Christian sin continues in the boys' idolatrous worship of the Beast, the "Lord of the Flies" (a translation of the Hebrew Ba'al zevuv—"Beelzebub" in Greek, the Lord of Filth and Dung), an allegorical representation of ubiquitous evil.

The boys' situation has also been interpreted as a "political nightmare" in which the forces of rational democracy are overthrown by an irrational dictatorship. In this interpretation, the boys' actions represent the large-scale actions of the nations of the world. Ralph, with the rationally thinking Piggy by his side, represents democracy; Jack, with the cruel henchman Roger, represents demonic authoritarianism. In their microcosmic life on the island, the boys allegorically re-create the actions of warring nations through their acts of crafty deception, aggressive intimidation, and barbaric "man-hunting." In this way, *Lord of the Flies* may be seen as representing on some level the alarming rise of fascism and anti-intellectualism.

Socially, *Lord of the Flies* allegorizes the idea that life without "civilization" becomes brutish and cruel. This allegorical interpretation recognizes that the boys' regression from socially acceptable patterns of behavior and subsequent savagery parallel the inevitable degeneration of society when social boundaries become blurred or erased.

Psychologically, *Lord of the Flies* may be read as an allegory of the Freudian aspects of the psyche as represented by three of the main characters. In this reading, Jack appears as the id, representing animal desires; Ralph is the ego, trying to maintain some rational balance; and Piggy becomes the superego, the conscience of the adult world. (Baker 1988; Cox 1962; Hynes 1988; Johnston 1980; Oldsey 1965)

See also Golding, William.

THE LORD OF THE RINGS

Although J. R. R. Tolkien himself denied any allegorical intention in his work, many readers have tended to see in *The Lord of the Rings*, in particular, a complex allegorical structure. For such readers the struggle between the forces allied with the King and his city—including Frodo and the people of the Shire—and those infected by the dark power of Sauron and the ring is an allegory of the confrontation between the Allied and the Axis powers in World War II. A secondary level of allegory, involving the same two sides, would be the universal struggle between good and evil in the universe with ordinary people—represented by Frodo and the Shire—caught between the warring factions and called upon to declare themselves. Thus, the Wizard Gandalf and the disguised king, Strider, convince Frodo that he must destroy the ring that is the potential source of total evil in the world. Again, it is important to note Tolkien's denial—certainly of the first level. The second level seems more likely, as it grows directly out of the situation in the novel in which the Hobbit-hero Frodo must wrestle with the conflicting calls of evil and goodness represented by the beings he meets on his ring journey and by the ring itself, which attracts him even as he is called upon to destroy it for the good of humanity.

That *The Lord of the Rings* is not true allegory, however, is indicated by the fact that we are invariably held by the tale itself—by what Tolkien would call the "inner consistency of reality" within the fantasy world that is presented—rather than by any secondary meaning. (Hunter 1989)

See also Tolkien, J. R. R.

LUCIAN

Lucian or Loukianos (120–200 C.E.) was a Greek writer whose travel satire, *The Voracious History*, has often been seen as an ancestor of such later works as Voltaire's *Candide* and Swift's *Gulliver's Travels*.

LYLY, JOHN

John Lyly (1554–1606) received his M.A. from Oxford, went to London, and shortly thereafter published his first book, *Euphues* (1578). It was an instant success, and as a result Lyly gained the patronage of Queen Elizabeth I's lord treasurer. Lyly spent the greater part of the next decades writing plays for the entertainment of the queen and her court; many of these works have been identified by scholars as being, on some level, allegorical. Five of Lyly's comedies that have been so identified are *Campapse* (1584), *Sapho and Phao* (1584), *Gallathea* (1585), *Endimion* (1591), and *Love's Metamorphosis* (1601). Of these, *Endimion* is perhaps the most frequently anthologized play, and therefore the one most deserving of close attention.

See also Endimion.

 # MCCARTHY, CORMAC

See Paysage Moralisé.

 # MACDONALD, GEORGE

MacDonald (1824–1905) was a Scottish writer of fantasy both for children *(At the Back of the North Wind, The Light Princess, The Princess and the Goblin)* and for adults *(Lilith, Phantases)*. Born into a farmer's family in Aberdeenshire, MacDonald studied chemistry and natural philosophy before going on to become a Congregationalist minister. In his mid-twenties, however, he gave up his ministry to devote his full time to writing. He wrote poetry *(Within and Without)*, sermons, and popular novels about the life of Scots country people, in addition to the children's books and adult fantasies for which he is better known now. MacDonald achieved great popularity in his lifetime and was friendly with Tennyson and Lewis Carroll, among other literary greats, and was much admired by C. S. Lewis and J. R. R. Tolkien. Lewis describes his work as standing somewhere "between the allegorical and the mythopoetic." It seems accurate to describe MacDonald's fantasies as symbolic fictions that lack the one-to-one connection between object and idea that tends to characterize allegory proper. (MacNeice 1965)

See also The Light Princess; Lilith.

 # MACNEICE, LOUIS

In his *Varieties of Parable*, the British poet Louis MacNeice (1907–1963) traces the relationship between parable and allegory through Spenser and Bunyan to the Romantics and Victorians and moderns.

See also Parable as Allegory.

MACQUEEN, JOHN

In *Allegory* (1970), MacQueen studies the development of allegory from its philosophic and religious origins. He is concerned primarily with classical, biblical, and medieval allegory and with the relation of allegory to myth and to satire.

THE MAGIC MOUNTAIN

Published in 1924, *Der Zauberberg [The Magic Mountain]* is the most philosophical and perhaps most allegorical novel by Thomas Mann (1875–1955). The story takes place in a sanatorium on a mountain in Switzerland, where a young engineer, Hans Castorp, has gone to visit his cousin, Joachim. Once there, Hans realizes that on the "magic" mountain, ordinary time does not exist. He had intended to visit for a few days but he remains on the mountain for seven years of ordinary time. While there he finds himself pulled by two opposing forces, represented by the various characters at the sanatorium—the force of reason and that of decadence. At one point, lost in the snow, Hans has a vision of a beautiful temple surrounded by enlightened people, but inside the temple two hags are devouring a child. In the end Hans leaves the mountain and enters the trenches of World War I.

What is important about this novel is not the plot but the allegorical significance of the characters and incidents. The sanatorium, which is filled with people of the various nationalities of Europe, is Europe and Western civilization on the brink of World War I. That it is a sanatorium suggests both disease and decadence and the hope of a cure. The mountain itself stands for the aspirations of the higher life as opposed to the decadence in the world below. Characters such as the head doctor represent reason and healthy activity. Characters such as Clavdia, the woman with whom Hans falls in love, and the assistant doctor represent depravity and the unreason of the occult. Various specific ideologies are also represented. There is an Italian humanist, a hedonist, an absolutist who is somehow a Jewish Jesuit, a scientist, and so forth. The temple in the vision with the devouring women within stands for the ambiguity of beauty and art. Much the same allegory is perhaps contained in the figure of the beautiful but flawed Tazio in Mann's *Death in Venice*. When Hans returns to the "real" world and "real" time below, we understand that he returns to the "real" Europe of World War I.

See also Mann, Thomas; *Paysage Moralisé*.

MAGIC REALISM AND ALLEGORY

Magic realism is a form of fiction characterized by a surrealistic exaggeration of events and a great deal of local color. It is associated particularly with South

American novelists such as Isabel Allende *(House of the Spirits)* (1982) and most particularly Gabriel García Márquez (b. 1928). García Márquez would not call his work allegorical, but the evident symbolism of any surrealistic work suggests allegory in particular scenes and situations. In one memorable scene in Márquez's most famous novel, *One Hundred Years of Solitude,* there is a patriarch who serves up his rival for dinner. In another scene the same patriarch has overslept but cannot admit that he has done so. That what he would like to be morning is really afternoon is unacceptable to him. So, to restore the balance of things servants have to stand outside his windows during the night holding up cardboard cutouts of the sun. These scenes suggest the absurdity—the reversal of reality—in a social system marked by public corruption and private despair.

MAGNYFYCENCE

Magnyfycence is a secular morality play written in 1515 by John Skelton (1460–1529). It is an allegory whose protagonist is Magnyfycence, a representation of magnificence and of the playwright's patron, Henry VIII. Also in the play are characters called Felycyte (Felicity), Lyberte (Liberty), and Measure. These characters are countered by Counterfet Countenance (disguised as Sure Surveyance), Crafty Conveyance (disguised as Good Demeanance), Clokyd Colusyon (disguised as Sober Sadness), and Courtly Abusyon (disguised as Lusty Pleasure). The latter four represent the kind of politics prevalent in Renaissance courts. Magnyfycence loses power and happiness because he listens to them, but regains both with the help of Redresse, Circumspeccyon, and Perseverance. There are lessons in this allegory for Renaissance monarchs.

See also Morality Plays.

THE MAHABHARATA

The great Indian epic *The Mahabharata* has been in a state of continuous composition since the fifth century B.C.E. or earlier. It is a composite of myths, legends, poems, sermons, rules for the various classes, and long philosophical digressions, of which the famous *Bhagavad Gita* is one. Traditionally the author of the epic is one Vyasa (the "reviser"), whose actual existence is at least as questionable as Homer's. The central story of *The Mahabharata* is that of the struggle between the Kaurava family, whose actions suggest that they are the allegorical representation of evil, and the Pandavas, who, though flawed, are just as clearly representative of goodness and right action. The Kauravas are nominally led by the king Dhritarashtra, whose blindness marks him as the representative of ignorance.

In the long and destructive war between the two families, the world in a sense comes to an end and the ultimately victorious Pandavas—those favored of the gods—are finally reunited in heaven. At the deepest level, this war is an allegory of the nearly impossible quest for order in the face of inevitable chaos within the universe and ourselves.

But the most important allegory in *The Mahabharata* is to be found in the section known to us as the *Bhagavad Gita*. In this section, the Pandava warrior Arjuna questions the value of a destructive war with the Kauravas. Allegorically he questions the value of the endless struggle against evil. He is answered by his charioteer, who is Krishna, the greatest incarnation of the god Vishnu. As the Lord Krishna, the charioteer is the eternal Truth within us all, the chariot being the body. And as the potential but questioning warrior, Arjuna is everyman's soul in which the inner war takes place between good and evil. Krishna's urging him to fight represents the call of conscience, or the spirit within, to do what is right even if it is difficult and painful.

See also Bhagavad Gita; Epic as Allegory.

MAILER, NORMAN

Norman Mailer (b. 1923) was raised in Brooklyn and educated at Harvard. His service in World War II provided him with material to create his first novel, *The Naked and the Dead* (1948), a bitter war story and harsh commentary on American values. It was highly acclaimed as a war novel, and made Mailer an internationally famous writer.

Mailer's second novel, *Barbary Shore* (1951), has been interpreted as an allegory of politics as well as an allegory of life, death, and rebirth. The major conflict in the novel is between Hollingsworth, an FBI agent, and McLeod, a subversive Marxist theoretician. In a political context, Hollingsworth allegorically represents capitalism, McLeod is Bolshevism, Lannie and Lovett portray Trotskyism, and Guinevere represents the masses. In a more spiritual vein, McLeod allegorizes the savior who must be sacrificed so that others may be transformed and delivered from forces of evil.

Mailer's other works have also been recognized as containing allegorical elements. Begiebing argues that *The Deer Park* (1955), *An American Dream* (1965), *Why Are We in Vietnam?* (1967), *The Armies of the Night* (1968), and other works continue to expand Mailer's symbolic depictions of Life versus Death and Good versus Evil by allegorically connecting the journey of the individual soul to the journey of America. Mailer reveals his vision of a fragmented America through his heroes' quests for regeneration, existential growth, and the discovery of the true self. (Begiebing 1980)

MALORY, SIR THOMAS

Malory (1408–1471) is the English writer known primarily for the prose collection of Arthurian romances called *Le Morte d'Arthur* (1469). Malory, who was a member of Parliament, wrote the work while in prison for political offenses.

See also Le Morte d'Arthur.

THE MAN WHO WAS THURSDAY: A NIGHTMARE

This 1908 second novel of the writer G. K. Chesterton (1874–1936) is a fantasy-adventure tale about a conspiratorial council of seven European anarchists, each named for a day of the week, led by the mysterious man called Sunday. An English poet/policeman named Gabriel Syme is elected to the position of Thursday, and embarks on a bizarre adventure that leads to the discovery that all the supposed anarchist-conspirators are actually police detectives in disguise. Eventually, the exposed councilors pursue Sunday back to his garden estate, demanding to know his identity and the ultimate meaning of their council. Sunday is revealed to be an official of Scotland Yard, but in Chesterton's allegory he becomes, donned in a pure white gown, the sanctity of the Sabbath. His lecture to the other "days" on the holiness of Sunday has led critics to interpret the novel as a religious allegory that portrays order arising out of chaos and connects each man to the biblical interpretations of his day of the week. (Hunter 1979; Wills 1987)

See also Chesterton, G. K.

MANN, THOMAS

German novelist and Nobel laureate Thomas Mann (1875–1955) was concerned in his life and work with the struggle in art and life between Apollonian order and Dionysian inspiration. He was fascinated by the good and bad sides of both. In *Death in Venice*, for instance, he places a bourgeois writer who worships Apollonian self-control in a situation that brings out his suppressed Dionysian side and leads him to a tragic end. In *The Magic Mountain*, he concerns himself with the same duality in the context of the soul of Europe as a whole.

See also The Magic Mountain.

MANSFIELD PARK

This 1814 novel by Jane Austen (1775–1817) tells the story of Fanny Price, a young girl who leaves her poor family to join the household of her wealthy uncle, Sir Thomas Bertram. Although snubbed or ignored by most of the Bertrams, Fanny develops an attachment to her cousin Edmund, who treats her kindly. When Henry and Mary Crawford arrive in the village, they introduce vain and jaded city attitudes to the inhabitants of Mansfield Park. Edmund becomes fond of Mary, arousing the jealousy of his cousin Fanny. Julia and Maria Bertram vie for Henry's attention, but he falls in love with Fanny, who rejects his proposal. Maria marries a Mr. Rushworth, a rich man whom she does not love. Sir Thomas, angry with Fanny for rejecting Henry, urges her to accept Henry for her husband. Unable to please her uncle, Fanny returns to her parents' home for a visit. While there, she hears that Maria and Henry have run away together and are "living in sin." Mary's lack of concern upon hearing this shocking news alerts Edmund to her true moral character and he finally recognizes that Fanny is the right woman for him. They marry and live happily at the parsonage near Mansfield Park.

N. W. Miller has suggested that *Mansfield Park* may be read as a moral allegory depicting the virtues of a truly moral life and demonstrating the importance of avoiding spiritual sloth. Certain characters in *Mansfield Park* embody, to varying degrees, the Seven Deadly Sins (Sloth, Lust, Anger, Pride, Envy, Gluttony, and Greed). Through these depictions, and frequent allusions to Milton's *Paradise Lost,* Austen illustrates the necessity of living an actively moral life. To this end, Dr. Grant and young Tom represent gluttony; Mrs. Norris and Maria represent pride and greed; Lady Bertram embodies sloth; Edmund, Maria, Henry, and, to a lesser degree, Fanny demonstrate lust; and Julia personifies envy and anger. All the characters, to some extent, embody spiritual sloth. Even Fanny, the heroine of the novel and the most virtuous person at Mansfield Park, suffers initially from a sort of passive morality which could be considered slothful. But in the end, Fanny is rewarded for her moral improvement and more active morality, and others in the household undergo similar moral metamorphoses when they recognize and correct their sinful behaviors. Thus, Austen's novel becomes on one level a didactic moral lesson in which the virtuous are compensated and the sinful are punished. (Miller 1992)

See also Austen, Jane.

THE MARBLE FAUN

Critics have demonstrated that Nathaniel Hawthorne's last romance novel, *The Marble Faun* (1860), may be read as an allegory on several different levels. For example, critic Paul Lister suggests that the story is "an allegorical representation of Christ's redemption of mankind from Satan" (79). In this story of salvation, Kenyon represents God, Hilda is the Holy Spirit, Donatello represents Jesus Christ, Miriam becomes mankind, and the model is Satan.

Kenyon's allegorical representation of God is founded primarily on his role as a sculptor. Like the Creator who formed the first man out of clay, Kenyon fashions a clay version of his statue, and then delegates the actual carving to subordinates. Symbols of the Holy Spirit, especially the traditional symbol of the dove, are associated with Hilda throughout the novel. She lives in a high tower her associates call the "Dove-Cote," and she herself is actually referred to as "the Dove." The beautiful Donatello, an allegorical representation of Jesus Christ, is closely linked to Miriam, the woman of unknown ancestry who comes to represent mankind. Donatello exacts Miriam's "salvation" through his murder of the model, and the guilt he experiences as a result forges a bond between them. After Donatello and Miriam commit their "sin," their relationships with Kenyon and Hilda are abruptly and permanently severed, recalling the severed relationship between God and man after the Original Sin. Finally, the model allegorizes Satan in his perpetual stalking of Miriam (mankind), his shrinking from the torchlight in the catacombs (divine presence and grace), and his profound resemblance to the painting of the Demon in the Church of the Capuchins.

Other allegorical interpretations of *The Marble Faun* have focused on the idea of innocence before the Fall (Donatello as an animal innocent of knowledge, Hilda as an angel innocent of evil), as well as the allegorical myths to which the characters' identities are closely linked. (Johnson 1981; Lister 1978)

See also Hawthorne, Nathaniel; *The Scarlet Letter.*

MARDI

Herman Melville's difficult novel *Mardi* (1849) was a great disappointment to many fans of the popular travel narratives *Typee* (1846) and *Omoo* (1847). Consciously trying to distance himself from these "sailor yarns," Melville crafted *Mardi* as a satirical allegory perhaps meant to attack various social ills attributed to modern Western life. The story traces the adventures of the first-person narrator, an American sailor, who encounters a series of fantastic and highly allegorical characters on the islands of the imaginary Mardian archipelago in the Pacific.

Critics have interpreted the allegorical implications of *Mardi* in a number of different ways. Some emphasize the sociopolitical aspects of the novel, citing Melville's descriptions of many of the Pacific island cultures as thinly veiled commentary on various nations in the Western world. Cindy Weinstein interprets *Mardi* as an allegory of the industrializing trends of mid–nineteenth-century America, in that the novel reflects America's anxiety toward a "developing and increasingly mechanized market economy" (240), and that characters such as Oh-Oh and Jiji "come to be allegorical by virtue of their role within the market economy" (249). Stephen de Paul explains that *Mardi* may also be understood as a study of colonial power insofar as the novel may be read as an "allegory of America in its era of Manifest Destiny" (181).

Other critics choose to highlight the religious or philosophical implications of Melville's allegory. In this context, the beautiful white maiden Yillah may represent heavenly love or "Truth," the island of Serenia stands for human limitation, and the slain priest Aleema embodies all the negative aspects of organized religion. The narrator's quest for Yillah thus becomes an allegorical journey to find Truth and resist temptation in the form of the flower-maidens. (Branch 1986; de Paul 1988; Johnson 1982; Weinstein 1993)

See also The Confidence Man; Melville, Herman; *Moby-Dick.*

MARIE DE FRANCE

Marie de France (late twelfth century) was said to have been the half sister of King Henry II of England and she lived most of her life in England. As a poet she was famous for her verse narratives on Arthurian themes. Marie de France's collection of fables called *Ysopet* [*Little Aesop*] was a translation into French of an English version of the tales.

See also Aesop; Fable as Allegory.

MARLOWE, CHRISTOPHER

The English poet and playwright Christopher Marlowe (1564–1593) was a highly educated and talented artist who was killed at an early age in a tavern quarrel. He is best known for his fine blank verse and for his colorful and original development of the tragic drama that had come down from the Greeks by way of the Romans. His plays include *Tamburlaine, The Jew of Malta, Edward II*, and the somewhat allegorical *The Tragical History of the Life and Death of Dr. Faustus*.

See also Dr. Faustus.

THE MARROW OF TRADITION

Charles Chestnutt (1858–1932) was born in Cleveland, Ohio, to a family of free blacks originally from North Carolina. All of Chestnutt's fiction is characterized by the portrayal of black folk culture in the South, manipulating and often exploding the common stereotypes about blacks that were widely held by the mainstream white reading audience.

The Marrow of Tradition (1901) is partially based on the actual race riot of 1898 in Wilmington, North Carolina, in which more than 20 African Americans were killed and the town government was essentially overthrown by a small group of white supremacists. The novel intertwines the lives of two families: the Carterets, who represent the white aristocracy of the New South, and the Millers, a family of mixed racial identity who represent Chestnutt's image of the progressive New Negro. Philip Carteret, the editor of the town's white newspaper, defames blacks in his paper and conspires to overthrow the town government. Eventually, his actions lead to a violent race riot in which Dr. Adam Miller's son is killed. Later, Carteret is forced to ask Dr. Miller to help his own ill son. At first Miller refuses, but his wife persuades him to minister to the boy and embrace once again his role as a healer in the town. Several other subplots complicate the story of *The Marrow of Tradition* and involve many other minor characters who represent certain identity "types" that Chestnutt saw as vital to understanding the racial tensions in the post-Reconstruction South.

Critics have interpreted *The Marrow of Tradition* as an elaborate historical allegory of America's racial struggles. The Delamere family allegorizes the growing malevolence of white southern society; significantly, Mr. Delamere, the gentlemanly aristocrat and kindly ex-slaveowner, is old and feeble and rapidly losing strength.

Other white characters who contribute to the allegory of the novel include the cruel Captain McBane, who represents the intense racial hatred of poor southern whites. Ellis personifies the sincere but totally ineffective white liberal, and Mrs. Polly Ochiltree, Mrs. Olivia Carteret, and Miss Clara Pemberton collectively represent the class of female aristocrats who are so spoiled that they are incapable of taking care of themselves. Even the Carterets' young child plays a role in this allegory; he is a sickly boy who represents the weakened bloodline of rich white southern families.

Black characters, of course, also add to Chestnutt's allegory of American race relations. Sandy, the devoted servant, and Aunt Jane, the loyal "Mammy," represent those blacks who have accepted the social role of servant to such a degree that they are unable to contribute positively to the African-American quest for social equality. Jerry Letlow adds to this image, representing the child-like "Sambo" stereotype of the black servant. But there are other important allegorizations of black people in this novel beyond those of obedient servants. Dr. William Miller, the narrative focus of much of the novel, represents the emerging class of black bourgeoisie in post–Civil War America and allegorizes the assimilationist attitude of many blacks at the turn of the century. In contrast to Dr. Miller's more passive, moderate character, Josh Green is presented as a sort of precursor to the black nationalist movement of the 1960s and 1970s, personifying those blacks in favor of violently retaliating against racial oppression. Somewhere in between these two opposing figures lies the character of Dr. Miller's wife, Janet Green, whose compassion for others and acute sensitivity to white oppression combine to create Chestnutt's consummate allegorical representation of black separatism.

As a whole, *The Marrow of Tradition* represents Chestnutt's belief that true benevolence in white southern America has died, and that the cherished hope of a few enlightened whites and a few capable black leaders working together to solve America's racial conflict is unrealizable. While Chestnutt perhaps portrays Janet Miller's ideology of racial separation as superior to either Dr. Miller's conservative pacifism or Josh Green's militant vengefulness, his allegory of racial strife certainly offers no absolute or easy answers to America's painful racial dilemma. (Giles 1984)

See also Chestnutt, Charles.

MARTIANUS CAPELLA

Martianus lived in the fifth century C.E. He wrote *De Nuptiis Mercurii et Philologiae*, an allegorical interpretation and survey of the liberal arts in the context of the marriage of Mercury and Philology.

MARVELL, ANDREW

The reputation of Andrew Marvell (1621–1678) as a poet has slowly grown; today, he is viewed as an important contributor to the canon of seventeenth-century English literature. Many of Marvell's poems have been interpreted as historical or political allegory. For example, "The Nymph Complaining for the Death of her Fawn" may be read as an allegory of the execution of the Royal Martyr, King Charles I. The slain fawn represents, of course, Charles; the huntsman who presented the fawn to the nymph is King James I, Charles's father; and the nymph herself represents a bereaved England, traumatized over the gruesome death of her monarch. Other examples of political allegory may be found in "The Mower, against Gardens," in which the mower becomes an allegorical figure of King Charles, and "Upon Appleton House," which suggests encroaching civil war.

It has also been argued that many of Marvell's poems may be interpreted as structurally allegorical; poems in which a fall of some kind is followed by an ascent or a triumph may allegorically suggest the "fortunate fall" of mankind (fortunate in the sense that the sin of Adam and Eve led to the coming of Jesus and redemption). For example, in "An Horatian Ode" the beheading of Charles is placed in the center of the poem, followed by the ascendance of Cromwell to lead the nation. Yet in other poems, such as the "Mower" poems, the "fall" is not followed by any sort of ascent; these poems may suggest a despair deeply rooted in the political turmoil of England at the time. (Griffin 1992; Sandstroem 1990)

MARXIST ALLEGORY

See Brecht, Bertolt; Epic Theatre.

MAUS

Art Spiegelman's graphic novels *Maus: A Survivor's Tale* and *Maus II* (1991), a two-volume cartoon history of the Holocaust, may be seen as allegorical insofar as the visual depictions of the Nazis as cats and the Holocaust victims as mice suggest meanings that extend beyond what the narrative itself indicates. It is important to recognize, however, that the story of *Maus* is not allegorical; that is, the tale itself is not an allegory of the Holocaust, but an actual story about the Nazis and the death camps. Nevertheless, the portrayal of the ruthless Nazis/cats who prey upon the defenseless prisoners/mice adds a level of meaning to the story that would not necessarily be achieved in a more traditional text. In this way, many graphic texts (or comic books), while not strictly allegorical, may be understood to contain particular visual elements that function emblematically or allegorically.

MEDIEVAL ART AND ALLEGORY

The medieval mind tended to see the world allegorically. Nature itself was allegorical; by contemplating it one could read God's mind. But it was in the works made by humans to celebrate God's glory that medieval Christian allegory is most evident. Any medieval church is, as John MacQueen has suggested, "a historical allegory written in stone, glass, and wood." A visitor to one of the great medieval cathedrals such as the one at Chartres will soon discover this fact. The Latin cross shape of the Gothic church itself, with its sanctuary-head, its narthex-feet, and its outstretched transept-arms, is the body of Christ. The stained glass windows and the countless carvings inside and out reflect a Christian rather than a secular view of history, and a Christian view of the war between the forces of Satan and those of God. They also reflect the typological allegory of the period, the Christian reading of the Old Testament stories as allegories of later Christian events. A depiction of the flood might be placed next to a depiction of baptism. Moses on the mountain might be seen near Jesus on the mountain, the tree in the garden with its forbidden fruit becomes an allegory for the cross-tree and the new nourishing food it bears, and so on.

See also Church Architecture and Allegory; Painting and Sculpture, Allegorical.

MELVILLE, HERMAN

Herman Melville (1819–1891) came from a New York family of some pretensions but little money. To make a living he took many jobs, including that of seaman, which provided him with much of the background for his later work as a writer of such novels as *Typee* and his masterpiece, *Moby-Dick*. Melville's premier position in the canon of nineteenth-century American fiction is due not only to the success of *Moby-Dick*, but also to that of his shorter novels and to his short stories as well. Like his novels, many of Melville's short stories have been subjected to allegorical interpretations. While few scholars find Melville's tales to be purely allegorical, many stories do include important allegorical aspects. A few representative examples of these partially allegorical readings are included here.

Melville's mysterious adventure tale "Benito Cereno" (1856) has been interpreted as incorporating certain allegorical elements. The story, set in 1799, tells the story of Captain Amasa Delano, an American sea captain of the sealing ship *Bachelor's Delight*. While anchored off the coast of Chile, Delano encounters a ship that is in apparent distress. He goes aboard and finds that the ship is a Spanish merchant ship carrying slaves. The captain, Benito Cereno, explains to the innocent Delano that their ship had met with much misfortune, and that many officers had been killed. Cereno, who is constantly attended by a slave, Babo, seems physically and mentally unwell. Delano, puzzled by the inconsistencies in Cereno's stories and Babo's relentless attention, prepares to leave the ship to return to his own. Suddenly, Cereno jumps into Delano's whaleboat, and Delano realizes that the slaves had been holding Cereno captive. Delano and his sailors later pursue and capture the ship of slaves, and

Cereno eventually testifies to the barbarous cruelties that the slaves committed in their mutiny.

Allegorically, "Benito Cereno" has been read as the story of the slave controversy in mid–nineteenth-century America, in which Delano represents the shallow liberal idealism that cannot fully comprehend the complexities of slavery. Critics are divided over the racial implications of "Benito Cereno"; some maintain that Babo represents the savagery and barbarism of blacks, while others assert that he is a heroic figure exercising his human right to rebel and achieve his freedom.

Another of Melville's tales that has been read allegorically is the posthumously published "Billy Budd, Sailor" (1924), which tells the story of an innocent, guileless sailor who, after being falsely accused of conspiring to mutiny onboard an English warship, strikes and kills his accuser, a superior officer named Claggart. Billy Budd is convicted of murder by the captain of the ship and is sentenced to hang the following morning. As Billy is placed beneath the yardarm before his execution, he blesses Captain Vere, who he realizes has no choice but to adhere to military regulations. Strangely, Billy's body never twitches during the hanging, but remains as calm as Billy remained in life. For years after, sailors remembered the remarkable Billy Budd and made much of the yardarm upon which he was hanged.

"Billy Budd, Sailor" is most commonly interpreted as a Christian allegory of the crucifixion of Jesus Christ, in which Billy, as Christ, suffers for the sins of others. An alternate allegorical reading of this story suggests that "Billy Budd" is a political allegory of America. Billy, born in 1776, represents the young United States of America. His loss of innocence in the face of Claggart's accusations reflects America's loss of innocence as a result of industrialized civilization (represented by the king and his military force). Melville's tale reveals a world in which natural law and the rights of man are sacrificed in order to preserve military and political principles of order.

Melville's 1854 short story "The Lightning-Rod Man," while never very well received by critics or readers, is yet another example of Melville's propensity for Christian allegory. The story itself, which takes place during a fiery electrical storm, involves the confrontation between a salesman of lightning rods and a townsman (the narrator) who refuses to buy one. Allegorically, the story tells of a confrontation between Good and Evil; the salesman represents Satan and the narrator represents pious man who overcomes devilish temptation by adhering to his faith. The salesman makes three attempts to lure the narrator away from the warmth and safety of his hearth (allegorically, the warmth and brotherhood of man). He fails in each of these attempts, due to the shrewdness of the narrator and his insistence that he will "stand at ease in the hands of my God." The narrator expels the salesman from his house; allegorically readers may infer that while faithful man has triumphed over evil, he has not destroyed evil. Presumably, the salesman/Satan is still free to roam the land and prey upon unsuspecting victims. (Davis 1984; Verdier 1981)

See also The Confidence Man; Mardi; Moby-Dick.

MENCIUS

Mencius (372–289 B.C.E.) was a Confucian philosopher who, in the ancient tradition of Chinese education, made much use of extended metaphors, parables, fables, and simple allegories. One of the primary Confucian teachings suggests that the essential virtue of humanity can only be revived by hard work. Mencius employs allegory to make this point. It is common enough for a man to go searching for a lost animal, he says, but, regrettably, he almost never goes in search of his lost self.

See also Parable as Allegory.

MENIPPUS OF GADARA

Mennipus was a third-century B.C.E. Cynic philosopher from whose work and name we derive the term *Menippean satire,* the best example of which is the allegorical satire by Jonathan Swift called *A Tale of a Tub.*

See also *A Tale of a Tub.*

METAPHOR AS ALLEGORY

In Elizabethan times, allegory was commonly defined as "a long and perpetual metaphore," what we today would call "extended metaphor." Beginning from that definition, the English medievalist C. S. Lewis suggests that "we cannot speak, perhaps we can hardly think, of an 'inner conflict' without a metaphor; and every metaphor is an allegory in little." There are those who would suggest that to equate allegory with metaphor even "in little" is to dilute the definition of allegory. A metaphor is an implied comparison in which a general idea or abstraction is compared to something concrete and specific—for example, "life is a bowl of cherries" or "all the world's a stage"—in order that the abstraction or general idea can become somehow present to the reader. Clearly this metaphorical process is related to allegory, and the second of these examples is closer to allegory than the first, but the purpose of allegory is not so much to make us experience an abstraction or general idea as to understand its meaning or significance. We watch the character Everyman in the medieval morality play *Everyman* as he represents all of us in his confrontation with death. The comparison between Everyman and us is not implied but explicit, and its purpose is didactic rather than aesthetic. Having said this, it is important to note that in much modern allegory, such as Kafka's *The Trial,* the allegory is more veiled than it is in the medieval tradition. But even in *The Trial* it would be fair to say that the character "K" is an allegorical personification of rather than merely a metaphor for Franz Kafka or humankind.

See also *Everyman;* Extended Metaphor; Kafka, Franz.

MILTON, JOHN

Generally considered one of the very greatest of English poets, John Milton (1608–1674) is best known for his literary epic, *Paradise Lost*. Milton came from a middle-class London family, was educated first privately and then at St. Paul's School and at Cambridge University. He built on his formal education by several years of independent study followed by a long tour in Europe. In the civil war of the period, Milton sided with the Puritans and became Oliver Cromwell's Latin secretary, a job that involved correspondence with the other nations of Europe to justify the Commonwealth that followed the beheading of Charles I. The combination of his work for Cromwell and his own writing led to blindness. His greatest achievements—*Paradise Lost, Paradise Regained*, and *Samson Agonistes*—were dictated. If one theme stands out in the work of this great Puritan poet, it is, not surprisingly, temptation. Certainly this is true of *Paradise Lost* and of his one particularly allegorical work, the masque *Comus*.

See also *Comus*.

MISS LONELYHEARTS

The short novel *Miss Lonelyhearts* (1933) by Nathanael West (1903–1940) tells the story of a man who takes a job writing a newspaper advice column as a joke, while waiting for a more desirable job opportunity to come along. But when the narrator (referred to only as Miss Lonelyhearts) starts to receive sincere letters from profoundly troubled, victimized, or otherwise pitiable people, writing the column becomes for him a complicated burden to bear. Through a series of encounters with his girlfriend Betty, his editor Shrike, Shrike's wife Mary, and a bizarre couple called the Doyles, Miss Lonelyhearts faces countless manifestations of human suffering and violence that culminate in his accidental murder.

Critics have interpreted *Miss Lonelyhearts* as a religious allegory, in which Miss Lonelyhearts, the son of a Baptist minister, adopts the characteristics of a Christ-figure suffering for others. Those anonymous readers who write to the advice column for help, describing wrenching and usually ghastly situations, allegorize the despair and anguish of modern humanity in general. Yet this allegorical interpretation takes a dark twist; unlike Christ, Miss Lonelyhearts finds himself completely incapable of alleviating anyone's suffering. As a result, critics have suggested that West's novel may actually allegorize the failings rather than the achievements of Christ to "save" humankind. (Herbst 1971; Hyman 1986; Light 1971)

See also *The Day of the Locust;* West, Nathanael.

MOBY-DICK

Herman Melville's classic American novel *Moby-Dick* (1851) has endured decades of scholarly attempts to classify it as some form of allegorical writing.

While most scholars agree *Moby-Dick* cannot be seen as a true allegory, many elements of the novel have been interpreted as allegorical to some degree. For example, the painting in the Schooner Inn may be read as an allegorical emblem that suggests Ishmael's fate. Captain Ahab's monomaniacal pursuit of the whale has also been interpreted as allegorical insofar as he is on some version of a heroic quest; indeed, Ahab himself may be said to interpret the whale as an allegorical incarnation of evil. Bainard Cowan examines a different allegorical aspect in his explanation that the "distance gained from land on the 'exiled waters' of his voyage allows Ishmael to reenvision the Western past and the natural present, freed from their enforced New England interpretations, as an allegory" (6). Other scholars have noted the distinction between explicit allegory (such as that found in "The Monkey Rope") and implicit allegory (the *Pequod* as a microcosm). (Cowan 1982; Dettlaff 1986; Ziarek 1989)

   See also The Confidence Man; Emblems; *Mardi*; Melville, Herman; The Quest as Allegory.

"THE MONKEY"

Known as Karen Blixen in Denmark, the Danish writer Isak Dinesen (1885–1962) spent much of her life in Africa. Her novel *Out of Africa* (1937) was made into a successful film and has become perhaps her best-known work. Her most allegorical text, however, is a short story called "The Monkey," which is included as one of *Seven Gothic Tales* (1934). "The Monkey" is the story of a virgin prioress in a secular convent called Closter Seven, who has a pet monkey from Zanzibar. The Prioress is visited by her nephew, Boris, who has been implicated in a scandalous homosexual affair and has decided to marry in order to salvage his reputation. The Prioress chooses Athena, the daughter of a Polish count, to be Boris's bride. However, Athena is an innocent but fierce virgin who has no interest in marrying anyone. The Prioress stages an elaborate seduction scene between the masculine Athena and her effeminate nephew, during which Boris gets two teeth knocked out in a struggle with the girl but does succeed in obtaining one kiss. The next morning, the Prioress tricks Athena into believing that she may be pregnant and therefore obliged to marry Boris. Just then the monkey breaks into the room, attacks the Prioress, and reveals itself to be the real Prioress. The other Prioress was actually the monkey masquerading as a woman. Boris and Athena are thus bound together for life, for they have shared the terrifying experience of seeing evil in the face of good, and they realize that they must forever keep their guilty secret from the rest of the world.

   Critics have interpreted "The Monkey" as "a witty allegory of the way in which nature (the monkey) and culture (the Prioress) cooperate to bring about the sexual relation and to channel it into marriage" (Mishler, 231). Other allegorical interpretations emphasize the topics of sexual identity (natural homosexuality versus socially mandated heterosexuality), order and chaos (the Prioress versus the monkey), the relationship between generations (Boris and

Athena versus the Prioress), and the biblical role of guilt in the establishment of human love. (Aiken 1990; Langbaum 1975; Mishler 1993)

See also Dinesen, Isak.

MORAL ALLEGORY

Also called tropological allegory, this is the level of "fourfold allegory" that speaks to the question of the reader's moral welfare. Thus, for example, Jerusalem is a literal place, and on a simple allegorical level it represents the Church. On the level of moral or tropological allegory it might represent the worthy soul or spiritual wholeness.

See also Fourfold Allegory.

MORALITY PLAYS

Medieval morality plays made use of allegorical personifications of vices, virtues, and other aspects of the human condition. Their purpose was clearly to teach the values and dogmas espoused by the Church by pitting vice against virtue for power over the human soul. These plays probably had ancestors in the now-lost allegorical "Paternoster Plays" of fourteenth-century England and similar French plays, which pitted the virtues against the vices. The morality play emerged as a recognizable genre in the fifteenth century, continued to develop in the sixteenth, and clearly influenced minor secular playwrights such as John Skelton, author of *Magnyfycence,* and John Bale, who wrote *John, King of England* (1540)—which contains such characters as Private Wealth and Usurped Power—and such major secular playwrights as Marlowe, Shakespeare, and Jonson. Marlowe's *Dr. Faustus,* Shakespeare's *As You Like It* and *King Lear,* and Jonson's *Volpone* all have characteristics of the morality play. They are at once ripe with lessons and marked by the possibility of allegorical interpretation. When Faustus sells his soul to the devil for pleasure and knowledge and Lear is deprived of all earthly power before he can understand his sin and his true identity, we are not so terribly far from the world of the morality plays like *Everyman* (1500), *Mankind* (1473), and *The Castle of Perseverance* (1425). French versions are *Bien avise, mal avise [Well Advised, Ill Advised]* and *L'Homme juste, et l'homme mondain [The Righteous Man and the Worldly],* both of the fifteenth century. An important theme of many morality plays is that of the journey that the hero must make in order to achieve salvation. This theme would be taken up by later allegorists such as John Bunyan in his *Pilgrim's Progress.*

See also The Castle of Perseverance; Dr. Faustus; Everyman; King John; Magnyfycence; The Pilgrim's Progress.

LE MORTE D'ARTHUR

Written by Sir Thomas Malory (1408–1471), *Le Morte d'Arthur* was an important source for allegorical works such as Spenser's *Faerie Queene* and Tennyson's *Idylls of the King.* It was written while Malory was in jail (ca. 1469) and pub-

A page from a 1529 edition of Sir Thomas Malory's *Le Morte d'Arthur*

lished by William Caxton in 1485. The work is really eight separate romances in English prose based on many sources, both English and French. The purpose behind the writing was not allegorical. Malory was primarily a storyteller who wished to give new life to the old Arthurian characters and incidents—Arthur, Sir Lancelot, Merlin, the Holy Grail (Sangreal), the love between Lancelot and Guinevere, the death of King Arthur. If the work is at all

179

allegorical, it is because its characters and events as a whole represent an age and a tradition of chivalry that had been eclipsed by Malory's time.

See also Arthurian Allegory; Malory, Sir Thomas.

MOSES, MAN OF THE MOUNTAIN

Critics have suggested that the novel *Moses, Man of the Mountain* (1939) by Zora Neale Hurston (1891–1960) may be read as an allegory of the struggles of black Americans to be free. The novel is a retelling of the biblical legend of Moses, using African instead of Hebrew characters. The children of Israel are the black slaves, Egypt represents the South, the Egyptians are white Americans, and Exodus becomes the First Migration. The Pharoah's palace is likened to the luxurious plantation mansions of the South, and the Hebrews' homes mirror the conditions found in slave quarters. Hurston adheres to the essentials of the biblical story of Moses and the Israelites, but her modern version of the tale manages both to demystify the figure of Moses and to establish him as a black folk hero. (Howard 1980; Jackson 1986)

See also Hurston, Zora Neale.

MR. WESTON'S GOOD WINE

This 1927 novel by the British writer T. F. Powys (1875–1953) is, as Louis MacNeice suggests, allegory of an "old-fashioned kind" (115). The book is concerned with the larger questions of life—death and other eternal questions— but also with the morality of village life. The setting is an English village in the center of which is "the oak tree bed" where village girls are seduced by village youths. The village is an allegorical representation of the world, into which comes God disguised as a typically British traveling salesman. The salesman and his sidekick, a disguised angel, sell wine of two sorts: one type makes people love each other; the other is the wine of death, for which Mr. Weston (God) says, "we allow no credit." (MacNeice 1965)

See also Powys, T. F.

MUMBO JUMBO

Ishmael Reed was brought up in Buffalo, New York. He has taught at many American universities, most recently at the University of California in Berkeley. He is a noted poet and novelist who has been concerned with the condition of African Americans. His novel, *Mumbo Jumbo*, has been seen by many as an allegory using events of the Harlem Renaissance of the 1930s to represent aspects of the 1960s Black Arts movement. Henry Louis Gates, Jr., in his *Signifying Monkey*, suggests that the book is also an allegory of the "history and nature of writing itself, especially that of the Afro-American tradition." By calling attention in the text of the novel to his own writing, Reed represents by the writing itself his main character's quest for a text that can give meaning to his life. (Gates 1988)

See also Allegoresis.

MUSIC AND ALLEGORY

There are several areas of contact between music and allegory. The Renaissance masque was allegorical in that it used stereotypical classical plots and characters, backed up by music and spectacle, to represent and justify the political status quo and to praise particular leaders. In the typical masque we find an allegorical struggle, supported by appropriate music—between personified virtues and vices. Insofar as the music is linked in style to the action, it is at least in part allegorical, in the sense that movie musical scores convey meaning to support the events and situations displayed on the screen.

There is also a deeper sense in which music can be discussed as allegory. Many musical theorists—Albert Schweitzer and Leonard Bernstein among them—have suggested a connection between aspects of music and aspects of human emotion. Thus a descending scale might suggest pain; minor keys, flats, and sharps might speak to anxiety; and ascending scales to joy. Bernstein, working from theories of the linguist Noam Chomsky, spoke of the "deep structure" of musical modes, structures that resemble the archetypes of Jung's "collective unconscious" and are linked with the universal human experience.

So-called program music—music that announces its illustrative relationship to particular scenes, stories, people, and so forth—is, of course, allegorical to varying degrees. Schumann's *Carnaval*, for example, is an allegory of a carnival, of a carnival of emotions, and of a particular love affair, all hidden in the details of the composition. The so-called leitmotifs of Wagner's operas can be said to refer to particular people or incidents. In *The Seasons,* Vivaldi's music surely refers to aspects of the seasons. Beethoven's *Eroica* Symphony is perhaps more evocative than representative of the historical events of the early nineteenth century. (Bukofzer 1939–1940; Fletcher 1964; Frye 1957)

MYSTERY PLAYS

See The Second Shepherd's Play.

MYTH AS ALLEGORY

It has been argued that the origins of allegory are in mythology. Traditionally, myths are narratives containing mysteries that are interpreted by priests or by the initiates of a given cult. The pre-Socratic Greeks, for instance, practiced the art of discovering *hyponoia* or the hidden meaning behind mythic narratives.

Plato refers to the *hyponoia* of myths, and by the second century C.E. we learn from Plutarch that the *hyponoia* of myths are now being called *allegoriai*. By definition, myths are code language that explains or reveals the unknown. By definition they are allegorical. One of the many functions of myths has been to explain and/or reveal the origins of certain phenomena and experiences that are important to humans—love, rain, spring, and so forth. Myths, on at least one level, then, are frequently allegorical in that aspects of the narratives in question precisely represent aspects of existence. It might be suggested, in fact, that myths more often than not have at least two allegorical levels. Many scholars have suggested that on the literal or material level the famous myth of Persephone stands as an explanation of the seasons or as a representation of the process of planting and germination. On a spiritual or archetypal level, the Persephone myth, like any other myth of descent into the underworld, is an allegory of the lost and redeemed self.

There is a long mythological tradition in which particular deities are personifications of abstractions. In the eighth century B.C.E., in *Theogony* and *Works and Days*, the Greek poet Hesiod was clearly working within this tradition, with such characters as Prometheus, meaning "forethought," Themis, meaning "Justice," and Pandora, meaning "all-giving." The Hellenistic Greeks and the Romans developed the allegorical tradition, creating such figures as Natura (Nature) and Fortuna (Fortune). There was a tendency to allegorize older deities as well. So it was, for instance, that old Kronos (Time) became the Roman Saturn and then the familiar Father Time.

See also Allegory; Attis Myth; Boccaccio, Giovanni; *Cupid and Psyche*; Fortuna; *Hyponoia*; Persephone Myth; Personification; Prometheus Myth; Sallustius.

NABOKOV, VLADIMIR

Given his fondness for word games, purposeful ambiguities, and self- and reader-directed ironies, the Russian, and later American, novelist Vladimir Nabokov (1899–1977) can be seen as a contributor to the postmodern exercise of allegoresis, in which the text itself becomes an allegory of the struggle for meaning between the author and the reader. The ambiguities and wordplay of *Ada* (1969), for example, reflect the process by which the author struggles to bring the reader to an understanding of the nature of time and memory. In the same way, the very absurdity of the texts of such novels as *Pale Fire* (1962) and *Pnin* (1953) speaks to the whole question of language as a means of communicating ideas. (Toker 1989)

See also Allegoresis.

NASREDDIN HODJA

Nasreddin Hodja, or Mullah Nassr Eddin in the original Persian tradition, is a legendary trickster/wiseman who is well known throughout the Middle East. Nasredin is his Turkish name. A *hodja* is a teacher—especially a wise Islamic teacher—yet Nasreddin constantly does things that are illogical and even foolish. He rides his donkey backwards, mistakes his beautiful echoing voice in the *hamam* (Turkish bath) for his real voice, and sometimes even steals and tells lies. Given the proximity of Nasreddin's "home town" of Akshehir to the city of Konya, where the Mevlevi Sufis (Whirling Dervishes) of the great Persian mystic poet Jalal al-din Rumi (1207–1273) established their center, and given the implication of wisdom in even the most absurd tales told by a *hodja*, it is tempting to read in the Nasreddin tales allegorical meanings associated with the teachings of Rumi.

According to Rumi, those who follow conventions simply because they have been inherited are, in fact, acting illogically. True logic demands that we overcome the automatic responses of our conditioning. The Sufi appears illogical to ordinary people because he lives beyond convention at several levels of experience at once. When during the *sema* (ceremony) he whirls in mystical abandonment, he defies the logic of gravity and ordinary fatigue even though, as a carpenter or teacher or bureaucrat in everyday life, he understands these principles well enough. The *hodja* stories—and Rumi himself often used such stories as parables to illustrate his points—are comic allegories of the paradoxical nature of the mystical understanding.

In one of the better-known tales we learn that the *hodja's* donkey had strayed and could be found nowhere. Yet, as the *hodja* ran about town looking for him, he cried out repeatedly, "Allah be praised!" The townsfolk who searched with him were confused by the teacher's words.

"Your donkey is lost, Hodja; why do you praise Allah for that?" they asked.

"I praise God," answered Nasreddin, "because I was not riding the donkey when he got lost, for if I had been on his back then, we would without doubt both be lost."

At least two levels of allegory are, of course, possible here. There is the representation of the illogical logic—the paradoxical truth—of the mystical path, and there is the inherently allegorical nature of the word "lost" in a moral or religious sense. The donkey is representative, in this sense, of the human's (*hodja's*) animal nature. To be attached to the back of one's animal nature when it is "lost" in sin is a fate from which the holy man might well praise God for saving him.

There is a wonderful allegory implicit in the grave in Akshehir that is said to be Nasreddin Hodja's. The gravestone stands behind an iron gate secured by a huge padlock. Yet there is no fence or wall on either side of the gate, nothing to prevent the visitor from walking around the locked gate to the gravestone itself. This arrangement would seem to be meaningful. The Sufi knows that those who do not understand truth will search for the logic that will unlock the gate or they will propose a bribe that might unlock it, while those who understand the illogical logic of the mystic will know that the truth is there for the taking, that locked gates are only for those who do not look around them. There is a small hole in the Hodja's gravestone, from which, the people say, he looks out to see what is going on in the world. It seems likely—allegorically speaking—that he looks out to laugh at those who stand fretting at the gate and to welcome those who have walked around it to the truth. (Leeming 1979)

¶ NATIVE AMERICAN ALLEGORY ¶

Allegory permeates the costumes, dwellings, and ceremonies of Native Americans. For the Navajo, the traditional dwelling place—the small, dome-shaped hogan—is an allegory for the sacred world itself, with its east-facing door waiting each morning for the entrance of the source of energy and light, the Sun Father. In the same way, the sandpaintings used in curing ceremonies are allegories of creation. As the patient sits in the painting and hears the shaman chanting the creation story, he or she is re-created to a new life as surely as the universe was created in the first days.

The *kiva*, the underground chamber of the Hopi and Pueblo peoples, is also allegorical, an appropriate place for sacred ceremonies because it is a metaphor for creation and for the womb of Mother Earth herself. On the floor of the kiva is a small hole, or *sipapu*, the navel hole leading down to the original place of creation. Different levels of the building represent the second and third worlds inhabited by the ancient peoples. A hole in the roof leads to the fourth world of creation outside the *kiva*. The ceremonies in the *kiva* are sacred dramas in which the initiate undergoes the process of spiritual re-creation reflected by the building itself.

Native American tales and myths, too, are often allegorical. A common practice among traditional storytellers was to personify aspects of nature, as in the case of this Ojibwa tale of the coming of corn as the resurrected Mondawmin.

WUNZH

In times past, a poor Indian was living with his wife and children in a beautiful part of the country. He was not only poor, but inexpert in procuring food for his family, and his children were all too young to give him assistance. Although poor, he was a man of a kind and contented disposition. He was always thankful to the Great Spirit for everything he received. The same disposition was inherited by his eldest son, who had now arrived at the proper age to undertake the ceremony of the *Keiguishimowin*, or fast, to see what kind of a spirit would be his guide and guardian through life. Wunzh, for this was his name, had been an obedient boy from his infancy, and was of a pensive, thoughtful, and mild disposition, so that he was beloved by the whole family. As soon as the first indications of spring appeared, they built him the customary little lodge at a retired spot, some distance from their own, where he would not be distrubed during this solemn rite. In the meantime he prepared himself, and immediately went into it, and commenced his fast. The first few days, he amused himself, in the mornings, by walking in the woods and over the mountains, examining the early plants and flowers, and in this way prepared himself to enjoy his sleep, and, at the same time, stored his mind with pleasant ideas for his dreams. While he rambled through the woods, he felt a strong desire to know how the plants, herbs, and berries grew, without any aid from man, and why it was that some species were good to eat, and others possessed medicinal or poisonous juices. He recalled these thoughts to mind after he became too languid to walk about, and had confined himself strictly to the lodge; he wished he could dream of something that would prove a benefit to his father and family, and to all others. "True!" he thought, "the Great Spirit made all things, and it is to him that we owe our lives. But could he not make it easier for us to get our food, than by hunting animals and taking fish? I must try to find out this in my visions."

On the third day he became weak and faint, and kept his bed. He fancied, while thus lying, that he saw a handsome young man coming down from the sky and advancing towards him. He was richly and gaily dressed, having on a great many garments of green and yellow colors, but differing in their deeper or lighter shades. He had a plume of waving feathers on his head, and all his motions were graceful.

"I am sent to you, my friend," said the celestial visitor, "by that Great Spirit who made all things in the sky and on the earth. He has seen and knows your motives in fasting. He sees that it is from a kind and benevolent wish to do good to your people, and to procure a benefit for them, and that you do not seek for strength in war or the praise of warriors. I am sent to instruct you, and show you how you can do your kindred good." He then told the young man to arise, and prepare to wrestle with him, as it was only by this means that he could hope to succeed in his wishes. Wunzh knew he was weak from fasting, but he felt his courage rising in his heart, and immediately got up, determined to die rather than fail. He commenced the trial, and after a protracted effort, was almost exhausted, when the beautiful stranger said, "My friend, it is enough for once; I will come again to try you;" and smiling on him, he ascended in the air in the same direction from which he came. The next day the celestial visitor reappeared at the same hour and renewed the trial. Wunzh felt that his strength was even less than the day before, but the courage of his mind seemed to increase in proportion as his body became weaker. Seeing this, the stranger again spoke to him in the same words he used before, adding, "Tomorrow will be your last trial. Be strong, my friend, for this is the only way you can overcome me, and obtain the boon you seek." On the third day he again appeared at the same time and renewed the struggle. The poor youth was very faint in body, but grew stronger in mind at every contest, and was determined to prevail or perish in the attempt. He exerted his utmost powers, and after the contest had been continued the usual time, the stranger ceased his efforts and declared himself conquered. For the first time he entered the lodge, and sitting down beside the youth, he began to deliver his instructions to him, telling him in what manner he should proceed to take advantage of his victory.

"You have won your desires of the Great Spirit," said the stranger. "You have wrestled manfully. To-morrow will be the seventh day of your fasting. Your father will give you food to strengthen you, and as it is the last day of trial, you will prevail. I know this, and now tell you what you must do to benefit your family and your tribe. To-morrow," he repeated, "I shall meet you and wrestle with you for the last time; and, as soon as you have prevailed against me, you will strip off my garments, throw me down, clean the earth of roots and weeds, make it soft, and bury me in the spot. When you have done this, leave my body in the earth, and do not disturb it, but come occasionally to visit the place, to see whether I have come to life, and be careful never to let the grass or weeds grow on my grave. Once a month cover me with fresh earth. If you follow my instructions, you will accomplish your object of doing good to your fellow creatures by teaching them the knowledge I now teach you." He then shook him by the hand and disappeared.

In the morning, the youth's father came with some slight refreshments, saying, "My son, you have fasted long enough. If the Great Spirit will favor you, he will do it now. It is seven days since you have tasted food, and you must not sacrifice your life. The Master of Life does not require that." "My father," replied the youth, "wait till the sun goes down. I have a particular reason for extending my fast to that hour." "Very well," said the old man, "I shall wait till the hour arrives, and you feel inclined to eat."

At the usual hour of the day the sky-visitor returned, and the trial of strength was renewed. Although the youth had not availed himself of his father's offer of food, he felt that new strength had been given to him, and that exertion had renewed his strength and fortified his courage. He grasped his angelic antagonist with supernatural strength, threw him down, took from him his beautiful garments and plume, and finding him dead, immediately buried him on the spot, taking all the precautions he had been told of, and being very confident, at the same time, that his friend would again come to life. He then returned to his father's lodge, and partook sparingly of the meal that had been prepared for him. But he never for a moment forgot the grave of his friend. He carefully visited it throughout the spring, and weeded out the grass, and kept the ground in a soft and pliant state. Very soon he saw the tops of the green plumes coming throught the ground; and the more careful he was to obey his instructions in keeping the ground in order, the faster they grew. He was, however, careful to conceal the exploit from his father. Days and weeks had passed in this way. The summer was now drawing towards a close, when one day, after a long absence in hunting, Wunzh invited his father to follow him to the quiet and lonesome spot of his former fast. The lodge had been removed, and the weeds kept from growing on the circle where it stood, but in its place stood a tall and graceful plant, with bright-colored silken hair, surmounted with nodding plumes and stately leaves, and golden clusters on each side. "It is my friend," shouted the lad; "it is the friend of all mankind. It is *Mondawmin*....We need no longer rely on hunting alone; for, as long as this gift is cherished and taken care of, the ground itself will give us a living." He then pulled an ear. "See, my father," said he, "this is what I fasted for. The Great Spirit has listened to my voice, and sent us something new...and henceforth our people will not alone depend upon the chase or upon the waters."

He then communicated to his father the instructions given him by the stranger. He told him that the broad husks must be torn away, as he had pulled off the garments in his wrestling; and having done this, directed him how the ear must be held before the fire till the outer skin became brown, while all the milk was retained in the grain. The whole family then united in a feast on the newly-grown ears, expressing gratitude to the Merciful Spirit who gave it. So corn came into the world....(Schoolcraft 1856 as quoted by Leeming 1981, pp. 103–106)

The human hero of this story, the boy Wunzh, who undergoes a vision quest—a rite of passage from boyhood to manhood—is the prototype of Henry Wadsworth Longfellow's Hiawatha. Wunzh represents the institution of shamanism, as through his mystical experience with the spirit world he achieves a great boon for his people. It could also be said that the wrestling match between Wunzh and Mondawmin is an allegory of the struggles present in any rite of passage and of the difficulties involved in any kind of birth or rebirth, whether physical, psychological, or spiritual.

The Cherokees tell an allegorical tale about the immense strength of winter as represented by Ice Man. It is said that once there was a great fire in the Smoky Mountains—a fire that enveloped a large poplar tree and burnt it down into its roots until a huge burning hole formed and the people thought the fire would burn so deeply into the earth as to destroy it.

A wise chief decided to send two messengers to the wild north to beg Ice Man for help. A perilous and long road finally led the two men to Ice Man, an ancient being with two immensely long braids. After hearing the story of the fire, Ice Man agreed to help. He unbraided his hair, and by grasping part of it in one hand and thrashing that part against the other he produced a cold wind, icy rain, and then snow. He sent the villagers home and promised to follow soon. In a few days Ice Man delivered on his promise: a huge blizzard flew in from the north and buried the fire in the deep hole. After the storm the people found a fine lake where the hole had been. As a personification of winter, Ice Man is clearly an allegorical figure.

The Chippewa Indians, too, use the Ice Man character as a personification of winter. In this story he plays a role in the explanation of the coming of spring, whose persona is that of a young man. Ice Man had grown very old and had lost much of his power. He was sitting sadly by his wigwam when a young man came by. The youth was lively, smiling, and handsome. He was decked in flowers. Feeling lonely, Ice Man invited the young man in: "Who are you, and why are you here?" he asked. "I come as a messenger," the youth answered. What followed was a friendly boasting contest. Ice Man and the messenger smoked the peace pipe lit from the last coals of Ice Man's almost dead fire, and Ice Man told of his powers—how with his breath he could turn water to glass and the soft ground to rock. With a shake of his hair he could bring blizzards. The youth smiled. "My breath turns the ice to water, the frozen earth to soft earth. A shake of my hair causes sweet rain to fall and the flowers to bloom." As the stranger talked, the things he had spoken of happened, and Ice Man grew smaller until he was nothing but a white flower called Spring Beauty—the first of the new season. (Bierhorst 1985; Leeming 1994)

THE NEW JERUSALEM

See Jerusalem.

NUMBERS AND ALLEGORY

In many cultures, numbers are seen as somehow magical. Not surprisingly, then, meanings have been attributed to particular numbers, meanings that go beyond their immediate significance as quantitative symbols. Numbers have been considered astrologically important and have also been associated with larger cosmic understandings. Early Christians based cosmological systems on the number three because it represented the Trinity, the very basis of ultimate reality. Later, an argument against Galileo's discovery that there were more than seven planets was based on number allegory. Francesco Sizzi pointed out that there were "seven windows in the head"—nostrils, ears, eyes, mouth—and that there must, therefore, be seven corresponding windows in the heavens. (Fletcher 1964)

O'CONNOR, FLANNERY

Flannery O'Connor (1925–1964) was born and raised in Georgia and spent most of her life in the South. Her father died of lupus when she was 16; the following year, O'Connor entered Georgia State College for Women (now Georgia College). In 1945 she left Georgia to study at the Writers' Workshop of the State University of Iowa (now the University of Iowa) and began writing short stories. Later, she spent time in New York and Connecticut while working on her first novel, *Wise Blood* (1952). In 1950, during a Christmas visit with her family, O'Connor was stricken with her first attack of lupus. Weakened, she moved back to Georgia to live with her mother and her uncle. For the next 13 years, O'Connor lived quietly on her family's farm, writing and raising peafowl. Surgery in 1964 reactivated the lupus; O'Connor died that August at the age of 39. She is remembered mostly for her collections of short stories, *A Good Man Is Hard To Find, and Other Stories* (1955), and *Everything That Rises Must Converge* (1965), but her novels have also received a great deal of critical attention for their often grotesque visions of Catholicism and southern life.

See also The Violent Bear It Away.

ODETS, CLIFFORD

Clifford Odets (1906–1963), an American playwright, was born in Philadelphia to middle-class Jewish immigrant parents. In 1931 he helped to found the Group Theatre in New York, initially participating only as an actor. After winning a contest for one-act plays with his 1935 hit *Waiting for Lefty,* the Group Theatre began producing many of Odets's plays, effectively launching his career. A member of the Communist party for a short time, Odets was a champion of the working classes and incorporated the experiences of underprivileged Americans in many of his plays. His greatest commercial success was *Golden Boy* (1937), which has allegorical aspects; other important plays in Odets's canon include *Awake and Sing!* (1935), *Paradise Lost* (1935), *Rocket to the Moon* (1938),

Flannery O'Connor

Night Music (1940), *Clash by Night* (1941), *The Big Knife* (1949), *The Country Girl* (1950), and *The Flowering Peach* (1954).

   See also *Golden Boy*.

THE ODYSSEY

While certainly not an allegory per se, Homer's *Odyssey* is a quest epic and, as such, is to some extent allegorical. The poem tells the story of the journey of Odysseus from Troy to his home in Ithaca. Each step of his perilous journey can be said to have allegorical meaning. In the Land of the Lotus-Eaters he faces the human tendency to give up, to choose mindless ease over perseverance; on Circe's island, in an archetypal patriarchal incident, he overcomes what men have seen as the power of women to deprive them of their being; by visiting the Land of the Dead he expresses the need to face mortality before true self-realization can be achieved; and by focusing always on home and his faithful wife, Penelope, Odysseus stands for his culture's sense that full identity can only be realized in the context of home and family.

   See also Epic as Allegory; Homer; The Quest as Allegory.

OLD FORTUNATUS

The play *The Pleasant Comedy of Old Fortunatus* (1599) by Thomas Dekker (ca. 1572–1632) is a rambling exemplum intended as moral instruction for the au-

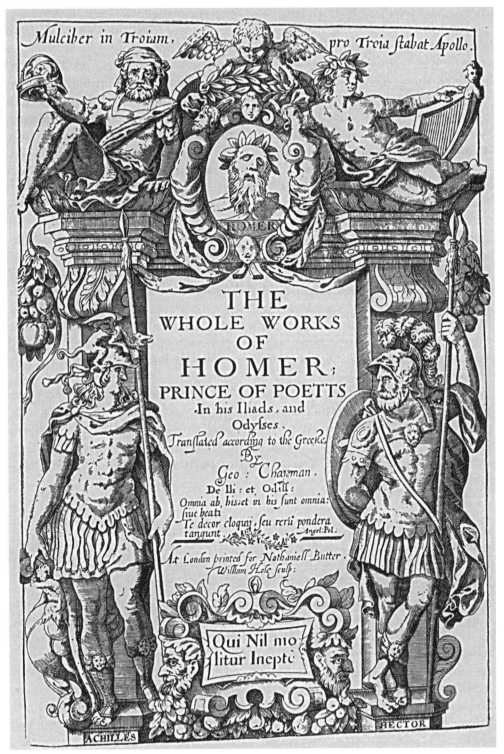

Title page of the 1616 edition of *The Whole Works of Homer*

dience at Queen Elizabeth I's court. An inherently allegorical tale, it describes the misfortunes that befall a beggar and his sons when they choose riches from all the benefits offered to them by the goddess Fortune.

Old Fortunatus, a poor man with two sons, is one day approached in the forest by the goddess Fortune. She offers him his choice of strength, beauty, health, long life, riches, or wisdom. He chooses riches, believing that from wealth all other virtues will flow. Fortune gives him a magic purse that will always contain ten gold pieces and will last until he and his sons are dead. Fortunatus shares his treasure with his sons and proceeds to travel around the world. After many adventures, Fortunatus returns home only to hear Fortune warn him of his imminent death. He pleads to change his wish from wealth to wisdom for his sons, but he is denied.

After Old Fortunatus dies, his sons, Ampedo and Andelocia, betray their father's wishes and separate the magic purse from the magic wishing hat (acquired during Fortunatus's travels to Babylon). Ampedo is a virtuous youth who is victimized by his younger brother Andelocia, the wastrel, who follows the same profligate lifestyle of his father. After several encounters with the figures of Virtue and Vice, it is Andelocia who eventually brings about the deaths of both himself and his brother. The play ends with a trial scene in which Vice flees, Fortune bows to the superiority of Queen Elizabeth I, and Virtue places herself at the mercy of Her Majesty, the living embodiment of virtue.

Old Fortunatus is quite clearly a morality play, intended to warn Queen Elizabeth I's courtiers against the evils of greed, sloth, and wastefulness. Furthermore, the moral dangers of material wealth are depicted both through the misadventures of Ampedo and Andelocia and through the struggles and rivalries among the allegorical characters of Fortune, Virtue, and Vice. (Price 1969)

See also Dekker, Thomas; Morality Plays.

ONE FLEW OVER THE CUCKOO'S NEST

One Flew over the Cuckoo's Nest, the popular 1962 novel by Ken Kesey (b. 1935), is the story of a prison convict, McMurphy, who feigns insanity in order to be sent from a work farm to a psychiatric hospital. In the ward, McMurphy constantly combats the tyrannical forces of Big Nurse and the Combine (which represent the repressive and mechanistic forces of society). McMurphy manages to arouse the emasculated and cowed psychiatric patients into a state of rebellion, and through a series of darkly comic events the patients begin to reassert their individual identities. Before their transformation is complete, however, Big Nurse exacts her revenge on McMurphy by subjecting him to a series of electric shock treatments and, finally, to a lobotomy. In an act of mercy, the narrator of the story, a patient at the hospital and a friend of McMurphy's, suffocates him to death and then flees the hospital in a quest for personal autonomy and freedom.

One Flew over the Cuckoo's Nest has been read as an allegory insofar as McMurphy may be interpreted as a Christ-figure. Numerous images in the novel support this reading: at one point McMurphy is accompanied by 12 followers (his "disciples") on a fishing trip; his shock treatments are administered on a table shaped like a cross, discharging a "crown of electric sparks in place of thorns"; and, most importantly, he willingly risks his life to save the others. He teaches the other patients that their lives can be meaningful, and that they are obliged to battle the social forces (Big Nurse and the Combine as symbols of American society in general) that try to dehumanize them. These important and hopeful lessons live on in the other patients after McMurphy's incapacitation and are directly responsible for the narrator's compassionate mercy killing and subsequent escape. (Hipkiss 1976; Leeds 1981; Safer 1988)

See also Kesey, Ken.

O'NEILL, EUGENE

Eugene O'Neill (1888–1953) has come to be known as one of America's most talented and creative twentieth-century playwrights. As a child, he toured with his popular actor-father, James O'Neill, and was educated at a Catholic boarding school. After spending one year at Princeton University, O'Neill worked at a series of odd jobs before beginning to write seriously. He became a highly acclaimed playwright beginning with *Beyond the Horizon* (1920) and *Anna Christie* (1921), yet his three Pulitzer Prizes for drama between 1920 and 1928 did not protect O'Neill from critics and skeptics who adamantly resisted some of the playwright's controversial depictions of issues such as interracial marriage, drug addiction, infanticide, abortion, and adultery. He was awarded the Nobel Prize in 1936; by this time he was suffering tremendously from what would eventually be diagnosed as Parkinson's disease. After a 12-year absence from the theater, O'Neill released *The Iceman Cometh* (1939; first performed 1946). This was followed by his Pulitzer Prize–winning *Long Day's Journey into Night* (1941; first performed 1956) and a continuation of the story of one of the characters in *Long Day's Journey* called *A Moon for the Misbegotten* (1943; first performed 1957). Ultimately, O'Neill's writing career was cut short due to the debilitating effects of Parkinson's disease; however, his vision of triumph and tragedy in the lives of "ordinary" people effectively transformed both American theater and literature. Several of his plays support allegorical readings.

See also *The Great God Brown; The Hairy Ape.*

OPERATION SIDEWINDER

The 1970 play *Operation Sidewinder* by Sam Shepard (b. 1943) has been recognized by some critics as a postmodern allegory of the conflicts between materialism and spiritualism in 1960s American culture. Noted as one of Shepard's early attempts at writing a serious political tract, *Operation Sidewinder*

illustrates the struggle between a power-hungry, technologically driven military force and a band of counterculture black radicals who want to use drugs to take over the country. When a government computer disguised as a giant sidewinder and designed to track UFOs lands in the desert, a band of Hopi Indians mistakes it for a snake-god that will reunite their physical selves with their spiritual selves. Both the military forces and the young radicals represent, in some way, American materialism, while the Hopis represent true spirituality. In the middle of this struggle appears Young Man, who represents the hippie everyman of the 1960s, and his girlfriend, Honey, who embodies the innocence and optimism of American youth. Critic Leonard Wilcox explains that *Operation Sidewinder* "follows the allegorical pattern of a trek through hell to the vision of the holy city we find in Dante and Bunyan, and this pattern is played out in Young Man . . . who moves . . . from self-absorption and materialism to spiritualism" (46). (DeRose 1992; Wilcox 1993)

See also Shepard, Sam.

ORPHEUS MYTH

A relatively late classical myth, most fully told by the Roman poet Ovid in his *Metamorphoses* (X), the Orpheus myth is a perversion of much earlier myths associated with the cult of Orphism in Greece. As it has come down to us, the story has gathered allegorical meaning.

Orpheus was the greatest of poets and musicians. His teachers were Apollo and the Muses, and his instrument was the lyre (from which we take the word "lyric" and thus "lyric poetry"). With his music Orpheus charmed not only humans but nature itself.

Upon returning from the journey of the Argonauts, described by Apollonius of Rhodes, Orpheus married Eurydice (Agriope). One day, as she escaped from the unwanted advances of one Aristaeus, she stepped on a poisonous snake and was fatally bitten by it. In death she sunk into Tartarus, the underworld of Hades.

Using the power of his music to charm the guardians of the underworld, the grief-stricken Orpheus descended to the depths in search of his love. He even charmed dark Hades himself so that the god allowed Eurydice to follow her husband back to the upper world, but under the condition that Orpheus was not to look back until Eurydice had completed her journey.

It seems likely that in the ancient versions of the myth, Orpheus and Eurydice succeeded in their conquest of death as the Orphic rites with which the myth would originally have been associated were in all likelihood shamanic and based on the idea of resurrection. According to the popular version as told by Ovid, however, Orpheus did look back and Eurydice was lost forever. The possible earlier ending especially suggests an allegorical meaning, which would have been essential not only to the Orphic cult but later to Christians, who would see in Orpheus (who in another myth became a sacrificial victim) a pagan prefiguring of Christ. According to the allegorical interpretation, Orpheus and his music are representative of the possibility of redemption. Eurydice is mortality. The quest of Orpheus and his eventual sacrifice stand for the necessary agonies the soul must suffer in order to redeem the mortal self which it loves. For Christians, the story of Orpheus and Eurydice is an allegory of Christ's redemptive powers. We are Eurydice and Orpheus-Christ is our salvation. It has been suggested by scholars that Orpheus's allegorical journey into Hades was the source for the journey into the underworld taken by so many epic heroes, from Odysseus to Dante. It seems more likely that such a journey is essentially archetypal, and that as such it predates even Orpheus. The Sumerian hero Gilgamesh had long before taken the journey, for example. Ultimately, the journey into the underworld is an allegory for the "night journey" or "dark night of the soul" that mystics associate with losing the self in order to find the self, or psychoanalysts see as the necessary and dangerous journey into the subconscious world a patient must undertake in order to achieve wholeness or individuation. (Frye 1957; MacQueen 1970)

ORWELL, GEORGE

George Orwell was born Eric Arthur Blair on 25 June 1903 in Bengal, India. He was taken to England by his mother as a young child while his father finished his job as a minor colonial officer in the Indian Civil Service. The Blairs were a middle- to upper-class family, and Eric, the middle child between two sisters, recalled a relatively happy childhood. He attended two preparatory schools: St. Cyprian's and then Eton. His grades were not high enough to win him a scholarship to college, so in the early 1920s he took a job with the Indian Imperial Police in Burma. After leaving the Imperial Service in 1927, he traveled to Paris to become a writer. For the next two decades, Orwell (who assumed his pseudonym upon publishing his first book, *Down and Out in Paris and London,* in 1933) wrote book reviews, articles, letters, essays, and 11 books. The allegorical novel *Animal Farm* was first published in 1945, in spite of many rejections from publishers who, considering England's alliance with Russia since 1941, thought the book too incendiary. However, *Animal Farm* became a huge success, making Orwell both internationally famous and financially secure. Orwell lived to complete one other masterpiece, *Nineteen Eighty-Four* (1949), before he died of tuberculosis in 1950.

See also Animal Farm.

THE OWL AND THE NIGHTINGALE

The Owl and the Nightingale is an anonymous Middle English poem of about 1,800 lines, probably composed sometime between 1180 and 1200. The entire poem consists of a conversation between an owl and a nightingale; for decades scholars have been fiercely divided on the meaning of this multifaceted conversation. It has been read as a political allegory, in which the owl is Thomas à

Becket, Archbishop of Canterbury, and the nightingale is King Henry II. It has also been interpreted with a radically different political twist: the owl as Geoffrey, Archbishop-elect of York, and the nightingale as King Richard I, Geoffrey's half brother. Still others have seen this poem through a more philosophical lens: the owl is gloom and seriousness while the nightingale is youth and cheerfulness; the owl is Philosophy while the nightingale is Art; the owl is the serious while the nightingale is the aesthetic. The possibility of religious allegory in this poem has not been ignored, either. Some maintain that the owl represents Christian wisdom and the nightingale represents physical love. On a literary level, some have argued that the allegory is based on poetics: the owl represents the older style of didactic poetry and the nightingale represents the newer form of secular, courtly poetry. Allegorical meaning has even been found in the context of music: the owl symbolizes the Gregorian chant while the nightingale embodies music influenced by the troubadours. Clearly, critics have been unable to come to any real sense of agreement on the specific allegorical meanings of this puzzling poem; nevertheless, scholars continue to consider *The Owl and the Nightingale* as some form of an allegory. (Hume 1975)

PAINTING AND SCULPTURE, ALLEGORICAL

Painting and sculpture have always been popular vehicles for allegory. As in the case of literary allegory, the allegorical painting or sculpture, to be ultimately effective, must work as an object of art in itself even as it is didactic. A book on allegorical painting and sculpture would resemble one on allegorical literature in that it would include examples that were obvious with those that were highly obscure. In very ancient times we find examples of allegorical art. A stone carving of the third millennium B.C.E. from Sumer shows the goddess Inanna (Ishtar) controlling two serpents as she stands upon two mammals whose appendages resemble a phallus and a stalk of grain. Any time we see a work of art which contains aspects that are somehow unrealistic, we assume an artistic purpose that has to do not with verisimilitude but with a meaning that is understandable to the culture out of which the work of art emerges. A student of Sumerian mythology would in all likelihood assume that the work just described reflects Innana's role as goddess of fertility.

The uninitiated visitor to any Hindu temple will be astounded by the proliferation of sculpture that covers the given building's walls. Most surprising of all will be the seemingly sacrilegious depictions of sexual intercourse. We recognize that such depictions must mean something other than what they literally depict. And, indeed, with help from one who can read the allegory we learn that the many depictions of sexual intercourse stand for various ways in which a god unites with his shakti—his other half—to achieve wholeness. By extension we achieve wholeness by seeking union with our spiritual side.

In Western classical art, to the extent that certain gods represent aspects of natural phenomena and human nature, depictions of them can be called allegorical—especially when isolated aspects of the depiction point to the quality in question. Thus, a famous fifth-century B.C.E. bronze figure from Dodona presents Zeus about to hurl a thunderbolt, suggesting his ancient storm god aspect (see illustration on page 197).

The medieval period is, not surprisingly, particularly rich in allegorical art. Over the south door of the great Byzantine church of St. Sophia in what is now

Istanbul we find a mosaic in which a woman enthroned holds a young child as a man on her right presents what appears to be a model of a church and one on her left presents a model of city walls. To any Byzantine Christian the allegory would have been clear. The woman is, of course, the Virgin Mary, the child is Jesus, the man on the Virgin's right is the Emperor Justinian presenting her with the great church itself while the Emperor Constantine on her left presents the city of Constantinople. The work speaks on a deeper level to the question of the Virgin's role as the Mother of and intercessor with God, represented in this case by her son.

The cathedrals of Western Europe were even more allegorical in their decorations than those of the Christian East. A modern visitor to the Cathedral of Chartres, especially one not versed in Judeo-Christian scriptures, might well wonder at the unrealistic scenes in the famous stained glass windows. In the south transept there are scenes in which four men are carrying four other men on their shoulders, the way a father might carry a child. It requires the allegorical analysis of the initiate to inform us of the meaning of these windows. Only when the allegory is made clear can the picture become "realistic"—at least in the context of the dogma to which it speaks. The cathedral guide reminds us that there were four Christian evangelists or gospelers—Matthew, Mark, Luke, and John—and that the vision of these men can be seen as an extension of the understanding of four great Old Testament prophets, Isaiah, Ezekiel, Daniel, and Jeremiah. The fact that the New Testament evangelists ride high on the shoulders of the Old Testament prophets suggests, according to Emile Male, one of the most important interpreters of medieval allegory, that "from their spiritual vantage-ground they have a wider outlook" (9).

Allegorical art continued to be popular in the Renaissance and in the transitional period between the Middle Ages and the Renaissance, as indicated, for example, in the famous series of paintings by Angiolotto Giotto (1267–1337) called the *Allegory of the Virtues and Vices.* A particularly popular abstraction in the Renaissance was Time. The Father Time we still associate with the end of the old year at New Year's Eve is a Renaissance mixing of the idea of Time itself with the classical Saturn, the brutal devourer of his own children. The Renaissance Time is an aged winged Saturn who carries a sickle or a scythe with which he sometimes clips the wings of Cupid—itself an allegorical act. An hourglass is also sometimes seen in association with him. Usually he is driven relentlessly forward on a cart pulled by antlered beasts. Sometimes he appears as a decrepit old man with a crutch, as in the painting by Jocopo Pesellino entitled *The Triumph of Time.*

Personification continued to mark the allegorical paintings of the seventeenth century. Cesare Ripa published his *Iconographia* early in the century. It was an illustrated encyclopedia of allegories that influenced all of the allegorical thought of the century. And in Rembrandt's famous painting *Bellona, Goddess of War*, if the face of Bellona does not appear to be particularly warlike, her costume—particularly the Gorgon on the shield—marks her clearly enough.

The early and mid-nineteenth century has its share of allegorical art. Often, as in the great historical works of Jacques Louis David, it is used to further

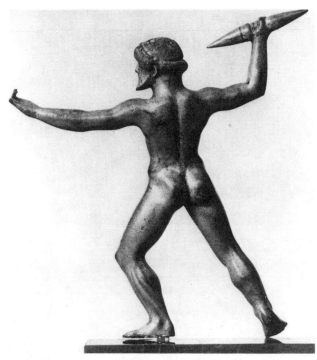

Arms outstretched, Zeus prepares to hurl a thunderbolt in this archaic Greek bronze from Dodona.

A window at the Cathedral of Chartres shows Isaiah bearing St. Matthew.

The mosaic over the south door of the Byzantine church St. Sophia depicts the Virgin Mary receiving a model of the church from Emperor Justinian (left) and a model of the city from Emperor Constantine (right).

Paul Delaux's *Phases of the Moon*, 1939

The Course of Empire IV: Destruction by Thomas Cole

political ideology. In the case of the American painter Thomas Cole, allegory is used to comment on such questions as aging and the "Course of Empire." Again, the sure sign of allegory is the presence of unrealistic objects or activities or a general sense of exaggeration, both of which suggest the need for explanation that leads to allegorical interpretation. In Cole's painting *The Course of Empire IV: Destruction* (see facing page), we see the fourth of five paintings in a series that describes the inevitable passage of empires from hopeful and bucolic beginnings to ruin; it clearly suggests the ultimate price to be paid by empires. The painting works as a painting but there is no question that the painter's intention is to use his work to represent an idea rather than any particular event or place.

Allegorical painting becomes more obscure as we move into the later part of the nineteenth century and eventually into twentieth-century modernism. With the advent of Surrealism, especially, influenced as it is by psychoanalysis and dream symbolism, we sense an art form that is almost by definition allegorical. The strange placing of real objects and people in mysterious or distorted contexts demands explanation, and even when we fail to understand, we feel that there is hidden meaning present, rather as we do when we look at early medieval allegorical art, characterized as it is by objects that are clearly allegorical. In the famous painting by Paul Delaux called *Phases of the Moon* (see facing page), we know from the title what the allegory is, but the details of the painting, the bow on the seated nude, the globe, the rocks on the ground, the two men who somehow look like psychiatrists, all demand attention as parts of an enigma to be solved. (Male 1958)

See also Ripa, Cesare.

 # PALIMPSEST

Originally, *palimpsest* referred to a manuscript that had been written on more than once, with the earlier text incompletely erased and still legible. In *The Madwoman in the Attic,* Sandra Gilbert and Susan Gubar use the word *palimpsest* to describe the way that women writers produce "works whose surface designs conceal or obscure deeper, less accessible (and less socially acceptable) levels of meaning. Thus these authors manage the difficult task of achieving true female literary authority by simultaneously conforming to and subverting patriarchal literary standards" (73). Palimpsestic works, then, can be interpreted as allegorical insofar as they tell two stories simultaneously; the "surface" story, complete in itself, masks the more "hidden," allegorical meaning. (Gilbert and Gubar 1984)

PANCHATANTRA

See Bidpai; Fable as Allegory.

PARABLE AS ALLEGORY

For some, notably Louis MacNeice in his *Varieties of Parable*, "parable" can be roughly equated with the word "allegory." In fact, the *Oxford English Dictionary* defines it as "any saying or narration in which something is expressed in terms of something else." In common practice, however, primarily because of its use in the New Testament, the parable has become a distinct type of allegory, a simple story that illustrates a moral lesson. Yet it should be pointed out that in keeping with an older tradition of the Hebrew prophets, parables can be complex—more like riddles than fables. Even in the New Testament, Jesus finds he must explain his parables, of which three examples follow. In Mark 4, we find the famous story of the sower with Jesus' allegorical interpretation.

> And he began again to teach by the sea side: and there was gathered unto him a great multitude, so that he entered into a ship, and sat in the sea; and the whole multitude was by the sea on the land. And he taught them many things by parables, and said unto them in his doctrine, Hearken; Behold, there went out a sower to sow: And it came to pass, as he sowed, some fell by the way side, and the fowls of the air came and devoured it up. And some fell on stony ground, where it had not much earth; and immediately it sprang up, because it had no depth of earth: But when the sun was up, it was scorched; and because it had no root, it withered away. And some fell among thorns, and the thorns grew up, and choked it, and it yielded no fruit. And other fell on good ground, and did yield fruit that sprang up and increased; and brought forth, some thirty, and some sixty, and some an hundred. And he said unto them, He that hath ears to hear, let him hear. And when he was alone, they that were about him with the twelve asked of him the parable. And he said unto them, Unto you it is given to know the mystery of the kingdom of God: but unto them that are without, all these things are done in parables: That seeing they may see, and not perceive; and hearing they may hear, and not understand; lest at any time they should be converted, and their sins should be forgiven them. And he said unto them, Know ye not this parable? and how then will ye know all parables? The sower soweth the word. And these are they by the way side, where the word is sown; but when they have heard, Satan cometh immediately, and taketh away the word that was sown in their hearts. And these are they likewise which are sown on stony ground; who, when they have heard the word, immediately receive it with gladness; And have no root in themselves, and so endure but for a time: afterward, when affliction or persecution ariseth for the word's sake, immediately they are offended. And these are they which are sown among thorns; such as hear the word, And the cares of this world, and the deceitfulness of riches, and the lusts of other things entering in, choke the word, and it becometh unfruitful. And these are they which are sown on good ground; such as hear the word, and receive it, and bring forth fruit, some thirtyfold, some sixty, and some an hundred. And he said unto them, Is a candle brought to be put under a bushel, or under a bed? and not to be set on a candlestick? For there is nothing hid, which shall not be manifested; neither was any thing kept secret, but that it should come abroad. If any man have ears to hear, let him hear. And he said unto them, Take heed what ye hear: with what measure ye mete, it shall be measured to you: and unto you that hear shall more be given. For he that hath, to him shall be given:

and he that hath not, from him shall be taken even that which he hath. And he said, So is the kingdom of God, as if a man should cast seed into the ground; And should sleep, and rise night and day, and the seed should spring and grow up, he knoweth not how. For the earth bringeth forth fruit of herself; first the blade, then the ear, after that the full corn in the ear. But when the fruit is brought forth, immediately he putteth in the sickle, because the harvest is come. And he said, Whereunto shall we liken the kingdom of God? or with what comparison shall we compare it? It is like a grain of mustard seed, which, when it is sown in the earth, is less than all the seeds that be in the earth: But when it is sown, it groweth up, and becometh greater than all herbs, and shooteth out great branches; so that the fowls of the air may lodge under the shadow of it. (Mark 4:1–32)

In the well-known parable of the Prodigal Son in Luke 16, the explanation comes before the story.

And he spake this parable unto them, saying, What man of you, having an hundred sheep, if he lose one of them, doth not leave the ninety and nine in the wilderness, and go after that which is lost, until he find it? And when he hath found it, he layeth it on his shoulders, rejoicing. And when he cometh home, he calleth together his friends and neighbours, saying unto them, Rejoice with me; for I have found my sheep which was lost. I say unto you, that likewise joy shall be in heaven over one sinner that repenteth, more than over ninety and nine just persons, which need no repentance. Either what woman having ten pieces of silver, if she lose one piece, doth not light a candle, and sweep the house, and seek diligently till she find it? And when she hath found it, she calleth her friends and her neighbours together, saying, Rejoice with me; for I have found the piece which I had lost. Likewise, I say unto you, there is joy in the presence of the angels of God over one sinner that repenteth. And he said, A certain man had two sons: And the younger of them said to his father, Father, give me the portion of goods that falleth to me. And he divided unto them his living. And not many days after the younger son gathered all together, and took his journey into a far country, and there wasted his substance with riotous living. And when he had spent all, there arose a mighty famine in that land; and he began to be in want. And he went and joined himself to a citizen of that country; and he sent him into his fields to feed swine. And he would fain have filled his belly with the husks that the swine did eat: and no man gave unto him. And when he came to himself, he said, How many hired servants of my father's have bread enough and to spare, and I perish with hunger! I will arise and go to my father, and will say unto him, Father, I have sinned against heaven, and before thee, And am no more worthy to be called thy son: make me as one of thy hired servants. And he arose, and came to his father. But when he was yet a great way off, his father saw him, and had compassion, and ran, and fell on his neck, and kissed him. And the son said unto him, Father, I have sinned against heaven, and in thy sight, and am no more worthy to be called thy son. But the father said to his servants, Bring forth the best robe, and put it on him; and put a ring on his hand, and shoes on his feet: And bring hither the fatted calf, and kill it; and let us eat, and be merry: For this my son was dead, and is alive again; he was lost, and is found. And they began to be merry. Now his elder son was in the field: and as he came and drew nigh to the house, he heard musick and dancing. And he called

Jesus as portrayed in *The Pilgrim's Progress*

one of the servants, and asked what these things meant. And he said unto him, Thy brother is come; and thy father hath killed the fatted calf, because he hath received him safe and sound. And he was angry, and would not go in: therefore came his father out, and intreated him. And he answering said to his father, Lo, these many years do I serve thee, neither transgressed I at any time thy commandment: and yet thou never gavest me a kid, that I might make merry with my friends: But as soon as this thy son was come, which hath devoured thy living with harlots, thou hast killed for him the fatted calf. And he said unto him, Son, thou art ever with me, and all that I have is thine. It was meet that we should make merry, and be glad: for this thy brother was dead, and is alive again; and was lost, and is found. (Luke 15:3–32)

Luke, in chapter 10, also reports the parable of the Good Samaritan:

And he answering said, Thou shalt love the Lord thy God with all thy heart, and with all thy soul, and with all thy strength, and with all thy mind; and thy neighbour as thyself. And he said unto him, Thou hast answered right: this do, and thou shalt live. But he, willing to justify himself, said unto Jesus, And who is my neighbour? And Jesus answering said, A certain man went down from Jerusalem to Jericho, and fell among thieves, which stripped him of his raiment, and wounded him, and departed, leaving him half dead. And by chance there came down a certain priest that way: and when he saw him, he passed by on the other side. And likewise a Levite, when he was at the place, came and looked on him, and passed by on the other side. But a certain Samaritan, as he journeyed, came where he was: and when he saw him, he had compassion on him, And went to him, and bound up his wounds, pouring in oil and wine, and set him on his own beast, and brought him to an inn, and took care of him. And on the morrow when he departed, he took out two pence, and gave them to the host, and said unto him, Take care of him; and whatsoever thou spendest more, when I come again, I will repay thee. Which now of these three, thinkest thou, was neighbour unto him that fell among the thieves? And he said, He that shewed mercy on him. Then said Jesus unto him, Go, and do thou likewise. (Luke 10:27–37)

Parables are not limited to the Judeo-Christian tradition. The Buddha, for instance, used them in much the same way Jesus did. In the Dhammapada, a collection of the Buddha's words, we find many such parables. This one is the story of the elephant; again, with allegorical interpretation provided by the "Exalted One."

THE ELEPHANT

I shall suffer hard words
as the elephant suffers arrows in battle.
People are people,
most of them ill-natured.

Only the tamed elephant goes into battle,
the king rides only a tamed elephant;
he who tames himself is best among men,
he suffers hard words patiently.

Tamed mules are excellent,
Sindhu horses of good breeding, excellent;
excellent are elephants of war.
Most excellent, however, is the self-tamer.

For no animals take one to Nirvana,
only the tamed self sees that untrodden land.

Consider the elephant Dhanapalaka,
temples glistening with rutting juice;
restless, he does not eat,
he pines for the elephant grove.

The glutton and the sluggard,
lapped in foolish sleep,
like hogs wallowing in filth,
find birth again and again.

There was a time when my mind wandered
freely, doing what it pleased;
now I must rule it, like the mahout
with his hook ruling the rutting elephant.

Check your mind.
Be on your guard.
Pull yourself out
as an elephant from mud.

If you have a friend sober, pure, and wise,
let nothing hold you back—
find delight and instruction in his company.

If you do not have a friend sober, pure, and wise,
walk alone—like a king who has renounced a conquered kingdom,
or an elephant roaming free in the forest.

Better aloneness than the friendship of a fool.
Walk alone like an elephant roaming free in the forest.
Be undemanding. Stay away from sin.
Friends give pleasure when needed.
Friendship is good when mutual.
Virtue's a friend when one dies.
Giving up sorrow gives virtue.

To be a mother is happy,
to be a father is happy.
It is happy to be a recluse,
it is happy to be a saint.

Happy is virtue that lasts,
happy is well-rooted faith,
happy it is to be wise,
happy to avoid sin.

The Zen Buddhists have a parable-like tradition in their use of brief para-doxical riddles called koans, which are meant to demonstrate the limitations of logic and the incomprehensibility of truth. The most famous example is a question a Zen master asks of his pupil: "You know how to make the sound of two hands clapping, but what is the sound made by one hand?" A koan that more closely resembles the parable—because it has a narrative aspect—is the well-known one called "Mu." There was a Chinese Buddhist monk who came to the famous Zen Master Joshu and asked him whether a dog could possess the Buddha-nature. Joshu answered simply, "Mu!" "Mu" means "no" or "not." But "mu" can also refer to the dynamic Buddha-nature. According to the Zen Master Yasutani, the paradox of this koan expresses the fact that the mystery of "Mu" can only be discovered within the inner self; intellectual analysis or con-ceptions can be of no help.

To understand a koan the student of Zen must practice extreme concentra-tion; it stands as a challenging spiritual barrier which must be overcome if enlightenment is to be achieved.

Something much like the parable exists in the Chinese tradition as well. The *Chuang-tsu*, along with the *Tao te Ching*, the major collections of Taoist thought, contains many parables, as do the works of Confucius and Mencius. (MacNeice 1965; MacQueen 1970; Rollinson 1981)

See also The Bible and Allegory; Lao Tsu; Mencius; Plato.

THE PARLEMENT OF FOULES

The Parlement of Foules, a dream vision, was written by Geoffrey Chaucer (ca. 1343–1400) probably in the years between 1374 and 1381. It was based on Cicero's *Dream of Scipio*. A gentle satire of the traditions of courtly love, the *Parlement of Foules* immediately addresses its main theme, opening with the narrator's comments on the difficulties and mysteries of love. The narrator soon falls fast asleep, and in his dream he is approached by Scipio Africanus, a character in a book the narrator was reading. Scipio becomes the dreamer's guide, leads him to the gate of a beautiful garden, and pushes him through. The two men find themselves amidst every kind of tree and bird imaginable, as well as many other animals. The dreamer visits the temple of Venus located in the garden and sees the personifications of Jealousy, Venus, Bacchus, and others (allegorical representations of the extremes of love). Returning to the garden, he sees the beautiful Dame Nature, surrounded by all the birds. It is Saint Valentine's Day, and the birds are eager to choose their mates. Dame Nature declares that the bird with the highest rank, the tercel (male) eagle, shall be allowed to choose first.

The eagle chooses the formel (female) eagle perched on Nature's hand; two other lower-ranking tercels challenge his choice, claiming that they also love her and deserve her as a mate. All the birds, allegorically representing the various levels of English society (the clergy, the bourgeoisie, the peasants), debate the issue at length. None of the birds offers an acceptable solution to the problem, so Nature intervenes and decides that the formel eagle may choose the mate she loves best (often interpreted as a pointed message to the arrangers of court marriages). The formel begs to be permitted to wait a year before she decides, for she feels she is too young to marry. Nature acquiesces, and at last the rest of the birds can choose their mates. Before they part, the birds sing a roundel in praise of summer and Saint Valentine. The noise that the birds make as they fly away awakens the dreamer, and the poem comes to an end. (Piehler 1988)

See also *The Canterbury Tales;* Chaucer, Geoffrey; Cicero; *The Hous of Fame.*

PAUL AS AN ALLEGORIST

Saint Paul (Saul of Tarsus) frequently used allegory as a device in his letters (the New Testament Epistles) to the early Christian churches. One such example is in his letter to the Galatians, in which Paul criticizes the Christians of the Jewish tradition, as opposed to the Gentiles, for attempting to bring Jewish law and practice into the Church. In that letter (Galatians 4), he compares the seed of Hagar, the slave, to that of Sarah. The child of the slave is the Old Law; the child of Sarah is the New Covenant of grace through Christ. (Honig 1966; MacQueen 1970)

See also The Bible and Allegory.

PAYSAGE MORALISÉ

This is a French term commonly used by literary critics to describe an allegorized landscape in fiction. In the "moralized landscape," particular kinds of settings are associated with particular values. Angus Fletcher suggests a *paysage moralisé* in Zane Grey's fiction. In *Black Mesa,* the Desert of Bitter Sleeps reflects the moral state of the characters who find themselves in it (5–7). The works of Cormac McCarthy lend themselves easily to the *paysage moralisé* approach as do the earlier works of Ernest Hemingway. The stark and forbidding landscape of McCarthy's *Blood Meridian* is a perfect reflection of the inner landscapes of the tortured characters who travel through it. In both *A Farewell to Arms* and *The Sun Also Rises,* by Ernest Hemingway, the morally good life is found in the hills, while the emptiness and ennui of the period between the wars is found in the valley towns and cities below. (Fletcher 1964)

PEAKE, MERVYN

Mervyn Peake (1911–1968) was a British poet, painter, and writer of fantasy novels—most notably, the *Gormenghast Trilogy*. While some critics have considered the trilogy to be allegorical in that it refers meaningfully back to our world, most would probably agree that the end result differs from real allegory in that the connections between the elements of the fiction and any secondary meaning are subjective and personal rather than objective and general. At most we can say that the highly ritualized castle in the novels stands for an order in the world—albeit a mysterious order—which the villain Steerpike undermines in the first novel. Steerpike, thus, stands for irrational evil. In the second and third novels of the trilogy, Titus is the hero; he finally leaves the castle to face a world which, without the castle and its rituals, is spiritless and perverted and overly mechanical. (Clifford 1974; Hunter 1989)

THE PEARL

An anonymously composed poem of fourteenth-century England, *The Pearl* is a visionary allegory. It begins with the despairing poet looking in a garden for his lost pearl. It is Reason and Nature personified who attempt to restore peace of mind to the distraught poet. That Nature teaches the poet the possibilities of the peace of Christ is significant because it is through death and life, the rhythm of Nature, that the great miracle of resurrection expresses itself. *The Pearl* is, of course, a Christian allegory, the lost pearl perhaps representing lost faith. The poem contains a mysterious figure, the pearl maiden, who, as the representative of the poet's soul or divine inspiration, must remind us of other important allegorical women such as Una in Spenser's *Faerie Queene* and Beatrice in Dante's *Divine Comedy*. (Piehler 1971)

PERSEPHONE MYTH

The myth of the rape of Core, or Persephone (Proserpina), the daughter of Demeter (Ceres), by the god Hades (Aidoneus, Dis, Pluto), is one of the most popular of classical myths. It was told first by the Greeks (in the "Homeric Hymn to Demeter"), then by the Romans (Ovid, *Metamorphoses*, Book V), and has been retold or referred to by countless later poets and writers, including Shakespeare (*A Winter's Tale*, IV, 4, 116–127) and Milton (*Paradise Lost*, IV, 268–272).

When the god of the underworld, Hades, asked his brother Zeus for permission to marry his daughter Persephone, Zeus was reluctant. What father would want his daughter to live her life in the darkness of the underworld, even if her husband were king there? And there was the question of the girl's mother, the agriculture goddess Demeter, who would never agree to such a marriage. Yet, Hades was powerful, and Zeus did not want to offend him. Zeus's unfortunate solution was to give tacit approval to the match by not interfering with it.

One day the beautiful young Persephone was out in one of her mother's fields happily picking flowers. The followers of Demeter say the field was in Eleusis, where the sacred mystery cult of the corn goddess would be established later.

In delight, Persephone reached out to grasp a particularly beautiful bunch of flowers. These had been magically cultivated by Hades himself to entice his prey, and as the girl leaned over, the earth opened and out sprang the dark god. He took the screaming girl into his golden chariot which, drawn by immortal horses, took the couple into the land of the dead. No one heard the cries of the raped maiden but the ancient witch-moon goddess, Hecate, who, with Demeter, convinced the sun to reveal that the abductor had been Hades and that Zeus had had knowledge of his brother's intentions.

In great anger, Demeter refused to keep company with the Olympian gods and withdrew her powers from the earth, so that the fruits and trees and crops dried up and humankind was on the brink of extinction. Demeter established herself at Eleusis and waited, lamenting all the while for her lost daughter.

Seeing the destruction wrought by his original inaction, and unhappy about the loss of sacrifices and offerings that would result from it, Zeus sent Hermes to Hades to ask for the return of Persephone. Hades agreed, but before the departure of his wife he forced her to eat of the food of the underworld, the fertile pomegranate seed, and so it was that she would be forced to return to her husband for one third of each year.

Demeter rejoiced to see her daughter and became reconciled to Zeus, although she regretted having to give up her child for a third of each year. When Persephone was with her the fields flourished, but when she was with Hades Demeter grieved and the fields died.

The Persephone tale has nearly always been seen as an allegory. In Greek, the word *Demeter* could be used to mean bread and in Latin *Ceres* could mean grain. Hades was equated with earth and Persephone with the seed planted in earth. In terms of the Eleusinian mysteries of Demeter, the myth, then, was an allegory of the germination process for which Demeter was responsible. Persephone is literally planted in the dark earth for one third of each year only to reemerge each spring. The myth at this level is an allegorical explanation of the seasons.

It seems likely that there would have been another allegorical level of meaning for the initiates of the Eleusinian mysteries. Persephone could have represented the human soul taken by Death (Hades) and redeemed by the great cult Mother (Demeter).

Later cultures would use the myth for their own allegorical purposes. For the Christian poet Milton, the rape of Persephone was a model for the fall of Adam and Eve, in which Hades represents Satan and Demeter the Christ who redeems humanity. (Leeming 1990; Leeming and Page 1994; Piehler 1971)

See also Myth as Allegory.

PERSONIFICATION

Personification *(prosopoeia)* is a literary device in which abstract ideas are represented by animate—usually human—characters. In the medieval play

Everyman, the character Good Deeds represents the abstract concept of good deeds. It could be argued that personified abstractions are the basis of the purest form of allegory. Such personifications do not result in complex characterizations, but they create illusions of personality that are sufficient to bring abstractions to life for the reader. There are cases, for example in Dante's *Divine Comedy*, in which the author does use complex characters for allegorical purposes in what might be called reverse personification. In such cases actual people—such as Paolo and Francesca—are treated, to quote Angus Fletcher, "in a formulaic way so that they become walking ideas" (28).

In recent years, personification has become the subject of renewed discussion by poststructuralist and postmodernist critics such as Paul de Man, Maureen Quilligan, and Lynette Hunter. It might be said, as James Paxon suggests, that personification has been rehabilitated by these critics. He also points out that "the deconstructive theory of personification (like the deconstructive theory of 'allegory') seems to expand to the point where it encompasses all narrative or lyric" (1). (de Man 1979; Fletcher 1964; Hunter 1989; Paxon 1994; Quilligan 1979)

See also Allegoresis; de Man, Paul; *The Divine Comedy*; Quilligan, Maureen.

PETER THE CHANTER

The Chanter was a master at the University of Paris and a church cantor (Chanter) in the late twelfth century. He was also the author of *The Distinctiones Abel*. A *distinctiones* was a literary form through which various allegorical meanings of words were distinguished; it was a sort of glossary of allegorical terms. The first word in Peter's alphabetically arranged book was Abel, thus the title. Each word to be discussed was placed to the left of the page. Explanations were placed to the right. (Bloomfield 1981)

PHILOSOPHICAL ALLEGORY

See Plato.

"THE PHOENIX AND THE TURTLE"

Shakespeare's poem contains examples of "pure allegory," in which abstractions are directly personified and even given emotions. For example, "Propertie was thus appalled" or "Reason in itself confounded,/Saw Division grow together. . . ." The whole poem is really a funereal poem in which birds have congregated to mourn the death of the phoenix and the turtle dove, who stand for resurrection and fidelity, truth and beauty, and are united in death: "Truth and beauty buried be." Shakespeare uses allegory here to comment on the paradox by which death divides lovers but cannot divide their love.

PHORNUTUS

See Cornutus, Annaeus.

THE PICTURE OF DORIAN GRAY

Oscar Wilde's (1854–1900) only novel, *The Picture of Dorian Gray* (1891), tells the story of a young artist named Basil Hallward, his handsome friend Dorian Gray, and a shallow and manipulative aesthete called Lord Henry Wotton. Basil paints a beautiful portrait of Dorian, who remarks, upon seeing the painting, that he would give his soul if he could remain young while the portrait itself aged. Lord Henry and Dorian soon become close friends, and through the older man's influence Dorian embarks on an Epicurean life of sensation and pleasure. After coldly ending a brief romance with a young actress named Sibyl (who subsequently commits suicide), Dorian discovers that while his own appearance remains unchanged, his portrait now reveals a certain cruelty in his face. Recognizing that the painting has become the true record of his debauched life, he hides it away in a locked room and continues his reckless and immoral lifestyle. Some years later, Basil comes to Dorian in an attempt to persuade him to change his depraved behavior. Dorian shows him the painting, and Basil is horrified to see how dreadfully the portrait has changed. In a rage, Dorian stabs Basil to death and then blackmails an acquaintance into concealing his crime by destroying the body.

Later, after one of his frequent visits to an opium den, Dorian encounters Sibyl's brother, Jim, who has vowed revenge on his dead sister's betrayer. Dorian convinces him that he is not to blame for Sibyl's death, for he is far too young to have been involved with a woman who died 18 years previously. After Dorian leaves, a woman in the opium den explains to Jim that, mysteriously, Dorian's appearance has not changed in many years. Some time later, while watching Dorian at his country estate, Jim is accidentally killed by a group of hunters.

Eventually, Dorian decides that he must destroy the painting, which constantly reminds him of his guilt. He stabs the painting with the knife he used to kill Basil, and the servants hear a terrible scream. When they enter the room they find on the wall a painting of their master as he had looked in his youth, and an old, wrinkled, unrecognizable body lying on the floor with a knife in its breast. After examining the jewelry on the corpse, they identify the body as the decrepit remains of Dorian Gray.

The Picture of Dorian Gray has been interpreted as containing elements of social and religious allegory. Socially, the novel allegorizes the problems of aestheticism through Dorian's attempt to realize his life as art. One critic suggests the possibility that "Wilde's allegory exposes the severe, life-denying limitations of aestheticism in practice" (San Juan, 67). By depicting the relentless disintegration of Dorian's moral sensibilities, Wilde reveals the shortcomings of his aesthetic view. In Dorian's misguided effort to eliminate his artistic representation and thereby alleviate his guilt, he kills himself.

As a religious allegory, *The Picture of Dorian Gray* is the story of man's fall from innocence into self-knowledge. Lord Henry Wotton is a figure of temptation, who propels Dorian toward evil but who never actually follows his own advice. Dorian is the proud, hedonistic sinner who refuses to repent, regardless of his troubled conscience and his knowledge of his wicked behavior. Basil is a Christ-figure, who implores Dorian to atone for his sins and save his corrupted soul and who is mercilessly sacrificed for trying to save his selfish friend from his own destruction. (Roditi 1969; San Juan 1967)

See also Wilde, Oscar.

PIERS PLOWMAN

The religious allegory *The Vision of Piers Plowman,* by the Englishman William Langland (ca. 1330–1387), is set in the poet's native Malvern Hills area. *Piers Plowman* survives in three distinct versions that are commonly called the A-, B-, and C-Texts. The A-Text is the shortest and most incomplete (about 2,400 hundred lines), the B-Text revises the A-Text and adds to it over 4,000 lines, and the C-Text is a revision of the B-Text. Although many earlier manuscripts still exist, *Piers Plowman* was first printed in 1550 and acquired an especially wide readership during the sixteenth century. From the start it was considered a controversial text; some even believe that its sympathy for the poor and its attack on all forms of corruption prophesied the English Reformation.

Piers Plowman has challenged readers for centuries with its complicated tale of man's quest for salvation and religious understanding. The story is told through a series of dream visions in which the relationship between man and God is explored and the nature of man's own intellect is examined. The character of Piers Plowman, an allegorical depiction of Christ, appears throughout the poem and holds together the loose series of visions and stories that compose the work.

The narrator begins his story by explaining that in a dream he envisioned a "fair feeld ful of folk," living on a plain between a castle on a hill and a dungeon in a valley. Langland's description of this community reflects his vision of actual fourteenth-century English society's inability to live according to truly Christian values. In the dream, a beautiful woman named Holy Church descends from the castle and explains to the dreamer that the lord of the castle is Truth and the lord of the dungeon is the Father of Falsehood. The dreamer asks Holy Church how he may save his soul; she answers him that Truth is best. Allegorically, the vision suggests that people must decide to whom they will pledge their faith—to Truth (God), or to False[hood] (the Devil).

The next section of *Piers Plowman* is an elaborate vision of a trial of a woman named Lady Meed. In medieval times, "meed" signified money used as wages, rewards, payments, and gifts, as well as money used to bribe and therefore to corrupt. Thus, Lady Meed becomes a complex allegorical figure who simultaneously represents Just Reward and Bribery. In the vision, Lady Meed is about to marry False. A character called Theology protests the match and suggests that the issue be tried in the king's court. The king chides Lady Meed for nearly marrying False and proposes instead that she marry one of his knights, Conscience. Conscience refuses, citing Lady Meed's power to corrupt, and maintains that conscience and bribery cannot be reconciled. The king summons Reason to mediate the dispute and eventually invites Reason and Conscience to help him rule his kingdom as Chancellor and Justice, respectively. The scene suggests Langland's dark view that the country is overrun with corruption, but that the counsel of Conscience and Reason may yet save the nation.

The next vision reveals Reason preaching to the people to be true to their duties—the common people should work hard, the clergy should follow their own preachings, and the rulers of the land should uphold the law fairly. His sermon moves the people to repent their sins; even the seven deadly sins confess their trespasses against Truth. A thousand people want to reform their lives and allegorically "go to Truth," but they lack leadership and guidance. A leader emerges from their ranks—a lowly but infinitely virtuous plowman named Piers. Piers teaches the people that the Ten Commandments mark the path to Truth and offers to lead them to Truth's castle if they will first help him plow his half-acre field. The people begin this labor, initially working cooperatively, in accordance with their social positions. But soon the effort falls apart, as the people cannot live up to their vows of repentance. Allegorically, this scene depicts the value of an ideal Christian society working for the common good, but at the same time demonstrates how impossible it is for actual society to maintain this level of camaraderie and cooperation. The dream continues as Truth hears of the events in the field and issues a pardon to Piers and to all those who helped him. After a priest looks at the pardon and comments that it does not resemble any pardon he has ever seen, Piers angrily tears it in two, thus ending this dream.

The dreamer's third vision continues the quest for Truth. The dreamer (called "Will" for the first time in this section) encounters a number of allegorical figures, including Thought, Patience, Study, etc., who represent different aspects of the internal, mental journey toward Truth. Thought divides the search for Truth into three lives, or states: Do-Well, Do-Better, and Do-Best. Through a series of encounters and with the guidance of conscience, Will learns that Do-Well involves honesty, obedience, fear of God, and love of one's fellow man. Do-Well is what common people must strive for if they wish to search for Truth. Do-Better describes the state of the priest, who must live according to his preachings and guide others to search for Truth. Do-Best falls to the bishops, who have the responsibility of living up to the requirements of Do-Well and Do-Better, as well as running the Church wisely and honestly.

As the character of Piers Plowman continues to appear throughout the work, it becomes progressively clearer to the reader that he is an allegorical representation of Jesus Christ. Although presented at first as merely a virtuous and hardworking man, by the end of the poem Piers-as-Jesus has explained the nature of the Tree of Charity and the Trinity of God. He also appears as the Good Samaritan, the builder of the Church, and a fighter willing to joust against

Satan. Furthermore, Langland chronicles many biblical events in his poem, from the story of Eden to the crucifixion of Jesus, thus reinforcing the strong Christian elements of the work.

Christians must decide to place their loyalties either with God (Truth) or with Satan; *Piers Plowman* allegorizes this important decision. Langland creates for the reader a series of allegorical confrontations between such abstract elements as Truth, Conscience, Reason, and others that depict the complexities of this decision and then inserts the simple, honest plowman, Piers—the perfect Christian—to serve as teacher and guide. The vision of medieval Christianity that *Piers Plowman* offers its readers serves to illustrate the journey-quest for salvation that is ultimately inseparable from the examination of one's own soul. (Aers 1975; Barney 1988; Johnson 1992)

See also Langland, William; The Quest as Allegory.

THE PILGRIM'S PROGRESS

The Pilgrim's Progress by John Bunyan (1628–1688) is one of the most famous and important Christian allegories, praised both for its adventurous episodes of human drama and its sensitive portrayal of a man trying to make the journey to Heaven. Bunyan uses the familiar metaphor of life as a journey to evoke in his readers a genuine connection between the trials of the hero, Christian, and the trials of every good Christian. His tale reflects the difficulties as well as the rewards of following a truly Christian path, as seen through the eyes of his impressionable narrator.

The story begins with the author falling asleep; the events of the allegory itself occur as a dream vision. The dream begins with the main character, Christian, grieving for the imminent destruction of his family and his community which he discovers through reading the Bible. Christian is soon approached by Evangelist, the preacher of Christianity, who presents him with a scroll that explains that Christian should flee from God's wrath, leaving the City of Destruction for the City of Zion. This command fills Christian with hope and he runs to his family and neighbors to ask them to make this journey with him. They think he is ill or has gone mad and refuse to listen to his entreaties. Finally, Christian ignores his family's pleas to stay with them and runs away toward a light in the distance under which he believes he will find the entrance to the City of Heaven.

Presently, Christian meets Pliant and Obstinate, who distract him from his journey and cause him to fall into the Slough of Despond. Christian cannot climb out of the Slough because of the weight of the sins he carries on his back. Eventually, he is rescued by Help and is released from the bog, but soon afterward he encounters Mr. Worldly Wiseman, who tells Christian that he could lead a happier life if he abandons his journey toward the light and settles down to a life in town. Evangelist reappears, fearing that Christian might be persuaded by Mr. Worldly Wiseman's entreaties, and shows Christian the faults of his arguments.

Shortly thereafter, Christian meets Good-Will, who explains to him that if he knocks on the closed gate before him, he will be allowed to enter. Christian knocks, enters the gate, and is invited by Interpreter into the gatekeeper's house. There, Christian learns the meanings of many Christian mysteries and sees pictures of Christ, Passion, Patience, Despair, and the Day of Judgment. Christian is filled with both fear and hope but resolves to continue his journey. Soon he comes to the Holy Cross and the Sepulchre of Christ, where his burden of sins falls off, allowing him to persevere in his quest with increased strength.

Christian soon encounters Sloth, Simple, Presumption, Formalism, and Hypocrisy, but they do not tempt him away from his journey. Christian becomes tired and falls asleep; upon waking, he forgets to take with him the scroll that Evangelist had given him. Later realizing his mistake, Christian runs back to the place where he has left the paper, then continues quickly on his way, trying to make up the time he has lost. Suddenly, he is confronted by two lions. His fright subsides when a porter explains that the lions are chained and cannot hurt him. The porter invites Christian into his home, where he is treated kindly and shown some biblical relics by four virgins: Discretion, Prudence, Piety, and Charity. They offer him sound advice and send him away, armed with the sword and shield of Christian faith.

Christian arrives in the Valley of Humiliation, where he is forced to battle a giant devil named Apollyon, whose body is covered with the scales of pride. Christian is hurt in the fight but manages to chase away the devil. Later, he heals his wounds with leaves from the Tree of Life. He then travels into the Valley of the Shadow of Death, where he must pass one of the gates of Hell. He protects himself from the devils who accost him by reciting some of the verses from the Psalms.

Christian's next challenge is to pass by the caves of the old giants, Pope and Pagan. After he does so, he meets a fellow traveler named Faithful. The two men continue together and soon reencounter Evangelist. He warns them of the dangers they will face in the town of Vanity Fair, a place where many men have been lured away from the path to Heaven. In Vanity Fair, all the vanities of the world are available, and the townspeople are ignorant, cruel, and do not care for travelers such as Christian and Faithful. The two companions promise Evangelist that they will be careful and avoid temptation.

When Christian and Faithful arrive in Vanity Fair, they are arrested for refusing to buy any of the town's goods. Faithful is condemned to be burned alive, and Christian is thrown in prison. When Faithful dies in the flames, a chariot descends from Heaven to take him to God. Christian escapes from prison, meets a man named Hopeful who is moved by Faithful's heavenly reward, and the two leave the town.

Christian and Hopeful travel through the Valley of Ease, where they are tempted to dig in a silver mine that is free for everyone. Leaving the valley, they see the pillar of salt that was once Lot's wife. They soon become lost and are captured by a giant named Despair. He takes them to his home, the Doubting Castle, and locks them in vaults beneath the castle walls. There they remain until Christian remembers that he has a key called Promise in his pocket. With this key, they escape from their prison.

The cave where two giants, the Pope and the Pagan, dwelt in Bunyan's *Pilgrim's Progress*.

Continuing their journey, the two pilgrims meet four shepherds named Knowledge, Experience, Watchful, and Sincere, who show them the Celestial Gate and caution them against the paths to Hell. Soon after, Christian and Hopeful pass the Valley of Conceit, where they meet Ignorance and other characters who have strayed from the path to Heaven. They then travel to the country of Beulah, where they can see the beautiful gates of Heaven in the distance. Elated, the two men lie down and rest.

Later, as they continue their journey toward the gates, they arrive at the River of Death. They walk into the river and try to wade across, but Christian becomes frightened. The more frightened he becomes, the more dangerous the waters around him become. Hopeful calls to him to have faith and hope, and Christian, cheered by his friend's words, becomes less afraid. The swirling waters recede, and the two men ford the river safely. Reaching the other side, they run up the hill toward Heaven, where they are welcomed by angels who lead them through the gates.

The Pilgrim's Progress allegorizes every Christian's journey through life toward either Heaven or Hell by chronicling the adventures of Christian, the naïve, gullible, and well-meaning main character. The work clearly preaches the dangers that such pitfalls as Vanity, Pride, and Despair can present to Christians, but because Bunyan teaches his lessons through an appealing, exciting adventure story, the allegory avoids becoming merely a dry sermon. *The Pilgrim's Progress* is an excellent example of seventeenth-century allegory, recounting the popular story of personal Christian salvation through unambiguous language and unmistakable characterizations. (Swain 1993)

See also Bunyan, John; *The Life and Death of Mr. Badman;* The Quest as Allegory.

PINTER, HAROLD

Harold Pinter (b. 1930) is a British playwright and screenplay writer whose plays are in some sense allegories. Martin Esslin notes that *The Birthday Party* "has been interpreted as an allegory of the pressures of conformity" and suggests that it might "equally well be seen as an allegory of death." This play and others by Pinter—for instance, *The Caretaker* and *The Homecoming*—are certainly representative in some way of the degeneration of modern life. But Pinter's characters and situations have such individuality and originality and the plays work so well as pure drama, without any need to attach a didactic intention, that the allegory label seems questionable. Pinter himself has made this clear: "I think it is impossible—and certainly for me—to start writing a play from any kind of abstract idea . . ." (Esslin 1961, 241). (Esslin 1961; MacNeice 1965)

See also *The Birthday Party.*

THE PLAGUE

Albert Camus (1917–1960), the 1957 Nobel Prize–winner from France, was an intellectual leader whose work wrestled with the complexities of the human conscience. *La Peste [The Plague]* (1947), published at the end of World War II, is the story of a town stricken with the deadly bubonic plague, and the reactions of the various townspeople to this calamity. Written as a chronicle, the narrator is eventually revealed to be one of the main characters in the story, Dr. Rieux. Other important characters include a journalist, a priest, an idealist, a suspected criminal, and a suicidal clerk. Camus's tale demonstrates how the victims cope with the devastation of plague either through human means (as the doctor does) or through spiritual means (as the priest does). Significantly, the medical victory over the epidemic is the result of the entire town's working together, perhaps suggesting the importance of human solutions over abstract, theological salvation.

Critics have interpreted *The Plague* as an allegory of the German occupation during World War II, specifically re-creating the horror and subsequent denial of the Holocaust. The horrible epidemic suggests the horror of the war through its potential to cause widespread, indiscriminate death. Critic Shoshana Felman explains that the huge number of deaths wrought by the plague (World War II) "deprive[s] the very loss of life of any tragic import, reducing death . . . to a statistical abstraction" (98). The world's unresponsive reaction to the millions of Holocaust victims killed at the hands of the Nazis testifies to this abstraction, just as the plague victims' inability to believe the extent of the disease's toll mirrors the Holocaust victims' inability to believe in the existence of the gas chambers. Life in the quarantined town of *The Plague* becomes an allegory of life in a concentration camp, and the medical volunteers who risk their lives to battle the ravages of the epidemic represent the European resistance groups that fought against Nazi domination. Finally, the townspeople deny and forget the horrors of the plague immediately after it subsides, allegorizing Europe's sweeping denial of the existence of the Holocaust as soon as the war came to an end. (Felman 1992)

See also Camus, Albert.

PLATO

Plato, or Platon (ca. 427–348 B.C.E.), was a philosopher born to a wealthy Athenean family. At first he was interested in politics but later became disillusioned, especially because of the murder of his teacher, Socrates. Plato was an ardent traveler and he never tired of attempting to influence the leaders of the societies he visited. His primary philosophical concern was the unity behind the apparent changes of the universe. Plato wrote, among many other works, the *Republic*, the *Apology*, and the *Symposium*. His works are for the most part written in dialogue form, suggesting conversations between Socrates and his pupils. Within these "Socratic dialogues" are myths that convey much of Plato's philosophy allegorically. For some, Plato is the father of allegory as we know it. Plato's myths are concerned with the soul, the mediator between unity and appearances through which true knowledge is attained. In the *Phaedrus*, for example, the soul, or reason, is a charioteer who must control the spiritual and sensual steeds.

The most famous Platonic myth of the soul in relation to unity and appearance—treated by Plato as a parable—is the myth of the cave, found in the sixth book of the *Republic*. Plato asks us to imagine some men living since childhood in an underground space reached by a long passage with an entrance that opens to the light. The men are chained by the neck so that they can only see what is in front of them. Above and behind them is the light caused by a burning fire and between them and the fire there is a track with a wall below it that is like the screen that hides the puppeteers at a puppet show. There are people behind the wall moving objects which appear on the track above it. These are models of objects, animals, humans, and so forth; they are given voices when appropriate by the people who move them. As for the prisoners, they cannot see the fire and the wall and track; they can only see the shadows caused by the firelight on the cave wall facing them and can hear only the echoes of any voices the puppeteers care to give to their figures. Their condition resembles ours, says Plato, giving an indication of the allegorical level. If the prisoners talk to each other about what they are seeing, which presumably they do, they can only refer to the shadows—not to the actual objects behind them. In short, the prisoners will recognize reality only in the shadows and echoes of artificial models.

Now the philosopher asks us to imagine that one of the prisoners is set free and made to turn and walk toward the light and to look at the models that had cast the shadows on the cave wall. Seeing these artificial objects, the confused former prisoner will probably consider the familiar shadows to be more real than the models. And if he is forced to look into the firelight his eyes will hurt at first and he will prefer to turn back to the clearer images on the cave wall.

We are asked next to imagine that the freed prisoner is forced to go up the long passageway to the sunlight. Once in the light of day, he will surely be so dazzled as to make any real vision impossible. He will see nothing of what he is now told is reality. It will be necessary for him to gradually get used to the new light; first he will see shadows and then images reflected in water and then the things themselves. Next he will be able to watch the moon and the stars at night and only later the sun itself in daylight. Finally, he will assume that the magnificent sun is the cause of the seasons and of everything in the visible world and even of the shadows on his old cave wall.

The freed man will remember his fellow prisoners down in the cave. He will feel sorry for them in their ignorance, praising each other for their knowledge of the shadows and their movements. But the man will not miss the praise of his fellows; like Achilles in *The Odyssey*, he would rather be a hired servant above than a king below living in the old way.

But suppose the man is forced to return to his old seat. The sudden change from light to darkness will cloud his vision. When asked his opinions, as in the old days, of the shadows on the wall, he will be unable to react as he once had. And the other prisoners will make fun of his ignorance. Obviously, from their point of view, an ascent to the upper world is useless and they might even kill anyone who tried to force them to make the climb.

Plato tells us at the outset that the myth of the cave-prison is a parable to "illustrate the degrees in which our nature may be enlightened or unenlightened," and after the myth he explains the allegory in detail. The prison-cave is the world we perceive by sight. The climb to the passage opening is the ascent of the soul to the world of the truly intelligible. The ability to look at the radiance of the sun itself is the ability to contemplate the "Form of Goodness"—the true light, the source of all real wisdom. The freed man's reluctance to return to the prison—the life of the mere senses—is the reluctance of those who have "seen the light" to return to ordinary life. And when such a soul returns to the prison of life, it necessarily appears awkward. As one who has seen reality, he seems foolish when he attempts to discuss the shadows of mere models of reality with those who have never seen the light.

In short, Plato tells his listeners, it is important to remember that the soul may be confused either by moving from darkness to light or from light to darkness. In terms of education in a new republic, then, it must be remembered that knowledge cannot be conveyed to a soul without proper preparation. The myth means that just as the body must be turned around so that light can be experienced rather than darkness, the soul must be turned away from the changing world of the senses in order that it might learn to contemplate the ultimate reality—the Good. Too often humans confuse the changing world with what is unchanging and eternal. In the new perfect republic, says Plato, intelligent beings must be forced, for their own good, to climb to the light, to the Eternal Good. But when they have seen the light, these new philosophers must be made to leave the heights and return to the ordinary prisoners below in the interest of the community as a whole. They must do their share of the work in the community. (MacQueen 1970; Plato 1993)

PLATO'S CAVE MYTH

See Plato.

THE PLEASANT COMEDY OF OLD FORTUNATUS

See *Old Fortunatus*.

PLUTARCH

See *The Life of Coriolanus*.

POE, EDGAR ALLAN

Edgar Allan Poe (1809–1849) lived a life fraught with disappointment, alcoholism, poverty, and frustration. Yet he managed to carve for himself a permanent

Edgar Allan Poe

place in the canon of American literature, a legacy as the "father of the detective story," and a lasting popularity among readers of every generation. During his lifetime Poe vehemently rejected the notion of didactic literature, yet in spite of his scathing condemnation that "in defense of allegory . . . there is scarcely one respectable word to be said," many critics remain convinced that important allegorical elements exist in much of Poe's fiction. Allegorical interpretations of his stories and poems vary widely, ranging from the religious to the psychological to the historical.

Critics have suggested that the short story "The Masque of the Red Death" (1842) adheres to many of the patterns of allegory as outlined by Angus Fletcher. Poe's story incorporates ritualistic repetitions (of color sequences, the chimes of the clock, and so forth), a demonic central figure (Prince Prospero), and an unspecified setting. Various scholars claim that Prince Prospero allegorically represents time, that the Red Death is actually the plague of rationalism sweeping through mid–nineteenth-century America, and even that the Red Death equals life itself, or at least the mortality of mankind from which there can be no escape.

"William Wilson: A Tale" (1839) has been interpreted as an allegory of a disintegrating psyche, as the narrator contends with what most critics believe to be his hallucinatory double. The ending may be read as either an allegory of the death of the narrator or a sort of spiritual death signified by the narrator's psychological decay. Like Stevenson's tale of *Dr. Jeckyll and Mr. Hyde*, "William Wilson" is an important example of the allegorical use of doubles to suggest a divided self. (Ruddick 1985; Ware 1989)

See also Dr. Jeckyll and Mr. Hyde; Fletcher, Angus.

POLITICAL ALLEGORY

In the course of human history, allegory has frequently been placed in the service of politics. In *The Faerie Queene*, Spenser uses allegory to support the politics of Elizabeth I and the English Church over those of the Pope and the Roman Catholic Church. In *Gulliver's Travels*, Swift uses the allegory of Lilliput and Brobdingnag to comment on the political conflict between Whigs and Tories in England. Totalitarian regimes have always used allegory to "educate" their masses. The literature and cinema of the old Soviet Union and the Cultural Revolution days of the People's Republic of China are marked by a strong tendency to personify political abstractions derived from the thought of Marx, Lenin, and Mao. Certain characters clearly represent "the People" and others the "bourgeois criminal." The landscape itself becomes allegorically politicized. The young Chinese or Soviet peasant couple driving their tractor into the red sunset form as allegorical a picture as any we can find in the morality plays of the Middle Ages.

For an important discussion of the political uses of allegory, see Kenneth Burke's *A Rhetoric of Motives*, Part III, in which the author examines the question of "symbolic action" as it applies to political questions. (Burke 1950; Fletcher 1964)

See also *Absalom and Achitophel;* Brecht, Bertolt; *The Faerie Queene; Gulliver's Travels.*

 # POSTMODERNIST ALLEGORY

In his *Postmodernist Fiction* (1987), critic Brian McHale discusses the increasing role that allegory has played in late–twentieth-century fiction and the impact that critics such as Honig, Fletcher, Quilligan, and de Man have had in "rehabilitating" the image of allegory. The allegorical or partially allegorical postmodernist novels of authors such as Thomas Pynchon, Ishmael Reed, John Barth, and many others attest to the resurgence of allegorical writing in the past few decades. McHale explains that this trend may be attributed partly to the notion that "allegory offers itself as a tool for exploring ontological structure and foregrounding ontological themes" (141). He maintains that Kafka, Beckett, and Joyce have established the dominant mode of postmodernist allegory, and that while "ancient psychomachias characteristically pitted personified Good against personified Evil . . . the postmodernist versions tend to prefer the Nietzschean opposition between the Apollonian and Dionysian principles, rational order vs. mindless pleasures" (142). (McHale 1987)

POTTER, BEATRIX

To illustrate the lengths to which allegorical interpretation can go, suggesting that all literary commentary when carried to extreme limits becomes allegorical, Angus Fletcher quotes some examples of a *Church Times* contest for "absurdly serious" (and, therefore, allegorical) interpretations of the work of British children's book author Beatrix Potter (1866–1943). One of these parodies considers the well-known *Tale of Peter Rabbit,* in which Peter experiences the temptations and the harsh realities of Mr. McGregor's garden. The interpreter sees the tale as a "poignant allegory" about adolescence, in which the rabbit burrow is the safety of childhood from which Peter emerges only to be faced with a choice between respectability (doing what his mother says) and the adventure of the "fatal garden," in which lurks the "great Foe." (Fletcher 1964)

POWYS, T. F.

T. F. Powys (1875–1953) was a British novelist who spent his life in a small Dorset village and wrote somewhat sardonically about village life. His novel, *Mr. Weston's Good Wine,* can be treated allegorically. (Benet 1965)

See also *Mr. Weston's Good Wine.*

PROMETHEUS MYTH

As told by the Greek poet Hesiod in the eighth century B.C.E. in his *Theogony* and *Works and Days*, the Prometheus tale is profoundly allegorical, the names of the characters in Greek meaning certain abstractions. Prometheus (Forethought) was born of Themis (Justice), which is to suggest that the quality of forethought grows out of a sense of justice. His brother Epimetheus (Afterthought) was a lesser being who married Pandora (All-Giving). Prometheus had the forethought to make the first humans and to give them the gift of fire, for which he was brutally punished by Zeus. His son Deucalion married brother Epimetheus's daughter Pyrrha. Because of the forethought of Prometheus, Deucalion and Pyrrha were able to survive the flood which the angry Zeus sent to destroy humanity. In *Prometheus Bound*, the version of the story told by the Greek playwright Aeschylus (515–456 B.C.E.), Zeus's punishment of Prometheus is carried out by his close henchmen, the obviously allegorical Kratos (Strength) and Bia (Force). (MacQueen 1970)

See also Myth as Allegory.

PROPHETIC ALLEGORY

See The Bible and Allegory.

PRUDENTIUS, AURELIUS CLEMENS

Prudentius (ca. 348–ca. 410) was the Roman author best known for his short, allegorical epic poem the *Psychomachia*, which uses the device of personification to give life to the vices and virtues. The work of Prudentius had a strong influence on medieval depiction of the war between vice and virtue. During the Romanesque period in particular, artists used Prudentius as a basis for their depictions of the great struggle against sin.

The title, *Psychomachia*, refers, then, to the battle within the soul—essentially a psychological battle. From the beginning of the poem there is a clear use of allegory in this context. Prudentius reminds us, for instance, of the story of how the biblical patriarch Abraham saved his nephew Lot, who had been imprisoned by hostile peoples in the Cities of the Plain (Genesis 14). He makes it clear that Lot represents the flawed aspects of the soul while Abraham, who is an allegory for Faith, represents the higher aspect. The invading kings who capture Lot are the sins of the world, which Abraham (Faith) can and must overcome if the soul is to attain wholeness. (Fletcher 1964; MacQueen 1970; Rollinson 1981)

PSYCHOANALYSIS AND ALLEGORY

An essential assumption of psychoanalysis is that images and ideas brought forth by the patient in dreams, or free association, or even in "slips" of speech, have meanings that extend beyond the literal. A character conjured up in a dream stands for some aspect of the dreamer's psyche, as do the actions of the character. In short, the dreamer and the free-associating patient are by definition natural allegorists.

See also Dream and Allegory; Freud, Sigmund.

PSYCHOMACHIA

See Prudentius, Aurelius Clemens.

PYNCHON, THOMAS

Thomas Pynchon lives a reclusive life, and few important details about his life are known beyond the facts that he was born in 1937, attended Cornell University, and has written several of the more critically acclaimed twentieth-century American novels, including *V* (1963), *The Crying of Lot 49* (1966), *Gravity's Rainbow* (1973), and *Vineland* (1990). In her extensive study *The Postmodernist Allegories of Thomas Pynchon*, Deborah L. Madsen explains that allegory reveals absolutist ideologies which, in Pynchon's vision, are seen as "oppressive of both the individual and the whole of culture" (114). While each of the aforementioned novels has been interpreted as a postmodern allegory, an examination of *The Crying of Lot 49* may serve as an example of Pynchon's allegorical approach to the oppression of modern society.

See also The Crying of Lot 49.

 QUARLES, FRANCIS

Francis Quarles (1592–1644) was an English metaphysical poet of the same school as George Herbert. He is best known for his illustrated allegorical book of poetry, *Emblemes*. (Benet 1965)

See also Emblems; Herbert, George.

 THE QUEST AS ALLEGORY

All quest stories can be said to be allegorical in that they inevitably represent in some way the human passage along the "road of life." Not surprisingly, then, the quest motif has often been the basis of allegory. The Grail romances and other medieval romances such as *Sir Gawain and the Green Knight* (ca. 1375–1400), *Pilgrimage of the Life of Man* by Guillaume de Deguileville (1294–1360), and major allegories such as Edmund Spenser's *Faerie Queene* and Bunyan's *Pilgrim's Progress* are all examples of allegorical writing that depend on the quest. The meaning of the quest story, whether Twain's *Huckleberry Finn* or the romances of the Holy Grail, always has to do with the human journey to knowledge, wisdom, or individuation.

See also Aeneid; Epic as Allegory; *The Faerie Queene; The Odyssey; Sir Gawain and the Green Knight.*

 QUILLIGAN, MAUREEN

In her important book, *The Language of Allegory* (1979), Professor Quilligan attempts to establish allegory as a definable literary genre. In so doing she reminds us, quoting the *American Heritage Dictionary*, that a genre is "a category of art distinguished by a definite style, form, or content" and that some genres can be recognized by content and some by form. Thus a sonnet is a genre because of its 14 lines and an elegy is a genre because by way of its content it creates a sense of mourning. Allegory is a genre in the second sense. Quilligan makes the further point that allegory speaks to the human ability to decode; it appeals to us as "readers of a system of signs" (24). In her definition of the genre, Quilligan moves beyond the traditional idea that allegory is a genre in which words mean something other *(allos)* metaphorically than what they say literally. She stresses instead the idea of the "problematical process of meaning multiple things simultaneously with one word." "Allegory" as a term "defines a kind of language significant by virtue of its verbal ambidextrousness," she says. In short, unlike most commentators on the genre, Quilligan focuses on the language of allegory itself rather than on the structure of extended metaphor hidden beneath the literal surface of the text. (Quilligan 1979)

See also Allegoresis.

QUINTILIAN

Quintilian (37–100 C.E.) was a Roman writer who discussed a concept of allegory in his *Institutio Oratoria*. For him, allegory was the art of saying one thing and meaning another. He compares allegory to metaphor and suggests that it has an ironic aspect. Quintilian strongly influenced medieval ideas on the subject. Isidore of Seville (560–636 C.E.), for instance, in his *Etymologiae* presents Quintilian's view almost exactly.

In his consideration of the ironic aspect of allegory, Quintilian seems to have been influenced by the Roman poet Horace (65–8 B.C.E.) who used allegory for satirical purposes. To describe his longing for the country, for example, Horace used Aesop's fable of the country mouse who found misery during his visit to the town mouse, thus satirizing his own unhappiness in Rome.

Quintilian uses Horace to make sense of his own definition of allegory, pointing out that in his *Odes* (I, xiv), when Horace refers to the ship, the storm, and the harbor he really means the state, the civil wars, and tranquility. (Fletcher 1964; MacQueen 1970)

RABELAIS, FRANÇOIS

A French monk, clergyman, doctor, and writer, Rabelais (1494–1553) is best known for his long satirical fantasy, *Gargantua and Pantagruel*. Coleridge regarded this work as in part allegorical. While it is true that Rabelais uses the escapades of his benevolent giants, Gargantua and Pantagruel, to comment on the society of his time and to make fun of many of his contemporaries, the characters he depicts are far too individualized to be considered allegories. One remembers them for themselves rather than for what they might represent. This would not be the case, for instance, with the characters in Spenser's *Faerie Queene*. Rabelais himself was certainly no adherent of allegory, which he considered a medieval art form as opposed to what he saw as his more modern approach. In fact, he was fond of criticizing allegorizers. In the preface to *Gargantua* he speaks somewhat scathingly of the classical tradition of reading Homer allegorically, suggesting that Homer was no more likely to have thought of his epics as allegories than Ovid was to have thought of his *Metamorphoses* as allegories of the "Gospel sacraments." (Fletcher 1964; Szeznac 1953)

   See also Coleridge, Samuel Taylor; *Gargantua and Pantagruel*.

RAMAYANA

The second of the great Indian epics, the *Ramayana* is a story of the hero Rama, who like Krishna is an incarnation of the great god Vishnu. It is a poem attributed to the second Indian "Homer," Valmiki, and parts of it date back to 500 B.C.E. The plot of the *Ramayana* is much more organized than that of the significantly longer *Mahabharata*. It is a quest story that tells how, after Rama won his bride Sita by bending the bow of the god Rudra, he was exiled, and his wife was taken off by Ravana, the demon king of what is now Sri Lanka and once was Ceylon. Rama rescues Sita, but not without the help of the demon's brother and an invasion of Sri Lanka led by the Monkey God Hanuman and his loyal troupe of monkeys, who build a bridge across the straits between India and Sri Lanka. But Rama and his people fear that Sita has been defiled by Ravana and she is sent into exile, where in the forest she is protected by the poet Valmiki himself. There she gives birth to Rama's sons and finally is welcomed back by him. As proof of Sita's doubted virtue, the earth Mother herself takes Sita off to the land of the gods.

The *Ramayana* is allegorical in the sense that any quest epic is. That is, the journey and search of the hero is our quest for the wholeness represented by the reunion of Rama and Sits. Sita can rightfully be called Rama's soul or psychic energy (what Hindus would call his *sakti*). At a simpler level, Rama is Justice and Sita is Truth and Virtue. Justice without Truth and Virtue is useless, and Truth is all too often doubted and forced to prove itself in the dark forest of pain and denial.

At still another level there is the allegory of human will as opposed to Fate or the will of the gods. (Benet 1965)

See also The Mahabharata; The Quest as Allegory.

REED, ISHMAEL

See Mumbo Jumbo.

RELIGIOUS ALLEGORY

See Aquinas, Thomas.

RESURRECTION

See Tolstoy, Leo.

REVELATION, THE BOOK OF

This is the only apocalyptic book of the New Testament or Christian section of the Bible. It was written by a man called John, probably in about 95 C.E. The Book of Revelation is visionary and symbolic, and at times allegorical. In chapter 6, for example, in the vision of the seven seals, Christ opens each of the seven seals of a scroll and as he does so, disasters take place on earth. The first four seals would seem to be allegorical. As they are opened, out come four horsemen, said to represent war, revolution, famine, and death. In chapter 12 there is a dragon who persecutes a pregnant woman. The dragon is traditionally seen as Satan, the woman as the new Christian church.

For the most part, however, Revelation is a symbolic work rather than an allegorical one. The various figures and incidents have all of the ambiguity of symbolism and little of the direct reference of traditional allegory. (Harris 1985)

RIPA, CESARE

Cesare Ripa was the author of the *Iconologia or Moral Emblems* (1603), a major source for Italian allegories of the seventeenth and eighteenth centuries. The book instructs artists on how to personify abstractions. In talking about the figure of Truth, for example, Ripa writes: "Truth has to be represented quite naked, because her nature is simplicity itself. . . . She holds up the sun to signify that she loves the light and is herself the light. . . . The globe is under her feet to show that she is more precious than all the riches of the world. . . ." Emile Male suggests that this description was the basis for Bernini's great statue (see illustration on following page) of Truth (193). (Male 1949; Panofsky 1939; Seznec 1953)

See also Johnson, Barbara; Painting and Sculpture, Allegorical.

RITUAL AS ALLEGORY

Rituals are often—perhaps always—allegorizations. The strange actions of ritual participants—actions that are strange because they stand out from everyday life in their use of special language, costumes, movement, and so forth—take on specific and significant meaning for those "in the know," those who are aware of the particular mythical context out of which the rituals spring. So, for example, the breaking of a glass at a Jewish wedding might seem strange and wasteful to a Hindu or an animist from Siberia, but for the Jew the act has particular cultural and theological meanings. In the same way, baptism might appear to the outsider to be a peculiarly inefficient bath, while for the Christian it has specific allegorical meanings having to do with the story of the death and resurrection of Jesus.

When the unwell Navajo is placed within the confines of a sandpainting while a shaman sings the creation myth over him or her, the significance of the situation is unclear to the non-Navajo without explanation, but to the Navajo the ritual process is clearly allegorical; it relates to a reestablishing of harmony with the spirit world and with the cosmos itself.

One of the most complex and striking allegories is that of the Christian Eucharist or Mass—the service of Holy Communion. The people gathered for the liturgy (*liturgy* comes from the Greek *leiturgia*, or "public work," thus the church "service") represent the body of Christ. This assembled body will undergo the act of sacrifice with Jesus by giving of itself physically (money, wine, bread, other offerings) and spiritually through prayer and meditation. The breaking of the bread is an allegory for the breaking of Christ's body at the crucifixion, and the act of eating the bread and drinking the wine (allegorically, the blood of Christ) is the means by which the people re-experience (represent) not only the last meal of Jesus and his disciples (the "Last Supper") but the death of Jesus and, as in baptism, the death of the old sinful self. In the re-newal that comes through this act, there is allegorical participation

Bernini's statue of *Truth*

in Jesus' resurrection. Finally, in the blessing after the communion, the priest metaphorically is Jesus, the people his disciples receiving his blessing before he ascends to heaven.

The whole purpose of rituals like this is to carry a particular group, allegorically, out of the ordinary into the real world of their belief, their mythology—usually for purposes of physical or spiritual healing, or remembering. (Hardison 1965; Quilligan 1979)

ROBINSON CRUSOE

Daniel Defoe (ca. 1660–1731) did not begin to write his series of adventure tales, of which *The Life and Strange Surprizing Adventures of Robinson Crusoe* was only the first, until he was nearly 60 years old. *Robinson Crusoe* appeared in 1719, to a lukewarm response from upper-class readers and an enthusiastic reception from his own middle class. His fictional autobiographies of exciting and interesting characters, including *Captain Singleton* (1720), *Moll Flanders* (1722), *Colonel Jack* (1722), and *Roxana* (1724), have offered readers throughout the centuries both adventurous tales and remarkable insights into the consciousness of individuals who are either physically or spiritually isolated.

The story of *Robinson Crusoe* is familiar to many readers of today. As a young man, the title character defied the wishes of his father and took to the sea. He was a trader, a captive slave, and a plantation owner before he was shipwrecked on a deserted island off the coast of South America. It was on this isolated island that Crusoe was to spend the next 28 years of his life.

Salvaging what materials he could from the destroyed ship, Crusoe went about making a home for himself on the island. He fashioned shelter and crude furniture, kept a journal, grew corn and other grains, and studied the Bible. During his twenty-fourth year of solitude, he was greatly disturbed and deeply frightened by some grisly evidence that savages had landed on the island, enjoyed a cannibalistic feast, and then departed. When the savages eventually returned to the island, Crusoe shot some of them, frightened away the rest of them, and managed to rescue one of their prisoners. This man, whom Crusoe named "Friday" after the day he was rescued, became his faithful servant and friend.

After four more years and further adventures involving the cannibals on the neighboring island, Crusoe and Friday were delivered from their exile by an English ship and brought to Crusoe's homeland. Crusoe had been away from England for 35 years, 28 of which were spent almost entirely alone. Crusoe found out that most of his family had died during this time, but his income from the plantation he owned had been saved, and he was now a wealthy man. He married and fathered three children in England, but when his wife died Crusoe and Friday again took to the sea, traveling back to their island home and bringing gifts to those who now inhabited it. Friday was later killed in an attack onboard the ship, and Crusoe, after an excursion to China and

Two Englishmen keep watch over the island in *Robinson Crusoe*.

Siberia, finally returned home to England, where he remained for the rest of his life.

Allegorically, *Robinson Crusoe* has been interpreted in several different ways. Some critics read Defoe's tale as a religious/spiritual allegory that tells the story of sin, the fall of man, repentance, and salvation. Crusoe's initial disregard of his father's wishes when he goes to sea represents the "original sin" of disobedience. Shipwreck is the result of his "fall from grace"; as punishment for his defiance, he is imprisoned on the island in order to repent his sin and lead a more holy life. This interpretation finds justification in Crusoe's study of the Bible, his dreams, and his spiritual meditations. Finally, after many years, Crusoe is permitted to return to society as a wealthy man who is free to live any sort of life he pleases. Allegorically, this suggests Crusoe's achievement of grace; he is ultimately rewarded for his penance on the solitary island.

A historically allegorical interpretation of Defoe's text develops a political connection between *Robinson Crusoe* and the historical events in England during the time of Crusoe's exile. Crusoe lives on the island from 1659 until 1686, arriving in England in June 1688. These years overlap the 28 years of restored Stuart rule in England, before the Glorious Revolution of 1688 and the ascendancy of William III. Defoe's family suffered under Stuart rule, and if he had been older, Defoe himself would have surely resisted the sovereignty of King Charles II. Allegorically, the time frame of the story suggests that the 28 years of Crusoe's "reign" over his island "nation" represents what Defoe perceived to be 28 lost years in England's history. Crusoe is, in many ways, an "island king"; he rules his "kingdom" and represents the ideals of England even though he is exiled from it for a great part of his life. As an absentee Englishman, he is not compromised by Stuart rule, as Defoe perceived true Englishmen to be. Instead, Crusoe represents the preservation of the English value system during a historical period in which Defoe believed the English spirit to be politically "exiled." (Foster 1993; Seidel 1981)

See also Defoe, Daniel.

ROJAS ZORRILLA, FRANCESCO DE

See Auto Sacramentale.

ROMANCE AS ALLEGORY

Traditionally the romance form has been a comfortable home for allegory. Whether in fairy tales, the medieval Grail romances, or the later, more ironic versions of the genre, such as Cervantes's *Don Quixote* or offshoots such as Ibsen's *Peer Gynt*, the essence of romance is the heroic quest. Although the adventure story itself often overpowers any allegorical intention in good romance, there is a natural tendency among writers and readers to place didactic meanings on the questor and the goal of the quest as well as on those characters who stand in the way of the hero's success and those who would help him. For instance, it is the story and the atmosphere of *Sir Gawain and the Green Knight* that most holds our attention, yet the strikingly unusual nature of the knight's quest and the events that befall him suggest an allegorical meaning and seem to demand that we search for it. (Frye 1957)

See also Fairy Tales and Allegory; The Quest as Allegory; *Sir Gawain and the Green Knight*.

THE ROMANCE OF THE ROSE

Le Roman de la Rose in the French original, *The Romance of the Rose* is a thirteenth-century allegorical romance that looks back to Ovid's *Ars Amatoria [The Art of Love]*. It is, in fact, a study of courtly love, as Ovid's work was a study of the art of love in Roman times. The poem is in two parts: the first 4,000 lines are by Guillaume de Lorris (early thirteenth century) and the next 18,000 lines are by Jean de Meung (late thirteenth century). If, in his part of the romance, Guillaume stresses the role of women in courtly love, Jean de Meung favors Nature as the source of goodness.

The allegory in *The Romance of the Rose* is based on personification. The central plot involves the quest of the Lover for his Rose, representing the quest of courtly love. It is Leisure who guards the Garden of Roses, signifying the fact that courtly love is a pursuit only of the aristocracy. The garden is inhabited by such figures as Good-Looks, Pleasure, and Wealth. Poverty is distinctly left outside of its wall. In the garden the Lover finds a rosebud for which he longs but is prevented from picking it by Cupid, who reminds him of the necessary trials of courtly love. Various personified qualities—Danger, Slander, and Shame—try to prevent the Lover from seeking to gain his beloved Rose, but Welcome encourages him before Jealousy blocks his path. The dangers of the courtly love process are thus depicted. In Jean de Meung's part of the poem, Nature helps in the overcoming of Fear, Danger, and Shame, and the Lover finally wins his Rose.

An interesting aspect of the Jean de Meung continuation of the poem is that in its use of satire, it represents a bourgeois reaction against the upper-class and religious power structure of the time, and against the whole system of courtly love. (Fleming 1969; Lewis 1938; Piehler 1979)

See also Chopinel, Jean; de Lorris, Guillaume; Romance as Allegory.

ROSICRUCIANS AND ALLEGORY

See The Chemical Wedding.

RUMI, JALAL AL-DIN

The Persian Sufi poet and Muslim mystic, Jalal al-din Rumi (1207–1273), is best known as the author of the long poem the *Mathnavi* and as the founder of the Whirling Dervish sect centered in Konya in Turkey. Rumi's central theme is always the love that empowers the universe. In Rumi's poetry there is often allegory associated with the sun, which stands for that love which is true understanding:

> Intelligence is the shadow of objective Truth.
> How can the shadow vie with sunshine.

In his teaching, Rumi also used stories—some of them comic parables such as those involving the trickster figure Nasreddin Hodja—to illustrate his points. (Eliade 1987; Shah 1970)

See also Nasreddin Hodja.

R.U.R.

R.U.R. is a play by the Czech writer Karel Capek. First published in 1923, it is about a futuristic state in which robots rebel against their human masters. It was this play that gave us the word *robot*, and which perhaps influenced Aldous Huxley's *Brave New World* and its depiction of the horrors of twentieth-century mechanization and spiritual sterility.

Robots were perfected by the Rossum Universal Robot Factory. These beings were designed to have no feelings. Their only purpose was work. When Helena Glory, daughter of the country's president, is sent to achieve better "living conditions" for the robots, she has difficulty believing they are not human, they seem so real. Helena tries to make the robots understand their "rights," but they seem not to care whether they live or die, and when they act in a peculiar way they are, in fact, taken apart and recycled. The factory manager, Harry Domin, tries to convince Helena of the value of the robots and of the correctness of using them in spite of the fact that they do sometimes act strangely, almost as if they were individuals. To Helena this behavior suggests a developing consciousness or soul. She tries to convince the executives of the danger of having robots do the work that humans have done—millions of people would be put out of work and rendered superfluous. When Alquist, the head of the works department, agrees with her, he is voted down. Strangely, Helena accepts Domin's proposal of marriage.

Many years pass and the robots are causing a great deal of trouble, a fact the managers try to hide from Helena Glory. There are robot wars and rebellions all over the world. Helena begs Domin to close the factory. He refuses; only Alquist agrees with her. Both he and Helena know that humans have stopped reproducing. The psychiatrist, Dr. Gall, knows that the robots are developing feelings, but Domin and his followers care only about their profits and do nothing about the situation.

A war between men and robots develops; the robots see humans as parasites, vow to kill them all, and attack the factory. Helena confesses that she has given them souls, and now, ironically, they act with the same brutality that had plagued humankind.

Only Alquist was spared by the robots because he had worked with them. But Helena, before her death, destroys the robot-building formula and now the robots, too, begin to die. But Alquist finds hope in two robots, a male called Primus and a female made in Helena's image. The two robots had fallen in love and were happy to die together. Now Alquist realizes that their love will bring about the regeneration of life.

In terms of allegory, the robots stand for the mechanization and the humans for the spiritual sterility of our century. It is the "mechanization of the Proletariat," as Capek put it, that will undermine the human spirit in our time. Helena Glory, as her name indicates, is a spark of the old human spirit. Harry Domin's name suggests domination and a lack of that spirit. The factory is, obviously, our civilization. The robot couple at the play's end represents a new Adam and Eve.

See also Capek, Karel.

RUSHDIE, SALMAN

See Haroun and the Sea of Stories.

SALLUSTIUS

Sallustius was a Roman philosopher of the fourth century C.E. A friend of the emperor Julian, he worked against the Christianization of the empire and was an apologist for the Greco-Roman gods, whom he tended to consider allegorically, as in his *About the Gods and the World*.

Sallustius suggests that all people can appreciate the gods but few can understand them. Myths are veils that clothe mysteries. It is for the philosopher to discover the mysteries, the allegories. There are, he says, levels of allegory in myth: theological, physical, psychic, and material.

For instance, Sallustius uses the myth of Kronos, the ancient father god who ate each of his children as they were born. At the level of theological allegory, this myth contemplates the essence of God, suggesting that God is intellectual and that "all intyellect returns into itself." On the physical level, the level that refers to God's activities in this world, Kronos is Time, the segments of which he swallows. On the psychic level, the myth speaks to the activities of the soul; the thoughts of the soul are within the thinker. On the material level Kronos is seen simply as an embodiment of time or of water, the way Earth is Isis or wine Dionysus. (MacQueen 1970)

See also Attis Myth; Myth as Allegory.

SARTOR RESARTUS

Thomas Carlyle (1795–1881) was a Scottish historian, biographer, and social critic known for his many writings concerning contemporary issues. His 1835 philosophical satire *Sartor Resartus* (literally, "the tailor reclothed") is a kind of sermon on silence, work, and duty, among other topics. The narrator is an English editor who faces the monumental task of sorting and commenting on six paper sacks of disorderly writings from an imaginary German philosopher, Professor Diogenes Teufelsdröckh ("Devil's dung") from a town called Weissnichtwo ("Don't-Know-Where"). One of Teufelsdröckh's important philosophical tracts is the "Clothes Philosophy"—the idea that the "clothes" (traditional institutions, customs, and religions) of society are "ill-fitting" and must be stripped away in order for the soul to express itself in new ways. *Sartor Resartus* has been interpreted as an allegory of the rise and teachings of German transcendentalism, and Teufelsdröckh himself has been read as an allegorical figure of Adam, whose spiritual development evolves not in an Edenic landscape but in the morally barren wasteland of the modern world. (Cumming 1988; Tennyson 1965)

SATIRE AND ALLEGORY

It has been suggested by John MacQueen and others that allegory has a close relative in satire, that allegory can often be better understood by considering its satirical aspect. Thus, for instance, the allegory in *Gulliver's Travels* is understood when we realize what aspects of the human condition are being satirized by Swift. MacQueen notes that in William Blake's poetry and in the novels of Henry Fielding and Jane Austen, satire and allegory are intricately entwined. So it is that Tom Jones's lack of wisdom in *Tom Jones* is satirized even as he pursues his allegorical quest for that quality as embodied in his beloved Sophia, whose name, of course, means wisdom. And in employing titles like *Pride and Prejudice, Sense and Sensibility*, and *Persuasion*, Jane Austen literally announces allegorical quests even as in the novels she satirizes the questors.

THE SCARLET LETTER

The student of allegory will have no difficulty discovering commentaries on Hawthorne's *Scarlet Letter* in connection with that genre. Yvor Winters calls the novel "pure allegory." Richard Chase makes essentially the same claim, reminding us that as a writer of prose romance, Hawthorne tended toward "mythic, allegorical, and symbolist forms." *The Scarlet Letter,* he wrote, "is an allegorical novel." Other Hawthorne critics have generally complained that what Richard Fogle called the modern "prejudice against allegory" has prevented us from reading this novel properly. Yet those not so prejudiced have written articles and books on *The Scarlet Letter* as an allegory of the American experience, of American history, and of the American conscience.

The protagonist of the novel is Hester Prynne. Hester has lived in the seventeenth-century Puritan colony of Boston for some years. Her husband has remained behind in Europe, and many assume he is dead. Meanwhile, Hester has become pregnant and given birth to Pearl. For her sin and her refusal to name the child's father, she has been imprisoned. Upon her release at the novel's opening, she suffers public condemnation as she stands on a pillory wearing an embroidered scarlet *A* on her breast. A stranger now appears in the town, one Roger Chillingworth, whom Hester realizes is, in fact, her husband. Chillingworth forces Hester not to reveal his identity and begins the process of taking revenge against the still-unknown father of Hester's child. Before long, using his almost supernatural instincts, Chillingworth realizes that the father is none other than the young and seemingly very pious minister, Arthur Dimmesdale. When Hester and Arthur attempt to escape to Europe in order to escape Chillingworth's diabolical mental harassment, Chillingworth prevents them from doing so. Now to achieve liberation from Chillingworth, Dimmesdale confesses his sin on the same pillory on which Hester had been humiliated and dies in Hester's arms.

Those who find moral allegory in this tale have seen Hester's prison as an embodiment of fate and the scarlet letter, of course, as a symbol of adultery. The pillory has been interpreted as an allegory of the cross, Chillingworth as Death or Satan disguised. Dimmesdale's concealed sin is the original sin we all embody. It might be said that only by accepting what we are can the moral poison represented by Chillingworth be overcome.

Hawthorne himself spoke of his "inveterate love of allegory." But to see his novel as simple allegory is to underrate its complexity. In fact, part of the work's irony lies in the fact that those who would punish Hester—Chillingworth and the other Puritans—attempt to deal with life's ambiguities by confronting them with simplistic allegorical understandings and tactics. Thus, Hester is pregnant, she must have sinned, she must be made into an example, she must become an emblematic allegory of Adultery by being forced to wear the letter *A*. Hawthorne, however, is not of Hester's time, and his novel is much more than a prose fiction version of a morality play. The author takes us deeply into the souls of his characters and forces us to comment mentally on the absurdity of the literalist or allegorical approach of Hester's society. We are not far into the novel before we are led to wonder whether the letter *A* should stand in our minds for Adultery or Angel, whether Hester's "sin" is not really a stand, albeit a hopeless one, against the absurdities of Puritanism or of modern hypocrisies Puritanism might serve to represent. In this light the novel becomes not so much an allegory as a psychological study of four characters, whose meanings we can never fully know.

Richard Chase is perhaps the most convincing supporter of the idea that *The Scarlet Letter* is allegory, but the allegory he sees is not a moral allegory of sin and damnation but an allegory of the novelist's mind, in which Chillingworth, the "wronged" husband who uses his powers to discover Hester's "partner in sin," is the novelist's "probing intellect," the "guilty" Reverend Dimmesdale his "moral sensibility," Hester his "fallible human reality," and their daughter Pearl his "demonic poetic faculty." (Flores 1987; James 1986; Merrill 1981; Waggoner 1979)

See also Emblems; Hawthorne, Nathaniel; *The Marble Faun.*

SCHREINER, OLIVE

Olive Schreiner (1855–1920), a South African writer and feminist, is best remembered for her novel *Story of an African Farm* (1883). It recounts the life stories of three farm children in South Africa as they grow to maturity. Emily ("Em") is a gentle girl who aspires to a domestic life, Waldo is a "dreamer,"

and Lyndall, the true heroine of the story, is a fiercely independent girl who struggles against the repressive Victorian gender roles that threaten to stifle her. Critics have argued that Schreiner's penchant for allegory colors her entire novel; it is most explicitly noted in an episode that has come to be known as the "allegory of the Hunter." At the precise midpoint of the novel, a Stranger arrives at the farm and tells the 15-year-old Waldo a story about the search for absolute truth. In the story, a Hunter leaves his village in search of the Bird of Truth, whose image he had seen reflected in a lake. Wisdom tells the Hunter that when a person sees the Bird of Truth, he can never rest until he finds her. The Hunter asks Wisdom how he might find this Bird; Wisdom replies that he has not yet suffered enough. To find the Bird of Truth, the Hunter must first travel to the Land of Absolute Negation and Denial, climb the mountains of Stern Reality, and then perhaps he will find Truth. The Hunter begins his journey by traveling through the woods, where he is tempted by the twins of Sensuality but refuses to join them. He reaches the mountain range and begins to climb. Years pass as he toils up the vertical cliff, carving stairs and laughing at the Echoes of Despair that mock his attempts. Finally, the Hunter realizes that he is dying but understands that others might someday climb the stairs that he carved and find Truth through him. The Hunter dies on the mountain clutching a feather from the Bird of Truth in his hand, never recognizing how close to Truth he had been. This classically allegorical tale of an arduous journey and seductive temptations illuminates the conflict between good and evil, the struggle for freedom, truth, and integrity that informs the rest of the novel, and the nineteenth-century belief in scientific rationalism.

Schreiner relied on allegory in many of her other writings; she published a number of "dream allegories" such as "The Sunlight Lay across My Bed," "Three Dreams in a Desert," and "A Dream of Wild Bees," which depict the contrasts between actual and ideal reality. On a more social level, her allegory "The Salvation of a Ministry" is a political tract which contrasts Christian ethics with the political actions of the Cape Colony government. *Dreams* (1893) and *Trooper Peter Halket of Mashonaland* (1897) include many of Schreiner's allegories published during her lifetime; *Stories, Dreams, and Allegories* (1923), *From Man to Man; or, Perhaps Only . . .* (1927), and *Undine* (1929) are allegorical tales that were published posthumously. (Berkman 1989; First 1980; Gorak 1992; Monsman 1985)

THE SECOND SHEPHERD'S PLAY

A medieval mystery play in the comic tradition, *The Second Shepherd's Play* was written by the so-called Wakefield Master, probably at the end of the fourteenth century. Mystery plays were performed by guilds, sometimes on pulled wagons (pageant wagons), usually on the Christian feast of Corpus Christi (Body of Christ). The source of the word "mystery" in this context lies in the word *ministerium*, referring to the "mysteries" accomplished by the expertise of the guild members in their ordinary work, and in the word *mysterium*, refer-ring to the deep mysteries of religion.

The Second Shepherd's Play is mildly allegorical in that it contains a parody of the nativity scene and in that the plot moves from the pain and sadness of winter to the "spring" which is Christ's birth.

SHEPARD, SAM

Born Samuel Shepard Rogers in Illinois in 1943, Sam Shepard is an accom-plished playwright, actor, and screenwriter who comments through his work on the American scene in such symbolic—some would say expressionistic—works as *Fool for Love*, *True West*, and *Buried Child*, all of which might be called allegories of the failure of family life. A more clearly allegorical play is *Opera-tion Sidewinder*. Shepard has won the Pulitzer Prize and several other awards for his work as a playwright.

See also Operation Sidewinder.

SIGNIFYING AND ALLEGORY

Signifying is a term that refers to a tradition in African and African-American vernacular of playing tricks with language in order to convey indirectly and metaphorically—allegorically—certain information meant only for those "in the know." (Gates 1988)

See also African-American Music as Allegory.

SIR GAWAIN AND THE GREEN KNIGHT

Written sometime in the fourteenth century by the so-called Gawain poet, of whom little is known except that he was from the north of England, *Sir Gawain and the Green Knight* is one of the masterpieces of English romance.

The story is that of the testing of the ideal knight—the representation of chivalry and courtly love—in King Arthur's court. The testing devices are adul-tery and a beheading.

At the new year celebrations the Green Knight appears and challenges any knight to chop off his head if he, the Green Knight, may be allowed to respond in a like manner the next year. Gawain takes up the challenge and cuts off the knight's head only to watch in amazement as the knight picks up his head and rides off.

After a year has passed, Gawain goes in search of the Green Chapel where he is to meet the Green Knight. One day he comes upon a castle, where he is richly entertained by Lord Bercilak. Bercilak suggests and Gawain accepts the terms of a game; each day the lord will go hunting and will give his guest the

The inscription below the chivalrous Sir Gawain reads "Now passed Sir Gawain on Gods behalf through the realms of Logres."

meat he has won. Gawain will give Bercilak whatever he has won in the castle during his host's absence.

For two days while the host is away, his beautiful wife attempts to seduce Gawain. Twice he refuses. But when on the third day he accepts a magic green sash from the lady—one that supposedly will help him against the Green Knight—he neglects to inform his host of the gift.

Now Gawain goes off to find the Green Knight. When they meet in the Green Chapel, Gawain prepares to meet his death. The first two blows do not touch Gawain, perhaps because of his two nights of resisting the lady of the castle, but the third blow wounds him slightly, because of his having accepted the sash. The Green Knight is, of course, Lord Bercilak, who is a follower of Morgan Le Fay, the ambiguous instigator of the whole Green Knight affair.

Gawain returns to Arthur's court and wears the green sash to remind him of his sin. The other knights also vow to wear green sashes to honor their colleague's bravery.

There have been many allegorical readings of *Sir Gawain and the Green Knight*, but none of them seems to speak to the complexity of characterization and action that marks this romance. While it is true that Gawain can be seen as an everyman and as a representation of chivalry and the lady of the castle as a personification of adultery, the Green Knight, himself, is much too ambiguous to be an allegory, and the whole beheading game seems to defy an allegorical reading. The most we can say is that the romance is an allegory of original sin, represented by Gawain's lapse, and the triumph of chivalry over evil.

SIR ORFEO

The anonymous medieval poem *Sir Orfeo* is a retelling of the classical myth of Orpheus. Sir Orfeo is a medieval king whose wife, Heurodis, is abducted by fairies as she sleeps beneath a tree in the garden. Orfeo, in his anguish over his great loss, takes his harp and leaves his court to live in the woods like a wild man. For ten years Orfeo roams the woods, plays his harp to the animals, and searches for his wife. One day he comes upon a group of fairy-creatures; he follows them and soon encounters the fairy king. This king is so enchanted with Orfeo's harp-playing that he offers him anything he wants. Orfeo requests his wife, and the couple subsequently leave the fairy world together and return to the court. After Orfeo, still looking like a wild man, tests his steward who was left in charge of the kingdom, he regains his position as king.

Sir Orfeo has been interpreted as containing elements of both religious and political allegory. As a Christian allegory, *Sir Orfeo* is the story of the journey of the soul from sin to redemption through the expiation of vice. Orfeo is a penitent pilgrim, whose transformation into a "hairy anchorite" of the wilderness represents the self-imposed suffering he must endure in order to absolve himself from the sin of pride. By stripping away all the trappings of vanity from his life, Orfeo achieves a sort of "rebirth," which is represented by the return of his beloved Heurodis.

Politically, *Sir Orfeo* is a story of medieval kingship, and the allegory encompasses the values and lessons to which a good king must adhere. Orfeo's initial failure in rescuing his wife forces him to learn that he is not omnipotent and cannot defeat Death. The work may be interpreted as a parable about power, and Orfeo himself is forced to learn, from painful experience, that a king must rise above the sin of pride and humble himself in the face of his human limitations. (Grimaldi 1981)

SLAVE SONGS AND ALLEGORY

See African-American Music as Allegory.

THE SONG OF SONGS

The Song of Songs or Song of Solomon is one of the Festival Scrolls (*Megillot*) of the Hebrew Bible. Traditionally it is associated with the Feast of Passover. What follows is an excerpt from the first two chapters of the Song in the Revised Standard Version. The song clearly revels in the erotic relationship between a man and his sister-spouse, a fact that suggests that the poem's origins might be in Egyptian marriage poetry (Egyptian pharoahs married their sisters).

1

The Song of Songs, which is
Solomon's.

2 O that you would kiss me with the
    kisses of your mouth!
For your love is better than wine,
3   your anointing oils are fragrant,
your name is oil poured out;
    therefore the maidens love you.
4 Draw me after you, let us make
    haste.
    The king has brought me into his
    chambers.
We will exult and rejoice in you;
    we will extol your love more than
      wine;
    rightly to they love you.

5 I am very dark, but comely,
    O daughters of Jerusalem,
like the tents of Kedar,
    like the curtains of Solomon.
6 Do not gaze at me because I am
    swarthy,
because the sun has scorched me.
My mother's sons were angry with
    me,
    they made me keeper of the
      vineyards;
    but, my own vineyard I have not
      kept!
7 Tell me, you whom my soul loves,
    where you pasture your flock,
    where you make it lie down at
      noon;
for why should I be like one who
    wanders
    beside the flocks of your
      companions?

8 If you do not know,
    O fairest among women,
follow in the tracks of the flock.
    and pasture your kids
    beside the shepherds' tents.

9 I compare you, my love,
    to a mare of Pharaoh's chariots.

¹⁰ Your cheeks are comely with
    ornaments,
    your neck with strings of jewels.
¹¹ We will make you ornaments of
    gold,
    studded with silver.

¹² While the king was on his couch,
    my nard gave forth its fragrance.
¹³ My beloved is to me a bag of myrrh,
    that lies between my breasts.
¹⁴ My beloved is to me a cluster of
    henna blossoms
    in the vineyards of En-ge'di.

¹⁵ Behold, you are beautiful, my love;
    behold, you are beautiful;
    your eyes are doves.
¹⁶ Behold, you are beautiful, my
    beloved,
    truly lovely.
Our couch is green;
¹⁷ the beams of our house are cedar,
    our rafters are pine.

2

I am a rose of Sharon,
a lily of the valleys.

² As a lily among brambles,
    so is my beloved among maidens.

³ As an apple tree among the trees
    of the wood,
    so is my beloved among young
    men.
With great delight I sat in his shadow,
    and his fruit was sweet to my taste.
⁴ He brought me to the banqueting
    house,
    and his banner over me was love.
⁵ Sustain me with raisins,
    refresh me with apples;
    for I am sick with love.
⁶ O that his left hand were under my
    head,
    and that his right hand embraced
    me!
⁷ I adjure you, O daughters of

Jerusalem,
    by the gazelles or the hinds of the
    field,
that you stir not up nor awaken
    love
    until it please.
⁸ The voice of my beloved!
    Behold, he comes,
leaping upon the mountains
    bounding over the hills.
⁹ My beloved is like a gazelle,
    or a young stag.
Behold, there he stands
    behind our wall,
gazing in at the windows,
    looking through the lattice,
¹⁰ My beloved speaks and says to me:
"Arise, my love, my fair one,
    and come away;
¹¹ for lo, the winter is past,
    the rain is over and gone.
¹² The flowers appear on the earth,
    the time of singing has come
and the voice of the turtledove
    is heard in our land
¹³ The fig tree puts forth its figs,
    and the vines are in blossom
    they give forth fragrance.
Arise, my love, my fair one,
    and come away.
¹⁴ O my dove, in the clefts of the rock,
    in the covert of the cliff,
let me see your face,
    let me hear your voice
for your voice is sweet,
    and your face is comely.
¹⁵ Catch us the foxes,
    the little foxes,
that spoil our vineyards,
    for our vineyards are in blossom"

¹⁶ My beloved is mine and I am his,
    he pastures his flock among the
    lillies
¹⁷ Until the day breathes
    and the shadows flee,
turn, my beloved, be like a gazelle,
    or a young stag upon rugged
    mountains.

When the early Christians brought together the Hebrew Bible, or Old Testament, with their own scriptures, the New Testament, they inevitably treated in an allegorical manner a book that was somewhat embarrassing to them. In educational or Sunday school editions of the Christian Bible, we typically find the allegory spelled out in detail. The traditional Christian explanation of the Song of Songs sees the lover as Christ and his beloved as the Church. It should be pointed out that Jews have interpreted the same work allegorically as a representation of Yahweh's love for his chosen people.

Here is the chapter-by-chapter King James Version of the Christian allegory, with arabic numerals referring to the Old Testament verses quoted on page 245:

> I 1 The church's love unto Christ. 5 She confesseth
> her deformity, 7 and prayeth to be directed to his
> flock. 8 Christ directeth her to the shepherds'
> tents: 11 and giveth her gracious promises.
> II 1 The mutual love of Christ and his church.
> 14 Christ's care of the church. 16 The profession of
> the church, her faith and hope.

This is an example of a type of allegory that occurs after the fact. The original words were not allegorical—at least not in the sense that they were interpreted later by Christians. The allegory is attached to the words to make them tolerable to a particular culture. In the same way, a modern secular humanist who wishes to take the irrational out of the Christian nativity "myth" while preserving its essential "truth," might interpret it as an allegory of the process of individuation, the psychological birth of the self within the individual. (Fletcher 1964; MacQueen 1970; Piehler 1971)

See also The Bible and Allegory.

THE SPACE TRILOGY

Sometimes called *The Space Trilogy*, three novels by C. S. Lewis (1898–1963) are linked together by Christian allegory and a central character with the allegorical name Ransom. The components of the trilogy are *Out of the Silent Planet* (1938), *Perelandra* (1943), and *That Hideous Strength* (1945). In all three novels, Ransom, a university don and a man of ordinary mental and physical powers, is the chosen everyman who, like Frodo in the fantasy work of Lewis's friend, J. R. R. Tolkien, is called upon to do the impossible in the great struggle between good and evil—between the way of God and the way of Satan. He is to be, like Christ or any "good" Christian, the ransom paid for the world's salvation. Kidnapped in *Out of the Silent Planet* by the evil physicist Weston and his materialist companion Devine, Ransom is taken off in a spaceship to Malacandra (Mars). There he is able to help prevent the infection of Malacandra that had already occurred on Earth as a result of the forces represented by Weston and Devine.

In *Perelandra* Ransom is called by a higher being—the Oyarsa—to travel to the planet of Perelandra (Venus), which is being threatened by the same dark forces that have corrupted earth. Perelandra is a floating world populated by a queen and a king—Adam and Eve figures in their utter innocence. The female figure is being threatened by evil in the form of the physicist Weston—the reincarnation of the Edenic serpent—and once again, Ransom's role is to play Christ to Weston's Satan and to prevent from happening in Perelandra what had happened to the first parents on Earth.

That Hideous Strength takes place on Planet Earth. Ransom, now older and the leader of a group that stands for good, finds himself in the most difficult battle yet. This time the antagonist is still Weston, whose disembodied brain—the mind of Satan—is contained at the heart of an organization for materialism and perverted science called NICE. This time Ransom is given help by a figure from the ancient past, the Arthurian magician Merlin, and after great difficulty NICE and its energy source are overcome.

See also *The Chronicles of Narnia*; Lewis, C. S.

SPIEGELMAN, ART

See *Maus*.

SPENSER, SIR EDMUND

The author of *The Faerie Queene*, one of the greatest allegorical works in English, Edmund Spenser (1552–1599) was a product of the political, religious, and aesthetic turmoil of the Elizabethan age in England. Born in London to an adamantly anti-Catholic, pro-Protestant family, his earliest memories included the persecution of Protestants by Mary Tudor in the 1550s. To Spenser and people like him, the ascendancy of Elizabeth to the throne marked the return of moral, political, and historical legitimacy to Britain but did not eliminate the danger of an ever-present and ever-devious Catholic threat to this legitimacy. At Cambridge University, a center for the most radical Protestant thought in the late sixteenth century, Spenser would find intellectual justification for his moral and political positions and encouragement for his growing belief that his talent for poetry could be put to good practical use.

The Shepheardes Calender (1579) was Spenser's first major work and can be seen as a logical predecessor to *The Faerie Queene*. A collection of 12 pastoral eclogues—dialogues between shepherds—in the tradition of Virgil, the work reflects the interest of the English Renaissance poets such as Sir Philip Sidney, Christopher Marlowe, and Spenser himself in things classical, and provides the poet—also in the tradition of Virgil—with an opportunity to comment, through the dialogues, on political and moral issues that will later form the basis of the allegory in *The Faerie Queene*.

See also *The Faerie Queene*.

STATIUS, PUBLIUS PAPINIUS

A Latin poet, Statius (45–96 C.E.) wrote epics on Greek themes. Critics in his time tended to consider his works allegories on religious and social questions. Most readers now would disagree. Statius's most important work is probably the *Thebaid,* and when we read it today—though people rarely do—we find a work that is allegorical only in that the myths it makes use of are allegorical. The same can be said of the fragment called the *Achilleid.*

STEVENS, WALLACE

Wallace Stevens (1879–1955) is an interesting and unusual figure among American poets, partially as a result of his loyalty to his position as an insurance executive in Connecticut. He won the Pulitzer Prize and the National Book Award in 1955, and his highly visual and aurally appealing poetry has secured for him a permanent place in modern American poetry.

Several critics have suggested that some of Stevens's poetry makes use of allegorical images. For example, "Thirteen Ways of Looking at a Blackbird" has been read as an allegory of death, specifically the inseparable nature of life and death. In this interpretation, the blackbird, as the figure of death, brings awareness to the reader (or mankind) that in our universe of flux, death is always present. It is important to add, however, that this allegorical reading is only one of many valid critical interpretations of the poem. (Blessing 1970)

STEVENSON, ROBERT LOUIS

The author of *Treasure Island* (1884), *Dr. Jeckyll and Mr. Hyde* (1886), *Kidnapped* (1886), *The Mystery of Ballantrae* (1888), and several popular novels, Stevenson (1850–1894) was born in Scotland and spent a great deal of his life traveling in search of health and adventure. He spent the last five years of his life on the South Sea island of Samoa on a plantation.

See also Dr. Jeckyll and Mr. Hyde.

STORY OF AN AFRICAN FARM

See Schreiner, Olive.

SUFIS

See Nasreddin Hodja; Rumi, Jalal al-din.

SUMMA

See Aquinas, Thomas.

SWIFT, JONATHAN

Jonathan Swift was born in Dublin, Ireland, in 1667, to English parents. Through the generosity of a wealthy uncle, he was educated at Kilkenny School and Trinity College, Dublin. He relocated to England in 1689, after James II invaded Ireland, and lived with Sir William Temple, a relative of Swift's and a friend of King William's. Swift remained a member of Sir Temple's household for about ten years, during which time he read voraciously, became a clergyman, and began writing satirical pieces on religion, politics, and learning. *A Tale of a Tub* and *The Battle of the Books* were published in 1704. In 1699, Swift returned to Ireland as chaplain to the lord justice, the Earl of Berkeley; he lived unwillingly in Ireland for nearly the rest of his life.

Swift was a devoted Anglican and used his pen to attack any group or institution that he believed threatened his Church. Politically, Swift was originally a Whig, but abandoned his party and vehemently allied himself with the Tories in 1710, after deeming the Whigs too indifferent to the welfare of the Anglican Church. His loyalty to his religion, however, did not earn him the English bishopric he deeply desired, but the deanship of St. Patrick's Cathedral in Dublin. He served as dean from 1713 until 1739, when, at 72 years of age, the crippling effects of what we now recognize as Ménière's disease rendered him incapable of performing his duties. After six more unhappy years, Swift died in 1745.

Although perhaps best remembered for his masterful *Gulliver's Travels* (1726), Swift also wrote a series of shorter but equally biting allegories attacking the politics of his time. "Story of an Injured Lady" (1707) is an allegory of England's unjust treatment of Ireland, contrasted with England's generous treatment of Scotland under the terms of the Union of 1707. In "Story," the relationship among the three nations is represented by the relationship among a man and his two lovers. In another allegorical piece, "An Account of the Court and Empire of Japan" (1728), Swift recounts English political history from the Revolution to the rise of King George II. Swift uses anagrams in the "Account" to thinly disguise the actual identities of his characters; for example, the character representing George II is called "Regoge." (Lock 1980)

See also *Gulliver's Travels; A Tale of a Tub.*

SYMBOL

Symbols are aspects of literature or other art that are integral to the work in question but that seem to stand out in such a way as to demand special attention as to their meaning or significance. The lighthouse in Virginia Woolf's *To the Lighthouse* is a symbol and so are Hester Prynne's letter *A* in Hawthorne's *Scarlet Letter* and the whiteness of the whale in Melville's *Moby-Dick*. Some critics have made a special case of the distinction between symbol and allegory. There are degrees of symbolism. Some symbols add richness to a text merely by adding mystery and ambiguity; it seems unnecessary to discover the specific meaning, for example, of Woolf's lighthouse, so we hesitate to speak of the lighthouse as allegory. We might be more tempted to understand the white whale allegorically—partly because its meaning is addressed in the text. If we turn to a work that is clearly allegorical, we move away from symbol to allegorical figure or emblem. We have no doubt as to the meaning of the figures of Duessa and Una in Spenser's *Faerie Queene,* for example. It is necessary that we recognize their meaning to truly understand the text in question. We do not, however, need to understand in a one-to-one manner the meaning of Henry James's golden bowl, a symbol in the novel of that name. (Frye 1957)

See also Coleridge, Samuel Taylor.

THE SYSTEM OF DANTE'S HELL

This autobiographical fiction by Amiri Baraka (b. 1934) is a long prose poem that looks back to Dante's *Inferno* from the perspective of an African American who feels he has "sinned" by allowing himself to be sucked in by American and Western cultural values. The characters in this highly abstract work can be said to be allegories of the author's experience. They stand for particular black leaders whom Baraka does not respect, representing, almost as if this were a modern morality play, characteristics such as Pride and Prosperity, though these characteristics take their meaning from a value system that is not the same as Dante's or what Baraka sees as the Western world's. So it is that Prosperity is associated with one Dolores Morgan because she has an illegitimate child, and Pride is embodied in the man who fathered the child. The people in the lowest ring of this Hell are those who have denied their real identity as African Americans and become "white."

See also Baraka, Amiri; *The Divine Comedy.*

A TALE OF A TUB

Jonathan Swift's *A Tale of a Tub* (1704) is considered by many to be one of the more important English satires on religion and learning. The work itself has two extensive dedications—one a distinctly allegorical one to "Prince Posterity"—a preface, 12 subsequent sections that are made up of the tale proper, entire sections of "digressions," and a conclusion. *A Tale of a Tub* allegorizes the corruption of the Christian religion through its story of three brothers. The interspersed digressions parody corruption in learning by exposing scholars, critics, and theologians who misapply their knowledge and contaminate society.

Part I, the Introduction, cautions readers to be aware of the allegory that follows. Part II begins the actual *Tale,* introducing a set of triplets: Peter, Martin, and Jack. Peter represents St. Peter, and therefore the Roman Catholic Church. Martin is Martin Luther, and allegorizes the Lutheran and Anglican Churches. Jack, or John Calvin, depicts the Calvinist Dissenters. The story begins as their father (God), on his deathbed, bequeaths each son a simple coat to be worn but never altered, representing the New Testament doctrines. After their father dies, the brothers decide to make their coats more fashionable by embellishing them with gold lace, silver fringe, shoulder knots, and other decorations. Peter cleverly finds new ways to interpret their father's will in order to justify these forbidden alterations.

Part III leaves behind the allegory to attack abuses in learning by parodying critics who look only for defects in the work of others. The allegory of the brothers resumes in Part IV, in which Swift denounces various Roman Catholic institutions such as purgatory, penance, celibacy, confession, and holy water, among others. The allegory remains primarily concerned with Peter, who takes on the title of Lord Peter and claims to be superior to Martin and Jack. The other brothers, justifiably angry at Peter, obtain a copy of their father's will, which proves them to be equal heirs. Peter, incensed, expels them from the house they had always shared. Allegorically, the *Tale* parallels the events of the English Reformation.

The next part digresses from the allegory in order to attack modern writers and their tendencies to glorify their own work while mocking the Ancients. Part VI returns to the story of the brothers, specifically the dilemma of Martin and Jack. Martin decides to remove the decorations from his coat; after careful work, the garment is nearly back to its original state. Jack also decides to remove his embellishments, but in his haste and carelessness he tears his coat to shreds. Jack then covets Martin's coat, and the two have a terrible argument. This development allegorizes the historical split between Luther and the more fanatical Calvinist reformers.

Another digression in Part VII ironically assaults modern writers who plagiarize and digress in their writing, instead of adhering to ideals of originality and style. Part VIII returns to the story of the brothers, dealing primarily with Jack and his followers. Swift allegorizes the verbose, egotistical, and "windy" preachings of the Calvinist ministers as he describes Jack and his followers as "Aeolists," wind-worshippers who admire man for his ability to produce "wind" at both ends of his body.

Both Parts IX and X are digressions from the *Tale,* which attack (among other issues) man's lack of common sense and the hypocrisy of modern writers. Part XI returns for the last time to the tale of the brothers; Swift's allegory mocks the fanatic Calvinists and their notions of predestination, their avoidance of church music, and their insistence on simplicity. Jack's affectations come to resemble those of his brother Peter; this disturbs them both.

Swift ends *A Tale of a Tub* with a long-winded conclusion that celebrates his successful defense of commonsense approaches to issues of religion and learning through his mockery of the foibles of modern scholars and religious sects. (Swift's mockery also aims specifically at one man, William Wotton, a scholar whose furious reactions to the *Tale* were added to subsequent editions of the work.) The allegorical tale of Peter, Martin, and Jack reveals Swift's strong bias toward the Church of England's position as a middle course between the more radical Roman Catholics and Calvinists. And, just as importantly, it offers readers moral lessons on the conduct of a true Christian humanist, in Swift's terms. (Clark 1970)

See also Swift, Jonathan.

TAOISM

See Lao Tsu.

TENNYSON, ALFRED, LORD

Alfred, Lord Tennyson (1809–1892), considered by many to be the greatest Victorian poet, was the fourth son in a family of 12 children. His father, the Reverend Dr. George Tennyson, was a well-educated man born to a wealthy landowning family. But instead of inheriting his family's estate, George was disinherited in favor of his younger brother and was forced to seek a career in the clergy. He became an often violent drunkard, but managed to tutor his sons so that they could enter the university.

Alfred Tennyson began composing and publishing poetry at an early age, and at Cambridge University he found many supportive friends who encouraged his writing. He published several volumes of poetry (1830, 1832, 1842) and when his great elegy *In Memoriam* appeared in 1850, his popularity and importance as a poet were sealed. Later that year he succeeded William Wordsworth as England's poet laureate. The rest of Tennyson's career brought many more poetic successes; *Maud,* a long experimental poem, appeared in 1855, and *Idylls of the King,* which occupied much of his later career, was published in its entirety in 1888. Tennyson died in 1892, the most popular poet of his time.

See also *The Idylls of the King.*

THEOGONY

An allegorical work by the Greek poet Hesiod (eighth century B.C.E.), the *Theogony* is the primary source for the ancient Greek understanding of the creation and early stages of the cosmos. It traces the history of the immortals from the days of the first father god, Uranos, to the reign of his grandson Zeus. Two basic kinds of allegory are present in this story. The first is allegory by personification. For instance, during the war between Zeus and the Titans, the Titan Styx deserts to Zeus's side with her children, whose names are Glory, Victory, Power, and Strength, all attributes admired by the Olympian gods (and their creators, the Greeks) and taken over by them in their ultimate victory over the Titans. The second sort of allegory is more complex.

In the beginning, says Hesiod, there was only the Void and then Mother Earth, who produced from herself an equal being called Uranos (Sky). But the male principle Uranos became arrogant and powerful and at Mother Earth's suggestion was castrated by his son Kronos (Time). The allegory would seem to point to the establishment of the power of time in the universe over that of the timelessness represented by the original Void and Sky. That Earth supports the rise of time suggests the dominance of this world rather than the world of the immortal sky god. This ancient mythological arrangement coincides with early pre-Aryan agricultural Mother rite traditions in Greece that were later overcome by warriors from the north who carried with them the tradition of the War-Sky god embodied in Zeus. In the *Theogony,* Kronos eats his children. Allegorically, he is Time, who thus deprives his offspring of immortality and condemns them to the time-dominated world of Mother Earth. But when the baby Zeus is about to be swallowed, a rock is substituted for him and he remains alive to defeat his father. Thus Zeus overcomes the power of time and becomes immortal and liberates his swallowed brothers and sisters as well. When these new and powerful Sky-Warrior gods destroy the earth-bound offspring of the old powers, represented by the Titans, they establish the male-dominated Sky religion of the Olympian gods in Greece.

See also Hesiod; Myth as Allegory.

THEOLOGICAL ALLEGORY

See Aquinas, Thomas.

THOMPSON, FRANCIS

An English Roman Catholic poet whose work is often mystical, Thompson (1859–1907) was best known for his allegorical poem "The Hound of Heaven," in which an individual attempts to escape a pursuing hound. The poem begins:

> I fled Him, down the nights and down the days;
> I fled Him, down the arches of the years;
> I fled Him, down the labyrinthine ways
> Of my own mind.

It is clear that the poet's intentions are allegorical here. If the title is not sufficient to make the point, the word *him* is capitalized throughout, indicating clearly that the hound is God. The pursued is the poet or any human being who thinks he or she can escape God. That this is no mere story of a reversed hunt is evident in a phrase like "arches of the years," which takes the chase out of the literal into the world of metaphor. And when we hear that the hunt takes place in the "labyrinthine ways/Of my own mind," we know that the poet refers to the inner struggles involved in the "call" of faith. (MacNeice 1965)

THROUGH THE LOOKING GLASS

The continuation by Lewis Carroll (1832–1898) of his more famous *Alice's Adventures in Wonderland, Through the Looking Glass* (1871) takes place in a world where chess pieces, flowers, and insects talk. The events of the story have to do with chess moves, and many have found allegorical meaning in the strange events surrounding such characters as the White King and Queen, the Red King and Queen, the White and Red Knights, Tweedledum and Tweedledee, and Humpty Dumpty.

When Alice and her black kitten pass through the looking glass into the world behind the mirror, everything looks like our world but everything is different. The countryside, for instance, is a huge chessboard, and the Red Queen tells Alice she can be the White Queen's Pawn. It is a land in which you have to run as fast as you can to stay in the same place and twice as fast as you can to get anywhere. There is a train in this land, but it is full of talking insects and Alice does not have a ticket. She meets two fat men, Tweedledum and Tweedledee, who say things that always have double meanings. They recite a poem about a Walrus, a Carpenter, and Oysters. They tell Alice that she is only real in the Red King's dream; Alice cries when she hears this. The White Queen comes along; she is a person who lives in reverse, remembering things that have not yet happened, for example. Knitting needles change to oars in this world, and an egg becomes Humpty Dumpty. Humpty talks to Alice in riddles. The Red and the White Knights try to capture her, and later she passes a certain test and becomes a Queen. There is a party for her and the White Queen becomes a leg of mutton.

Adult analysts have found in *Through the Looking Glass* a subtle commentary on the nature of logic and of reality. More in keeping with Carroll's disillusionment with the Victorian world, Alice, as the commonsense figure, is an allegorical pawn on the chessboard of the game of life; it is with Alice that the author identifies and sympathizes. Life as seen by Carroll is characterized by an absurd logic; our world is the looking-glass world from which Carroll longed to escape.

See also **Alice's Adventures in Wonderland; Carroll, Lewis.*

THURBER, JAMES

See Fable as Allegory.

THE TIME MACHINE

See Wells, H. G.

TINY ALICE

Edward Albee's play *Tiny Alice* (1964), like *Who's Afraid of Virginia Woolf?*, tackles the formidable human dilemmas of loneliness, hypocrisy, and illusion. It tells the story of Miss Alice, the wealthiest woman in the world, who donates two billion dollars to the Catholic Church. The Cardinal's assistant, a lay-brother named Julian, moves into Alice's castle to expedite the transaction. Once there, the innocent Julian finds himself entangled in a confusing web of deceit collectively spun by Miss Alice, her lawyer, and her butler. Julian eventually marries Miss Alice, only to discover that she is merely impersonating the *real* Alice. In the final scene, Miss Alice and her two conspirators abandon the mortally wounded Julian, leaving him to face his fears, the destruction of his beliefs, and the spirit of Alice.

The most allegorical element in *Tiny Alice* is undoubtedly a model castle, which is the major stage prop throughout most of the play. It is a miniature, dollhouse version of Alice's real castle, which, the play suggests, houses the spirit of Alice. When a fire breaks out in the chapel, a corresponding fire appears in the model. When one is extinguished, the other disappears as well. Through this mysterious correlation between reality and its replica, and Julian's ultimate acceptance that the miniature castle is in fact the "real" one, critics suggest that the model functions like the Platonic allegory of the cave. That is, for Julian to accept the model castle as reality and the larger castle as merely a false illusion, he undergoes the same disorientation that Plato's man in the cave did. Thus, Albee may be allegorically suggesting that what we consider to be the truth about reality may in fact be only an illusion that can be stripped away. (Bigsby 1975; Hayman 1973)

See also Albee, Edward; Plato; *Who's Afraid of Virginia Woolf?*

TOLKIEN, J. R. R.

An English scholar and professor of medieval philology, Tolkien (1892–1973) is best known as the author of the fantasy trilogy *The Lord of the Rings* and its forerunner, *The Hobbit*.

See also The Lord of the Rings.

TOLSTOY, LEO

Count Lev Nikolayevich Tolstoy (1828–1910), Russian novelist and social reformer, is best known for the great realist novels *War and Peace* and *Anna Karenina*. But by the mid-1880s, Tolstoy had denied the validity of nondidactic art—including his own early work. Instead of realist fiction about life among Russian aristocrats, Tolstoy began to write works that illustrated his newfound commitment to what he saw as original Christian principles. He wrote parables—often based on Russian folktales—such as "How Much Land Can a Man Own?," in which a peasant's greed, representing human greed in general, leads to his death. And he wrote longer fiction that spoke somewhat allegorically to moral questions. *The Death of Ivan Ilyich* is the story of how a man's slow and painful death leads him, with the help of a peasant's instinctive gentleness, to the joy of salvation. Tolstoy's last novel, with the allegorical title *Resurrection,* represents the mystical redemption of a selfish and worldly man through genuine confession and sacrifice.

With the exception of some of the more simplistic parables, however, Tolstoy's works are not properly called allegories. Even in his late works Tolstoy remains a realist, albeit a didactic one. His work has none of the surreal quality that marks the more evidently allegorical work of moderns like Kafka and Borges.

TOM JONES

The greatest work of the English novelist Henry Fielding (1707–1754), *Tom Jones* is not an allegory, but it does contain obvious allegorical aspects. It is the story of how a foundling, Tom Jones, is wrongly expelled from the house of one Squire Allworthy and travels as a result across England, experiencing many adventures. Only after his difficulties does Tom achieve sufficient maturity and knowledge to prove himself innocent of the crimes of which he has been

Mark Twain

accused and to return, redeemed, to the all-worthy squire. The squire makes Tom his heir, indicating allegorically his worthiness at last to marry the beautiful Sophia, whose name, not insignificantly, means "wisdom."

See also Fielding, Henry.

THE TRIAL

See Kafka, Franz.

TROPOLOGICAL ALLEGORY

See Moral Allegory.

TWAIN, MARK

Mark Twain (1835–1910) was born Samuel Langhorne Clemens in Missouri and was raised in the Mississippi River town of Hannibal. His experiences growing up in Hannibal provide the basis for his descriptions of St. Petersburg, the fictional town where Tom Sawyer and Huckleberry Finn lived. Although Mark Twain is often envisioned in American folklore as a warm, avuncular man with a sharp wit and a penchant for humor, scholars now understand that Twain was a complicated figure torn between writing solely to make money and writing in order to expose the injustice he witnessed around him. As a result, the scope of Twain's work is unusually broad. For example, he wrote *The Prince and the Pauper* (1882) partly to demonstrate his ability to accommodate the tastes of genteel readers, yet a few years later published *A Connecticut Yankee in King Arthur's Court* (1889), which satirize the conditions of the powerful rich and the oppressed poor. *The Adventures of Huckleberry Finn* (1885) is considered to be Twain's most allegorical work, and scholars have offered a number of different interpretations of this story of the child/outcast who searches for a way to reconcile what society teaches him and what he knows in his heart to be true.

See also *The Adventures of Huckleberry Finn.*

TYPOLOGICAL ALLEGORY

Typological allegory is concerned with allegorical connections between figures of different periods. Thus Adam is a type for Christ, the "New Adam." For early Christians, especially, typological allegory provided a meaningful link between the Old and New Testaments, the old and new laws. (Honig 1966)

See also Bede, The Venerable; The Bible and Allegory; The Song of Songs.

THE UNIVERSAL BASEBALL
ASSOCIATION, INC., J. HENRY WAUGH, PROP.

The second novel by Robert Coover (b. 1942), *The Universal Baseball Association* (1968) uses baseball as the vehicle to allegorize American attitudes toward religion. The story describes the mundane life of Henry Waugh, a lonely 56-year-old bachelor and accountant, who invents a baseball game played with dice and charts on an imaginary field. Henry creates each player's fictional biography, and, over time, his game becomes so exciting to him that he loses interest in every other aspect of his life. Eventually forgetting that the Universal Baseball Association is just an invention, Henry starts to believe in the actual existence of his players. He becomes particularly attached to one talented young player, Damon Rutherford, who becomes for Henry the son he never had. Henry's life is shattered when a roll of the dice one day dictates that Rutherford be killed by a pitched ball. In revenge, Henry tries to destroy Jock Casey, the pitcher who fatally struck Damon. But Casey becomes stronger and more powerful, until finally Henry intervenes and intentionally places the three dice in the six-six-six configuration that determines Casey's death by a line drive. The final, eighth chapter of the novel ends not with Henry's story, but with the story of the imaginary baseball players of Henry's Association, 100 years after the deaths of Rutherford and Casey.

Naturally, critics have interpreted the extensive biblical imagery, names, numerical allusions, and events in *The Universal Baseball Association* as a complicated religious allegory. Indeed, critics have been quick to note the appropriateness of Coover's allegory in that baseball has become a sort of American religion, and ballparks are treated, by many, with the respect and sanctity often accorded churches. Henry's initials J. H. W. suggest the Hebrew god Yahweh; Henry, like Yahweh, takes on the role and responsibility of becoming the Creator of his world. In keeping with this biblical connection, Jock Casey, J. C., becomes the sacrificial Jesus Christ figure whose life is the price for the salvation of the U.B.A. Significantly, Casey's life is ended with a six-six-six roll of the dice, recalling the number of the beast in Revelation. Richard Andersen suggests that "Jock Casey's death not only redeems his brothers in the association, as Christ's death atoned for the sins of his fellow man, but he saves Henry, his creator, from turning his back on his fiction and participating in the real world. . . . Vomiting a rainbow of pizza over his altered universe, Henry provides his ballplayers with a sign of the covenant he has made with them" (69).

Furthermore, some critics recognize the politically allegorical elements evident in Coover's novel. The U.B.A. becomes the U.S.A.; Swanee Law becomes Lyndon B. Johnson; Rutherford, the young hero struck down, becomes John F. Kennedy or Martin Luther King, Jr.; and Henry's story becomes the story of 1960s America. Critic Jackson Cope invites us to recognize that the "Kennedy myth of national renewal aborted is reflected in a series of killings following upon Henry's assassination of Jock after the death of Damon. . . . We are directed to read through the layer of the accountant Jehovah to the history of the USA in the sixties, to see the sacrifice of Casey, the consequent helpless commitment of Henry and the chancellor as Vietnam, to hear the surge of revolution rolling in from the future. Politics and war are, after all, the great American games" (42–43). (Andersen 1981; Cope 1986; Gordon 1983)

VARGAS LLOSA, MARIO

Mario Vargas Llosa (b. 1936) is one of South America's leading novelists. In recent years he has been criticized for what many have seen as right-wing leanings. Generally he has been an advocate of democracy in his native Peru and at one point was offered the position of prime minister—a position he refused. While not an allegorist, Vargas Llosa makes use of what seems to be allegory in his novel *The War at the End of the World*.

See also *The War at the End of the World*.

VATHEK

Vathek, a novel by the Englishman William Beckford (1794–1844), is a Gothic allegory. Vathek is an Arabian prince who, somewhat Faust-like, is a devotee of the senses and of the mysteries of science and the occult. He builds a dark tower in which his evil mother makes burnt sacrifices to the spirits of the dark world. When Vathek is given some sabres bearing mysterious letters that change daily, he becomes sure that the words hold the key to power and riches in the "dark kingdom." A mysterious stranger called Giaour reveals to Vathek that he will understand the writings only after he has made a sacrifice. Vathek brutally murders 50 children to please Giaour, and the people turn on him in anger. Still, Vathek and his mother persist in their evil and un-Moslem ways. On his way to the Mountain of Isatakhar, where Vathek hopes to discover more secrets of the dark world, he is entertained by the holy prince Fakreddin, and he falls in love with his daughter, Nouronihar, already bethrothed to her cousin, Gulchenrouz. Vathek plots to abduct the young woman. When the plot is discovered, Fakreddin has his daughter and her betrothed drugged so that they will seem to be dead. Then he hides them away, and when they awake they think they have been dead and have awakened in Paradise.

Unfortunately, Nouronihar strays from her hiding place one day and is seduced by Vathek. She becomes his favorite wife and his accomplice in the attempt to discover and control the riches of the dark powers. When the couple arrive at the dark mountain, they are welcomed by its lord and the riches are revealed along with the horrors of that world. When Vathek's mother arrives she is consumed by flames, as are Vathek and his evil spouse. But the 50 murdered children are taken away to an earthly paradise.

Vathek himself stands for evil and his quest becomes, ironically, an allegory for the process by which we come to recognize the nature of evil. Thus Nouronihar stands for the fall from innocence, and her father for goodness, which has only so much power in the face of determined evil. Most critics agree, however, that Beckford had enough of the Vathek character within himself to appreciate his hero's debaucheries more than the moral lesson for which his demise seems to stand. (Magill 1976)

See also Beckford, William.

VICTORY

Victory (1915) is a novel by Joseph Conrad (1857–1924) that tells the story of a loner called Axel Heyst, who comes to the assistance of a young woman called Lena and takes her to his isolated South Sea island. On the island Heyst and Lena discover love and achieve a kind of victory over their isolation in life. But the victory costs a great deal, as Lena dies for it in a terrible confrontation with a certain Mr. Jones and his evil henchman.

Not surprisingly, the novel has been read allegorically. The island becomes a new Garden of Eden, with Heyst and Lena as Adam and Eve and Mr. Jones as Satan, who invades their paradise and brings death to it.

See also Conrad, Joseph; *Heart of Darkness*.

THE VIOLENT BEAR IT AWAY

Flannery O'Connor (1925–1964) was born and raised in Georgia and spent the majority of her life in the South. Most readers remember her for her collections of short stories, *A Good Man Is Hard To Find, and Other Stories* (1955), and *Everything That Rises Must Converge* (1965), but the grotesque visions of Catholicism and southern life that characterize her novels have also received much critical attention and acclaim.

Critics have noted that O'Connor's second novel, *The Violent Bear It Away* (1960), has particularly strong allegorical qualities. The novel tells the story of Tarwater, a 14-year-old adolescent torn between his connection to the religious fanaticism of his late great-uncle Mason Tarwater, a crazed prophet/hermit, and to the secular beliefs of his living uncle Rayber, a schoolteacher, social scientist, and Mason's estranged son. After leaving the backwoods home he and Mason had shared, Tarwater is determined to deny his late uncle's wish that he realize his calling as a prophet by baptizing Bishop, his retarded cousin and Rayber's son. Rayber attempts to instill a more intellectual system of beliefs in the boy, but ultimately Tarwater cannot deny his prophetic election. Against Rayber's emphatic orders, Tarwater baptizes Bishop, but in doing so he drowns the idiot child.

Interpreters of *The Violent Bear It Away* as a religious allegory recognize that Mason Tarwater, who believes himself to be descended from the Old Testament prophets, represents fundamental Christianity, and Rayber, who denies any spiritual life whatsoever, represents modern, intellectual man. The ideas of baptism and the bread of life figure prominently in young Tarwater's struggle to decide in which uncle's vision he will place his loyalties. Ultimately, he becomes the new prophet—a virtual reincarnation of his great-uncle—and his story of self-discovery allegorizes the powerful struggle between religious piety and secular humanism. (Baker 1992)

See also O'Connor, Flannery.

VIRGIL

The greatest Roman poet Publius Vergilius Maro (70–19 B.C.E.) was born near Mantua. His prosperous family sent him to Rome to study rhetoric. Rome, however, did not please Virgil, and he returned to his father's farm to study Greek philosophy and poetry. During the chaos that followed the assassination of Julius Caesar, Virgil's poetry came to the attention of the influential Maecenas, who urged the poet to expand and publish his eclogues as the *Bucolics* and later, his observations of farm life, the *Georgics*, both of which owe something to Hesiod's *Works and Days*. Virgil then began his most famous work, the *Aeneid*, the great epic of the founding of Rome, which he never quite completed. The epic contains allegorical elements. In the Middle Ages, Virgil himself became an allegorical figure, serving Dante in *The Divine Comedy*, for example, as an appropriate guide through Hell and Purgatory because he represented human wisdom or true poetry. Much of the allegorical lore that developed around Virgil himself was the result of a Christian allegorical reading of his fourth *Eclogue* (39 B.C.E.). In this short work, one of ten pastoral poems in the style of the Greek poet Theocritus, Virgil predicts the birth of a child who will usher in a golden age of peace and prosperity. Virgil was, of course, referring to a Roman child who would be born to one of his patrons or to the future emperor, Octavian. Or perhaps he was telling a flattering story, after the fact, of the birth of Octavian himself. Medieval Christians, however, saw in the fourth *Eclogue* a prophecy of the Messiah, the Christ. When we read this John Dryden translation of the *Eclogue*, we can see why the temptation to read the poem allegorically might have been overwhelming:

THE FOURTH ("MESSIANIC") ECLOGUE

Sicilian Muse, begin a loftier strain!
Though lowly shrubs and trees that shade the plain
Delight not all, Sicilian Muse, prepare
To make the vocal woods deserve a consul's care.

The last great age, foretold by sacred rhymes,
Renews its finished course: Saturnian times
Roll round again, and mighty years, begun

From their first orb, in radiant circles run.
The base, degenerate iron offspring ends;
A golden progeny from heaven descends.
O chaste Lucina, speed the mother's pains,
And haste the glorious birth! Thy own Apollo reigns!
The lovely boy with his auspicious face
Shall Pollio's consulship and triumph grace.
Majestic months set out with him to their appointed race.
The father banished virtue shall restore,
And crimes shall threat the guilty world no more.
The son shall lead the life of gods, and be
By gods and heroes seen, and gods and heroes see.
The jarring nations he in peace shall bind,
And with paternal virtues rule mankind.

    Unbidden earth shall wreathing ivy bring
And fragrant herbs, the promises of spring,
As her first offerings to her infant king.
The goats with strutting dugs shall homeward speed,
And lowing herds secure from lions feed.
His cradle shall with rising flowers be crowned;
The serpent's brood shall die; the sacred ground
Shall weeds and poisonous plants refuse to bear;
Each common bush shall Syrian roses wear.

    But when heroic verse his youth shall raise,
And form it to hereditary praise,
Unlabored harvests shall the fields adorn,
And clustered grapes shall blush on every thorn.
The knotted oaks shall showers of honey weep,
And through the matted grass the liquid gold shall creep.
Yet of old fraud some footsteps shall remain:
The merchant shall still plow the deep for gain;
Great cities shall with walls be compassed round,
And sharpened shares shall vex the fruitful ground;
Another Tiphys shall new seas explore;
Another Argo land the chiefs upon the Iberian shore.
Another Helen other wars create,
And great Achilles urge the Trojan fate.

    But when to ripened manhood he shall grow,
The greedy sailor shall the seas forgo.
No keel shall cut the waves for foreign ware,
For every soil shall every product bear.
No laboring hind his oxen shall disjoin;
No plow shall hurt the glebe, no pruning hook the vine;
Nor wool shall in dissembled colors shine.
But the luxurious father of the fold
With native purple or unborrowed gold

Beneath his pompous fleece shall proudly sweat;
And under Tyrian robes the lamb shall bleat.

    The Fates, when they this happy web have spun,
Shall bless the sacred clew and bid it smoothly run.

    Mature in years, to ready honors move,
O of celestial seed! O foster son of Jove!
See, laboring Nature calls thee to sustain
The nodding frame of heaven and earth and main!
See to their base restored earth, seas, and air;
And joyful ages from behind in crowding ranks appear.
To sing thy praise, would Heaven my breath prolong,
Infusing spirits worthy such a song,
Not Thracian Orpheus should transcend my lays,
Nor Linus crowned with never-fading bays,
Though each his heavenly parent should inspire,
The Muse instruct the voice, and Phoebus tune the lyre.
Should Pan contend in verse, and thou my theme,
Arcadian judges should their god condemn.

    Begin, auspicious boy, to cast about
Thy infant eyes, and with a smile they mother single out.
Thy mother well deserves that short delight,
The nauseous qualms of ten long months and travail to requite.
Then smile. The frowning infant's doom is read:
No god shall crown the board, nor goddess bless the bed.

(Fletcher 1964; MacQueen 1970)
   See also Aeneid; The Divine Comedy.

THE VISION OF PIERS PLOWMAN

See Piers Plowman.

VOLTAIRE

Voltaire was the pen name of François Marie Arouet (1694–1778), the influential and controversial French philosopher and writer, whose most famous works are the satirical novels *Candide* and *Zadig*. Voltaire was notoriously antireligious and scorned the blind use of reason deprived of common sense. Both *Candide* and *Zadig* are allegorical in that the characters and situations they are about are used didactically to represent certain universals, abstractions, and Voltairian ideas. Voltaire was an irritant to those in authority around him, and he spent time in prison and in exile for his views. Eventually he moved to an estate called Ferney, just across the French border, from which position he could be as critical as he wished. Voltaire died at the age of 84, a man much admired all over Europe.

See also Candide; Zadig.

 # WAITING FOR GODOT

The Irish playwright Samuel Beckett (1906–1989) was first recognized as an important writer when *Waiting for Godot*, a despairing yet funny play, was produced in 1952. The story line of *Waiting for Godot* is utterly simple: two tramps named Vladimir and Estragon are waiting for a figure named Godot, who has promised to meet them but who never appears. The two vagabonds talk, complain, sing, try to prove that they actually exist in the world, and share a few brief encounters with three other characters: Pozzo, Lucky, and a Boy. At the end of the play the two tramps are still waiting for Godot.

Waiting for Godot is sometimes interpreted as a religious allegory of man's need for salvation. Estragon and Vladimir believe that when Godot appears they will be "saved," thus suggesting a fairly obvious connection between Godot and either God or some other, perhaps ironical manifestation of the Second Coming of Christ. Even the two-act structure of the play has been paralleled with the Old and New Testaments in the Bible. But not all allegorical interpretations of this play are based on religion; critics have also suggested existential readings (demonstrating man's sense of loss after the death of God), and Freudian readings (in which Estragon represents the id and Vladimir represents the ego) as valid explanations of the play's meaning. (Kennedy 1989; Mercier 1977)

See also Beckett, Samuel; *Endgame.*

 # WAITING FOR THE BARBARIANS

J. M. Coetzee (b. 1940), a native of South Africa, incorporates allegorical elements into several of his novels, including *Waiting for the Barbarians* (1980). This novel tells the story of an unnamed magistrate who is in command of a tiny frontier settlement on the edge of the Empire. Unwilling to recognize the impending war between the surrounding colonies of barbarians and his own Empire, the Magistrate is deposed by the Empire's forces. In an act of rebellion intended to preserve his own human dignity, as well as that of the barbarians who have been abused at the hands of the government, the Magistrate is imprisoned as an enemy of the state.

Waiting for the Barbarians has been interpreted as a political allegory of the struggle between the oppressor and the oppressed. As critic Dick Penner explains, "at the heart of Coetzee's allegory is a dialectic concerning the relationships between empire and colony, master and slave-rebel, man and woman, blindness and sight, law and barbarism, and expediency and ethics" (76). As is the case in many allegories, the time frame of *Waiting for the Barbarians* is unidentifiable, the setting is remote, and the powerful forces are unnamed. While there are certainly connections between the world of Coetzee's novel and recent situations in South Africa, the Empire, embodied in the character of Colonel Joll, may represent any form of tyrannical injustice (particularly colonialism), and the Magistrate may represent any person who feels morally obliged to examine his or her own complicity with cruel and unconscionable regimes. (Penner 1989)

See also Coetzee, J. M.; *Foe; In the Heart of the Country.*

THE WAR AT THE END OF THE WORLD

An allegorical novel by the Peruvian Mario Vargas Llosa, *The War at the End of the World* takes place in the remote northeast corner of Brazil in the nineteenth century. A messiah figure, the Counselor, is a holy man who has gathered followers and prophesied an apocalypse at the millennium, 1900. When a republic is formed in the country at large and its leaders announce plans for a census, the Counselor and his followers suspect the reinstitution of slavery and denounce the republic as the "anti-Christ." The Counselor takes his people to the city of Bel Monte—a "new Jerusalem" in Canudos. There he announces that there will be "four fires." Three will be put out, but the fourth will consume their world. A certain peasant woman, who has been raped by a revolutionary, comes to town with two seemingly allegorical figures, a storyteller dwarf whose stories no one will buy and a journalist whose broken glasses distort his vision of history in the making. In the defeat of Bel Monte 30,000 people are killed, but the disappearance of the Counselor's body stands as a symbol of hope and redemption. An old woman asks the leader of the invaders whether he wants to know where the body is. When he says he does, she tells him that the messiah has gone: "The archangels took him up to heaven: I saw them," she says. The allegory here and elsewhere in the novel is not as specific as the allegorical reader might wish. There are genuine ambiguity and development in the characterization. Yet the connection—perhaps ironical—between the Counselor and Christ is obvious. The journalist with the broken glasses would seem to suggest the failure of our world to convey the truth of history, and the dwarf whose stories are refused speaks to the question of society's denial of the writer's value. In the end one feels that the real allegorical message in this novel is that all messianic dreams are suspect.

See also Vargas Llosa, Mario.

WATERSHIP DOWN

Watership Down (1972) is the best-known novel of British author Richard Adams. It developed out of a tale made up by Adams to entertain his daughters during long car rides. While not altogether an allegory, the book does, like most fantasies, have allegorical moments. The story is that of a rabbit warren made up of individuals who represent all aspects of humanity. There are good rabbits, bad rabbits, leaders and followers, rabbits who are brave and loyal, rabbits who are not. Everything in the story takes place in the context of an encroaching human housing development that threatens the old life of the warren. There is at least an implicit allegorical comment here on the loss of old established ways in the face of modern "progress," but the book is really more about perseverance and bravery.

See also Adams, Richard.

WELLS, H. G.

Herbert George Wells (1866–1946) was a prolific English writer best known for *The Time Machine* (1895) and *The War of the Worlds* (1898), two of his many science fiction novels. A great many of Wells's works have been recognized as allegorical by critics, who also note, as Robert P. Weeks explains, that Wells's fiction often adheres to a basic pattern of "disentanglement from an imprisoning reality, followed by exhilaration, then disillusionment or defeat" (Draper 35). This pattern provides the structure for Wells's caustic examinations of the many imperfections of humanity, and the barbaric underpinnings of modern civilization.

The Time Machine tells the story of a Time Traveller who journeys to the year 802701. There he encounters a world divided between the decadent, childlike society of the Eloi, who pursue comfort and beauty, and the brutal society of the Morlocks, who live and labor underground and who prey on the frail Eloi. It is suggested that the Eloi descended from the elite strata of society, and the Morlocks descended from the class of manual laborers. The entire novel has been read as an allegory of man's exploitation of man, and a vitriolic denunciation of the modern hierarchical class system that divides rich and poor.

The Island of Doctor Moreau (1896), *Mr. Blettsworthy on Rampole Island* (1928), and *The Croquet Player* (1936) are three satirical novels in which Wells incorporates allegorical elements to examine the nature of evil and the folly of mankind. Their remote settings allow the reader to examine moral and social issues from the perspective of an outsider, thereby making visible what is too often invisible. The allegories in each of these novels equate mankind with animals and serve as reminders of the bestial nature inherent in all of us.

Other allegorical or partly allegorical works include several short stories, such as "The Pearl of Love," "The Country of the Blind," and "The Beautiful Suit," as well as the novella *The Brothers* (1938). In each of these Wells articulates, through allegorical characters and events, the pitfalls of modern society and the evil inherent in the nature of mankind. Yet his pessimistic outlook often leads the reader not to total despair, but to an understanding of the need for improvement and endurance, and of the dangers of complacency and apathy. (Bergonzi 1976; Draper 1988; Hammond 1979)

WERFEL, FRANZ

Franz Werfel (1890–1945) was an extremely prolific and popular Austrian writer during his lifetime, but has been largely neglected since his death. He was born in Prague and died in exile in California; he is best remembered for his best-selling novel *The Song of Bernadette* (1941), based on the life of Saint Bernadette of Lourdes and later made into an Academy Award–winning film. He made major contributions to German expressionist poetry, and his novels, plays, and poetry made him famous in German-speaking countries. He first became known in the United States when his play *Goat Song [Bocksgesang]*, written in 1921, was produced in New York in 1926; shortly thereafter many of his other works were translated into English. Werfel fled from Austria to France in 1938 and arrived in the United States in 1940, where he spent the remainder of his life in exile.

See also Goat Song.

WEST, NATHANAEL

Nathanael West (1903–1940), originally Nathan Wallenstein Weinstein, was born in New York and attended Brown University. Many critics believe that West, killed in a tragic car accident at the age of 37, may have become one of America's premier novelists had he lived a longer life. Nevertheless, West's short writing career produced several novels that capture the dark, often grotesque underside of American life. Several of his works, including his well-known *Miss Lonelyhearts* and *The Day of the Locust*, have been recognized as incorporating elements of the allegorical to depict the hopelessness and meaningless of modern life.

See also The Day of the Locust; Miss Lonelyhearts.

WHO'S AFRAID OF VIRGINIA WOOLF?

The 1962 Broadway debut of *Who's Afraid of Virginia Woolf?* solidified Edward Albee's position as a dramatist of major importance and widespread popularity. The play, which contains virtually no action, is composed mainly of conversations between two married couples. Martha, the 52-year-old daughter of a college president, is married to George, a 46-year-old history professor who never rose through the professional ranks as Martha had hoped he would.

Their guests are Nick, a young biology professor who has just joined the faculty, and his wife, Honey, a plain, petite, thoroughly insipid woman. The entire play details the events of one drunken evening spent at George and Martha's home, during which the audience witnesses the shocking callousness and cruelty that these characters display toward one another. Only during the final scene do George and Martha connect on an intimate level, but it is only to acknowledge their common fear of living in a world devoid of the fantasies they have concocted in order to make life bearable.

Who's Afraid of Virginia Woolf? has been interpreted as a loose allegory of the cultural decline of America and its inability to live up to the ideals of its founders. The main characters are named after the Washingtons, the "parents" of America, which suggests a comparison between the George and Martha of the American Revolution and the George and Martha of modern America. Yet the modern George and Martha are not parents in any sense, which suggests that, unlike their revolutionary forebears, they are incapable of leading future generations to any realization of higher truths. In fact, the modern George and Martha intentionally blunt their moral convictions and revolutionary tendencies with alcohol or intellectualism, and inhabit a world entirely lacking in real values or national identity. Thus, allegorically, *Virginia Woolf* may be interpreted as a depiction of America's social collapse, mirrored in the failure of individuals to overcome their hedonistic impulses and profound loneliness in order to treat one another with anything like compassion. (Clurman 1975; Hayman 1973; Trilling 1975)

See also Albee, Edward; *Tiny Alice.*

THE WILD DUCK

A play by the Norwegian playwright Henrik Ibsen (1828–1906), *The Wild Duck* has often been interpreted allegorically. In this play, the central symbol, a wounded wild duck, lives in the attic of an essentially dysfunctional family, itself wounded by society. The attic of the Ekdals has been seen almost as a *paysage moralisé*, reflecting the predicament of the have-not classes who have been "wounded" by the capitalist class, represented here by old Mr. Werle, who had wronged old Mr. Ekdal, and Gregers Werle, his naïve and dangerously idealistic son, who while aiming to help the Ekdals in effect destroys them. One critic, Wolfgang Sohlich, has gone so far as to see in the play a "materialist"—that is to say Marxist—allegory of modern life in the technological age. His starting point is the existence in the Ekdal household of a photographer and a photographer's studio. Photos, says Sohlich, "misrepresent a reality in which human interactions are mediated by a depersonalized technology" (101). The studio and the cameras "refer to the intrusion of instrumental market relations into the family interior" (114).

As in the case of so many modernist writers—for example, Joyce, Woolf, and Lawrence—who have been approached allegorically, it seems worthwhile to caution the reader to differentiate between symbol and allegory. That the camera, the studio, and the duck in *The Wild Duck* are symbols is clear. As places and/or objects they stand out from the text. But it might well be argued that they do so ambiguously in such a way as to bring complexity and depth to the text rather than specific meaning. There may well be allegorical moments in Ibsen, but his intention was clearly to write realist rather than allegorical plays. (Haugen 1979; Sohlich 1992)

See also Ibsen, Henrik; *Paysage Moralisé.*

WILDE, OSCAR

Born Fingal O'Flahertie Wills, the Irish poet and playwright Oscar Wilde (1854–1900) was a popular writer who publicly endorsed the theories of John Ruskin's and Walter Pater's "aesthetic movement" and who enjoyed his image as a flamboyant "dandy." He achieved his greatest successes as a writer with his witty plays, including *Lady Windermere's Fan* (1892), *A Woman of No Importance* (1893), and *The Importance of Being Earnest* (1895). But also in 1895, Wilde, who was married and a father at the time, was tried and convicted on charges of homosexuality. His adoring public in England and America denounced him, and Wilde, released from prison two years later, was a ruined man. He lived out the final three years of his life under an assumed name in France, ostracized from his past life and supported only by the kindness of his friends.

See also The Picture of Dorian Gray.

WILLIAMS, CHARLES

A friend of J. R. R. Tolkien and C. S. Lewis, Charles Williams (1886–1945) wrote Christian fantasies, morality dramas in prose. The best known of his works are *Descent into Hell, War in Heaven,* and *All Hallows Eve.* Williams's novels are, in a sense, "thrillers," and they work well on that level. To call them allegories would be inaccurate for that reason. In short, although we sense a strong didactic moral symbolism in the works, we cannot attach particular allegorical meanings to each character and incident.

See also All Hallows Eve.

THE WIND IN THE WILLOWS

The classic children's story *The Wind in the Willows* (1908), by Kenneth Grahame (1859–1932), was based on stories the author told his young son, Alastair. This novel-length animal tale relates the adventures of a collection of friends, most importantly Rat, Mole, Toad, and Badger. Critics have recognized the allegorical qualities of the tale, specifically in the context of the social class system prevalent in Britain during Grahame's time. According to this interpretation, Badger represents the aristocratic upper class, Mole is the lower-class figure,

Oscar Wilde

Rat is middle-class, and Toad, also middle-class, additionally suggests qualities of the nouveau riche. *The Wind in the Willows* is the story of an arcadian landscape that maintains, at any cost, the status quo. As critic Peter Hunt explains, by the end of the tale, "the ruling order has been restored: the lower middle classes represented by Mole have been absorbed, the nouveau-riche perhaps represented by Toad have been brought into life, the working classes of the Wild Wood have been put back in their place. Arcadia is safe again" (77).

Other critics have offered different interpretations of Grahame's allegory, including a Freudian reading that suggests that Toad represents the id, Badger is the superego, and the combined forces of Rat and Mole are the ego. Another allegorical interpretation suggests a more mythic reading of *The Wind in the Willows;* in this context, the story of the animals searching for and creating their homes retells the mythic journey-quest of Odysseus trying to return to his home. (Hunt 1994; Kuznets 1987)

See also Grahame, Kenneth; The Quest as Allegory.

THE WONDERFUL WIZARD OF OZ

L. Frank Baum's classic tale *The Wonderful Wizard of Oz* (1899) was written primarily as a children's story. Yet Baum (1856–1919), a supporter both of William Jennings Bryan's quest for the 1896 presidency and of abandoning the gold standard, uses his fantasy tale to allegorize the political happenings in late–nineteenth-century America.

Baum's story is kept alive today mostly because of the 1939 movie *The Wizard of Oz.* Although the screenwriters kept much of the story intact, there were several changes made in the story's transition to film that alter the allegorical meaning. For example, in the film version, the shoes that eventually allow Dorothy to return home are ruby slippers, but in the book, Dorothy wears silver shoes. For an authentic look at the allegory that Baum presents, it is important to look at the original text, rather than rely solely on the movie version of Dorothy Gale's adventures.

Critics suggest that *The Wonderful Wizard of Oz* presents a deeply allegorical picture of William Jennings Bryan's attempt to win the presidential election of 1896, move the county toward a bimetallic standard of currency, and become more receptive to the needs of ordinary citizens. In this interpretation, Dorothy Gale represents Bryan himself; both were young (Bryan was only 36 when he was nominated for president), poor (Bryan's lack of funds probably contributed to his political defeat), and compiled an eclectic assortment of supporters to help them overcome many obstacles.

In the story, Dorothy's first supporter is the Scarecrow, the personification of the American farmers. American farmers, suffering from falling farm prices, supported Bryan and believed that the bimetallic monetary standard would increase the money supply and help to alleviate their financial troubles. The Scarecrow believes that he has no brain—an image in keeping with popular prejudices against farmers. But throughout the story it is the Scarecrow who often comes up with solutions to Dorothy's problems, and at the end of the book it is he who is placed in control of the Emerald City. Thus Baum allegorically rewards the farmers for their integral part in America's future.

The second "recruit" in Dorothy's support team is the Tin Woodsman, who represents the industrial workers. In Baum's original story, the Tin Woodsman was once a real person, but the Wicked Witch of the East placed an evil spell on his axe, causing him to chop himself to pieces. He was repaired by a tinsmith, but he was no longer a true human being because his new body lacked a heart. This grisly story suggests Baum's (and Bryan's) abhorrence of the way American industrial workers had been dehumanized by capitalism. Bryan turned to the industrial working class for support during his political campaigns, but in fact they did not endorse him as fully as he had hoped.

Dorothy's third companion, the Cowardly Lion, allegorizes the Populist party. In 1896 the Populists had to decide whether to support Bryan and thereby risk losing their own party's identity, or to run a candidate against Bryan. They chose to endorse Bryan's Democratic nomination, a move that was deemed "cowardly" by many members who wanted to run an independent presidential campaign.

Together, Dorothy, her lifelong canine friend Toto (the Democratic party), the Scarecrow, the Tin Woodsman, and the Cowardly Lion manage to overcome many obstacles on their way to the Emerald City. But when they reach the Wizard of Oz and make their requests, they are denied, just as Bryan was denied the presidency in 1896. But Bryan immediately looked ahead to the election of 1900, and Dorothy and her entourage looked ahead to overcoming one more obstacle and thereby earning their wishes. All they had to do was slay the Wicked Witch of the West (William McKinley).

At this point in the story, Baum shifts from allegorizing the politics of the past to predicting the events of the future. Writing in 1899, he could not have known the outcome of the 1900 presidential campaign, but he felt confident that Bryan and the bimetallic system would triumph. In his tale, Dorothy and her friends are assaulted by all forms of terrible creatures, including wolves, crows, and killer bees. Finally, the Witch resorts to the powers of her golden cap to send swarms of flying monkeys to attack the little group. The monkeys capture Dorothy, scatter the Scarecrow's stuffing, hurl the Tin Woodsman onto a pile of rocks, and enslave the Cowardly Lion.

Nevertheless, Dorothy's encounter with the Wicked Witch of the West proves to be victorious. The Witch fears the power of Dorothy's silver shoes, and Dorothy destroys her in a battle for possession of them. Dorothy collects her friends and frees the Witch's slaves who, in gratitude, fashion for the Tin Woodsman a gold and silver axe. Dorothy takes to wearing the Witch's golden cap as well as her silver shoes, and the combined force of the gold and silver keep her safe for the rest of the story.

Returning to the Emerald City, Dorothy and her companions expose the Wizard to be a fake whose reclusive habits have fooled his citizens into believing he has extraordinary powers. Baum's vision of the Wizard as a recluse represents the antisocial, solitary lives of many late–nineteenth-century

Dorothy (Judy Garland) is guided to the yellow brick road by Glenda, the Good Witch of the North (Billie Burke), in the 1939 movie *The Wizard of Oz*.

presidents. In spite of his confession of powerlessness, the Wizard of Oz pretends to grant the little company their wishes and abdicates his throne. Dorothy's silver shoes take her home to her uncle's farm, and Baum's vision of Populist victory and the bimetallic standard comes to an end.

Other allegorical interpretations of *The Wonderful Wizard of Oz* have been developed, including a vision of Baum's tale as an allegory of institutionalized religion. In this interpretation, critics link Dorothy's journey to the Emerald City to the mythic quest for the Holy Grail. Arriving at the cathedral-like domain of the Wizard, Dorothy asks the doorkeeper if she and her friends may see the Great Oz, only to be told that she may not, for no one has ever seen him. Dorothy's next question, "Then how do you know he exists?," challenges the root of institutional faith in an invisible deity. Through the ensuing series of adventures, Dorothy and her friends eventually learn that the godlike figure of the Wizard is merely a myth, which establishes an allegorical connection between the Wizard and God. Yet, although Baum's tale reveals a god-figure as merely a human projection, all the characters discover within themselves what they thought they lacked (the Scarecrow's brain, the Tin Woodsman's heart, the Lion's courage) simply by believing in the myth of the Wizard. Thus, the story suggests that religious quests may satisfy very important human needs regardless of their grounding in absolutely provable truths. (Downing 1984; Geer 1993; Littlefield 1964)

See also Baum, L. Frank.

WOOLF, VIRGINIA

One of the greatest English novelists of the modernist tradition, Virginia Woolf (1882–1914) was a genuine innovator, especially known for her use of the "stream-of-consciousness" technique in such novels as *To the Lighthouse* and *The Waves*. Woolf was one of the leaders of a literary-artistic circle known as the Bloomsbury Group. She and her husband, Leonard Woolf, founded the Hogarth Press, which first published T. S. Eliot and E. M. Forster. Woolf was not usually an allegorist, but in *Between the Acts*, her last novel, we find a significant amount of allegorizing.

See also Between the Acts.

WORKS AND DAYS

Works and Days, by the eighth-century B.C.E. Greek poet Hesiod, differs from his other great work, the *Theogony,* in that it is more concerned with the life of the present—that is, his life on the farm in Boetia—than in the origins of the universe. In some ways the book is a kind of *Farmer's Almanac.* But the gods are very much present in Hesiod's world, and so is some allegory. At the beginning of the poem, for instance, he talks about the two Strifes, Good and Bad, that affect us. Good Strife he personifies positively as the elder daughter of

Virginia Woolf

Night, who "pushes the shiftless man to work." Bad strife, who is negative, "builds up evil wars and slaughter" (Hesiod 1959, 19). In *Works and Days*, Hesiod tells the story of Pandora and how she released the evil contained in her magic box. (Hesiod 1959)

See also Hesiod; *Theogony.*

YEATS, WILLIAM BUTLER

The Anglo-Irish poet William Butler Yeats (1865–1939) spoke of a passage in his career from allegory to symbol. He was to distinguish often between symbol, which he saw as a revelatory device, and allegory, which was "one of many possible representations of an embodied thing." In short, Yeats shared the distaste of many modernists for allegory. This having been said, it must be pointed out that critics have often found allegory in his work. J. Hillis Miller says that "all of Yeats's poetry from one end of his career to the other is generated by an unreconciled opposition between natural image and allegorical emblem" (Bloomfield, 365). And others have focused on the allegorical aspects of his plays. Many readers have seen in *Cathleen ni Houlihan*, for instance, an allegory in which Cathleen embodies the spiritual reality of Ireland in the face of English oppression. (Bloomfield 1981; Chadwick 1986; Yelton 1967)

"THE YELLOW WALL-PAPER"

Charlotte Perkins Gilman (1860–1935) was a prolific writer, both in fiction and in sociological analysis. In her own lifetime, she was best known for her sociological studies of women's roles in society, especially *Women and Economics* (1898). Today she is considered to be an intellectual leader in the women's movement from 1890 to 1920, and her classic short story, "The Yellow Wall-Paper," is regarded as a significant text in the canon of nineteenth-century American literature.

"The Yellow Wall-Paper" (1892) tells the story of an unnamed female narrator who, suffering from "a slight hysterical tendency," must endure a "rest-cure" under the supervision of John, her physician-husband. John takes her to a secluded house in the country, where she is kept in isolation in the nursery-room on the top floor. There, as weeks go by, the narrator finds that the hideous yellow wallpaper covering her room begins to absorb all her attention. As her mental condition deteriorates, she becomes increasingly aware of a female figure trapped behind the maddening pattern on the walls. In the climactic final scene, the narrator strips the wallpaper from the walls to free the woman, and herself, as John faints away in horror.

Allegorically, "The Yellow Wall-Paper" may be interpreted as the story of a woman who battles against the expectations of her society, choosing madness over acquiescence to traditionally female roles. In this interpretation, John represents the tyrannical male social figure; he is an utterly rational, empirical physician who cruelly condescends to his wife and scoffs at anything imaginative or creative. In contrast, the narrator symbolizes the imaginative literary force that subverts, through writing, the rigid hierarchy that society attempts to impose on every nineteenth-century woman. The nursery, with its disturbing yellow wallpaper, becomes the battleground for these two conflicting forces; male dominance and female rebellion clash in a struggle for control.

On a very different level, "The Yellow Wall-Paper" may also be interpreted as a religious allegory in which the narrator suffers a sort of living hell as punishment for her sins. Locked in her room, she is effectively barred from the lush, Edenic garden surrounding the house and is forced to contemplate her own guilty failings as a wife and mother. She sleeps on a bed nailed to the floor, suggesting what critic Greg Johnson calls a "sexual crucifixion," and gazes at the tortured faces and bulging eyes of suicides embedded in the pattern on the walls. Significantly, the woman caring for the narrator's child during the course of this "rest-cure" is named Mary, implying a supremely perfect mother-figure that the narrator cannot emulate. This interpretation, Johnson argues, justifies the namelessness of the narrator; since she has no identity and no role to play in the structure of this theological allegory, she has no need for a name.

Many readings of "The Yellow Wall-Paper" place Gilman herself at the center of the allegory. Her personal anger at being subjected to her doctor's prescribed "rest-cure" comes to life in the fictional rendering of her narrator's situation. The physical confinement of the woman in the nursery reflects Gilman's sense of the psychological confinement that nineteenth-century society exercised over women, especially creative women. And the chilling conclusion of the story, as the narrator crawls over and over her husband's senseless body, suggests the extraordinary lengths to which women must go in order to "free" themselves from the stranglehold of societal, gender-based constraints. (Jackson 1989)

See also Gilman, Charlotte Perkins.

ZADIG

The story of *Zadig*, by the French satirist Voltaire (1694–1778), is subtitled *Destiny*. As in *Candide*, Voltaire's purpose in this novel is purely didactic. The handsome, rich, and good Babylonian, Zadig, discovers through various adventure-traps laid for him by the author that the world is an evil place and that evil is a necessary component of reality. Only when—with the help of an angel—he learns this lesson can Zadig achieve wisdom and happiness. Inasmuch as Zadig is, like Candide, an "innocent" everyman, and inasmuch as his adventures represent the real world as understood by our somewhat pessimistic author, *Zadig* can be said to be allegorical.

Carol Sherman has proposed a postmodernist allegorical reading of *Zadig* that could be applied to *Candide* as well. She points out that the title, *Zadig, or Destiny*, suggests a reading on two levels, fictional and philosophical, and that both the narrator and the main character indulge in lesson-giving as well as lesson searching, even as the text itself undermines what they say. Sherman suggests that *Zadig*, therefore, is both against and about interpretation, and she sees the work as an "allegory of (mis)reading" (32). (Sherman 1984)

See also Allegoresis; *Candide;* Quilligan, Maureen; Voltaire.

APPENDIX A
TITLES FEATURED IN THE TEXT

The following titles appear as entries in this encyclopedia. Titles of all literary works mentioned in this volume are to be found in the general index.

Absalom and Achitophel (1681)
The Advancement of Learning (1605)
The Adventures of Huckleberry Finn (1885)
Aeneid (19 B.C.E.)
Aesop's Fables (4th century B.C.E.)
Alice's Adventures in Wonderland (1865)
All Hallows Eve (1948)
The Allegory of Love (1936)
Animal Farm (1945)
Argenis (1636)
The Art of Love (12th century)
The Beautyful Ones Are Not Yet Born (1969)
"Below the Mill-Dam" (1902)
Beowulf (8th century [?])
Between the Acts (1941)
Bhagavad Gita (ca. 3d century B.C.E.)
The Birthday Party (1958)
The Book of Margery Kempe (15th century)
The Book of Thel (1789)
Candide (1759)
The Canterbury Tales (ca. 1386)
The Castle of Perseverance (15th century)
The Caucasian Chalk Circle (1944)
The Chemical Wedding (1616)
"Childe Roland to the Dark Tower Came"
    (1852)
The Chronicles of Narnia (1950–1956)
Comus (1634)
The Confidence Man (1857)
The Consolation of Philosophy (ca. 524)

The Crying of Lot 49 (1966)
Cupid and Psyche (2d century)
The Day of the Locust (1939)
Dead Souls (1842)
The Divine Comedy (ca. 1300–1321)
Dr. Faustus (Marlowe) (1588)
Dr. Jeckyll and Mr. Hyde (1886)
The Dynasts (ca. 1900)
Emblemes (1635)
Endgame (1958)
Endimion (1591)
Endymion (1817)
Enuma Elish (3d millennium B.C.E.)
Erec and Énide (12th century)
Erewhon (1872)
Everyman (ca. 1500)
A Fable (1954)
The Faerie Queene (1590–1609)
The Family Reunion (1939)
Foe (1986)
The French Revolution (1837)
Gargantua and Pantagruel (1532–1553)
Gilgamesh (ca. 2000 B.C.E.)
Goat Song (1921)
The Golden Ass (2d century)
Golden Boy (1937)
The Great God Brown (1926)
The Great Theater of the World (ca. 1637)
Grimm Brothers: *Fairy Tales* (1812 ff.)
Gulliver's Travels (1726)

The Hairy Ape (1922)
Haroun and the Sea of Stories (1990)
Heart of Darkness (1902)
Henderson the Rain King (1959)
The Holy War (1682)
Homeric Allegories (1st century)
The Hotel New Hampshire (1981)
The Hous of Fame (1374–1380)
"Howl" (1956)
The Idylls of the King (1859–1885)
In the Heart of the Country (1977)
Invisible Man (1952)
King John (before 1536)
The Life and Death of Mr. Badman (1680)
The Life of Coriolanus (1st century)
The Light Princess (1950s [?])
Lilith (1895)
Lord of the Flies (1954)
The Lord of the Rings (1954–1955)
The Magic Mountain (1924)
Magnyfycence (1515)
The Mahabharata (5th century B.C.E. [?])
The Man Who Was Thursday: A Nightmare (1908)
Mansfield Park (1814)
The Marble Faun (1860)
Mardi (1849)
The Marrow of Tradition (1901)
Maus (1991)
Miss Lonelyhearts (1933)
Moby-Dick (1851)
"The Monkey" (1934)
Le Morte d'Arthur (1469; pub. 1485)
Moses, Man of the Mountain (1939)
Mr. Weston's Good Wine (1927)
Mumbo Jumbo (1972)
The Odyssey (ca. 8th century B.C.E.)
Old Fortunatus (1599)
One Flew over the Cuckoo's Nest (1962)
Operation Sidewinder (1970)
The Owl and the Nightingale (ca. 1180–1200)
The Parlement of Foules (ca. 1374–1381)

The Pearl (14th century)
"The Phoenix and the Turtle" (1601)
The Picture of Dorian Gray (1891)
Piers Plowman (ca. 1362–1387)
The Pilgrim's Progress (1678–1684)
The Plague (1947)
Ramayana (500 B.C.E. ff.)
The Book of Revelation (ca. 95 C.E.)
Robinson Crusoe (1719)
The Romance of the Rose (13th century)
R.U.R. (1923)
Sartor Resartus (1835)
The Scarlet Letter (1850)
The Second Shepherd's Play (ca. late 14th century)
Sir Gawain and the Green Knight (14th century)
Sir Orfeo (14th century)
The Song of Songs (ca. 10th century B.C.E.)
The Space Trilogy (1938–1945)
The System of Dante's Hell (1965)
A Tale of a Tub (1704)
Theogony (8th century B.C.E.)
Through the Looking Glass (1871)
Tiny Alice (1964)
Tom Jones (1744)
The Universal Baseball Association, Inc., Henry Waugh, Prop. (1968)
Vathek (1786)
Victory (1915)
The Violent Bear It Away (1960)
Waiting for Godot (1952)
Waiting for the Barbarians (1980)
The War at the End of the World (1984)
Watership Down (1972)
Who's Afraid of Virginia Woolf? (1962)
The Wild Duck (1748)
The Wind in the Willows (1908)
The Wonderful Wizard of Oz (1899)
Works and Days (8th century B.C.E.)
"The Yellow Wall-Paper" (1892)
Zadig (1748)

TITLES FEATURED IN THE TEXT, LISTED BY DATE

Enuma Elish (3d millennium B.C.E.)
Gilgamesh (ca. 2000 B.C.E.)
The Song of Songs (ca. 10th century B.C.E.)
The Odyssey (ca. 8th century B.C.E.)
Theogony (8th century B.C.E.)
Works and Days (8th century B.C.E.)
Ramayana (500 B.C.E. ff.)
The Mahabharata (5th century B.C.E. [?])
Aesop's Fables (4th century B.C.E.)
Bhagavad Gita (ca. 3d century B.C.E.)
Aeneid (19 B.C.E.)
Homeric Allegories (1st century)
The Life of Coriolanus (1st century)
The Book of Revelation (ca. 95 C.E.)
Cupid and Psyche (2d century)
The Golden Ass (2d century)
The Consolation of Philosophy (ca. 524)
Beowulf (8th century [?])
The Art of Love (12th century)
Erec and Énide (12th century)
The Owl and the Nightingale (ca. 1180–1200)
The Romance of the Rose (13th century)
The Pearl (14th century)
Sir Gawain and the Green Knight (14th century)
Sir Orfeo (14th century)
The Second Shepherd's Play (late 14th century)
The Divine Comedy (ca. 1300–1321)
Piers Plowman (ca. 1362–1387)
The Hous of Fame (1374–1380)
The Parlement of Foules (ca. 1374–1381)
The Canterbury Tales (ca. 1386)

The Book of Margery Kempe (15th century)
The Castle of Perseverance (15th century)
Le Morte d'Arthur (1469; pub. 1485)
Everyman (ca. 1500)
Magnyfycence (1515)
Gargantua and Pantagruel (1532–1553)
King John (before 1536)
Dr. Faustus (1588)
The Faerie Queene (1590–1609)
Endimion (1591)
Old Fortunatus (1599)
"The Phoenix and the Turtle" (1601)
The Advancement of Learning (1605)
The Chemical Wedding (1616)
Comus (1634)
Emblemes (1635)
Argenis (1636)
The Great Theater of the World (ca. 1637)
The Pilgrim's Progress (1678–1684)
The Life and Death of Mr. Badman (1680)
Absalom and Achitophel (1681)
The Holy War (1682)
A Tale of a Tub (1704)
Robinson Crusoe (1719)
Gulliver's Travels (1726)
Tom Jones (1744)
The Wild Duck (1748)
Zadig (1748)
Candide (1759)
Vathek (1786)
The Book of Thel (1789)
Grimm Brothers: *Fairy Tales* (1812 ff.)
Mansfield Park (1814)

Endymion (1817)
Sartor Resartus (1835)
The French Revolution (1837)
Dead Souls (1842)
Mardi (1849)
The Scarlet Letter (1850)
Moby-Dick (1851)
"Childe Roland to the Dark Tower Came"
 (1852)
The Confidence Man (1857)
The Idylls of the King (1859–1885)
The Marble Faun (1860)
Alice's Adventures in Wonderland (1865)
Through the Looking Glass (1871)
Erewhon (1872)
The Adventures of Huckleberry Finn (1885)
Dr. Jeckyll and Mr. Hyde (1886)
The Picture of Dorian Gray (1891)
"The Yellow Wall-Paper" (1892)
Lilith (1895)
The Wonderful Wizard of Oz (1899)
The Dynasts (ca. 1900)
The Marrow of Tradition (1901)
"Below the Mill-Dam" (1902)
Heart of Darkness (1902)
The Man Who Was Thursday: A Nightmare
 (1908)
The Wind in the Willows (1908)
Victory (1915)
Goat Song (1921)
The Hairy Ape (1922)
R.U.R. (1923)
The Magic Mountain (1924)
The Great God Brown (1926)
Mr. Weston's Good Wine (1927)
Miss Lonelyhearts (1933)
"The Monkey" (1934)
The Allegory of Love (1936)
Golden Boy (1937)

The Space Trilogy (1938–1945)
The Day of the Locust (1939)
The Family Reunion (1939)
Moses, Man of the Mountain (1939)
Between the Acts (1941)
The Caucasian Chalk Circle (1944)
Animal Farm (1945)
The Plague (1947)
All Hallows Eve (1948)
The Chronicles of Narnia (1950–1956)
The Light Princess (1950s [?])
Invisible Man (1952)
Waiting for Godot (1952)
The Lord of the Rings (1954–1955)
A Fable (1954)
Lord of the Flies (1954)
"Howl" (1956)
Endgame (1958)
The Birthday Party (1958)
Henderson the Rain King (1959)
The Violent Bear It Away (1960)
One Flew over the Cuckoo's Nest (1962)
Who's Afraid of Virginia Woolf? (1962)
Tiny Alice (1964)
The System of Dante's Hell (1965)
The Crying of Lot 49 (1966)
The Universal Baseball Association, Inc.,
 Henry Waugh, Prop. (1968)
The Beautyful Ones Are Not Yet Born (1969)
Operation Sidewinder (1970)
Mumbo Jumbo (1972)
Watership Down (1972)
In the Heart of the Country (1977)
Waiting for the Barbarians (1980)
The Hotel New Hampshire (1981)
The War at the End of the World (1984)
Foe (1986)
Haroun and the Sea of Stories (1990)
Maus (1991)

BIBLIOGRAPHY

Achtemeier, Paul J., ed. (1985) *Harper's Bible Dictionary.* San Francisco: Harper and Row.

Aers, David. (1975) Piers Plowman *and Christian Allegory.* New York: St. Martin's Press.

Aiken, Susan Hardy. (1990) *Isak Dinesen and the Engendering of Narrative.* Chicago: University of Chicago Press. 133–153.

Allen, Don Cameron. (1970) *Mysteriously Meant: The Rediscovery of Pagan Symbolism and Allegorical Interpretation in the Renaissance.* Baltimore: The Johns Hopkins University Press.

Alter, Robert E., and Frank Kermode, eds. (1987) *A Literary Guide to the Bible.* Cambridge, MA: Harvard University Press.

Andersen, Richard. (1981) *Robert Coover.* Boston: G. K. Hall & Co., 57–78.

Asimov, Issac, ed. (1980) *The Annotated* Gulliver's Travels. New York: Clarkson N. Potter, Inc.

Atwell, David. (1993) *J. M. Coetzee: South Africa and the Politics of Writing.* Berkeley: University of California Press, 104–112.

Auden, W. H. (1968) *Secondary Worlds.* London: Faber.

Auerbach, Erich. (1946) *Mimesis: The Representation of Reality in Western Literature.* Translated by Willard Trask. Reprint. Garden City, NY: Doubleday Anchor Books, 1957.

Augustine, St. (1957) *The City of God.* Translated by G. E. McCracken. Cambridge, MA: Loeb Classics.

Baker, J. Robert. (1992) "Flannery O'Connor's Four-Fold Method of Allegory." *The Flannery O'Connor Bulletin* 21: 84–96.

Baker, James R. (1988) "Why It's No Go." In *Critical Essays on William Golding,* edited by James R. Baker. Boston: G. K. Hall & Co., 22–30.

Barney, Stephen A. (1988) "Allegorical Visions." In *A Companion to* Piers Plowman, edited by John A. Alford. Berkeley: University of California Press, 117–133.

———. (1979) *Allegories of History, Allegories of Love.* Hamden, CT: Archon Books.

Beck, Avent. (1992) "The Christian Allegorical Structure of *Platoon.*" *Literature/Film Quarterly,* 20 (3): 213–222.

Becker, John E. (1971) *Hawthorne's Historical Allegory: An Examination of the American Consciousness.* Port Washington, NY: Kennikat Press.

Begiebing, Robert J. (1980) *Acts of Regeneration: Allegory and Archetype in the Works of Norman Mailer.* Columbia, MO: University of Missouri Press.

Benet, William Rose. (1965) *The Reader's Encyclopedia.* New York: Harper and Row.

Berek, Peter. (1962) *The Transformation of Allegory from Spenser to Hawthorne.* Amherst, MA: Amherst College Press.

Berger, Harry. (1957) *The Allegorical Temper: Vision and Reality in Book II of Spenser's* Faerie Queene. New Haven, CT: Yale University Press.

Bergonzi, Bernard. (1976) "*The Time Machine:* An Ironic Myth." In *H. G. Wells: A Collection of Critical Essays,* edited by Bernard Bergonzi. Englewood Cliffs, NJ: Prentice Hall, Inc., 39–55.

Berkman, Joyce Avrech. (1989) *The Healing Imagination of Olive Schreiner.* Amherst: The University of Massachusetts Press, 50–51; 214–215.

The Bestiary. (1960) Translated by T. H. White. New York, Putnam.

Bierhorst, John. (1985) *The Mythology of North America.* New York: William Morrow.

Bigsby, C. W. E. (1975) "Tiny Alice." In *Edward Albee: A Collection of Critical Essays,* edited by C. W. E. Bigsby. Englewood Cliffs, NJ: Prentice Hall, Inc., 124–134.

Blessing, Richard Allen. (1970) *Wallace Stevens' "Whole Harmonium."* Syracuse: Syracuse University Press, 25–26.

Bloom, Edward. (1951) "The Allegorical Principle." *Journal of English Literary History* 18: 163–190.

Bloomfield, Morton W., ed. (1981) *Allegory, Myth, and Symbol.* Cambridge, MA: Harvard University Press.

———. (1980) "Personification Metaphors." *Chaucer Review* 14: 287–297.

———. (1962–63) "A Grammatical Approach to Personification Allegory." *Modern Philology* 60 (3): 161–167.

———. (1968) *"Beowulf* and Christian Allegory: An Interpretation of Unferth." In *The* Beowulf *Poet: A Collection of Critical Essays,* edited by Donald K. Fry. Englewood Cliffs, NJ: Prentice Hall, Inc., 68–75.

Boardman, John, et al., eds. (1986) *The Oxford History of the Classical World.* New York: Oxford University Press.

Bodkin, Maud. (1934) *Archetypal Patterns in Poetry: Psychological Studies of Imagination.* London: Oxford University Press, 1963.

Boethius. (1943) *The Consolation of Philosophy.* Edited by Irwin Edman. New York: Modern Library.

Branch, Watson. (1986) "The Quest for Mardi." In *A Companion to Melville Studies,* edited by John Bryant. New York: Greenwood Press, 123–143.

Brenman-Gibson, Margaret. (1981) *Clifford Odets: American Playwright.* New York: Atheneum, 465–467.

Bronson, Bertrand H. (1947) "Personification Reconsidered." *Journal of English Literary History* 14: 163–167.

Brooke-Rose, Christine. (1965) *A Grammar of Metaphor.* London: Secker & Warburg (1958).

Bukofzer, Manfred. (1939–1940) "Allegory in Baroque Music." *Journal of the Warburg Institute* 3: 1–21.

Buning, Marius. (1992) "Allegory, the American Canon, and Thomas Pynchon's *The Crying of Lot 49."* In *Rewriting the Dream: Reflections of the Changing American Literary Canon,* edited by W. M. Verhoeven. Amsterdam: Rodopi, 141–156.

Burke, Kenneth. (1957) *The Philosophy of Literary Form: Studies in Symbolic Action.* New York: Vintage Books.

———. (1950) *A Rhetoric of Motives.* New York: Prentice-Hall.

Bush, Douglas. (1932) *Mythology and the Renaissance Tradition in English Poetry.* New York: W. W. Norton (1963).

Camille, Michael. (1989) *The Gothic Idol: Ideology and Image-Making in Medieval Art.* Cambridge: Cambridge University Press.

Campbell, Joseph. (1970) *The Masks of God: Occidental Mythology.* New York: Viking.

Carnochan, W. B. (1968) *Lemuel Gulliver's Mirror for Man.* Berkeley: University of California Press.

Cassirer, Ernst. (1955) *The Philosophy of Symbolic Forms.* New Haven: Yale University Press.

Cawley, A. C., ed. (1956) Everyman *and Medieval Miracle Plays.* New York: Dutton.

BIBLIOGRAPHY

Chadwick, Joseph. (1986) "Family Romance as National Allegory in Yeats's *Cathleen ni Houlihan* and *The Dreaming of the Bones.*" *Twentieth Century Literature: A Scholarly and Critical Journal* 32 (2): 155–168.

Chase, Richard. (1955) *The American Novel and Its Tradition.* Garden City, NJ: Doubleday & Co.

Clark, John R. (1970) *Form and Frenzy in Swift's* Tale of a Tub. Ithaca: Cornell University Press.

Clifford, Gay. (1974) *The Transformations of Allegory.* London and Boston: Routledge & Kegan Paul.

Clurman, Harold. (1975) "Who's Afraid of Virginia Woolf?" In *Edward Albee: A Collection of Critical Essays,* edited by C. W. E. Bigsby. Englewood Cliffs, NJ: Prentice Hall, Inc., 76–79.

Coleridge, Samuel Taylor. (1936) *Miscellaneous Criticism.* Edited by Thomas Middleton Raysor. London: Constable.

Comparetti, Domenico. (1908) *Vergil and the Middle Ages.* Translated by E. F. M. Benecke. Reprint. Hamden, CT: Archon Books, 1966.

Cope, Jackson I. (1986) *Robert Coover's Fictions.* Baltimore: The Johns Hopkins University Press, 35–58.

Cope, Kevin L., ed. (1993) *Enlightening Allegory: Theory, Practice, and Contexts of Allegory in the Late Seventeenth and Eighteenth Centuries.* New York: AMS Press.

Cowan, Bainard. (1982) *Exiled Waters:* Moby Dick *and the Crisis of Allegory.* Baton Rouge: Louisiana State University Press.

Cox, C. B. (1963) "Lord of the Flies." In *William Golding's* Lord of the Flies: *A Sourcebook,* edited by William Nelson. Indianapolis: The Odyssey Press, Inc., 82–88.

Cumming, Mark. (1988) *A Disimprisoned Epic: Form and Vision in Carlyle's* French Revolution. Philadelphia: University of Pennsylvania Press, 131–147.

Cundy, Catherine. (1993) "Through Childhood's Window: *Haroun and the Sea of Stories.*" In *Perspectives on the Fiction of Salman Rushdie,* edited by M. D. Fletcher. 1994. Amsterdam–Atlanta, GA: Rodopi B.V., 335–341.

Dale, Alzina Stone. (1988) *T. S. Eliot: The Philosopher Poet.* Wheaton, IL: Harold Shaw.

D'Amassa, Don. (1985) "Three by Bachman." In *Discovering Stephen King,* edited by Darrell Schweitzer. Mercer Island, WA: Starmont House, Inc., 123–130.

Damon, S. Foster. (1971) *A Blake Dictionary.* New York: Dutton.

Davis, R. Evan. (1984) "An Allegory of America in Melville's *Billy Budd.*" *Journal of Narrative Technique* 14 (3): 172–181.

Dawson, David. (1992) *Allegorical Readers and Cultural Revision in Ancient Alexandria.* Berkeley: University of California Press.

de Man, Paul. (1979) *Allegories of Reading: Figural Language in Rousseau, Nietzsche, Rilke and Proust.* New Haven, CT: Yale University Press.

de Paul, Stephen. 1988. "The Poetics and Politics of the 'Unmanageable': Cultural Crosscurrents in Melville's *Mardi." English Studies in Canada* 14 (2): 170–183.

DeRose, David J. (1992) *Sam Shepard.* New York: Twayne Publishers, 41–44.

Dettlaff, Shirley M. (1986) "Melville's Aesthetics." In *A Companion to Melville Studies,* edited by John Bryant. New York: Greenwood Press, 625–665.

Downing, David C. (1984) "Waiting for Godoz: A Post-Nasal Deconstruction of *The Wizard of Oz." Christianity and Literature* 33 (2): 28–30.

Doyno, Victor A. (1991) *Writing* Huck Finn: *Mark Twain's Creative Process.* Philadephia: University of Pennsylvania Press.

Draper, Michael. (1988) *H. G. Wells.* New York: St. Martin's Press, 35.

Drew, D. L. (1927) *The Allegory of the "Aeneid."*

Durix, Jean-Pierre. (1993) "'The 'Gardener of Stories': Salman Rushdie's Haroun and the Sea of Stories." In *Perspectives on the Fiction of Salman Rushdie,* edited by M. D. Fletcher. 1994. Amsterdam-Atlanta, GA: Rodopi B.V., 343–51.

Eco, Umberto, and Costantino Marmo, eds. (1989) *On the Medieval Theory of Signs.* Amsterdam and Philadelphia: John Benjamins.

Egri, Peter. (1984) "'Belonging' Lost: Alienation and Dramatic Form in Eugene O'Neill's *The Hairy Ape." In Critical Essays on Eugene O'Neill,* edited by James J. Martine. Boston: G. K. Hall & Co., 77–111.

Eliade, Mircea, ed. (1987) *Encyclopedia of Religion.* 16 vols. New York: Macmillan.

———. (1977) *Essential Sacred Writings from around the World (From Primitives to Zen).* San Francisco: Harper & Row (1967).

Eliade, Mircea. (1961) *Images and Symbols.* Translated by Philip Mairet. New York: Sheed and Ward (1952).

Empson, William. (1930) *Seven Types of Ambiguity.*

Erskine-Hill, Howard. (1993) *Landmarks of World Literature:* Gulliver's Travels. New York: Cambridge University Press.

Esslin, Martin. (1961) *The Theatre of the Absurd.* New York: Anchor.

Feidelson, Charles, Jr. (1953) *Symbolism and American Literature.* Chicago: Chicago University Press.

Felman, Shoshana, and Dori Laub, M.D. (1992) *Testimony: Crises of Witnessing, Psychoanalysis, and History.* New York: Routledge, Chapman and Hall, Inc., 93–119.

First, Ruth, and Ann Scott. (1980) *Olive Schreiner.* London: André Deutsch Ltd., 98–101; 182–194.

Fleming, John V. (1969) *The* Roman de la Rose: *A Study in Allegory and Iconography.* Princeton, NJ: Princeton University Press.

Fletcher, Angus. (1964) *Allegory: The Theory of a Symbolic Mode.* Ithaca, NY: Cornell University Press.

Flores, Ralph. (1987) "The Dead-Living Letter in Hawthorne's *The Scarlet Letter.*" *Criticism: A Quarterly for Literature and the Arts* 29 (3): 313–340.

Foster, James O. (1993) "Robinson Crusoe and the Uses of the Imagination." *Journal of English and Germanic Philology.* 91 (2): 179–202.

Frank, R. W. (1953) "The Art of Reading Medieval Personification Allegory." *English Literary History* 20: 239–250.

Fraser, Robert. (1980) *The Novels of Ayi Kwei Armah: A Study in Polemical Fiction.* London: Heinemann Educational Books, Inc., 15–29.

Freed, Richard C. (1985) "Hawthorne's Reflexive Imagination: *The Scarlet Letter* as Compositional Allegory." *American Transcendental Quarterly* 56 (March): 31–54.

Freud, Sigmund. (1956) *The Interpretation of Dreams.* Translated by James Strachey. New York: Avon.

Frye, Northrop. (1983) *The Great Code: The Bible and Literature.* New York: Harvest Books.

———. (1963) *Fables of Identity: Studies in Poetic Mythology.* New York: Harcourt, Brace & World.

———. (1957) *Anatomy of Criticism.* Princeton, NJ: Princeton University Press.

Frye, Roland M. (1961) "Swift's Yahoo and the Christian Symbols for Sin." In *A Casebook on Gulliver among the Houyhnnyms,* edited by Milton P. Foster. New York: Thomas Y. Crowell Company.

Gakwandi, Shatto Arthur. (1992) "Freedom as Nightmare: Armah's *The Beautyful Ones Are Not Yet Born.*" In *Critical Perspectives on Ayi Kwei Armah,* edited by Derek Wright. Colorado Springs, CO: Three Continents Press. 102–115.

Gates, Henry Louis, Jr. (1988) *The Signifying Monkey.* New York: Oxford University Press.

Geer, John G., and Thomas R. Rochon. (1993) "William Jennings Bryan on the Yellow Brick Road." *Journal of American Culture* 16 (4): 59–63.

Gilbert, Sandra M., and Susan Gubar. (1984) *The Madwoman in the Attic: The Woman Writer and the Nineteenth-Century Literary Imagination.* New Haven: Yale University Press, 73.

Giles, James R., and Thomas P. Lally. (1984) "Allegory in Chestnutt's *Marrow of Tradition.*" *Journal of General Education* 35 (4): 259–269.

Goldsmith, Margaret E. (1970) *The Mode and Meaning of* 'Beowulf.' London: The Athlone Press, 60–96.

Gorak, Irene E. (1992) "Olive Schreiner's Colonial Allegory: The Story of an African Farm." *Ariel: A Review of International English Literature* 23 (4): 53–72.

Gordon, Lois. (1983) *Robert Coover: The Universal Fictionmaking Process.* Carbondale, IL: Southern Illinois University Press, 34–50.

Gottlieb, Sidney. (1989) "Herbert's Political Allegory of `Humilitie.'" *Huntington Library Quarterly: A Journal for the History and Interpretation of English and American Civilization* 52 (4): 469–480.

Grant, Robert M. (1965) *A Short History of the Interpretation of the Bible.* London: Adam and Charles Black.

Greenblatt, S., ed. (1981) *Allegory and Representation: Selected Essays of the English Institute, 1979–80.* Baltimore, MD: The Johns Hopkins University Press.

Greenblatt, Stephen J. (1974) "Orwell as Satirist." In *George Orwell: A Collection of Critical Essays,* edited by Raymond Williams. Englewood Cliffs, NJ: Prentice–Hall, Inc., 103–118.

Griffin, Patsy. (1992) "Structural Allegory in Andrew Marvell's Poetry." *Journal of English and Germanic Philology* 91 (3): 325–343.

Grimaldi, Patrizia. (1981) "*Sir Orfeo* as Celtic Folk-Hero, Christian Pilgrim, and Medieval King." In *Allegory, Myth, and Symbol,* edited by Morton W. Bloomfield. Cambridge: Harvard University Press, 147–161.

Hall, James. (1974) *Dictionary of Subjects and Symbols in Art.* New York: Harper and Row.

Hamilton, A. C. (1961) *The Structure of Allegory in* The Faerie Queene. Oxford: The Clarendon Press.

Hammond, J. R. (1979) *An H. G. Wells Companion.* London: The Macmillan Press Ltd.

Hankins, John Erskine. (1971) *Source and Meaning in Spenser's Allegory: A Study of* The Faerie Queene. Oxford: The Clarendon Press.

Hanson, R. P. C. (1959) *Allegory and Event.* Richmond, VA: John Knox Press.

Hardison, O. B. (1965) *Christian Rite and Christian Drama in the Middle Ages: Essays in the Origin and Early History of Modern Drama.* Baltimore: The Johns Hopkins University Press.

Harris, John F. (1916) *Samuel Butler, Author of* Erewhon: *The Man and His Works*. London: Grant Richards Ltd.

Harris, Stephen A. (1985) *Understanding the Bible*. Palo Alto, CA: Mayfield.

Haugen, Einar. (1979) *Ibsen's Drama: Author to Audience*. Minneapolis: University of Minnesota Press.

Haviland, Beverly. (1987) "The Sin of Synecdoche: Hawthorne's Allegory against Symbolism in `Rappaccini's Daughter.'" *Texas Studies in Literature and Language* 29 (3): 278–301.

Haworth, Kenneth R. (1980) *Deified Virtues, Demonic Vices, and Descriptive Allegory in the "Psychomachia" of Prudentius*. Amsterdam: Adolf M. Hakkert.

Hayman, Ronald. (1973) *Edward Albee*. New York: Fredrick Ungar Publishing Co.

Headings, Philip R. (1982) *T. S. Eliot*. Revised edition. Boston: Twayne Publishers.

Heale, Elizabeth. (1987) The Faerie Queene: *A Reader's Guide*. Cambridge: Cambridge University Press.

Herbst, Josephine. (1971) "*Miss Lonelyhearts:* An Allegory." In *Twentieth Century Interpretations of* Miss Lonelyhearts, edited by Thomas H. Jackson. Englewood Cliffs, NJ: Prentice Hall, Inc. 97–98.

Hermann, John P. (1989) *Allegories of War: Language and Violence in Old English Poetry*. Ann Arbor: University of Michigan Press.

Hesiod. *The Works and Days and Theogony*. (1959) Translated by R. Lattimore. Ann Arbor: University of Michigan Press.

Higonnet, Margaret R., ed. (1993) *The Sense of Sex: Feminist Perspectives on Hardy*. Urbana: University of Illinois Press.

Hill, Christopher. (1989) *A Tinker and a Poor Man: John Bunyan and His Church, 1628–1688*. New York: Alfred A. Knopf, Inc., 240–259.

Hinks, Roger. (1939) *Myth and Allegory in Ancient Art*. London: Warburg Institute.

Hipkiss, Robert A. (1976) *Jack Kerouac: Prophet of the New Romanticism*. Lawrence, KS: The Regents Press of Kansas, 122–123.

Hogins, James Burl. (1974) *Literature: Mythology and Folklore*. Palo Alto, CA: SRA.

Holmer, Paul L. (1976) *C. S. Lewis: The Shape of His Faith and Thought*. New York: Harper and Row.

Honig, Edwin. (1966) *Dark Conceit: The Making of Allegory*. New York: Oxford University Press.

Houppert, Joseph W. (1975) *John Lyly*. Boston: Twayne Publishers.

Howard, Lillie P. (1980) *Zora Neale Hurston*. Boston: Twayne Publishers, 114–117.

Hume, Kathryn. (1975) "The Owl and the Nightingale": *The Poem and Its Critics*. Toronto: University of Toronto Press, 51–83.

Hunt, Peter. (1994) The Wind in the Willows: *A Fragmented Arcadia*. New York: Twayne Publishers, 48–77.

Hunter, G. K. (1962) *John Lyly: The Humanist as Courtier*. London: Routledge & Kegan Paul Ltd.

Hunter, Lynette. (1989) *Modern Allegory and Fantasy: Rhetorical Stances of Contemporary Writing*. New York: St. Martin's Press.

———. (1979) *G. K. Chesterton: Explorations in Allegory*. New York: St. Martin's Press, 64–74.

Hyde, Lewis, ed. (1984) *On the Poetry of Allen Ginsberg*. Ann Arbor: University of Michigan Press.

Hyman, Stanley Edgar. (1986) "Nathanael West." In *Nathanael West: Modern Critical Views*, edited by Harold Bloom. New York: Chelsea House Publishers, 11–40.

Hynes, Samuel. (1988) "[William Golding's *Lord of the Flies*]." In *Critical Essays on William Golding*, edited by James R. Baker. Boston: G. K. Hall & Co., 13–21.

Irvine, Martin. (1981) "Cynewulf's Use of Psychomachia Allegory: The Latin Sources of Some `Interpolate' Passages." In *Allegory, Myth, and Symbol*, edited by Morton W. Bloomfield. Cambridge: Harvard University Press, 39–62.

Jack, Ian. (1973) *Browning's Major Poetry*. Oxford: The Clarendon Press, 179–194.

Jackson, Blyden. (1986) "Moses, Man of the Mountain: A Study of Power." In *Zora Neale Hurston*, edited by Harold Bloom. New York: Chelsea House Publishers, 151–155.

Jackson, Greg. (1989) "Gilman's Gothic Allegory: Rage and Redemption in 'The Yellow Wall-Paper.'" *Studies in Short Fiction* 26 (4): 521–530.

James, Walter. (1986) "The Letter and the Spirit in Hawthorne's Allegory of American Experience." *ESQ: A Journal of the American Renaissance* 32 (1): 36–54.

Jenkins, Priscilla. (1969) "Conscience: The Frustration of Allegory." In Piers Plowman: *Critical Approaches*, edited by S. S. Hussey. London: Methuen & Co. Ltd, 125–142.

Johnson, Barbara. (1994) *The Wake of Deconstruction*. Cambridge, MA: Blackwell.

———. (1992) *Reading* Piers Plowman *and* The Pilgrim's Progress: *Reception and the Protestant Reader*. Carbondale, IL: Southern Illinois University Press.

Johnson, Claudia D. (1981) *The Productive Tension of Hawthorne's Art.* Tuscaloosa, AL: University of Alabama Press.

Johnson, Julie M. (1982) "Taji's Quest in Melville's *Mardi:* A Psychological Allegory in the Mythic Mode." *Colby Library Quarterly* 18 (4): 220–230.

Johnston, Arnold. (1980) *Of Earth and Darkness: The Novels of William Golding.* Columbia: University of Missouri Press, 8–21.

Jones, Joseph. (1959) *The Cradle of* Erewhon: *Samuel Butler in New Zealand.* Austin: University of Texas Press.

Jung, Carl G. 1953–1961. *The Archetypes and the Collective Unconscious.* In *Collected Works* Volume 9. Princeton, NJ: Princeton University Press.

Kallich, Martin. (1970) *The Other End of the Egg: Religious Satire in* Gulliver's Travels. Bridgeport, CT: University of Bridgeport Press.

Katzellenbogen, Adolf. (1939) *Allegories of the Virtues and Vices in Medieval Art.* New York: W. W. Norton & Co. (1964).

Kennedy, Andrew K. (1989) *Samuel Beckett.* Cambridge: Cambridge University Press, 24–66.

King, Kathleen. (1988) "Bellow the Allegory King: Animal Imagery in *Henderson the Rain King.*" *Saul Bellow Journal* 7 (1): 44–50.

King, Roma A., Jr. (1972) "A Fable: Everyman's Warfare." In *Religious Perspectives in Faulkner's Fiction: Yoknapatawpha and Beyond*, edited by J. Robert Barth. Notre Dame, IN: University of Notre Dame Press, 203–209.

Kitson, Peter. (1991) "Coleridge, James Burgh, and the Mad Ox: A Source for Coleridge's 'Recantation.'" *Notes and Queries* 38 (3): 299–301.

Koonce, B. G. (1966) *Chaucer and the Tradition of Fame: Symbolism in* The Hous of Fame. Princeton, NJ: Princeton University Press.

Kouwenhoven, Jan Karel. (1983) *Apparent Narrative as Thematic Metaphor.* Oxford: The Clarendon Press.

Kuhlmann, Susan. (1973) *Knave, Fool, and Genius: The Confidence Man as He Appears in Nineteenth-Century American Fiction.* Chapel Hill: University of North Carolina Press.

Kuznets, Lois R. (1987) *Kenneth Grahame.* Boston: Twayne Publishers, 100–107; 120.

Lamberton, Robert. (1986) *Homer the Theologian: Neoplatonist Allegorical Reading and the Growth of the Epic Tradition.* Berkeley, CA: The University of California Press.

Langbaum, Robert. (1975) *Isak Dinesen's Art: The Gayety of Vision.* Chicago: University of Chicago Press, 81–88.

Lawrence, D. H. (1932) *Apocalypse.* New York: Viking Press.

Leach, Elsie. (1971) *"Alice in Wonderland* in Perspective." In *Aspects of Alice: Lewis Carroll's Dreamchild as seen through the Critics' Looking-Glasses,* edited by Robert Phillips. New York: The Vanguard Press, Inc.

Leach, Maria, ed. (1984) *Standard Dictionary of Folklore, Mythology, and Legend.* New York: Harper and Row.

Lee, Robert A. (1969) *Orwell's Fiction.* Notre Dame, IN: University of Notre Dame Press, 105–127.

Leeds. Barry H. (1981) *Ken Kesey.* New York: Frederick Ungar Publishing Co., 13–43.

Leeming, David A. (1990) *The World of Myth.* New York: Oxford University Press.

———. (1979) "The Hodja." *Parabola* 4 (1): 84–89.

Leeming, David A., and Jake Page. (1996) *God: Myths of the Male Divine.* New York: Oxford University Press.

———. (1994) *Goddess: Myths of the Female Divine.* New York: Oxford University Press.

Leeming, David A., with Margaret A. Leeming. (1994) *Encyclopedia of Creation Myths.* Santa Barbara: ABC-CLIO.

Leonard, Frances McNeely. (1981) *Laughter in the Courts of Love: Comedy in Allegory, from Chaucer to Spenser.* Norman, OK: Pilgrim Books.

Leslie, Shane. (1971) "Lewis Carroll and the Oxford Movement." In *Aspects of Alice: Lewis Carroll's Dreamchild as seen through the Critics' Looking-Glasses,* edited by Robert Phillips. New York: The Vanguard Press, Inc.

Lettis, Richard, et al. (1962) *Huck Finn and His Critics.* New York: The Macmillan Company.

Levin, Samuel R. (1977) *The Semantics of Metaphor.* Baltimore: The Johns Hopkins University Press.

Lewis, C. S. (1938) *The Allegory of Love.* London: Oxford University Press.

Leyburn, E. D. (1956) *Satiric Allegory: Mirror of Man.* New Haven, CT: Yale University Press.

Light, James F. (1971) "The Christ Dream." In *Twentieth Century Interpretations of* Miss Lonelyhearts, edited by Thomas H. Jackson. Englewood Cliffs, NJ: Prentice Hall, Inc., 19–38.

Lindberg, Gary. (1982) *The Confidence Man in American Literature.* New York: Oxford University Press.

Lister, Paul A. (1978) "Some New Light on Hawthorne's *The Marble Faun.*" *Nathaniel Hawthorne Journal* 8: 79–86.

Littlefield, Henry. (1964) "The Wizard of Oz: Parable on Populism." *American Quarterly* 16: 47–48.

Lock, F. P. (1980) *The Politics of* Gulliver's Travels. New York: Oxford University Press.

MacCaffrey, Isabel G. (1976) *Spenser's Allegory: The Anatomy of Imagination.* Princeton, NJ: Princeton University Press.

McClennen, Joshua. (1947) *On the Meaning and Function of Allegory in the English Renaissance.* Ann Arbor: University of Michigan Press.

McCusker, Honor C. (1971) *John Bale: Dramatist and Antiquary.* Freeport, NY: Books for Libraries Press, 86–90.

McHale, Brian. (1987) *Postmodernist Fiction.* New York: Methuen, 140–143.

McNamee, M. B. (1963) "*Beowulf*—An Allegory of Salvation?" In *An Anthology of* Beowulf *Criticism,* edited by Lewis E. Nicholson. Notre Dame, IN: University of Notre Dame Press, 331–352.

MacNeice, Louis. (1965) *Varieties of Parable.* Cambridge: Cambridge University Press.

MacQueen, John. (1970) *Allegory.* London: Methuen.

Madsen, Deborah L. (1991) *The Postmodernist Allegories of Thomas Pynchon.* New York: St. Martin's Press.

Magill, Frank N., ed. (1989) *Cyclopedia of World Authors.* Englewood Cliffs, NJ: Salem Press.

———. (1976) *Masterplots.* Revised edition. Englewood Cliffs, NJ: Salem Press.

Malamud, Martha. (1989) *A Poetics of Transformation: Prudentius and Classical Mythology.* Ithaca, NY, and London: Cornell University Press.

Male, Emile. (1958) *The Gothic Image: Art in France of the Thirteenth Century.* Translated by Dora Nussey. New York: Harper.

———. (1949) *Religious Art: From the Twelfth to the Eighteenth Century.* New York: Noonday.

Matheson, Sue. (1988) "C. S. Lewis and the Lion: Primitivism and Archetype in the *Chronicles of Narnia.*" *Mythlore* 15 (1): 13–18.

Mayes, Herbert. (1928) *Alger: A Biography without a Hero.* New York: Macy-Masius.

Mendelson, Edward. (1975) "The Sacred, the Profane, and *The Crying of Lot 49.*" In *Individual and Community: Variations on a Theme in American Fiction,* edited by Kenneth H. Baldwin and David K. Kirby. Durham, NC: Duke University Press, 182–222.

Mercier, Vivian. (1977) *Beckett/Beckett.* New York: Oxford University Press, 171–175.

Merrill, Robert. (1981) "Another Look at the American Romance." *Modern Philology: A Journal Devoted to Research in Medieval and Modern Literature* 78 (4): 379–392.

Meyers, Valerie. (1991) *Modern Novelists: George Orwell*. New York: St. Martin's Press.

Michaels, Jennifer B. (1994) *Franz Werfel and the Critics*. Columbia, SC: Camden House, Inc., 41–43.

Miller, Gabriel. (1982) *John Irving*. New York: Frederick Ungar Publishing Co., 127–174.

Miller, J. Hillis. (1991) *Tropes, Parables, Performatives: Essays on Twentieth-Century Literature*. Durham, NC: Duke University Press.

Miller, Jordan Y., ed. (1965) *Playwright's Progress: O'Neill and the Critics*. Chicago: Scott, Foresman and Company.

Miller, N. W. (1992) "Sloth: The Moral Problem in Jane Austen's *Mansfield Park*." *International Journal of Moral and Social Studies* 7 (3): 255–266.

Mishler, William. (1993) "Parents and Children, Brothers and Sisters in Isak Dinesen's `The Monkey.'" In *Isak Dinesen: Critical Views*, edited by Olga Anastasia Pelensky. Athens: Ohio University Press, 225–249.

Monsman, Gerald. (1985) "The Idea of 'Story' in Olive Schreiner's *Story of an African Farm*." *Texas Studies in Literature and Language* 27 (3): 249–269.

Murray, Gilbert. (1951) *Five Stages of Greek Religion*. Boston: Beacon.

Murrin, Michael. (1980) *The Allegorical Epic: Notes on Its Rise and Decline*. Chicago: University of Chicago Press.

———. (1969) *The Veil of Allegory: Some Notes towards a Theory of Allegorical Rhetoric in the English Renaissance*. Chicago: University of Chicago Press.

Neuse, Richard. (1991) *Chaucer's Dante: Allegory and Epic Theater in* The Canterbury Tales. Berkeley: University of California Press.

Nugent, S. Georgia. (1985) *The Structure and Imagery of Prudentius' "Psychomachia."* London: Peter Lang.

Nuttall, A. D. (1967) *Two Concepts of Allegory*. London: Routledge & Kegan Paul.

Ogilvy, J. D. A., and Donald C. Baker. (1983) *Reading* Beowulf: *An Introduction to the Poem, Its Background, and Its Style*. Norman: University of Oklahoma Press.

Oldsey, Bernard S., and Stanley Weintraub. (1965) *The Art of William Golding*. New York: Harcourt, Brace & World, Inc., 30.

Padelford, Frederick Morgan. (1911) *The Political and Ecclesiastical Allegory of the First Book of* The Faerie Queene. Boston: Ginn and Company.

Panofsky, Erwin. (1955) *Meaning in the Visual Arts*. Garden City, NY: Doubleday.

———. (1939) *Studies in Iconology: Humanistic Themes in the Art of the Renaissance*. Reprint. New York: Harper, 1962.

Parker, A. A. (1943) *The Allegorical Drama of Calderon*. London: Dolphin Book.

Parker, M. Pauline. (1960) *The Allegory of* The Faerie Queene. Oxford: Oxford University Press.

Parry, Ann. (1988) "'Take Away That Bauble!' Political Allegory in 'Below the Mill Dam.'" *The Kipling Journal* 62 (248): 10–24.

Patch, H. R. (1935) *The Tradition of Boethius: A Study of His Importance in Medieval Culture*. New York: Oxford University Press.

Paxon, James J. (1994) *The Poetics of Personification*. Cambridge and New York: Cambridge University Press.

Peacham, Henry. (1954) *The Garden of Eloquence*. Gainesville, FL: Scholars Facsimiles & Reprints.

Peck, H. Daniel. (1977) *A World By Itself: The Pastoral Movement in Cooper's Fiction*. New Haven: Yale University Press, 15.

Penner, Dick. (1989) *Countries of the Mind: The Fiction of J. M. Coetzee*. Westport, CT: Greenwood Press, Inc., 75–87.

Piehler, Paul. (1988) "Myth, Allegory, and Vision in the *Parlement of Foules:* A Study in Chaucerian Problem Solving." In *Allegoresis: The Craft of Allegory in Medieval Literature,* edited by J. Stephen Russell. New York: Garland Publishing, Inc., 187–214.

———. (1971) *The Visionary Landscape: A Study in Medieval Allegory*. London: Edward Arnold.

Plato. *Republic*. Translated by Robin Waterfield. New York and Oxford: Oxford University Press.

Price, George R. (1969) *Thomas Dekker*. New York: Twayne Publishers, Inc., 40–49.

Priestley, F. E. L. (1973) *Language and Structure in Tennyson's Poetry*. London: André Deutsch Ltd.

Propp, Vladimir. (1958) *The Morphology of the Folktale*. Translated by Laurence Scott. Bloomington, IN: Indiana University Press.

Prudentius. *Psychomachia*. Translated by H. J. Thompson. London: Loeb Classical Library, 1949.

Quarles, Francis. *The Complete Works in Prose and Verse of Francis Quarles*. Edited by Alexander B. Grosart. New York: AMS Press, Inc., 1967.

Quilligan, Maureen. (1979) *The Language of Allegory: Defining the Genre.* Ithaca, NY: Cornell University Press.

Ranald, Margaret Loftus. (1984) *The Eugene O'Neill Companion.* Westport, CT: Greenwood Press.

Rans, Geoffrey. (1991) *Cooper's* Leatherstocking Tales: *A Secular Reading.* Chapel Hill: University of North Carolina Press, 216–239.

Reibetanz, John. (1982) "The Particular Vision of `The Whitsun Weddings.'" *Modern Language Quarterly* 43 (2): 156–173.

Reilly, Edward C. (1991) *Understanding John Irving.* Columbia: University of South Carolina Press, 81–99.

Reynolds, David S. (1988) *Beneath the American Renaissance.* Cambridge, MA: Harvard University Press.

Robertson, D. W., Jr. (1962) *Preface to Chaucer: Studies in Medieval Perspectives.* Princeton, NJ: Princeton University Press.

Robinson, E. M. (1917) *Tennyson's Uses of the Bible.* Baltimore: The Johns Hopkins University Press.

Roditi, Edouard. (1969) "Fiction as Allegory: *The Picture of Dorian Gray.*" In *Oscar Wilde: A Collection of Critical Essays,* edited by Richard Ellmann. Englewood Cliffs, NJ: Prentice Hall, Inc., 47–55.

Roheim, Geza. (1945) *Eternal Ones of the Dream.* New York: International Universities Press, Inc.

Rollinson, Philip. (1981) *Classical Theories of Allegory and Christian Culture.* Pittsburgh, PA: Duquesne University Press.

Ruddick, Nicholas. (1985) "The Hoax of the Red Death: Poe as Allegorist." *Sphinx: A Magazine of Literature and Society* 4 (16): 268–276.

Saccio, Peter. (1969) *The Court Comedies of John Lyly: A Study in Allegorical Dramaturgy.* Princeton, NJ: Princeton University Press.

Sadler, Lynn Veach. (1979) *John Bunyan.* Boston: G. K. Hall & Co., 81–85.

Safer, Elaine B. (1988) *The Contemporary American Comic Epic: The Novels of Barth, Pynchon, Gaddis, and Kesey.* Detroit: Wayne State University Press, 152–153.

Saintsbury, George. (1897) *The Flourishing of Romance and the Rise of Allegory.* New York: C. Scribner's Sons.

Sallustius. (4th cent.) *About the Gods and the World.* Appendix in *Five Stages of Greek Religion,* by Gilbert Murray. Boston: Beacon, 1951.

San Juan, Epifanio, Jr. (1967) *The Art of Oscar Wilde.* Princeton, NJ: Princeton University Press, 49–73.

BIBLIOGRAPHY

Sandstroem, Yvonne L. (1990) "Marvell's `Nymph Complaining' as Historical Allegory." *SEL: Studies in English Literature, 1500–1900* 30 (1): 93–114.

Sarkar, Subhas. (1972) *T. S. Eliot the Dramatist*. Calcutta: Minerva Associates.

Schilling, Bernard N. (1961) *Dryden and the Conservative Myth: A Reading of Absalom and Achitophel*. New Haven: Yale University Press.

Schlossman, Beryl. (1991) *The Orient of Style: Modernist Allegories of Conversion*. Durham, NC: Duke University Press.

Seidel, Michael. (1981) "Crusoe in Exile." *PMLA* 96 (3): 363–374.

Seznec, Jean. (1953) *The Survival of the Pagan Gods*. Translated by Barbara Sessions. New York: Harper.

Shah, Idries. (1971) *The Sufis*. New York: Anchor.

———. (1970) *The Way of the Sufis*. New York: Dutton.

Shaw, W. David. (1968) *The Dialectical Temper: The Rhetorical Art of Robert Browning*. Ithaca, NY: Cornell University Press, 126–135.

Sherman, Carol. (1984) "Voltaire's *Zadig* and the Allegory of (Mis)reading." *The French Review* 58 (1): 32–40.

Shulenberger, Arvid. (1955) *Cooper's Theory of Fiction: His Prefaces and Their Relation to His Novels*. Lawrence: University of Kansas Press, 46–48.

Smyer, Richard I. (1988) *Animal Farm: Pastoralism and Politics*. Boston: Twayne Publishers.

Smythe, Karen. (1990) "Imaging and Imagining: `The Jolly Corner' and Self-Construction." *Dalhousie Review* 70 (3): 375–385.

Solich, Wolfgang. (1992) "Allegory in the Technological Age: A Case Study of Ibsen's *The Wild Duck*." *Journal of Dramatic Theory and Criticism* 6 (2): 99–118.

Spivak, G. (1972) "Thoughts on the Principle of Allegory." *Genre* (4): 327–352.

Starkman, Miriam Kosh. (1950) *Swift's Satire on Learning in* A Tale of a Tub. Princeton, NJ: Princeton University Press.

Steadman, John M. (1974) *The Lamb and the Elephant: Ideal Imitation and the Context of Renaissance Allegory*. San Marino, CA: The Huntington Library.

Stillman, Clara G. (1932) *Samuel Butler: A Mid-Victorian Modern*. New York: The Viking Press.

Strayer, Joseph R. (1983) *Dictionary of the Middle Ages*. New York: Scribner's.

Swain, Kathleen M. (1993) *Pilgrim's Progress, Puritan Progress: Discourses and Contexts*. Urbana: University of Illinois Press.

Tennyson, G. B. (1965) *Sartor Called Resartus: The Genesis, Structure, and Style of Thomas Carlyle's First Major Work*. Princeton, NJ: Princeton University Press.

Thomas, W. K. (1978) *The Crafting of* Absalom and Achitophel: *Dryden's "Pen for a Party."* Waterloo, Ontario: Wilfrid Laurier University Press.

Todorov, Tzvetan. (1982) *Theories of the Symbol.* Translated by Catherine Porter. Ithaca, NY: Cornell University Press.

Toker, Leona. (1989) *Nabokov: The Mystery of Literary Structures.* Ithaca, NY: Cornell University Press.

Trilling, Diana. (1975) "The Riddle of Albee's *Who's Afraid of Virginia Woolf?*" In *Edward Albee: A Collection of Critical Essays,* edited by C. W. E. Bigsby. Englewood Cliffs, NJ: Prentice Hall, Inc., 80–88.

Trimpi, Helen P. (1987) *Melville's Confidence Men and American Politics in the 1850s.* Hamden, CT: The Connecticut Academy of Arts & Sciences.

Tuve, Rosemund. (1966) *Allegorical Imagery: Some Mediaeval Books and Their Renaissance Posterity.* Princeton, NJ: Princeton University Press.

Tyler, Hamilton A. (1964) *Pueblo Gods and Myths.* Norman: Oklahoma University Press.

Tymms, Ralph. (1983) "Doubles in Literary Psychology." In *The Definitive Dr. Jeckyll and Mr. Hyde Companion,* edited by Harry M. Geduld. New York: Garland Publishing, Inc., 77–79.

Urgo, Joseph R. (1989) *Faulkner's Apocrypha: A Fable, Snopes, and the Spirit of Human Rebellion.* Jackson: University of Mississippi Press, 105–111.

Van Dyke, Carolynn. (1982) "The Intangible and Its Image: Allegorical Discourse in the Cast of *Everyman.*" In *Acts of Interpretation,* edited by Mary J. Carruthers and Elizabeth D. Kirk. Norman, OK: Pilgrim Books, 311–324.

Varay, Simon. (1990) "Exemplary History and the Political Satire of *Gulliver's Travels.*" In *The Genres of* Gulliver's Travels, edited by Frederik N. Smith. Cranbury, NJ: Associated University Presses, 39–55.

Verdier, Douglas L. (1981) "Who Is the Lightning-Rod Man?" *Studies in Short Fiction* 18 (3): 273–279.

Vinaver, Eugene. (1971) *The Rise of Romance.* New York: Oxford University Press.

Wagener, Hans. (1993) *Understanding Franz Werfel.* Columbia: University of South Carolina Press, 49–51.

Waggoner, Hyatt H. (1979) *The Presence of Hawthorne.* Baton Rouge: Louisiana State University Press.

Wakefield, Gordon. (1992) *Bunyan the Christian.* London: HarperCollins Religious, 94–97.

Ware, Tracy. (1989) "The Two Stories of 'William Wilson.'" *Studies in Short Fiction* 26 (1): 43–48.

Warren, Austin, and Rene Wellek. (1949) *Theory of Literature*. New York: Harcourt, Brace.

Wedel, T. O. (1968) "On the Philosophical Background of *Gulliver's Travels*." In *Twentieth Century Interpretations of* Gulliver's Travels: *A Collection of Critical Essays*, edited by Frank Brady. Englewood Cliffs, NJ: Prentice Hall, Inc.

Weinstein, Cindy. (1993) "The Calm before the Storm: Laboring through *Mardi*." *American Literature: A Journal of Literary History, Criticism, and Bibliography* 65 (2): 239–253.

Wellek, Rene. (1955) *A History of Modern Criticism I*. New Haven: Yale University Press.

White, T. H. (1984) *The Book of Beasts*. New York: Dover Publications.

Whitman, Jon. (1987) *Allegory: The Dynamics of an Ancient and Medieval Technique*. Cambridge, MA: Harvard University Press.

Wilcox, Leonard. (1993) "The Desert and the City: *Operation Sidewinder* and Shepard's Postmodern Allegory." In *Rereading Shepard: Contemporary Critical Essays on the Plays of Sam Shepard*, edited by Leonard Wilcox. New York: St. Martin's Press, 42–57.

Williams, Anne. (1984) "Gracious Accommodations: Herbert's 'Love III.'" *Modern Philology: A Journal Devoted to Research in Medieval and Modern Literature* 82 (1): 13–22.

Williams, Kathleen. (1968) "Gulliver in Laputa." In *Twentieth Century Interpretations of* Gulliver's Travels: *A Collection of Critical Essays*, edited by Frank Brady. Englewood Cliffs, NJ: Prentice Hall, Inc., 60–69.

Wills, Garry. (1987) "*The Man Who Was Thursday*." In *G. K. Chesterton: A Half Century of Views*, edited by D. J. Conlon. Oxford: Oxford University Press, 335–342.

Wittkower, Rudolf. (1977) *Allegory and the Migration of Symbols*. London: Thames and Hudson.

Woodward, James B. (1978) *Gogol's* Dead Souls. Princeton, NJ: Princeton University Press.

Yelton, Donald C. (1967) *Mimesis and Metaphor: An Inquiry into the Genesis and Scope of Conrad's Symbolic Imagery*. The Hague: Mouton.

Ziarek, Ewa. (1989) "'Surface Stratified on Surface': A Reading of Ahab's Allegory." *Criticism: A Quarterly for Literature and the Arts* 31 (3): 271–286.

Zwicker, Steven N. (1972) *Dryden's Political Poetry: The Typology of King and Nation*. Providence, RI: Brown University Press.

Zwicker, Steven N. (1984) *Politics and Language in Dryden's Poetry: The Arts of Disguise*. Princeton, NJ: Princeton University Press.

ILLUSTRATION CREDITS

INDEX

Note: Page numbers in **boldface** denote major entry headings.

		DATE DUE		